ACC

Strategic Profession – Options

Advanced Performance Management (APM)

EXAM KIT

PUBLISHING

British Library Cataloguing-in-Publication Data

A catalogue record for this book is available from the British Library.

Published by:

Kaplan Publishing UK

Unit 2 The Business Centre

Molly Millar's Lane

Wokingham

Berkshire

RG41 2QZ

ISBN: 978-1-78740-111-2

© Kaplan Financial Limited, 2018

Printed and bound in Great Britain.

Acknowledgements

These materials are reviewed by the ACCA examining team. The objective of the review is to ensure that the material properly covers the syllabus and study guide outcomes, used by the examining team in setting the exams, in the appropriate breadth and depth. The review does not ensure that every eventuality, combination or application of examinable topics is addressed by the ACCA Approved Content. Nor does the review comprise a detailed technical check of the content as the Approved Content Provider has its own quality assurance processes in place in this respect.

Kaplan Publishing are constantly finding new ways to make a difference to your studies and our exciting online resources really do offer something different to students looking for exam success.

This book comes with free MyKaplan online resources so that you can study anytime, anywhere. This free online resource is not sold separately and is included in the price of the book.

Having purchased this book, you have access to the following online study materials:

CONTENT	ACCA (including FFA,FAB,FMA)		FIA (excluding FFA,FAB,FMA)	
	Text	Kit	Text	Kit
Eletronic version of the book	✓	✓	✓	✓
Check Your Understanding Test with instant answers	✓			
Material updates	✓	✓	✓	✓
Latest official ACCA exam questions*		✓		
Extra question assistance using the signpost icon**		✓		
Question debriefs using clock icon***		✓		
Consolidation Test including questions and answers	✓			

*   Excludes AB, MA, FA, LW, FAB, FMA and FFA; for all other subjects includes a selection of questions, as released by ACCA

** For ACCA SBR, AFM, APM, AAA only

*** Excludes AB, MA, FA, LW, FAB, FMA and FFA

How to access your online resources

Kaplan Financial students will already have a MyKaplan account and these extra resources will be available to you online. You do not need to register again, as this process was completed when you enrolled. If you are having problems accessing online materials, please ask your course administrator.

If you are not studying with Kaplan and did not purchase your book via a Kaplan website, to unlock your extra online resources please go to www.mykaplan.co.uk/addabook (even if you have set up an account and registered books previously). You will then need to enter the ISBN number (on the title page and back cover) and the unique pass key number contained in the scratch panel below to gain access.

You will also be required to enter additional information during this process to set up or confirm your account details.

If you purchased through Kaplan Flexible Learning or via the Kaplan Publishing website you will automatically receive an e-mail invitation to MyKaplan. Please register your details using this email to gain access to your content. If you do not receive the e-mail or book content, please contact Kaplan Publishing.

Your Code and Information

This code can only be used once for the registration of one book online. This registration and your online content will expire when the final sittings for the examinations covered by this book have taken place. Please allow one hour from the time you submit your book details for us to process your request.

Please scratch the film to access your MyKaplan code.

Please be aware that this code is case-sensitive and you will need to include the dashes within the passcode, but not when entering the ISBN. For further technical support, please visit www.MyKaplan.co.uk

CONTENTS

	Page
Index to questions and answers	P.5
Analysis of past exams	P.11
Exam technique	P.13
Exam specific information	P.15
Kaplan's recommended revision approach	P.17
Kaplan's detailed revision plan	P.21
Mathematical tables	P.27

Section

1	Practice questions – Section A	1
2	Practice questions – Section B	37
3	Answers to practice questions – Section A	141
4	Answers to practice questions – Section B	215

Features in this edition

In addition to providing a wide ranging bank of real past exam questions, we have also included in this edition:

- Details of examination format.

- Exam-specific information and advice on exam technique.

- Our recommended approach to make your revision for this particular subject as effective as possible.

   This includes step by step guidance on how best to use our Kaplan material (Study Text, Pocket Notes and Exam Kit) at this stage in your studies.

- Enhanced tutorial answers packed with specific key answer tips, technical tutorial notes and exam technique tips from our experienced tutors.

- Complementary online resources including full tutor debriefs and question assistance to point you in the right direction when you get stuck.

You will find a wealth of other resources to help you with your studies on the following sites:

www.MyKaplan.co.uk and http://www.accaglobal.com/uk/en/student.html

Quality and accuracy are of the utmost importance to us so if you spot an error in any of our products, please send an email to mykaplanreporting@kaplan.com with full details.

Our Quality Co-ordinator will work with our technical team to verify the error and take action to ensure it is corrected in future editions.

INDEX TO QUESTIONS AND ANSWERS

INTRODUCTION

Some past exam questions have been modified (sometimes extensively) to reflect the current APM syllabus.

KEY TO THE INDEX

ENHANCEMENTS

We have added the following enhancements to the answers in this exam kit:

Key answer tips

All answers include key answer tips to help your understanding of each question.

Tutorial note

All answers include more tutorial notes to explain some of the technical points in more detail.

ONLINE ENHANCEMENTS

 Question debrief

For selected questions, we recommend that they are to be completed in full exam conditions (i.e. properly timed in a closed book environment).

In addition to the examiner's technical answer, enhanced with key answer tips and tutorial notes in this exam kit, online you can find an answer debrief by a top tutor that:

- works through the question in full

- points out how to approach the question

- how to ensure that the easy marks are obtained as quickly as possible, and

- emphasises how to tackle exam questions and exam technique.

These questions are indicated with the 'clock' icon in the index.

 Online question assistance

Have you ever looked at a question and not know where to start, or got stuck part way through?

For selected questions, we have produced 'Online question assistance' offering different levels of guidance, such as:

- ensuring that you understand the question requirements fully, highlighting key terms and the meaning of the verbs used

- how to read the question proactively, with knowledge of the requirements, to identify the topic areas covered

- assessing the detail content of the question body, pointing out key information and explaining why it is important

- help in devising a plan of attack

With this assistance, you should then be able to attempt your answer confident that you know what is expected of you.

These questions are indicated with the 'signpost' icon in the index.

Online question enhancements and answer debriefs will be available on MyKaplan at:

www.MyKaplan.co.uk

SECTION A TYPE QUESTIONS

			Page number		
			Question	*Answer*	*Past exam*
1	Thyme		1	141	*Sept/Dec 17*
2	Dargeboard Services (DS)		4	147	*Mar/Jun 17*
3	Flack		7	153	*Mar/Jun 16*
4	Monza		10	159	*Sept/Dec 16*
5	Boltzman		13	165	*Dec 14 (A)*
6	Cantor		16	170	*Jun 14*
7	JHK Coffee Machines Co		19	176	*Jun 11 (A)*
8	Metis Restaurants		21	182	*Jun 12 (A)*
9	Kolmog Hotels		23	189	*Jun 13*
10	Lopten Industries	🕐	26	195	*Dec 13 (A)*
11	Merkland Sportswear		28	201	*Jun 15*
12	Iron Chicken		32	208	*Sept/Dec 15 (S)*

Note: (A) signifies that the question has been amended from the original, either to match the current syllabus or, more usually, to match the current format of the exam.

(S) signifies that the question was included in the Specimen Exam relevant from September 2018 onwards. The Specimen Exam questions and answers have been included in the Exam Kit. These are slightly different to the original exam questions and answers, with rewording in parts and restructuring with the breakdown of the scenario to include headings.

SECTION B TYPE QUESTIONS

A – STRATEGIC PLANNING AND CONTROL

| | | | Page number | | |
			Question	Answer	Past exam
13	Cuthbert		37	215	Mar/Jun 16
14	Framiltone		39	219	Sept/Dec 16
15	Briggs		41	223	-
16	Alflonnso		42	225	Sept/Dec 16
17	Godel		44	229	Jun 14 (A)
18	Dibble		46	232	Mar/Jun 16
19	Herman Swan & Co	🕐	47	236	Dec 12 (A)
20	Booxe		48	239	Jun 14
21	Ganymede University		50	241	Jun 12 (A)
22	Maxwell		51	244	Dec 14 (A)
23	ENT Entertainment Co		53	247	Jun 11 (A)
24	PLX Refinery Co		54	250	Pilot 10 (A)
25	FGH Telecom (FGH)		55	253	Dec 10 (A)
26	GMB Co	◩	57	256	Dec 07 (A)
27	Film Productions Co (FP)		58	259	Dec 10 (A)

B – IMPACT OF RISK AND UNCERTAINTY ON ORGANISATIONAL PERFORMANCE

| | | Page number | | |
		Question	Answer	Past exam
28	Sweet Cicely (SC)	59	262	Sept/Dec 17
29	Turing	60	266	Jun 14
30	Franchising For You Ltd (F4U)	62	270	Jun 09
31	The Equine Management Academy (EMA)	63	273	Jun 10
32	Stokeness Engineering	65	277	Jun 13 (S)

C – PERFORMANCE MEASUREMENT SYSTEMS AND DESIGN

| | | Page number | | |
		Question	Answer	Past exam
33	Nelson, Jody and Nigel (NJN)	67	281	Mar/Jun 17
34	Integrated Reporting	68	285	
35	Bluefin School	69	287	Dec 11 (A)
36	Quark Healthcare	71	290	Dec 13
37	Forion Electronics	72	293	Jun 15
38	Albacore	73	296	Pilot 10

D – STRATEGIC PERFORMANCE MEASUREMENT

Page number

39	Chicory		75	299	Sept/Dec 17
40	Tosemary and Rhyme Hospital (TRH)		77	303	Sept/Dec 17
41	Pitlane		78	307	Mar/Jun 17
42	Jenson, Lewis and Webb (JLW)		80	311	Mar/Jun 17
43	The Better Electricals Group (BEG)		81	315	Jun 10 (A)
44	Essland Police Force		83	318	Dec 13
45	Telecoms at Work (TAW)	🕐	85	321	Jun 08 (A)
46	Westamber		87	324	Pilot 07 (A)
47	Alpha Division		89	326	Dec 07
48	Beeshire Local Authority (BLA)		91	330	Dec 14
49	SSA Group		93	332	Dec 09 (A)
50	Local government housing department		94	336	Jun 10 (A)
51	Tench Cars		95	339	Dec 11 (A)
52	Thebe Telecom		96	342	Jun 12 (A)
53	Lincoln & Lincoln Advertising		97	345	Dec 12 (A)
54	Landual Lamps		101	349	Jun 13
55	Beach Foods		103	353	Jun 15
56	Posie Furniture		104	357	Sept/Dec 15
57	Universities in Teeland		106	362	Mar/Jun 16
58	Laudan Advertising Agency (LLA)		108	368	Sept/Dec 16
59	The Health and Fitness Group (HFG)	🕐	110	372	Jun 08 (A)

E – PERFORMANCE EVALUATION AND CORPORATE FAILURE

		Page number		
60	Royal Botanical Gardens	112	377	–
61	BLA	113	380	*Dec 03 (A)*
62	Culam	115	385	*Dec 14 (S)*
63	Performance pyramid	116	388	*Jun 06 (A)*
64	BPC	118	392	*Dec 07 (A)*
65	The Sentinel Company (TSC)	119	395	*Dec 08 (A)*
66	The Spare for Ships Company (SFS)	121	399	*Jun 10 (A)*
67	The Superior Business Consultancy (SBC)	122	402	*Jun 10(A)*
68	LOL Co	124	406	*Dec 10 (A)*
69	RM Batteries Co	125	409	*Dec 10*
70	APX Accountancy	126	412	*Jun 11 (A)*
71	Cod Electrical Motors	127	414	*Dec 11 (A)*
72	Callisto	129	418	*Jun 12 (A)*
73	Coal Creek Nursing Homes	130	421	*Dec 12 (A)*
74	Graviton Clothing	132	425	*Dec 13*
75	Victoria-Yeeland Logistics	133	429	*Jun 15*
76	Soup Rail Services	135	432	*Sept/Dec 15*
77	Pharmaceutical Technologies Co (PT)	137	437	*Pilot 10*
78	Bettaserve	138	439	*Pilot 07*

ANALYSIS OF PAST EXAMS

The table below summarises the key topics that have been tested in recent examinations to date.

	J12	D12	J13	D13	J14	D14	J15	S/D 15	M/J 16	S/D 16	M/J 17	S/D 17
SWOT							X					
Benchmarking	X					X						X
Mission					X						X	
CSFs and KPIs	X			X				X		X	X	
Role of management accountant		X										X
BCG												
Stakeholders						X						
Risk					X		X					X
Porter's 5 forces/PEST			X	X								
Budgeting		X	X			X		X	X	X		
BPR						X			X			
Complex business structures	X		X		X							
Services			X									
Information systems				X			X		X		X	
Qualitative factors						X						
Evaluation of a performance report	X		X		X				X		X	X
Wrong signals				X								
Human resource management		X			X		X		X		X	X
Financial performance evaluation	X	X							X	X		X
Divisional performance measurement	X	X			X		X	X		X	X	
Transfer pricing			X							X		
Value for money						X			X			X
Public sector league tables/targets	X			X					X			
Performance pyramid				X								
Balanced scorecard			X							X		
Building block			X								X	
NFPIs						X						X
Corporate failure		X				X						
Quality practices	X					X		X		X	X	X
Lean management				X						X	X	
Value chain							X					
Quality costs												X
EMA						X				X		

EXAM TECHNIQUE

- **Skim through the whole exam**, assessing the scope and level of difficulty of each question.

- **Divide the time** you spend on questions in proportion to the marks on offer:

  - There are 1.95 minutes available per mark in the examination.

  - Within that, try to allow time at the end of each question to review your answer and address any obvious issues.

  Whatever happens, always keep your eye on the clock and **do not over run on any part of any question!**

- **Decide the order** in which you think you will attempt each question:

  - A common approach is to tackle the question you think is the easiest and you are most comfortable with first.

  - Others may prefer to tackle the longest questions first as this has the most marks attributable and you cannot afford to leave this question to last and find that you have run out of time to complete it fully.

  - It is usual, however, that students tackle their least favourite topic and/or the most difficult question last.

  - Whatever your approach, you must make sure that you leave enough time to attempt all questions fully and be very strict with yourself in timing each question.

- At the beginning of each question, take time to:

  - read the question scenario and requirements **carefully** so that you understand them, and

  - **plan** your answers.

- Spend the last **five minutes** of the examination:

  - reading through your answers, and

  - **making any additions or corrections**.

- If you **get completely stuck** with a question:

  - leave space in your answer book, and

  - **return to it later.**

- Stick to the question and **tailor your answer** to what you are asked.

  - pay particular attention to the verbs in the question.

- If you do not understand what a question is asking, **state your assumptions**.

  Even if you do not answer in precisely the way the examiner hoped, you should be given some credit, if your assumptions are reasonable.

- You should do everything you can to make things easy for the marker.

  The marker will find it easier to identify the points you have made if your **answers are legible**.

- **Written questions:**

  APM marks are normally awarded for depth of explanation and discussion. For this reason, lists and bullet points should be avoided unless specifically requested.

  Your answer should:

  – Have a clear structure using sub-headings to improve the quality and clarity of your response.

  – Be concise: get to the point!

  – Address a broad range of points: it is usually better to write a little about a lot of different points than a great deal about one or two points.

- **Reports, memos and other documents:**

  Some questions ask you to present your answer in the form of a report or briefing notes. Professional marks are awarded for these questions so do not ignore their format.

  Make sure that you use the correct format – there could be easy marks to gain here.

- **Computations:**

  It is essential to include all your workings in your answers.

  Many computational questions can be answered using a standard step by step approach.

  e.g. ABC computations, budget analysis, risk and uncertainty.

  Be sure you know these steps before the exam and practice answering a range of questions using the same step by step approach.

  Always ensure that you try to interpret any figures calculated.

EXAM SPECIFIC INFORMATION

THE EXAM

FORMAT OF THE EXAM

	Number of marks
Section A: One compulsory question.	50
Section B: Two compulsory questions worth 25 marks each.	50
Total time allowed: 3 hours 15 minutes.	

Note that:

- Syllabus sections A, C and D are examinable in Section A.

- Section B will contain one question from syllabus section E. The other question will be from any other syllabus sections.

- There will be four professional marks available in Section A.

- Candidates will receive a present value table and annuity table.

- Questions will be based around a short scenario. It is important to refer back to this scenario when answering the question.

- There will be a mixture of written requirements and computational requirements.

- Earlier knowledge from previous exams will be drawn on at times.

PASS MARK

The pass mark for all ACCA Qualification examinations is 50%.

DETAILED SYLLABUS, STUDY GUIDE AND SPECIMEN EXAM

The detailed syllabus and study guide written by the ACCA, along with the Specimen Exam can be found at:

http://www.accaglobal.com/uk/en/student.html

KAPLAN'S RECOMMENDED REVISION APPROACH

QUESTION PRACTICE IS THE KEY TO SUCCESS

Success in strategic professional examinations relies upon you acquiring a firm grasp of the required knowledge at the tuition phase. In order to be able to do the questions, knowledge is essential.

However, the difference between success and failure often hinges on your exam technique on the day and making the most of the revision phase of your studies.

The Kaplan study text is the starting point, designed to provide the underpinning knowledge to tackle all questions. However, in the revision phase, pouring over text books is not the answer.

Kaplan online knowledge check tests help you consolidate your knowledge and understanding and are a useful tool to check whether you can remember key topic areas.

Kaplan pocket notes are designed to help you quickly revise a topic area, however you then need to practice questions. There is a need to progress to full exam standard questions as soon as possible, and to tie your exam technique and technical knowledge together.

The importance of question practice cannot be over-emphasised.

The recommended approach below is designed by expert tutors in the field, in conjunction with their knowledge of the examiner.

The approach taken for the applied knowledge and applied skills exams is to revise by topic area. However, with the strategic professional stage exams, a multi topic approach is required to answer the scenario based questions.

You need to practice as many questions as possible in the time you have left.

OUR AIM

Our aim is to get you to the stage where you can attempt exam standard questions confidently, to time, in a closed book environment, with no supplementary help (i.e. to simulate the real examination experience).

Practising your exam technique on real past examination questions, in timed conditions, is also vitally important for you to assess your progress and identify areas of weakness that may need more attention in the final run up to the examination.

In order to achieve this we recognise that initially you may feel the need to practice some questions with open book help and exceed the required time.

The approach below shows you which questions you should use to build up to coping with exam standard question practice, and references to the sources of information available should you need to revisit a topic area in more detail.

Remember that in the real examination, all you have to do is:

- attempt all questions required by the exam

- only spend the allotted time on each question, and

- get them at least 50% right!

Try and practice this approach on every question you attempt from now to the real exam.

EXAMINER COMMENTS

We have included the examiner's comments to the more recent examination questions in this kit for you to see the main pitfalls that students fall into with regard to technical content.

However, too many times in the general section of the report, the examiner comments that students had failed due to:

- 'not answering the question'

- 'a poor understanding of why something is done, not just how it is done'

- 'simply writing out numbers from the question. Candidates must understand what the numbers tell them about business performance'

- 'a lack of common business sense' and

- 'ignoring clues in the question'.

Good exam technique is vital.

THE KAPLAN APM EXAM REVISION PLAN

Stage 1: Assess areas of strengths and weaknesses

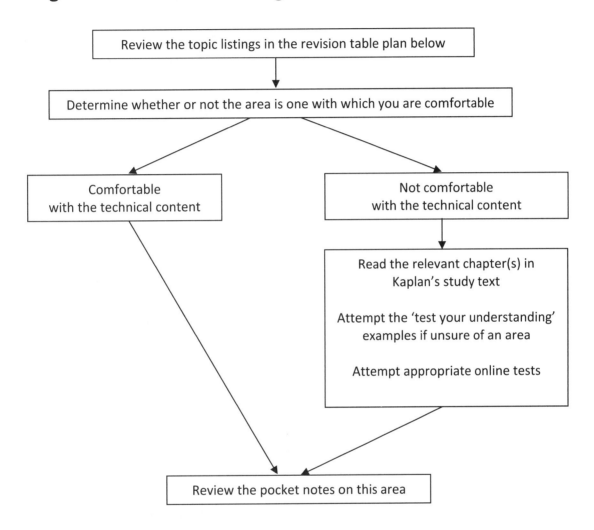

Stage 2: Practice questions

Ensure that you revise all syllabus areas as questions could be asked on anything.

Try to avoid referring to text books and notes and the model answer until you have completed your attempt.

Try to answer the question in the allotted time.

Review your attempt with the model answer and assess how much of the answer you achieved in the allocated exam time.

Fill in the self-assessment box below and decide on your best course of action.

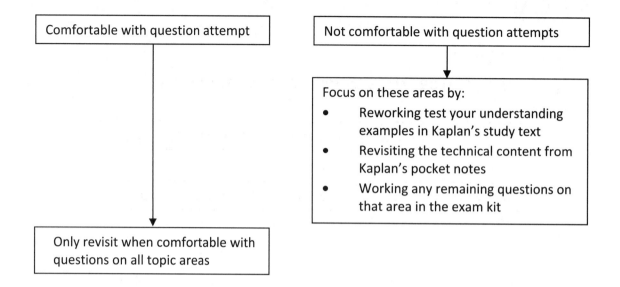

Note that:

 The 'signpost questions' offer online question assistance to help you to attempt your question confidently and know what is expected of you.

 The 'clock questions' have an online debrief where a tutor talks you through the exam technique and approach to that question and works the question in full.

Stage 3: Final pre-exam revision

We recommend that you **attempt at least one three hour and 15 minute mock examination** containing a set of previously unseen exam standard questions.

It is important that you get a feel for the breadth of coverage of a real exam without advanced knowledge of the topic areas covered – just as you will expect to see on the real exam day.

Ideally this mock should be sat in timed, closed book, real exam conditions and could be a mock examination offered by your tuition provider.

KAPLAN'S DETAILED REVISION PLAN

Introduction to strategic management accounting

Topic	Study Text Chapter	Pocket Notes Chapter	Questions to attempt	Tutor guidance	Date attempted	Self-assessment
– Benchmarking	1	1	5(iii), 21, 39(b)	Students should be prepared to perform a benchmarking exercise using given data and to also evaluate the method of benchmarking used compared to other methods.		
– Mission, CSFs and KPIs	1	1	2(i)(ii), 6(v), 10(i)(iii)(iv), 12(ii), 27, 50(a)	A core area that is commonly examined. It is important to complete a range of questions here. Mission may not be tested in isolation but, for example, you may need to consider the impact of a change in the mission statement on the KPIs of the organisation.		
– BCG	1	1	23, 55(c)	The classification from this model will be used to determine performance management issues and performance measures which are required depending on where in the matrix the division/product etc. falls.		
– Role of management accountant and integrated reporting	1	1	1(ii), 19(a), 34	It's important to consider the changes in the role of the management accountant and the role of the management accountant in integrated reporting.		
– SWOT	1	1	11(i)	Not commonly examined but do review one question on this.		

Topic	Study Text Chapter	Pocket Notes Chapter	Questions to attempt	Tutor guidance	Date attempted	Self-assessment
Environmental influences						
– Risk	2	2	28(b)(c), 29(a)(b), 31, 32(c)	Much of this is brought forward knowledge from PM but notice the change in emphasis of the questions – the calculations will be used to underpin your discussion rather than accounting for the majority of the marks.		
– Ethics and CSR	2	2	–	It is important to understand that the adoption of an ethical/ socially responsible approach can help (rather than hinder) an organisation in achieving its stated objectives.		
– Stakeholders	2	2	5(ii)	May not be tested in isolation but could be examined, say, alongside the Performance Pyramid.		
– PEST and Porter's 5 forces	2	2	10(ii), 28(a), 32(a), 43(a)	Consider PEST in the context of performance management. Consider Porter's 5 forces in the context of performance management.		
Approaches to budgets						
– Budgeting	3	3	14, 16(a)(b), 17, 18, 20, 26, 66	Do not overlook this area. Knowledge of the written areas of budgeting can help you to score relatively easy marks in the exam. In addition, make sure that you can do the basic calculations for budgets and variances.		
Business structure and performance management						
– BPR	4	4	13(a), 20	It is important to understand what BPR is and to consider its impact on systems development and performance improvement.		

KAPLAN PUBLISHING

Topic	Study Text Chapter	Pocket Notes Chapter	Questions to attempt	Tutor guidance	Date attempted	Self-assessment
– Services	4	4	9(i)	A straightforward area but be ready to distinguish service and manufacturing organisations.		
– Value chain	4	4	11(v)	It is important to understand that a focus on an organisation's activities (and the linkages between them) can help to improve performance.		
– McKinsey's 7s model	4	4	15	A relatively minor area but complete one question on this.		
– Complex structures	4	4	29(c), 72	The organisations in the exam are often more complex in nature – these complex structures will present their own problems.		
The impact of information technology						
– Information systems	5	5	3(v), 7(d)(e), 35-37, 51(d)	Think about the link between performance management and information systems. In particular, what information needs does the organisation have and what information systems should they implement as a result of these needs?		
Performance reports for management						
– Performance reports and qualitative factors	6	6	1(i), 2(iii), 3(i), 6(i), 8, 9(ii), 38(a)	A commonly examined area. Complete a number of questions to understand how it can be examined in a variety of contexts. It is important to be able to evaluate a performance report in the context of the organisation's mission and objectives.		

Topic	Study Text Chapter	Pocket Notes Chapter	Questions to attempt	Tutor guidance	Date attempted	Self-assessment
Human resource aspects of performance management						
– Reward	7	7	2(v), 13(b), 42(a)(b), 53	HR aspects can be overlooked but consider the impact of a number of HR issues and management styles on performance management. It is vital that managers are motivated to achieve the goals and KPIs of the organisation.		
– Management styles	7	7	38(b), 40(c), 55(c)			
Financial performance measures in the private sector						
– Assessing financial performance	8	8	30, 39(a)	Don't get too bogged down in the calculations. You need to be ready to assess financial performance in the context of the scenario given rather than simply calculating every single measure that you know.		
Divisional performance appraisal and transfer pricing						
– Divisional performance	9	9	3(ii)–(iv), 6(ii)–(iv), 12(i), 42(c), 47, 55, 59	A commonly examined area. Be ready to calculate and evaluate RI, ROI and EVA and to discuss VBM.		
– Transfer pricing	9	9	7(b)(c), 49, 54, 58	The transfer price negotiated between the divisions, or imposed by head office, can have a profound, but perhaps arbitrary, effect on the reported performance and subsequent decisions made.		

KAPLAN PUBLISHING

Topic	Study Text Chapter	Pocket Notes Chapter	Questions to attempt	Tutor guidance	Date attempted	Self-assessment
Performance management in not-for-profit organisations						
– Performance management in NFPOs	10	10	40(a)(b), 48, 51(b), 57(a)	Think about the problems and diversity of objectives and the different approaches to performance measurement in NFPOs.		
– League tables	10	10	44, 57(b)	A very topical issue. Be prepared to evaluate the use of league tables (benchmarking) and targets in the public sector.		
Non-financial performance indicators						
– Balanced scorecard	11	11	4(i), 9(iii)(iv), 60, 67, 75-77	A number of tools are available for measuring financial and non-financial performance. A		
– Building block	11	11	2(iv), 9(v), 61, 65, 70	core area – practise a number of questions so that you understand how these models can be		
– Performance pyramid	11	11	5(i), 43(c), 63, 71, 74, 78	examined in a range of contexts.		
Corporate failure						
– Corporate failure	12	12	62, 64, 69, 73	Be ready to discuss corporate failure, assess the likelihood of failure and discuss and evaluate models such as the Z score and Argenti.		
The role of quality in performance measurement						
– Quality practices	13	13	1(iii), 4(v), 5(iv), 33, 41, 51(b)(c), 52, 56	There are a number of quality practices. It is a good idea to complete a range of questions on these.		
– Quality costs	13	13	1(iv), 4(iv), 43(b), 45, 51(a)	Ensure you understand the different definitions of quality and cost classification.		

Topic	Study Text Chapter	Pocket Notes Chapter	Questions to attempt	Tutor guidance	Date attempted	Self-assessment
Environmental management accounting (EMA)						
– EMA	14	14	16(c), 22, 24, 25	A reasonably straightforward but very topical area. Be prepared to discuss the reasons for the implementation of EMA and to explain the techniques that can be used.		

Note: not all of the questions in the kit are referred to in the programme above. We have recommended a large number of exam standard questions and successful completion of these should reassure you that you have a good grounding of most of the key topics and are well prepared for the exam.

The remaining questions are available in the kit for extra practice for those who require more questions on some areas.

MATHEMATICAL TABLES

PRESENT VALUE TABLE

Present value of 1 i.e. $(1+r)^{-n}$ where r = discount rate, n = number of periods until payment

Periods					Discount rate (r)						
(n)	1%	2%	3%	4%	5%	6%	7%	8%	9%	10%	
1	0.990	0.980	0.971	0.962	0.952	0.943	0.935	0.926	0.917	0.909	1
2	0.980	0.961	0.943	0.925	0.907	0.890	0.873	0.857	0.842	0.826	2
3	0.971	0.942	0.915	0.889	0.864	0.840	0.816	0.794	0.772	0.751	3
4	0.961	0.924	0.888	0.855	0.823	0.792	0.763	0.735	0.708	0.683	4
5	0.951	0.906	0.863	0.822	0.784	0.747	0.713	0.681	0.650	0.621	5
6	0.942	0.888	0.837	0.790	0.746	0.705	0.666	0.630	0.596	0.564	6
7	0.933	0.871	0.813	0.760	0.711	0.665	0.623	0.583	0.547	0.513	7
8	0.923	0.853	0.789	0.731	0.677	0.627	0.582	0.540	0.502	0.467	8
9	0.914	0.837	0.766	0.703	0.645	0.592	0.544	0.500	0.460	0.424	9
10	0.905	0.820	0.744	0.676	0.614	0.558	0.508	0.463	0.422	0.386	10
11	0.896	0.804	0.722	0.650	0.585	0.527	0.475	0.429	0.388	0.350	11
12	0.887	0.788	0.701	0.625	0.557	0.497	0.444	0.397	0.356	0.319	12
13	0.879	0.773	0.681	0.601	0.530	0.469	0.415	0.368	0.326	0.290	13
14	0.870	0.758	0.661	0.577	0.505	0.442	0.388	0.340	0.299	0.263	14
15	0.861	0.743	0.642	0.555	0.481	0.417	0.362	0.315	0.275	0.239	15
(n)	11%	12%	13%	14%	15%	16%	17%	18%	19%	20%	
1	0.901	0.893	0.885	0.877	0.870	0.862	0.855	0.847	0.840	0.833	1
2	0.812	0.797	0.783	0.769	0.756	0.743	0.731	0.718	0.706	0.694	2
3	0.731	0.712	0.693	0.675	0.658	0.641	0.624	0.609	0.593	0.579	3
4	0.659	0.636	0.613	0.592	0.572	0.552	0.534	0.516	0.499	0.482	4
5	0.593	0.567	0.543	0.519	0.497	0.476	0.456	0.437	0.419	0.402	5
6	0.535	0.507	0.480	0.456	0.432	0.410	0.390	0.370	0.352	0.335	6
7	0.482	0.452	0.425	0.400	0.376	0.354	0.333	0.314	0.296	0.279	7
8	0.434	0.404	0.376	0.351	0.327	0.305	0.285	0.266	0.249	0.233	8
9	0.391	0.361	0.333	0.308	0.284	0.263	0.243	0.225	0.209	0.194	9
10	0.352	0.322	0.295	0.270	0.247	0.227	0.208	0.191	0.176	0.162	10
11	0.317	0.287	0.261	0.237	0.215	0.195	0.178	0.162	0.148	0.135	11
12	0.286	0.257	0.231	0.208	0.187	0.168	0.152	0.137	0.124	0.112	12
13	0.258	0.229	0.204	0.182	0.163	0.145	0.130	0.116	0.104	0.093	13
14	0.232	0.205	0.181	0.160	0.141	0.125	0.111	0.099	0.088	0.078	14
15	0.209	0.183	0.160	0.140	0.123	0.108	0.095	0.084	0.074	0.065	15

ANNUITY TABLE

Present value of an annuity of 1 i.e. $\dfrac{1-(1+r)^{-n}}{r}$ where r = discount rate, n = number of periods

Periods (n)	\multicolumn{10}{c}{Discount rate (r)}									
	1%	2%	3%	4%	5%	6%	7%	8%	9%	10%	
1	0.990	0.980	0.971	0.962	0.952	0.943	0.935	0.926	0.917	0.909	1
2	1.970	1.942	1.913	1.886	1.859	1.833	1.808	1.783	1.759	1.736	2
3	2.941	2.884	20829	2.775	2.723	2.673	2.624	2.577	2.531	2.487	3
4	3.902	3.808	3.717	3.630	3.546	3.465	3.387	3.312	3.240	3.170	4
5	4.853	4.713	4.580	4.452	4.329	4.212	4.100	3.993	3.890	3.791	5
6	5.795	5.601	5.417	5.242	5.076	4.917	4.767	4.623	4.486	4.355	6
7	6.728	6.472	6.230	6.002	5.786	5.582	5.389	5.206	5.033	4.868	7
8	7.652	7.325	7.020	6.733	6.463	6.210	5.971	5.747	5.535	5.335	8
9	8.566	8.162	7.786	7.435	7.108	6.802	6.515	6.247	5.995	5.759	9
10	9.471	8.983	8.530	8.111	7.722	7.360	7.024	6.710	6.418	6.145	10
11	10.37	9.787	9.253	8.760	8.306	7.887	7.499	7.139	6.805	6.495	11
12	11.26	10.58	9.954	9.385	8.863	8.384	7.943	7.536	7.161	6.814	12
13	12.13	11.35	10.63	9.986	9.394	8.853	8.358	7.904	7.487	7.103	13
14	13.00	12.11	11.30	10.56	9.899	9.295	8.745	8.244	7.786	7.367	14
15	13.87	12.85	11.94	11.12	10.38	9.712	9.108	8.559	8.061	7.606	15
(n)	11%	12%	13%	14%	15%	16%	17%	18%	19%	20%	
1	0.901	0.893	0.885	0.877	0.870	0.862	0.855	0.847	0.840	0.833	1
2	1.713	1.690	1.668	1.647	1.626	1.605	1.585	1.566	1.547	1.528	2
3	2.444	2.402	2.361	2.322	2.283	2.246	2.210	2.174	2.140	2.106	3
4	3.102	3.037	2.974	2.914	2.855	2.798	2.743	2.690	2.639	2.589	4
5	3.696	3.605	3.517	3.433	3.352	3.274	3.199	3.127	3.058	2.991	5
6	4.231	4.111	3.998	3.889	3.784	3.685	3.589	3.498	3.410	3.326	6
7	4.712	4.564	4.423	4.288	4.160	4.039	3.922	3.812	3.706	3.605	7
8	5.146	4.968	4.799	4.639	4.487	4.344	4.207	4.078	3.954	3.837	8
9	5.537	5.328	5.132	4.946	4.772	4.607	4.451	4.303	4.163	4.031	9
10	5.889	5.650	5.426	5.216	5.019	4.833	4.659	4.494	4.339	4.192	10
11	6.207	5.938	5.687	5.453	5.234	5.029	4.836	4.656	4.486	4.327	11
12	6.492	6.194	5.918	5.660	5.421	5.197	4.988	4.793	4.611	4.439	12
13	6.750	6.424	6.122	5.842	5.583	5.342	5.118	4.910	4.715	4.533	13
14	6.982	6.628	6.302	6.002	5.724	5.468	5.229	5.008	4.802	4.611	14
15	7.191	6.811	6.462	6.142	5.847	5.575	5.324	5.092	4.876	4.675	15

Section 1

PRACTICE QUESTIONS – SECTION A

> **Note:** From September 2018, Section A of the APM exam will only examine syllabus sections A, C and D. Some of the questions below were written before September 2018 and include requirements from other syllabus sections, i.e. B and E. These have been included since they serve as good revision of real past exam questions or exam standard questions and will also serve as good revision for Section B questions in the exam.

1   THYME (SEPT/DEC 17)

Thyme Engine Products (Thyme) manufactures jet aircraft engines for the commercial aircraft market. This is a worldwide business although Thyme's production and development are all based in the country of Beeland. Thyme is a listed company and its stated overall objective is to be 'a world-class jet engine manufacturer trusted by our customers to deliver excellent products'. Its promise to its shareholders is that it will maximise their returns. The strategy to achieve this is to use world-class engineering to design engines and high quality production and customer service in order to drive profitable growth.

Thyme's share price has recently suffered as a result of the failure of a new engine design which led to large cash losses and a difficulty in obtaining new financing. There has also been a bribery scandal involving a senior manager and one of its key customers. As a result, a new chief executive officer (CEO) has been employed and she has begun a major review of systems at Thyme.

The first area which the CEO wants to examine is the information given to the board for strategic decision-making in both the planning and controlling of the business. The government of Beeland has been encouraging information sharing between businesses and has recently sponsored awards for management accounting. The winner of the engineering sector has produced a sample dashboard template (with dummy figures) for an annual review and this is given in Appendix 1. The CEO realised that the winner had a very similar overall objective and strategies to Thyme and wants to know what it is about this dashboard that helped it win the award. She does not want a new dashboard for Thyme at this stage but there may be some useful, specific comments to make about the contents of the dashboard given Thyme's recent problems.

The CEO has also recently been reading about integrated reporting and in the light of this review of the dashboard, the CEO has also asked for your views on how integrated reporting might impact on the type of information prepared by the company's management accountants.

As high quality engineering products lie at the heart of Thyme's competitive advantage, there has been a total quality management (TQM) approach to the management of all resources and relationships throughout the business. Thyme currently has a project under consideration to develop a new simple jet engine which would compete in the crowded market for small corporate jets. In order to compete in this market, it is believed that a target costing approach to this new engine would be beneficial. The CEO wants you to calculate the target cost gap for the new engine using the data in Appendix 2. Next, she wants to know how the use of target costing would fit within the existing TQM approach for this new engine.

The new engine project has further raised the profile of quality as a broad issue at Thyme and the CEO wants your advice on the costs associated with quality. She needs to know the cost of each of the four categories of quality costs. She has gathered data in Appendix 3 for this exercise. She is happy that she has identified that prevention costs are complete but is worried that some of the possible costs for the other three categories are missing and needs suggestions of cost areas to be examined to identify these missing items. Finally, she needs advice on the relative importance to Thyme of each of the four categories.

Required:

Write a report to the CEO of Thyme to:

(i) Evaluate why the dashboard in Appendix 1 was award winning, as requested by the CEO.

(15 marks)

(ii) Explain broadly the role of the management accountant in providing information for integrated reporting. **(6 marks)**

(iii) Calculate the target cost gap for the new engine (using the data in Appendix 2) and assess how the use of this target cost will fit within the TQM approach. **(12 marks)**

(iv) Categorise and calculate the costs of quality at Thyme (given in Appendix 3). Suggest cost areas to be examined as required by the CEO, and evaluate the relative importance of each category to Thyme. **(13 marks)**

Professional marks will be awarded for the format, style and structure of the discussion of your answer. **(4 marks)**

(Total: 50 marks)

Appendix 1

Award winning performance dashboard

Report for the year to June 2017

	2015	2016	2017	Budget variance 2017	Growth 2016 to 2017	Budget 2018
Financial						
Revenue ($m)	10,652	11,213	11,500	234F	2.6%	11,776
Operating profit margin	16.2%	16.8%	17.2%	0.2 percentage points F	0.4 percentage points	17.2%
EVA™	746	774	815	48F	5.3%	803
Total shareholder return	6.5%	6.8%	11.1%	4.5 percentage points F	4.3 percentage points	7.5%
Design						
Class leading products in:						
fuel efficiency	3	3	3	0		3
noise levels	2	2	3	1F		3
chemical emissions	1	2	3	1F		3
Manufacturing						
Percentage of orders right first time	92.0%	92.4%	93.7%	0.7 percentage points F		93.0%
Delivery						
Deliveries on time	88.0%	89.9%	88.2%	0.2 percentage points F		88.0%
Marketshare (as percentage of market leader)	33.0%	35.2%	38.1%	1.1 percentage points F		39.0%

Commentary:

The revenue growth of the business remains strong above the average growth for the sector of 1·5%.

EVA™ is positive and growing indicating increased shareholder wealth.

Healthy and continuing growth in market share reflects an increased number of class-leading products and improvements in 'right on time' service to customers.

There have been no major new business risks arising during the period while market volume growth continues as expected.

Appendix 2

New jet engine

	$000/engine
Competitor price	2,500
Raw materials	200
Subcomponents bought in	600
Skilled labour	625
General labour	125
Production overheads	275
Planned profit margin 15%	

Notes:

1   Design and development has cost $120m and the engine is expected to sell approximately 1,200 units over its lifetime.

2   Sales and marketing costs are expected to be approximately 20% of the selling price.

3   The planned selling price is expected to match the competitor's price with the brand reputation of Thyme providing the competitive edge.

Appendix 3

Quality costs identified in current year

	$m
Repairs and replacements under customer warranties	223
Customer relationship management – complaint handling	56
Performance testing of final assembly	110
Performance testing of subcomponents from suppliers	28
Costs of re-inspection after repairs arising from final assembly testing	95
Training in quality control	11
Maintenance of inspection equipment	36

Notes:

1   The company spent $92m in the year buying higher quality raw materials to use in manufacture.

2   The company's revenue was $11,500m in the current year.

2   DARGEBOARD SERVICES (DS) (MAR/JUN 17)

Dargeboard Services (DS), a listed company, provides facilities management (FM) services where it manages such activities as cleaning, security, catering and building services on behalf of its clients. Clients can outsource to DS a single activity or often outsource all of these aspects in a full service contract.

The mission of DS is 'to give the shareholders maintainable, profitable growth by developing the best talent to provide world-class services with maximum efficiency.'

The board have asked the chief executive officer (CEO) to review the effectiveness of Dargeboard's systems for performance measurement and management. She has turned to you to begin this process by considering the strategic performance dashboard of DS. She has supplied the most recent example in Appendix 1.

She wants a report to the board which will cover three aspects of strategic performance reporting at DS. First, it should address whether the current set of key performance indicators (KPIs) measure the achievement of the mission by showing how each one links to all or part of the mission. She does not want suggestions of new indicators. Second, taking each of the current indicators in turn she wants the assumptions underlying the calculation of the indicators examined. There has been a suggestion made in the press that DS is producing a biased set of results aimed to mislead the markets. This would then artificially boost the share price and so boost the value of the senior management's share holdings. Third, the report should evaluate the other presentational aspects of the dashboard against best practice.

The idea of employee share ownership has always been at the heart of DS' remuneration schemes. Its aim is to   support an entrepreneurial culture and is a key differentiator in the market for new employees. The current reward system grants shares based on the appraisal of the individual by the line manager against vague categories such as leadership and entrepreneurship. The results of this scheme have been that only about 5% of staff received their maximum possible bonus in previous years and half of them received no bonus at all. Increasingly, this has led to the staff ignoring the reward scheme and describing it as 'only for the bosses' favourite people'.

In response to this, the board have been discussing methods of analysing and improving the rewards system at DS.   One non-executive director suggested using Fitzgerald and Moon's building block model. The CEO was asked to consider this as a project separate from the issues of performance measurement mentioned above. She will select suitable indicators from the dimensions but currently needs you to explain to the board what is meant by results and determinants in this context and how the dimensions link to standards and targets. Finally, she believes that there are two types of reward scheme which might suit DS and wants an evaluation of their relative strengths and weaknesses. The scheme details are given in Appendix 2.

Required:

Write a report to the board to:

(i) **Evaluate the links between the current key performance indicators at DS in Appendix 1 and its mission.** (8 marks)

(ii) **Assess the assumptions and definitions used in the calculation of the current set of key performance indicators in Appendix 1.** (12 marks)

(iii) **Evaluate the other aspects of reporting in the DS performance dashboard given in Appendix 1.** (8 marks)

(iv) **Explain how the building block model works as required by the CEO.** (6 marks)

(v) **Assess the two reward schemes given in Appendix 2.** (12 marks)

Professional marks will be awarded for the format, style and structure of the discussion of your answer. (4 marks)

(Total: 50 marks)

Appendix 1

Dargeboard Services: Strategic performance dashboard

Year to 31 December 2016

	Cleaning	*Security*	*Catering*	*Building services*	*Full service*	*Total*	*Total 2015*
Operating profit margin	6.5%	6.4%	6.5%	4.9%	5.9%	5.9%	5.8%
Secured revenue	76%	85%	92%	88%	93%	88%	87%
Management retention	86%	74%	87%	82%	89%	85%	87%
Order book ($m)	1,160	875	357	1,553	3,359	7,304	6,807
Organic revenue growth	7.1%	4.3%	5.0%	8.1%	7.9%	7.2%	4.6%
ROCE						17.2%	16%

KPI definitions and notes

1 Cleaning, security, catering and building services headings are for single service contracts.

2 No commentary is provided as the CEO talks the board through the dashboard at each board meeting.

3 Secured revenue is long-term recurring revenue. This is the percentage of budgeted revenue which is already contracted. The budget is often not completed until well into the year as it is a complex process. In 2016, the original budget showed revenue of $1,565m with the final budget signed off at the end of Q1 showing $1,460m. The secured (contracted) revenue for the period was $1,285m. The accounts show a year end revenue of $1,542m.

4 Management retention is the percentage of managers who were still employed throughout the whole year. The figure only includes those employees on full-time contracts (about 65% of all managers).

5 Order book is the total cash value of future contracted revenue. DS has contracts which run up to 10 years into the future.

6 Operating profit margin. This excludes exceptional items such as the reorganisation of the catering business which cost $55m in 2016, where revenue was $245m.

7 Organic revenue growth is calculated by using the total revenue figure as reported in the accounts. It includes net acquisitions which brought in revenue of $48m in 2016.

8 Return on capital employed (ROCE). Capital employed is total assets less current liabilities from the statement of financial position.

Appendix 2

The CEO is considering two schemes, one based on the current scheme and a new scheme.

Scheme 1 (based on the current scheme)

The reward system grants shares in DS based on the appraisal of the individual by the line manager against vague categories (leadership and entrepreneurship). The line managers have been informed that their bonus will in turn be partly dependent on how well they perform this appraisal. The expectation will be that as a result, 20% of staff will receive their maximum possible bonus and 20% will receive no bonus.

Scheme 2 (the new one)

Under scheme 2, employee targets are to be derived from the strategic indicators depending on the employee's area   of responsibility. The senior management (with help from line management where appropriate) will cascade down the strategic indicators to the relevant operational or tactical level for that employee.

There will be five targets set by senior and line management in consultation and the employee will then get up to 50% on top of their basic salary as a bonus (10 percentage points for each of the targets achieved).

3 FLACK (MAR/JUN 16)

Flack Supermarkets (Flack) is a multi-national listed business operating in several developing countries. The business is divided into two divisions: Metro, which runs smaller stores in the densely populated centres of cities and Hyper, which runs the large supermarkets situated on the edges of cities. Flack sells food, clothing and some other household goods.

Competition between supermarkets is intense in all of Flack's markets and so there is a constant need to review and improve their management and operations. The board has asked for a review of their performance report to see if it is fit for the purpose of achieving the company's mission of being:

'...the first choice for customers by providing the right balance of quality and service at a competitive price. We will achieve this through acting in the long-term interests of our stakeholders: earning customer loyalty, utilising all our resources and serving our shareholders' interests.'

This report is used at Flack's board level for their annual review. The divisional boards have their own reports. Also, there has been criticism of the board of Flack in the financial press that they are 'short-termist' and so the board wants your evaluation of the performance report to include comments on this. A copy of the most recent report is provided as an example at Appendix 1.

The board is considering introducing two new performance measures to address the objective of 'utilising all our resources'. These are revenue and operating profit per square metre. The CEO also wants an evaluation of these two measures explaining how they might address this aspect of the mission, what those ratios currently are and how they could be used to manage business performance. There is information in Appendix 1 to assist in this work.

There have been disagreements between Flack's divisional management about capital allocation. The divisions have had capital made available to them. Both sets of divisional managers always seem to want more capital in order to open more stores but historically have been reluctant to invest in refurbishing existing stores. The board is unsure of capital spending priorities given that the press comments about Flack included criticism of the 'run-down' look of a number of their stores. The board wants your comments on the effectiveness of the current divisional performance measure of divisional operating profit and the possibility of replacing this with residual income in the light of these problems.

As the company is opening many new stores, the board also wants an assessment of the use of expected return on capital employed (ROCE) as a tool for deciding on new store openings, illustrating this using the data in Appendix 2 on one new store proposal. The focus of comments should be on the use of an expected value not on the use of return on capital employed, as this is widely used and understood in the retail industry.

Finally, the CEO has proposed to the board that a new information system be introduced. She wishes to spend $100m on creating a loyalty card programme with a data warehouse collecting information from customers' cards regarding their purchases. Her plan is to use this information to target advertising, product range choices and price offers more efficiently than at present.

Required:

Write a report to the board of Flack to:

(i)	Evaluate the performance report of Flack, using the example provided in Appendix 1, as requested by the board.	**(14 marks)**
(ii)	Evaluate the introduction of the two measures of revenue and operating profit per square metre, as requested by the CEO.	**(8 marks)**
(iii)	Assess the proposal to change the divisional performance measure.	
	Note: No calculations of the current values are required.	**(8 marks)**
(iv)	Calculate the expected return on capital employed for the new store and assess the use of this tool for decision-making at Flack.	**(8 marks)**
(v)	Explain how the proposed new information system can help to improve business performance at Flack.	**(8 marks)**

Professional marks will be awarded for the format, style and structure of the discussion of your answer. **(4 marks)**

(Total: 50 marks)

Appendix 1: Board's performance report
Flack Year to 31 March

	Metro Budget 2016 $000	Metro Actual 2016 $000	Hyper Budget 2016 $000	Hyper Actual 2016 $000	Flack Budget 2016 $000	Flack Actual 2016 $000	Flack Actual 2015 $000	Change on PY $000
Revenue								
Food	1,093,521	1,104,567	5,431,277	5,542,119	6,524,798	6,646,686	6,513,752	2.04%
Clothes	765,465	773,197	3,801,894	3,879,483	4,567,359	4,652,680	4,536,363	2.56%
Other goods	328,056	331,370	1,629,383	1,662,636	1,957,439	1,994,006	1,964,096	1.52%
Total	2,187,042	2,209,134	10,862,554	11,084,238	13,049,596	13,293,372	13,014,211	2.15%
Cost of sales	1,994,583	2,014,730	10,199,937	10,408,099	12,194,520	12,422,829	12,186,796	1.94%
Gross profit	192,459	194,404	662,617	676,139	855,076	870,543	827,415	5.21%
Gross margins		8.80%		6.10%		6.55%		
Other operating costs	34,993	35,346	173,801	177,348	208,794	212,694	208,227	
Operating profit	157,466	159,058	488,816	498,791	646,282	657,849	619,188	6.24%
Operating margins		7.20%		4.50%		4.95%		
Finance costs					76,993	79,760	75,482	
Group profit before tax					**569,289**	**578,089**	**543,706**	6.32%
Tax					142,322	144,522	135,926	
Group profit after tax					**426,967**	**433,567**	**407,780**	6.32%
Total shareholder return						3.10%	2.70%	
Return on capital employed	13.2%	13.3%	13.2%	13.5%	13.2%	13.4%	13.2%	
Number of stores		533		208				
Total square metres		161,227		841,967				

Appendix 2: New store

The following data has been forecast by the marketing department for the new store based on Flack's existing experience. There are three possible scenarios:

Demand scenarios	Low	Medium	High
Revenue ($m)	12.5	13	13.5
Probability (%)	20	50	30
Forecast operating margin (%)	4.1	4.3	4.4

The new store is expected to cost $4.2m to buy, fit out and stock. The target ROCE for Flack has been set at 13%.

4   MONZA (SEPT/DEC 16)

Monza Pharma (Monza) is a developer and manufacturer of medical drugs, based in Beeland but selling its products all over the world. As a listed company, the overall objective of the company is to maximise the return to shareholders and it has used return on capital employed (ROCE) as its performance measure for this objective. There has often been comment at board meetings that it is good to have one, easily-understood measure for consideration.

The company has three divisions:

- the drug development division develops new drug compounds, taking these through the regulatory systems of different countries until they are approved for sale

- the manufacturing division then makes these compounds

- the sales division then sells them.

Monza's share price has underperformed compared to the market and the health sector in the last two years. The chief executive officer (CEO) has identified that its current performance measures are too narrow and is implementing a balanced scorecard (BSC) approach to address this problem. The current performance measures are:

- Return on capital employed

- Average cost to develop a new drug

- Revenue growth

The CEO engaged a well-known consulting firm who recommended the use of a BSC. The consultants began by agreeing with the board of Monza that the objective for the organisation's medium-term strategy was as follows:

- Create shareholder value by:

    - Innovating in drug development

    - Efficiency in drug manufacturing

    - Success in selling their products

The consulting firm has presented an interim report with the following proposed performance measures:

- Financial : ROCE

- Customer : Revenue growth

- Internal business process : Average cost to develop a new drug

- Learning and growth : Training days provided for employees each year

The CEO and the lead consultant have had a disagreement about the quality and cost of this work and as a result the consultants have been dismissed. The CEO has commented that the proposed measures lack insight into the business and do not appear to tackle issues at strategic, tactical and operational levels.

The CEO has decided to take this work in-house and has asked you as the performance management expert in the finance department to assist him by writing a report to the board to cover a number of areas. First, following the disagreement with the consultants, the CEO is worried that the consultants may not have been clear about the problems of using the BSC in their rush to persuade Monza to use their services.

Second, he wants you to evaluate the choice of performance measures currently used by Monza and those proposed by the consulting firm.

Third, there has been a debate at board level about how ROCE should be calculated. The marketing director stated that she was not sure what profit figure (of at least four which were available) should be used and why, especially given the large variation in result which this gives. She also wondered what the effect would be of using equity rather than all capital to calculate a return on investment. Some basic data has been provided in Appendix 1 to assist you in quantifying and evaluating these possibilities.

In addition to these concerns, the board is considering introducing a total quality management approach within Monza. Obviously, quality of output is critical in such a heavily regulated industry where the products can be a matter of life and death. There has been discussion about testing this idea within the manufacturing division. The CEO wants to understand, first, the costs associated with quality issues within that division. To aid your analysis, he has supplied some detailed information in Appendix 2. Next, the board requires an outline evaluation of how a total quality management (TQM) approach would fit within the manufacturing division.

Finally, the drug development divisional managers have been lobbying for a new information system which will assist their research chemists in identifying new drug compounds for testing. The new system will need to be capable of performing calculations and simulations which require high computational power and memory but will also need to have access to external data sources so that these scientists can keep up with developments in the field and identify new opportunities. The CEO is worried about the cost of such a new system and wants to know how it would fit within the existing lean management approach within that division.

Required:

Write a report to the board of Monza to:

(i)   Assess the problems of using a balanced scorecard at Monza.   **(8 marks)**

(ii) Evaluate the choice of the current performance measures and the consulting firm's proposed performance measures for Monza.   **(12 marks)**

(iii) Evaluate the effect of choosing different profit and capital measurements for different measures of return on investment and recommend a suitable approach for Monza.   **(11 marks)**

(iv) Analyse the current quality costs in the manufacturing division and then briefly discuss how implementation of total quality management would affect the division.   **(10 marks)**

(v)   Briefly advise on how the drug development division can aim to make the new information system 'lean'.   **(5 marks)**

Professional marks will be awarded for the format, style and structure of the discussion of your answer.   **(4 marks)**

(Total: 50 marks)

Appendix 1

Financial data for Monza for the most recent accounting period

	$m
Revenue	8,001
Costs	2,460
Gross profit	5,541
Other costs	3,248
Restructuring costs	482
Operating profit	1,811
Finance costs	266
Profit before tax	1,545
Tax	419
Profit after tax	1,126

Capital structure from the statement of financial position

Shareholders' equity	1,161
Long-term debt	8,739

Note: Restructuring costs relate to a major project which completed during the period.

Appendix 2

Cost information for the manufacturing division for the most recent accounting period

1   Batches rejected at factory valued at $17m which have a scrap value of $4m.

2   Training of factory staff which cost $8m.

3   Regulatory fines costing $5m (due to drug compounds being outside the specified range of mix of chemical ingredients).

4   Discounts given following customer complaints due to late delivery costing $22m.

5   Factory product testing department cost $12m.

6   Cost of raw materials was $1,008m.

5   BOLTZMAN (DEC 14 – AMENDED)

Boltzman Machines (Boltzman) is a listed, multinational engineering business. It has two divisions, one manufacturing aerospace parts and the other automotive parts. The company is known for innovation and it allows its managers much autonomy to run their own divisions and projects. There has been recent criticism at a shareholders' meeting of the executive management for not listening to shareholders' concerns and allowing this autonomy to run out of control. Therefore, the board at Boltzman have decided to create a framework which brings together all of the initiatives described below.

The chief executive officer (CEO) feels that the performance pyramid may be a suitable model for linking objectives and performance measures and has asked you to draft a report to the board to explain the model and how Boltzman's existing initiatives fit within it.

The initiatives which are running at present are:

1   An analysis of stakeholder influence at Boltzman leading to suitable strategic performance measures.

2   A benchmarking exercise of the performance measures from initiative 1 with Boltzman's main competitor, General Machines.

3   The introduction of quality initiatives bringing lean production methods to Boltzman.

The CEO also requires your input on each of these initiatives as they are all at various stages of progress:

First, a stakeholder analysis has been completed by one of Boltzman's managers (in Appendix 1) but she has gone on holiday and has not written up a commentary of her results. Therefore, the CEO wants you to take the information in Appendix 1 and explain the results and evaluate the suggested performance measures. The CEO has asked that you do not, at this stage, suggest long lists of additional indicators.

Second, the CEO wants you to use these suggested measures to benchmark the performance of Boltzman against General Machines. The CEO stated, 'Make sure that you calculate the measures given in Appendix 1. You should also add two justified measures of your own using the data provided. However, restrict yourself to these seven measures and don't drown us with detail about individual business units.' A junior analyst has gathered data to use in the benchmarking exercise in Appendix 2.

Third, the company has stated that one of its strategic aims is to be the highest quality supplier in the market place. In order to achieve this, the head of the aerospace division has already started a project to implement just-in-time (JIT) manufacturing. An extract of his email proposing this change is given in Appendix 3. The CEO feels that there are some important elements hinted at but not developed in this email. In particular, the CEO wants you to explain the problems of moving to JIT manufacturing.

Required:

Prepare a report to the board of Boltzman to:

(i) **Explain the four levels of the performance pyramid and discuss how the three initiatives relate to these levels.** (9 marks)

(ii) **Briefly justify appropriate management approaches to each of the stakeholders and, based on this analysis, evaluate the appropriateness of the performance measures suggested in Appendix 1.** (14 marks)

(iii) **Benchmark Boltzman against General Machines as suggested by the CEO, evaluating the approach to benchmarking used.** (16 marks)

(iv) **Explain the problems which will accompany a move towards just-in-time manufacturing at Boltzman.** (7 marks)

Professional marks will be awarded for the format, style and structure of the discussion of your answer. (4 marks)

(Total: 50 marks)

APPENDIX 1

Key stakeholders	Level of interest	Level of power
Shareholders	Low – institutions have delegated management to the board and are only interested in financial returns	High – ability to vote out existing management
Employees	Medium – in a high skill industry employees are interested in the new opportunities which the market can present	Low – although there is a group of key employees in product development whose skills must not be lost
Customers	Medium – some of the parts supplied by Boltzman are unique and specifically designed for the customer	High – as there are few major players in the aerospace and automotive businesses, the loss of a customer would have a significant impact on Boltzman
Suppliers	Medium – Boltzman is one of the large customers to many of the company's suppliers	Low – the suppliers are generally bulk component producers and there is significant competition for Boltzman's business

Suggested performance measures:

- Return on capital employed
- Economic value added
- Revenue growth
- Average pay per employee
- Net profit margin

Appendix 2

The figures are drawn from the financial statements for the year to September 2014.

	Boltzman $m 2014	General Machines $m 2014
Revenue	23,943	25,695
Cost of sales	18,078	20,605
Other costs	2,958	3,208
Operating profit	2,907	1,882
Financing costs	291	316
Tax	663	718
Net income	1,953	848

	Boltzman $m 2013	Boltzman $m 2014	General Machines $m 2013	General Machines $m 2014
Non-current assets	16,335	16,988	17,716	17,893
Current assets	10,618	11,043	11,515	11,630
	26,953	28,031	29,231	29,523
Equity	8,984	9,961	9,744	10,083
Non-current liabilities	9,801	9,739	10,629	10,405
Current liabilities	8,168	8,331	8,858	9,035
	26,953	28,031	29,231	29,523

		Boltzman 2014	General Machines 2014
Notes:			
No of employees		86,620	93,940
Staff costs	($m)	4,731	4,913
Revenue for 2013	($m)	22,506	25,438
Product development costs	($m)	2,684	2,630
No. of top 10 biggest potential customers where the business has top tier supplier status			
Aerospace		6	6
Automotive		7	8

A suitable cost of capital for both companies is 11%.

The tax rate is 28%.

Appendix 3

Extract of Head of Aerospace's email on his quality initiative:

In order to improve the quality and profitability of our products, we intend to begin by introducing a lean approach to manufacturing.

The first step in our move to lean manufacturing will be the introduction of JIT manufacturing. Although this will be a difficult process, the financial rewards in reduced working capital required and a decluttering of the workplace should be significant. We will have to consider how this change impacts up and down our supply chain with customers and suppliers.

6   CANTOR (JUN 14)

Cantor Group (Cantor) is a listed company with two subsidiaries, both involved in food and drink retailing in the small country of Deeland. Its mission is 'to maximise shareholder value through supplying good value food and drink in appealing environments for our customers'.

Cantor Cafes (Cafes) is the original operating company for the group and is a chain of 115 cafes specialising in different coffee drinks but also serving some simple food dishes. Cafes has been running successfully for 15 years and has reached the limit of its expansion as the cafe market is now considered to be saturated with competition. Further growth will occur only as the opportunity to obtain profitable, new sites is presented, although such opportunities are not expected to be significant over the next few years.

Cantor Juicey (Juicey) was started by the Cantor Group two years ago. Now, it is made up of 15 juice bars which serve a variety of blended fruit juice drinks and health snacks. The products served by Juicey have benefited from an increased awareness in Deeland of the need to eat and drink healthily. Cantor Group expects to increase the rate of property acquisition in order to feed the rapid growth of this business, intending to open 25 outlets per year for the next four years.

Cantor Group organises its two subsidiaries in a similar way, as they are involved in similar areas of business. There is one exception to this, namely in the arrangements over the properties from which the subsidiaries operate. Cafes rent their properties on the open market on standard commercial terms with a five-year lease at a fixed rental payable quarterly in advance. Juicey, on the other hand, has made a single arrangement with a large commercial landlord for all of its properties. Juicey has agreed that the rent for its sites is a percentage of the revenue generated at each site. Juicey believes that it can continue its expansion by obtaining more sites from this landlord under the same terms.

The board of Cantor is reviewing their performance reporting systems and would like your evaluation of the current report given in Appendix 1. This report contains information for both of the subsidiaries and the group and is used by all three boards. The CEO has advised you that the board does not require an evaluation of Cantor's performance. However, the CEO does want you to consider the cost structures at Cantor and advise on the implications of the mix of fixed and variable elements in the key cost areas of staff and property for performance management.

At a recent shareholder meeting of Cantor, one of the large shareholders expressed concern that the group lacks focus and suggested the introduction of value-based management (VBM) using economic value added (EVA™) as the measure of value. Cantor's CEO has asked you, their strategic management accountant, to give the board more information on the implications of this suggestion. She has asked you to do an example calculation of the EVA™ for the Group using the current data (Appendices 1 and 2) and explain how the shareholders might view the result. Next, the board needs to have the VBM system explained and evaluated to be able to make a decision about its use at Cantor.

Finally, the board is considering amending the mission statement to include more information on the ethical values of the company. The area being considered for inclusion in the overall mission is on the treatment of employees as it is felt that they should share in the progress and profitability of Cantor since a happy working environment will help them to better serve the customers.

The proposed new mission statement would read:

'to maximise shareholder value and to provide a fair deal to our employees by supplying good value food and drink in appealing environments for our customers.'

The CEO has asked you to consider how the Group's performance in the area regarding employees could be measured using the current management information at Cantor. You have obtained additional information from the management information system to assist with this task, given in Appendix 3.

Appendix 1

Cantor Group	Year to 31 March						Costs and profit as a % of revenue	
	Cafes	Cafes	Juicey	Juicey	Group	Group		
	Budget 2014	Actual 2014	Budget 2014	Actual 2014	Budget 2014	Actual 2014	Group	Industry average
	$	$	$	$	$	$		
Revenue								
Drink	47,437,500	46,521,000	5,130,000	5,398,000	52,567,500	51,919,000		
Food	15,812,500	15,913,000	570,000	582,000	16,382,500	16,495,000		
Total	**63,250,000**	**62,434,000**	**5,700,000**	**5,980,000**	**68,950,000**	**68,414,000**		
Cost of sales								
Drink	12,808,125	12,560,670	1,385,100	1,457,460	14,193,225	14,018,130		
Food	3,478,750	3,500,860	125,400	128,040	3,604,150	3,628,900		
Total	**16,286,875**	**16,061,530**	**1,510,500**	**1,585,500**	**17,797,375**	**17,647,030**	25.8%	
Gross profit	**46,963,125**	**46,372,470**	**4,189,500**	**4,394,500**	**51,152,625**	**50,766,970**	74.2%	72.8%
Staff costs	**16,128,750**	**15,920,670**	**1,453,500**	**1,524,900**	**20,082,250**	**21,345,000**	31.2%	30.9%
Other operating costs								
Rent	2,875,000	2,875,000	342,000	358,800	3,929,000	3,945,800		
Local property tax	920,000	920,000	60,000	60,000	980,000	980,000		
Insurance	276,000	282,000	18,000	18,400	294,000	300,400		
Utilities	874,000	861,000	61,500	62,900	935,500	923,900		
Marketing	6,957,500	6,888,000	627,000	750,000	7,584,500	7,638,000	11.2%	10.0%
Depreciation	4,427,500	4,427,500	353,400	353,400	4,780,900	4,780,900		
Total	**16,330,000**	**16,253,500**	**1,461,900**	**1,603,500**	**18,503,900**	**18,569,000**	27.1%	
Operating profit	**14,504,375**	**14,198,300**	**1,274,100**	**1,266,100**	**12,566,475**	**10,852,970**	15.9%	15.3%
Finance costs						798,000	801,000	
Group profit before tax					**11,768,475**	**10,051,970**	14.7%	
Tax						2,942,119	2,512,993	
Group profit after tax					**8,826,356**	**7,538,977**	11.0%	

Appendix 2

Additionally, you have discovered the following data about the group for the financial year:

1	Debt/Equity	30.0%
2	Cost of equity	15.7%
3	Tax rate	25.0%
4	Group ROCE	19.0%
5	Group capital employed: $53,400,000 at period start and $58,500,000 at period end.	
6	Pre-tax cost of debt	6.5%
7	There has been $2.1m of tax paid in the year.	
8	It is estimated that half of the marketing spend of $7.638m is building the Cantor brand long term.	
9	It is further estimated that there has been the same level of annual spending on long-term brand building in the years leading up to 2014.	

Appendix 3

Additional management information

No of employees	Cafes	Juicey	Group
At year start	1,495	96	1,611
Leavers	146	15	161
Joiners	152	35	187
At year end	1,501	116	1,637

Note:

1   Group numbers include Cafes, Juicey and head office numbers.

Required:

Write a report to the CEO of Cantor to:

(i)   Evaluate the current performance report in Appendix 1.   **(15 marks)**

(ii)   Assess the balance of fixed and variable elements of the CEO's two key costs in each of the two subsidiaries and the impact which this may have on performance management of these costs.

       Note: Detailed calculations are not required.   **(6 marks)**

(iii) Evaluate the economic value added (EVA™) of Cantor Group, justifying any assumptions made.   **(9 marks)**

(iv)   Explain how value-based management (VBM) could be implemented at Cantor and evaluate its potential impact on the group.   **(10 marks)**

(v)   Using the information in the appendices, provide justified recommendations for suitable performance measures to reflect the proposed change in the company's mission statement.   **(6 marks)**

Professional marks will be awarded for the format, style and structure of the discussion of your answer.   **(4 marks)**

(Total: 50 marks)

7 JHK COFFEE MACHINES CO (JUN 11 – AMENDED)

JHK Coffee Machines Co (JHK) manufactures coffee makers for use in bars and cafes. It has been successful over the last five years and has built and maintained a loyal customer base by making a high quality machine backed by a three-year warranty. The warranty states that JHK will recover and repair any machine that breaks down in the warranty period at no cost. Additionally, JHK always maintains sufficient spare parts to be able to quote for a repair of any of its machines made within the previous 10 years.

JHK is structured into two divisions: manufacturing/sales (M/S) and service. The board are now considering ways to improve coordination of the activities of the divisions for the benefit of the company as a whole.

The company's mission is to maximise shareholder wealth. Currently, the board use total shareholder return (TSR) as an overall corporate measure of performance and return on investment (ROI) as their main relative measure of performance between the two divisions. The board's main concern is that the divisional managers' performance is not being properly assessed by the divisional performance measure used. They now want to consider other measures of divisional performance. Residual income (RI) and economic value added (EVA™) have been suggested.

A colleague has collected the following data which will allow calculation of ROI, RI and EVA™.

	Manufacturing/sales	Service
	$m	$m
Revenue	880	17.0
Operating costs	494	11.0
Operating profit	386	6.0
Apportioned head office costs	85	1.0
Profit before tax	301	5.0
Capital employed	1,294	38.0

The notional cost of capital used is	9% pa
The current cost of debt is	5.5%
The tax rate is	30%

Operating costs include:

	Manufacturing/sales	Service
	$m	$m
Depreciation	88	2.7
Other non-cash expenses	4	0.3

All operating costs are tax deductible.

In addition to the divisional performance measures, the board want to consider the position of the service division. The standard costs within the service division are as follows:

	$
Labour (per hour)	18
Variable divisional overhead (per hour)	12
Fixed divisional overhead (per hour)	25

Overheads are allocated by labour hours

Currently, the service division does two types of work. There are repairs that are covered by JHK's warranty and there are repairs done outside warranty at the customer's request. The service division is paid by the customer for the out-of-warranty repairs while the repairs under warranty generate an annual fee of $10m, which is a recharge from the M/S division. The company sells 440,000 units per year and in the past, 9% of these have needed a repair within the three-year warranty. Parts are charged by the M/S division to the service division at cost and average $75 per repair. A repair takes two hours, on average, to complete.

The board are considering amending this existing $10m internal recharge agreement between M/S and service. There has been some discussion of tailoring one of the two transfer-pricing approaches (market price or cost plus) to meet the company's objectives.

Although the service division has the capacity to cover all of the existing work available, it could outsource the warranty service work, as it is usually straightforward. It would retain the out-of-warranty service work as this is a higher margin business. It would then begin looking for other opportunities to earn revenue using its engineering experience. A local engineering firm has quoted a flat price of $200 per warranty service repair provided that they obtain a contract for all of the warranty repairs from JHK.

Finally, the board are also considering a change to the information systems at JHK. The existing systems are based in the individual functions (production, sales, service, finance and human resources). The board are considering the implementation of a new system based on an integrated, single database that would be accessible at any of the company's five sites. The company network would be upgraded to allow real-time input and update of the database. The database would support a detailed management information system and a high-level executive information system.

Required:

Write a report to the finance director to:

(a) Evaluate the divisional performance at JHK and critically discuss the proposed measures of divisional performance. **(15 marks)**

(b) Outline the criteria for designing a transfer pricing system at JHK. **(5 marks)**

(c) Evaluate the two methods discussed of calculating the transfer price between the service and M/S divisions. (Perform appropriate calculations) **(12 marks)**

(d) Evaluate the potential impact of the introduction of the new information systems at JHK on performance management. **(10 marks)**

(e) Briefly describe the types of external information which the new system should seek to capture. **(4 marks)**

Professional marks will be awarded for the format, style and structure of the discussion of your answer. **(4 marks)**

(Total: 50 marks)

8   METIS RESTAURANTS (JUN 12 – AMENDED)

Metis is a restaurant business in the city of Urbanton. Metis was started three years ago by three friends who met at university while doing courses in business and catering management. Initially, their aim was simply to 'make money' although they had talked about building a chain of restaurants if the first site was successful.

The three friends pooled their own capital and took out a loan from the Grand Bank in order to fit out a rented site in the city. They designed the restaurant to be light and open with a menu that reflected the most popular dishes in Urbanton regardless of any particular culinary style. The dishes were designed to be priced in the middle of the range that was common for restaurants in the city. The choice of food and drinks to offer to customers is still a group decision amongst the owners.

Other elements of the business were allocated according to each owner's qualifications and preferences. Bert Fish takes charge of all aspects of the kitchen operations while another, Sheila Plate, manages the activities in the public area such as taking reservations, serving tables and maintaining the appearance of the restaurant. The third founder, John Sum, deals with the overall business issues such as procurement, accounting and legal matters.

Competition in the restaurant business is fierce as it is easy to open a restaurant in Urbanton and there are many competitors in the city both small, single-site operations and large national chains. The current national economic environment is one of steady but unspectacular growth.

The restaurant has been running for three years and the founders have reached the point where the business seems to be profitable and self-sustaining. The restaurant is now in need of refurbishment in order to maintain its atmosphere and this has prompted the founders to consider the future of their business. John Sum has come to you as their accountant looking for advice on aspects of performance management in the business. He has supplied you with figures outlining the recent performance of the business and the forecasts for the next year (see the performance report below). This table represents the quantitative data that is available to the founders when they meet each quarter to plan any short-term projects or initiatives and also, to consider the longer-term future. Bert and Sheila have often indicated to John that they find the information daunting and difficult to understand fully.

John Sum has come to you to advise him on the performance reporting at Metis and how it could be improved. He feels that the current report is, in some ways, too complex and, in other ways, too simple. He wants to look at different methods of measuring and presenting performance to the ownership group. As a starting point, he has suggested to you that you consider measures such as NPV, EVA™, MIRR as well as the more common profit measures. John is naive and wants the NPV and MIRR to be appraised as if the business was a three-year project up to 2012 so he knows the performance of the business to date. He has requested that other calculations in your performance review should be annual based on the 2012 figures although he is aware that this may be omitting in his words 'some important detail'.

At recent meetings, Sheila has been complaining that her waiters and waitresses are not responding well to her attempts to encourage them to smile at customers although her recent drive to save electricity by getting staff to turn off unnecessary lights seems to be working. Bert stated that he was not convinced by either of Sheila's initiatives and he wants her to make sure that food is collected from the kitchen swiftly and so delivered at the right temperature to the customer's table. Also, Bert has said that he feels that too much food is becoming rotten and having to be thrown out. However, he is not sure what to do about it except make the kitchen staff go through lengthy inventory checks where they review the food held in store. John is worried about these complaints as there is now an air of tension in the owners' meetings. He has been reading various books about performance management and has come across the quote, 'What gets measured, gets done.' He believes this is true but wants to know how it might apply in the case of his business.

Metis Performance Report

Metis Restaurant

			Year to 31 March		*Latest quarter to 31 March*	*Previous*
	Actual	*Actual*	*Actual*	*Forecast*	*2012*	*quarter*
	2010	*2011*	*2012*	*2013*	*(Q4 2012)*	*(Q3 2012)*
	$	$	$	$	$	$
Revenue						
Food	617,198	878,220	974,610	1,062,180	185,176	321,621
Wine	127,358	181,220	201,110	219,180	38,211	66,366
Spirits	83,273	118,490	131,495	143,310	24,984	43,394
Beer	117,562	167,280	185,640	202,320	35,272	61,261
Other beverages	24,492	34,850	38,675	42,150	7,348	12,763
Outside catering	9,797	13,940	15,470	16,860	2,939	5,105
Total	979,680	1,394,000	1,547,000	1,686,000	293,930	510,510
Cost of sales						
Food	200,589	285,422	316,748	345,209	60,182	104,527
Wine	58,585	83,361	92,511	100,821	17,577	30,528
Spirits	21,651	30,807	34,189	37,261	6,496	11,283
Beer	44,673	63,566	70,543	76,882	13,403	23,279
Other beverages	3,674	5,228	5,801	6,323	1,102	1,914
Outside catering	3,135	4,461	4,950	5,395	941	1,634
Total	332,307	472,845	524,742	571,891	99,701	173,165
Gross profit	647,373	921,155	1,022,258	1,114,109	194,229	337,345
Staff costs	220,428	313,650	348,075	379,350	66,134	114,865
Other operating costs						
Marketing	25,000	10,000	12,000	20,000	3,000	3,000
Rent/mortgage	150,800	175,800	175,800	193,400	43,950	43,950
Local property tax	37,500	37,500	37,500	37,500	9,375	9,375
Insurance	5,345	5,585	5,837	6,100	1,459	1,459
Utilities	12,600	12,978	13,043	13,173	3,261	3,261
Waste removal	6,000	6,180	6,365	6,556	1,591	1,591
Equipment repairs	3,500	3,658	3,822	3,994	956	956
Depreciation	120,000	120,000	120,000	120,000	30,000	30,000
Building upgrades				150,000		
Total	360,745	371,701	374,367	550,723	93,592	93,592
Manager salary	35,000	36,225	37,494	38,806	9,373	9,373
Net profit/loss before interest and corporate taxes	31,200	199,579	262,322	145,230	25,130	119,515
Net margin	3.2%	14.3%	17.0%	8.6%	8.5%	23.4%

Additional notes:

1   The business was founded with $600,000 which comprised $250,000 of equity from the founders and the remainder in a loan from Grand Bank. Under the terms of the loan, all principal is repayable in 10 years' time and interest is charged at a fixed rate of 8.4% per year.

2   John has estimated the overall cost of capital to be 12.5%.

3   The company earns 4.5% on any returns in its deposit account.

4   John wishes you to use the $600,000 original investment as the capital employed figure for analysis purposes as no new capital has been input and the owners have taken out all residual earnings so far as dividends.

5   The corporation tax rate for Metis is 30%, paid in the same year as profits are generated. Accounting depreciation is a tax allowable cost.

6   Marketing spending is for the short-term promotion of offers only.

Required:

Prepare a report to Mr John Sum addressing the following issues:

(a)   **Critically assess the existing performance report and suggest improvements to its content and presentation**   **(15 marks)**

(b)   **Comment on the performance of Metis using the data presented in the current performance report**   **(6 marks)**

(c)   **Calculate and briefly evaluate**

   (i)   **the use of John's suggested performance measures and**

   (ii)   **other profit-based measures, using the most recent year's actual figures where appropriate as examples**   **(15 marks)**

(d)   **Assess how the quote 'What gets measured, gets done' could apply to Metis.**

                                                                                                                                           (10 marks)

Professional marks will be awarded in question 1 for format, style, structure and clarity of the discussion.   **(4 marks)**

                                                                                                                                     (Total: 50 marks)

9   KOLMOG HOTELS (JUN 13)

Kolmog Hotels is a large, listed chain of branded hotels in Ostland. Its stated mission is: 'to become the No. 1 hotel chain in Ostland, building the strength of the Kolmog brand by consistently delighting customers, investing in employees, delivering innovative products/services and continuously improving performance'. The subsidiary aims of the company are to maximise shareholder value, create a culture of pride in the brand and strengthen the brand loyalty of all stakeholders.

The hotels in the Kolmog chain include a diverse range of buildings and locations serving different customer groups (large conference venues, city centre business hotels and country house hotels for holidays). For reporting purposes, the company has divided itself into the four geographical regions of Ostland as can be seen in a recent example of the strategic performance report for the company used by the board for their annual review (see appendix 1). At the operational level, each hotel manager is given an individual budget for their hotel, prepared in the finance department, and is judged by performance against budgeted profit.

Kolmog is planning a strategic change to its current business model. The board has decided to sell many of the hotels in the chain and then rent them back. This is consistent with many other hotel companies who are focusing on the management of their hotels rather than managing a large, property portfolio of hotels.

In order to assist this strategic change, the chief executive officer (CEO) is considering introducing the balanced scorecard (BSC) across Kolmog. He has tasked you, as a management accountant in the head office, with reviewing the preliminary work done on the development of the scorecard in order to ensure that it is consistent with the goal of meeting the strategic objectives of the company by tying operational and strategic performance measurement into a coherent framework.

The CEO is worried that the BSC might be perceived within the organisation as a management accounting technique that has been derived from the manufacturing sector. In order to assess its use at Kolmog, he has asked you to explain the characteristics that differentiate service businesses from manufacturing ones.

Senior executives at the head office of Kolmog have drawn up a preliminary list of perspectives and metrics as an outline of the balanced scorecard in table 1:

Table 1

Key strategic perspective	Metric
Strategic financial performance	– financial performance benchmarked to Kolmog's main competitors (share price and return on capital employed)
Customer satisfaction	– customer satisfaction survey scores
Hotel performance against budget	– variance analysis for each hotel
Employee satisfaction	– staff turnover

The history of rewards at Kolmog has not been good, with only 1% of staff receiving their maximum possible bonus in previous years and 75% of staff receiving no bonus. This has led to many complaints that targets set for the reward system are too challenging.

Under a new performance reward system, employee targets are to be derived from the above BSC strategic measures depending on the employee's area of responsibility. The new system is for hotel managers to be given challenging targets based on their hotel's performance against budgeted profit, industry wide staff turnover and the company's average customer satisfaction scores. The hotel managers will then get up to 30% of their basic salary as a bonus, based on their regional manager's assessment of their performance against these targets. The CEO wants you to use Fitzgerald and Moon's building block model to assess the new system. He is happy with the dimensions of performance but wants your comments on the standards and rewards being applied here.

Appendix 1

Strategic performance report for review

Kolmog Hotels year to 31 March 2013

	East region $m	West region $m	North region $m	South region $m	Total $m	Total 2012 $m	As % of revenue for 2013
Revenue	235	244	313	193	985	926	
Cost of sales	28	30	37	21	116	110	11.78%
Gross profit	207	214	276	172	869	816	
Staff costs	61	65	78	54	258	245	26.19%
Other operating costs							
hotels	68	70	97	54	289	270	29.34%
head office						158	150	16.04%
Operating profit	78	79	101	64	164	151	16.60%
Financing costs					78	73	7.92%
Profit before tax					86	78	8.73%

			Growth year on year
Capital employed	$1,132m	$1,065m	6.29%
EPS	$1.36	$1.27	7.09%
Share price	$12.34	$11.76	4.93%
ROCE	14.49%	14.18%	

Required:

Write a report to the CEO to:

(i)   explain the characteristics that differentiate service businesses from manufacturing ones, using Kolmog to illustrate your points   **(5 marks)**

(ii)   evaluate the current strategic performance report and the choice of performance metrics used (Appendix 1)   **(8 marks)**

(iii)   evaluate the outline balanced scorecard (Table 1) at Kolmog, suggesting suitable improvements   **(12 marks)**

(iv)   describe the difficulties in implementing and using the balanced scorecard at Kolmog   **(7 marks)**

(v)   explain the purpose of setting targets which are challenging, and evaluate the standards and rewards for the hotel managers' performance reward system as requested by the CEO.   **(14 marks)**

Professional marks will be awarded for the format, style and structure of the discussion of your answer.   **(4 marks)**

                (Total: 50 marks)

10   LOPTEN INDUSTRIES (DEC 13 – AMENDED)

  Question debrief

Lopten Industries is one of the largest, listed consumer durables manufacturers in the world, making washing machines, tumble dryers and dishwashers. It has recently expanded into Beeland which is a developing country where incomes have risen to the point where demand is increasing for Lopten's goods among the growing middle-class population.

Lopten believes in the economies of scale of large manufacturing sites with dispersed selling branches in the markets in which it operates. Therefore, it has entered the Beeland market by setting up a local sales force and supporting them with a national marketing campaign. The company is currently selling only two products in Beeland (both are types of washing machines):

- a basic product (called Cheerful) with functions which are comparable with the existing local competitors' output and

- a premium product (called Posh) which has functions and features similar to Lopten's products in other developed countries.

Both products are manufactured and imported from its regional manufacturing hub, which is in the neighbouring country of Kayland.

The competitive environment in Beeland is changing rapidly. The washing machine market used to be dominated by two large local manufacturers who make simple, cheap and reliable machines. There are two other major international manufacturers apart from Lopten. One of these has already opened a factory in Beeland and is producing machines similar to Cheerful to compete directly with the existing local producers. The government of Beeland has supported this new entrant with grants, as it is keen to encourage inward investment by foreign companies and the resulting expertise and employment which they provide. The other international competitor is now considering entering the Beeland market with more highly specified machines similar to Lopten's Posh brand.

Lopten's stated mission is to be the 'most successful manufacturer of its type of products in the world'. The board has set the following critical success factors (CSFs) for Lopten's Beeland operations:

1   to obtain a dominant market presence

2   to maximise profits within acceptable risk

3   to maintain the brand image of Lopten for above average quality products.

The board is considering using the following key performance indicators (KPIs) for each product: total profit, average sales price per unit, contribution per unit, market share, margin of safety, return on capital employed (ROCE), total quality costs and consumer awards won.

(**Note:** Margin of safety has been defined as [actual sales units – breakeven sales units]/actual sales units.)

The board has asked you as a consultant to assess its current performance measurement systems. They want a report which calculates the various indicators suggested above and then assesses how the key performance indicators address issues in the external environment. The report should assess the balance between planning and controlling represented by the KPIs as they want to ensure that these match what they should be doing at the strategic level in Lopten. Also, it should evaluate how the KPIs fit with the CSFs which have been selected. The data given in Appendix 1 has been collated for your use.

Finally, the board is considering two new marketing strategies going forward:

Plan A is to continue operations as at present allowing for 4% growth p.a. in volumes of both Cheerful and Posh.

Plan B is to dramatically reduce the marketing spend on Cheerful and to reallocate resources to focus the marketing on Posh. This is expected to lead to an anticipated growth in volume of 15% p.a. for Posh and flat sales for Cheerful.

The target operating profit for the Beeland operation in two years' time is set at $135m and the board wants an evaluation of these strategies in meeting that target.

Appendix 1: Beeland operation's information for the most recent financial year

	Cheerful	*Posh*	*Total*
Variable costs	$ per unit	$ per unit	
Materials	90	120	
Labour	60	80	
Overheads	40	50	
Distribution costs	45	45	
Quality costs	20	30	
Fixed costs	$m	$m	$m
Administration costs	18	18	36
Distribution costs	16	16	32
Quality costs	6	6	12
Marketing costs	80	80	160
Other data	$m	$m	$m
Revenue	448	308	756
Capital employed	326	250	576
	Units	Units	Units
Total market size (millions)	9.33	1.33	10.66
Beeland operation's sales (millions)	1.12	0.44	1.56

Notes:

1   Cheerful has won one best buy award from the Beeland Consumer Association.

2   Posh has won four best buy awards from the Beeland Consumer Association.

3   The allocations of fixed costs are based on a recent activity-based costing exercise and are considered to be valid.

Required:

Write a report to the board of Lopten which:

(i)   calculates the key performance indicators (KPIs) suggested by the board for the assessment of performance of the Beeland operations   **(11 marks)**

(ii)   uses PEST analysis to identify issues in the company's external environment and then evaluates the effectiveness of the suggested KPIs in addressing these issues
                                                                                            (11 marks)

(iii)   takes each critical success factor (CSF) in turn and evaluates how the suggested KPIs fit to the CSFs given   **(10 marks)**

(iv)   assesses the extent to which the suggested KPIs would be suitable for use in planning rather than controlling   **(5 marks)**

(v)   evaluates whether the two proposed marketing strategies result in Beeland hitting its operating profit target in two years' time.   **(9 marks)**

Professional marks will be awarded for the format, style and structure of the discussion of your answer.   **(4 marks)**

Note: All figures are real for the purpose of this scenario so that inflation can be ignored. Also, round to the nearest $million as appropriate.

                                                                                            (Total: 50 marks)

 Calculate your allowed time, allocate the time to the separate parts...............

11   MERKLAND SPORTSWEAR (JUN 15)

Merkland Sportswear (MS) is the market leader in sportswear in Ceeland, selling a variety of sportswear products under its own well-known brand. It is primarily a product development and marketing business as it contracts out all of its manufacturing to third parties around the world and it mostly sells its products through third-party retailers. It has only one store which is located in the capital city of Ceeland. The purpose of this store is to act as a centre for its marketing activities and to be a tangible representation of the MS brand. However, the main marketing activity for MS is the recruitment and promotion of star sports men and women as MS brand ambassadors. MS tries to have the most well-known sports star in each of the 10 most popular sports in Ceeland as an ambassador.

You are a performance management advisor to MS, brought into the company by the chief executive officer (CEO) to help the board with a number of issues. The first area which the board of MS requires your input is in a review of the existing performance dashboard for MS (Appendix 1). The dashboard is deliberately kept focused as it is for board use and the CEO has indicated that the three performance headings of 'financial, design and brand' will be kept at this time. The board has accepted that there may need to be up to two metrics for each of 'brand' and 'design' but they want to keep the number of financial metrics at three.

The mission statement of the business is designed to be broadly appealing. It is 'to inspire Ceelanders to compete'. From a business perspective, the aims are more focused, MS aims to grow as a business and to maximise shareholder wealth. The CEO further clarified the broad strategy to achieve these aims saying, 'We want to inspire competition not just in our customers but also within the company, to seek our greatest competitive advantage. We will achieve this by creating innovative products which provide reduced risk of injury and enhanced sporting performance supported by the best marketing operation in Ceeland.'

In order to assist in providing more detailed strategies to achieve these aims, the board has instituted a review of the competitive position of MS by commissioning a SWOT analysis (Appendix 2).

The CEO has asked that your first task be a review of the current dashboard metrics (Appendix 1). You should then review the SWOT analysis to suggest changes to the dashboard metrics within the constraints which the CEO has outlined.

Also, you are given details on a recent new development in the market. Nush Sportswear, one of the major competitors of MS, has recently suffered a scandal which has been widely reported. An investigative reporter discovered that one of the suppliers who manufactured sports shoes for Nush had been using child labour. The country in which the manufacturer worked had rules prohibiting child labour, but enforcement was very weak. This story has been widely covered in the media and has led to consumer boycotts and a review by the Ceeland business regulator into Nush's sourcing policies. It has been discovered that this is common practice in the sports footwear business where manufacturing is outsourced to such countries.

MS' shareholders have reacted with alarm to the potential damage that this could do to MS' brand. They have asked the board to consider changing their policy of outsourcing footwear manufacture. The board is considering two alternative responses:

1   Review and ensure that all outsourced footwear manufacture complies with appropriate employment terms and conditions (where necessary manufacturing would move to third-party companies in countries with appropriate regulation and enforcement); or

2   Create a manufacturing operation for MS in order to have full control of operations.

In response 1, the review of existing third-party manufacturers is being performed by a team from the procurement department. They have also considered the impact of moving all footwear sourcing to more strictly regulated environments. The results of this investigation are given in Appendix 3 and the board wants an evaluation of the qualitative and quantitative impact of this response.

In response 2, the board is considering setting up a factory for the manufacture of all MS footwear. They want to understand the impact of this on MS' existing performance metrics. First, they need a forecast of the profit from the factory as there are three distinct economic scenarios under which it might operate (see Appendix 4 for details).

Second, the board wants to know how the new factory will impact on the existing performance dashboard. However, since the probabilities of these economic scenarios are under debate, the board has said that they want this work to be independent of the results of the profit calculation from Appendix 4. Therefore, the board wants you to use an estimate of $103m profit before interest and tax from the new factory to evaluate the impact of the new factory on the dashboard. (This estimate is before product development and marketing costs as it only represents the manufacturing operation at the factory.)

Finally, the consultant who did the SWOT analysis has mentioned to the board that if they are thinking of reviewing their existing strategies, then they should consider using the value chain to secure competitive advantage. The CEO thinks that you should assess the implications of using the value chain for the performance management of MS. (An outline of the value chain is given in Appendix 5.)

Required:

Write a report to the board of MS to:

(i)   Assess the existing five metrics (Appendix 1). Using the SWOT analysis in Appendix 2, make suggestions for improvements within the constraints outlined by the CEO.

Note: You should ignore the impact of the Nush scandal in this part of the question.

(16 marks)

(ii)   Using the data in Appendix 3, assess the qualitative and quantitative impact on performance management at MS of response 1. (8 marks)

(iii)   Calculate the expected operating profit of the new factory and evaluate the use of this method of decision-making under risk. (6 marks)

(iv)   Using 2015 figures as a base, evaluate the impact of the new factory on the values and choice of metrics in the existing dashboard. (10 marks)

(v)   Explain the implications of using the value chain for performance management at MS. (6 marks)

Professional marks will be awarded for the format, style and structure of the discussion of your answer. (4 marks)

(Total: 50 marks)

Appendix 1

MS performance dashboard

Report for the year to March 2015

	2015	2014	2013	Change 2015/2014
Financial				%
Revenue ($m)	273	238	209	14.7%
Operating profit ($m)	71	60	54	18.3%
ROCE	41.7%	37.5%	36.0%	11.2%
Design				
Design awards won	2	2	1	0.0%
Brand				
Awareness	64%	63%	59%	1.6%

Notes:

Design awards are national clothing design awards which address both the look and technology in a product. Brand awareness is the percentage of those sampled who could identify the company's logo and can name at least one of its products.

Appendix 2

SWOT (completed before the Nush scandal was reported)

S:	W:
– High market share – Excellent brand awareness – Strong revenue growth (compared to industry average of 11%) – Supply chain management	– Loss of a key brand ambassador (who was injured when he tripped over the laces of his MS boots) – Weak IT expertise
O:	T:
– New products in the market for new sports (such as those being introduced at each World Championships)	– Growth of social media as main marketing channel

Appendix 3

Procurement review of new outsourced footwear manufacturers

Currently, MS buys 2 million pairs of shoes at an average of $21 per unit (a pair of shoes) and we assume an average selling price of $75. Cost per unit will increase by 10%. Additionally, there will be a need to perform annual audits of these suppliers which will cost $0.5m.

The change of policy will be marketed as sustaining the values of MS. The MS ethics code states 'We will play fair and source our goods responsibly.' This marketing will cost $0.8m p.a. but it is hoped that this will produce a gain in market share. However, the increase in sales cannot be estimated at this time as competitors are making similar moves. The reviewer commented, 'It would be helpful to know how many units we would need to sell in order to cover these increased costs so this can be used as a marketing target.'

Appendix 4

New factory

The data collected on the new factory depends on three possible economic scenarios in response to MS' change in sourcing policy:

	Bad	Medium	Good
Probability	30%	60%	10%
Units manufactured (000s)	1,800	2,000	2,200
Variable costs per unit ($)	21	22	23
Fixed costs ($000s)	2,500		
Capital required	$000		
Building and equipping	36,000		
Working capital	11,000		

Notes:

One unit is one pair of shoes.

Assume all units made are sold.

Assume an average selling price of $75.

The total Ceeland market for this type of shoe is estimated as 6.25m p.a.

Appendix 5

Value chain analysis

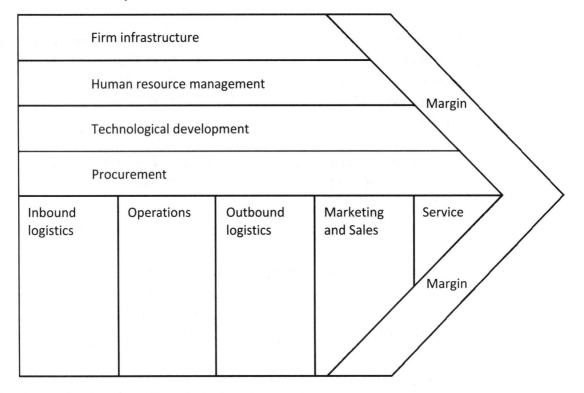

12 IRON CHICKEN (SEPT/DEC 15) (SPECIMEN 18)

Company information and mission

Iron Chicken (IC) is a multinational business which manufactures commercial building control systems. Building control systems include heating and air-conditioning systems, lighting controls, power and water monitoring and security systems (e.g. keypad access, alarms and CCTV). IC's manufacturing takes place at a number of factory sites where some products have a long product life and are simple and mass-produced while other products are complex and have a short product life due to changing technologies.

IC's mission statement is 'to create value for shareholders through control products which improve productivity, save energy and increase comfort and safety'.

A new chief executive officer (CEO) has been appointed to address a decline in IC's share price in the last three years. This CEO has identified that the business has grown through acquisition and as a result she stated, 'senior management have focused on making corporate deals and not making control systems.' The CEO has declared that the business must focus on optimising its value generation rather than just getting larger through acquisitions. She has developed an improvement programme for IC.

You are a performance management expert within IC and the CEO has tasked you with aiding her on four aspects of her improvement programme:

Economic value added (EVA™)

She wants your views on the use of EVA™ as the key performance metric at IC. You have been supplied with the current EVA™ calculation (Appendix 1) but there is some doubt about whether the junior management accountant who has done this work was sufficiently trained in the method.

Therefore, the CEO requires you to evaluate its accuracy and the assumptions which form part of the calculation and advise her on your results, providing calculations as needed.

Critical success factors (CSFs) and key performance indicators (KPIs)

The CEO believes that the poor performance of the company can be addressed by ensuring that the mission statement flows down into the performance management of the business. To that end, the following critical success factors (CSFs) and the associated current key performance indicators (KPIs) have been identified:

CSF	Associated current KPI
– Greater staff productivity	Units produced per labour hour
– Reduction of wastage in production	Power consumed per unit produced
– Greater innovation of products	Number of new products launched

The CEO wants you to briefly explain a weakness of the current KPI associated with each CSF and then provide a justified alternative KPI.

Improvement projects

In order to improve performance, the CEO plans to implement initiatives associated with 'lean' manufacturing. Specifically, there are three projects which have been suggested and the CEO needs your advice on these:

1   Move to just-in-time manufacturing

2   Use kaizen costing

3   Examine the costs of quality in achieving a 'zero defects' approach to manufacturing

The CEO has stated that she needs you to explain what the three improvement projects are, how they will help to meet the CSFs at IC and also how they will impact on the existing three KPIs.

New information system

The CEO is concerned about the implications of the improvement projects for IC's information systems as she feels that they are not currently suitable for the plan that she has. The current information systems of the company are based around the functional departments of the business such as manufacturing, marketing, finance and logistics. Each department has developed its own system although all feed into the finance system which is the main one used for strategic decision-making. In order that the department systems can all feed through to the current finance system, these current systems only handle quantitative data. The company is considering the implementation of a new information system. This new system will introduce networking technology in order to bring together all of the departmental systems into a new, single, corporate database.

Required:

Write a report to the CEO of Iron Chicken to:

(i)   Evaluate the EVA^{TM} calculation and the assumptions in Appendix 1 as required by the CEO.   **(15 marks)**

(ii)   Respond to the CEO's request for work on the KPIs, ensuring each of the three critical success factors are addressed.   **(6 marks)**

(iii)   Assess the three improvement projects as required by the CEO.   **(15 marks)**

(iv)   Assess the impact of the proposed, new information system on the three improvement projects.   **(10 marks)**

Professional marks will be awarded for the format, style and structure of the discussion of your answer.   **(4 marks)**

(Total: 50 marks)

Appendix 1

Economic value added

	$m	Note
Operating profit	551.4	
Add back		
Non-cash expenses	15.1	
Marketing capitalised	23.1	5
Less		
Tax	134.8	6
Lost tax relief on interest	24.5	7
	─────	
Net operating profit after tax (NOPAT)	430.3	
Capital employed		
From the statement of financial position	2,401.0	9
Marketing spend capitalised	23.1	5
	─────	
Adjusted capital employed	2,424.1	

WACC = (1/2 × 16%) + (1/2 × 6.8%) = 11.4%

EVA^{TM} = NOPAT – (WACC × Capital employed) = 154

Assumptions and notes:

1   Debt/Equity   100.0%

2   Cost of equity   16.0%

3   Tax rate   30.0%

4   Cost of debt (pre-tax)   6.8%

5   There has been $23.1m of marketing spent each year for the last two years in order to build the brand of IC long term.

6   Tax paid in the year was $130m while the tax charged per the accounts was $134.8m.

7   Interest charged in the period was $81.6m.

Lost tax relief on this interest was 30% × $81.6m.

8   The only research and development spending identified in the last five years was $10m expensed during this year on a new product.

The product has not been launched yet.

9   Capital employed during the period (from the statement of financial position):

Opening	2,282.0
Change in period	119.0
	————
Closing	2,401.0

Section 2

PRACTICE QUESTIONS – SECTION B

> **Note:** From September 2018, Section B of the APM exam will include one question from syllabus section E and one question from any other syllabus section. In addition, there will be two compulsory 25 mark questions in Section B. Previously, candidates chose 2 from 3 questions worth 25 marks each. Any reference to question choice (for example, in the Examiner's comments) relates to exams set prior to September 2018.

A – STRATEGIC PLANNING AND CONTROL

13 CUTHBERT (MAR/JUN 16)

Cuthbert is based in Ceeland and manufactures jackets for use in very cold environments by mountaineers and skiers. It also supplies the armed forces in several countries with variants of existing products, customised by the use of different coloured fabrics, labels and special fastenings for carrying equipment. Cuthbert incurs high costs on design and advertising in order to maintain the reputation of the brand.

Each jacket is made up of different shaped pieces of fabric called 'components'. These components are purchased by Cuthbert from an external supplier. The external supplier is responsible for ensuring the quality of the components and the number of purchased components found to be defective is negligible. The cost of the components forms 80% of the direct cost of each jacket, and the prices charged by Cuthbert's supplier for the components are the lowest in the industry. There are three stages to the production process of each jacket, which are each located in different parts of the factory:

Stage 1 – Sewing

The fabric components are sewn together by a machinist. Any manufacturing defects occurring after sewing has begun cannot be rectified, and finished garments found to be defective are heavily discounted, or in the case of bespoke variants, destroyed.

Stage 2 – Assembly

The garments are filled with insulating material and sewn together for the final time.

Stage 3 – Finishing

Labels, fastenings and zips are sewn to the finished garments. Though the process for attaching each of these is similar, machinists prefer to work only on labels, fastenings or zips to maximise the quantity which they can sew each hour.

Jackets are produced in batches of a particular style in a range of sizes. Throughout production, the components required for each batch of jackets are accompanied by a paper batch card which records the production processes which each batch has undergone. The batch cards are input into a production spreadsheet so that the stage of completion of each batch can be monitored and the position of each batch in the factory is recorded.

There are 60 machinists working in the sewing department, and 40 in each of the assembly and finishing departments. All the machinists are managed by 10 supervisors whose duties include updating the batch cards for work done and inputting this into a spreadsheet, as well as checking the quality of work done by machinists. The supervisors report to the factory manager, who has overall responsibility for the production process.

Machinists are paid an hourly wage and a bonus according to how many items they sew each week, which usually comprises 60% of their total weekly wages.

Supervisors receive an hourly wage and a bonus according to how many items their team sews each week. The factory manager receives the same monthly salary regardless of production output. All employees are awarded a 5% annual bonus if Cuthbert achieves its budgeted net profit for the year.

Recently, a large emergency order of jackets for the Ceeland army was cancelled by the customer as it was not delivered on time due to the following quality problems and other issues in the production process:

- A supervisor had forgotten to input several batch cards and as a result batches of fabric components were lost in the factory and replacements had to be purchased.

- There were machinists available to sew buttons onto the jackets, but there was only one machinist available who had been trained to sew zips. This caused further delay to production of the batch.

- When the quality of the jackets was checked prior to despatch, many of them were found to be sewn incorrectly as the work had been rushed. By this time the agreed delivery date had already passed, and it was too late to produce a replacement batch.

This was the latest in a series of problems in production at Cuthbert, and the directors have decided to use business process reengineering (BPR) in order to radically change the production process.

The proposal being considered as an application of BPR is the adoption of 'team working' in the factory, the three main elements of which are as follows:

1   Production lines would re-organise into teams, where **all** operations on a particular product type are performed in one place by a dedicated team of machinists.

2   Each team of machinists would be responsible for the quality of the finished jacket, and for the first time, machinists would be encouraged to bring about improvements in the production process. There would no longer be the need to employ supervisors and the existing supervisors would join the teams of machinists.

3   The number of batches in production would be automatically tracked by the use of radio frequency identification (RFID) tags attached to each jacket. This would eliminate the need for paper batch cards, which are currently input into a spreadsheet by the supervisors.

You have been asked as a performance management consultant to advise the board on whether business process reengineering could help Cuthbert overcome the problems in its production process.

Required:

(a) Advise how the proposed use of BPR would influence the operational performance of Cuthbert. **(14 marks)**

(b) Evaluate the effectiveness of the current reward systems at Cuthbert, and recommend and justify how these systems would need to change if the BPR project goes ahead. **(11 marks)**

(Total: 25 marks)

14 FRAMILTONE (SEPT/DEC 16)

Framiltone is a food manufacturer based in Ceeland, whose objective is to maximise shareholder wealth. Framiltone has two divisions: Dairy division and Luxury division. Framiltone began manufacturing dairy foods 20 years ago and Dairy division, representing 60% of total revenue, is still the larger of Framiltone's two divisions.

Dairy division

This division manufactures cheeses and milk-based desserts. The market in Ceeland for these products is saturated, with little opportunity for growth. Dairy division has, however, agreed profitable fixed price agreements to supply all the major supermarket chains in Ceeland for the next three years. The division has also agreed long-term fixed volume and price contracts with suppliers of milk, which is by far the most significant raw material used by the division.

In contrast to Luxury division, Dairy division does not operate its own fleet of delivery vehicles, but instead subcontracts this to a third party distribution company. The terms of the contract provide that the distribution company can pass on some increases in fuel costs to Framiltone. These increases are capped at 0.5% annually and are agreed prior to the finalisation of each year's budget.

Production volumes have shown less than 0.5% growth over the last five years. Dairy division managers have invested in modern production plant and its production is known to be the most efficient and consistent in the industry.

Luxury division

This division was set up two years ago to provide an opportunity for growth which is absent from the dairy foods sector. Luxury division produces high quality foods using unusual, rare and expensive ingredients, many of which are imported from neighbouring Veeland. The product range changes frequently according to consumer tastes and the availability and price of ingredients. All Luxury division's products are distributed using its own fleet of delivery vehicles.

Since the company began, Framiltone has used a traditional incremental budgeting process. Annual budgets for each division are set by the company's head office after some consultation with divisional managers, who currently have little experience of setting their own budgets. Performance of each division, and of divisional managers, is appraised against these budgets. For many years, Framiltone managed to achieve the budgets set, but last year managers at Luxury division complained that they were unable to achieve their budget due to factors beyond their control. A wet growing season in Veeland had reduced the harvest of key ingredients in Luxury's products, significantly increasing their cost. As a result, revenue and gross margins fell sharply and the division failed to achieve its operating profit target for the year.

Framiltone has just appointed a new CEO at the end of Q1 of the current year. He has called you as a performance management expert for your advice.

'In my last job in the retail fashion industry, we used rolling budgets, where the annual budget was updated to reflect the results of every quarter's trading. That gives a more realistic target, providing a better basis on which to appraise divisional performance. Do you think we should use a similar system for all divisions at Framiltone?', he asked.

You have obtained the current year budget for Luxury division and the division's Q1 actual trading results (Appendix 1) and notes outlining expectations of divisional key costs and revenues for the rest of the year (Appendix 2).

Appendix 1

Luxury division current year budget

C$000	Q1	Q2	Q3	Q4	Total	Q1 Actual
Revenue	10,000	12,000	11,000	7,000	40,000	10,400
Cost of sales	(6,100)	(7,120)	(6,460)	(4,720)	(24,400)	(6,240)
Gross profit	3,900	4,880	4,540	2,280	15,600	4,160
Distribution costs	(600)	(720)	(660)	(420)	(2,400)	(624)
Administration costs	(2,300)	(2,300)	(2,300)	(2,300)	(9,200)	(2,296)
Operating profit	1,000	1,860	1,580	(440)	4,000	1,240

Appendix 2

Expected key costs and revenues for remainder of the current year

1   Sales volumes are expected to be 2% higher each quarter than forecast in the current budget.

2   Average selling price per unit is expected to increase by 1.5% from the beginning of Q3.

3   The exchange rate between the Ceeland Dollar (C$) and the Veeland Dollar (V$) is predicted to change at the beginning of Q2 to C$1.00 buys V$1.50. For several years up to the end of Q1, C$1.00 has been equivalent to V$1.40 and this exchange rate has been used when producing the current year budget. Food produced in the Luxury division is despatched immediately upon production and Framiltone holds minimal inventory. The cost of ingredients imported from Veeland represents 50% of the division's cost of sales and suppliers invoice goods in V$.

4   The rate of tax levied by the Ceeland government on the cost of fuel which Luxury uses to power its fleet of delivery vehicles is due to increase from 60%, which it has been for many years, to 63% at the beginning of quarter 3. 70% of the division's distribution costs are represented by the cost of fuel for delivery vehicles.

5   The CEO has initiated a programme of overhead cost reductions and savings of 2.5% from the budgeted administration costs are expected from the beginning of Q2. Q3 administration costs are expected to be a further 2.5% lower than in Q2, with a further 2.5% saving in Q4 over the Q3 costs.

Required:

(a) **Using the data in the appendices, recalculate the current year budget to the end of the current year and briefly comment on the overall impact of this on the expected operating profit for the year.** **(12 marks)**

(b) **Evaluate whether a move from traditional incremental budgeting to a system of rolling budgets would be appropriate for Dairy and Luxury divisions.** **(13 marks)**

(Total: 25 marks)

15 BRIGGS

Briggs was started 5 years ago by Tom Briggs to offer lifestyle and (some) counselling services online. The company's initial strategy was to grow its share in the market and, given it had very few employees, its structure was very simple. There were very few formal systems, mainly because the company didn't need many at this time. Tom adopted a democratic but chaotic management style and attracted experienced staff who were adventurous and valued team work. Initial joiners were also offered shares in the company to help motivate them.

Since then the company has grown to become a large business with 400 employees and has now achieved a 50% market share in its domestic market. Its structure has changed and is now a well-oiled bureaucratic machine based on functional lines with strong service support. To facilitate this, Tom introduced new motivation, reward and control systems based on bonuses and specific individual targets, recruited experts in different fields and encouraged a culture of enthusiasm and excellence.

However, Tom has recently become concerned about the following:

• Trust and teamwork have disappeared due to so many new employees.

• He has been criticised for still trying the run the company as if it were a small business.

• There is no formal strategic planning process in place.

• To grow further Tom is considering expansion into foreign markets.

Required:

(a) **Briefly describe McKinsey's 7S model.** **(5 marks)**

(b) **Using McKinsey's 7S model, analyse the key performance management issues facing the firm.** **(14 marks)**

(c) **Assuming a divisional structure is set up for each country, suggest, with reasons, TWO critical success factors with ONE key performance indicator for each, that could be applied for each new country.** **(6 marks)**

(Total: 25 marks)

16   ALFLONNSO (SEPT/DEC 16)

Alflonnso is a large producer of industrial chemicals, with divisions in 25 countries. The agrochemicals division produces a chemical pesticide, known internally as 'ALF', to control pests in a crop which is of worldwide significance, economically and for food production. Pesticides such as ALF only remain effective for a limited time, after which pests become resistant to them and a replacement product needs to be found. A scientific study has shown that the current variant, ALF6, is becoming ineffective in controlling pests and in some places, it has accumulated in the soil to levels which may significantly reduce crop yields in the future if it is continued to be used. The agrochemicals division is evaluating three new products to find one replacement for ALF6.

ALF7

ALF7 is produced by a small chemical modification to the existing product and requires little research and development (R&D) resources to develop it. As it is closely related to the current variant, it is only expected to remain effective, and in use, for three years. It is unclear whether ALF7 will accumulate in the soil in the same way as ALF6 does.

Red

Red is a new type of pesticide which will incur large amounts of R&D expenditure to develop a commercial version. In addition, the agrochemicals division will have to fund a long-term scientific study into the effect of Red on the environment at a cost of $4m for each of the 15 years that the product will be in use, and for five years afterwards.

Production of Red generates large amounts of toxic by-products which must be treated in the division's waste treatment facility. The production plant used to produce Red must also be decommissioned for cleaning, at an estimated cost of $45m, at the end of the life of the product.

Green

Green is a form of a naturally occurring chemical, thought to be safe and not to accumulate in the environment. It is expected to remain in use for eight years. Production of Green requires relatively large amounts of energy. Significant R&D expenditure is also needed to produce an effective version, as Green remains active in the environment for only a short time. Because of this, Green is unsuitable for use in climates where crop production is already difficult.

The Global Food Production Organisation (GFPO) is a non-governmental organisation which funds new ways to increase global crop production, especially in regions where food for human consumption is already scarce. The GFPO has agreed to make a significant contribution to the R&D costs of producing a replacement for ALF6, but will be unwilling to contribute to the R&D costs for Green because it cannot be used in every region. Similarly, a number of governments, in countries where Alflonnso has licences to operate its other chemical businesses, have warned the company of the potential public disapproval should the agrochemical division choose to replace ALF6 with a product unsuitable for use in areas where food production is scarce.

The newly appointed chief financial officer (CFO) for the agrochemicals division has asked you as a performance management consultant for your advice. 'One of our analysts in the agrochemicals division', she said, 'has produced a single period statement of profit or loss (Appendix 1) to show the profitability of the three new products we are considering as replacements for ALF6.'

'I think the analyst's calculations are too simplistic', she continued. 'The costs of the waste treatment are apportioned based on the expected revenue of the new products. This is consistent with Alflonnso's traditional group accounting policy, but I don't think this gives an accurate costing for the new products. Also, I watched a presentation recently about the use of lifecycle costing and also how environmental management accounting (EMA) can help reduce costs in the categories of conventional, contingent and reputation costs and as a result improve performance.'

Appendix 1

Single period statement of profit or loss for the replacement products for ALF6[1]

	ALF7	Red	Green
Revenue per litre ($)	8.00	13.00	11.00
Quantity sold and produced (million litres)	100	85	75
	$m	$m	$m
Revenue	800	1,105	825
Direct material, labour and energy	(524)	(724)	(565)
Factory overheads	(80)	(122)	(74)
Environmental study	–	(4)	–
Waste treatment of toxic by-products[2]	(54)	(63)	(71)
Net profit[3]	142	192	115
Average profit per litre ($)	1.42	2.26	1.53

Notes to the statement of profit or loss:

[1] – All figures exclude the contribution from the GFPO towards the R&D costs of the new product.

[2] – Waste treatment is an overhead cost incurred in the division's waste treatment facility. Currently, costs of waste treatment are apportioned to products according to expected revenue. The total annual cost of the waste treatment facility, which processes a total of 55m litres of waste each year, is $300m. Any waste treatment capacity not used by any of the three new products can be used to treat waste created during the manufacture of other products in the division. One litre of waste by-product is produced for every 12.5 litres of ALF7 produced, for every 2.5 litres of Red produced and for every 100 litres of Green.

[3] – R&D costs are incurred in the division's R&D facility. In accordance with the group's accounting policy, R&D expenditure is not currently apportioned to individual products. The annual cost of the R&D facility is $60m and has a total of 30,400 R&D hours available, of which 800 hours would be required to develop ALF7, 8,500 hours to develop Red, and 4,000 hours to develop Green.

Required:

(a) (i) Explain how activity based costing may help the agrochemicals division in assessing the profitability of the three new products. **(5 marks)**

    (ii) Using activity based costing, and excluding the value of the grant from the GFPO, calculate the total R&D costs and waste treatment costs of the three new products. **(3 marks)**

(b) Using your answers from part (a) (ii), calculate the average net profit per litre of each of the three alternative new products over their expected lifecycles and comment on the results. **(9 marks)**

(c) Advise how environmental management accounting (EMA) may help improve the performance of the agrochemicals division. **(8 marks)**

(Total: 25 marks)

17 GODEL (JUN 14 – AMENDED)

Godel Goodies (Godel) manufactures a variety of own-label sweets for the two largest supermarket chains in Seeland. The business makes several different flavours of the same basic product. The strategy of the business has been to be a cost leader in order to win the supermarkets' business. The sales of Godel vary up and down from quarter to quarter depending on the state of the general economy and competitive forces.

Most of the sweet manufacturers have been in business for decades and so the business is mature with little scope to be innovative in new product development. The supermarkets prefer to sign suppliers to long-term contracts and so it is difficult for new entrants to gain a foothold in this market. The management style at Godel is very much command-and-control which fits with the strategy and type of business. Indeed, most employees have been at Godel for many years and have expressed their liking for the straightforward nature of their work.

The chief executive officer (CEO) of Godel has asked your firm of accountants to advise him as his finance director (FD) will be absent for several months due to a recently diagnosed illness. As the CEO is preparing for the next board meeting, he has obtained the operating statement and detailed variance analysis from one of the junior accountants (Appendix 1).

The CEO is happy with the operating statement but wants to understand the detailed operational and planning variances, given in Appendix 1, for the board meeting. He needs to know what action should be taken as a result of these specific variances.

The FD had been looking at the budgeting process before she fell ill. The CEO has decided that you should help him by answering some questions on budgeting at Godel.

Currently, the budget at Godel is set at the start of the year and performance is measured against this. The company uses standard costs for each product and attributes overheads using absorption costing based on machine hours. No variations are allowed to the standard costs during the year.

The standard costs and all budget assumptions are based on adjusting previous year figures, along with discussions with the relevant operational manager before being set. However, these managers grumble that the budget process is very time-consuming and that the results are ultimately of limited value from their perspective. Some of them also complain that they must frequently explain that the variances are not their fault. The CEO wants to know your views on whether this way of budgeting is appropriate and whether the managers' complaints are justified. He is satisfied that there is no dysfunctional behaviour at Godel which may lead to budget slack or excessive spending and that all managers are working in the best interests of the company.

Finally, in the last few months, the FD had been reading business articles and books and had mentioned that there were a number of organisations which were adopting zero-based budgeting to reduce planning variances. The CEO is concerned that he does not understand what budgeting does for the business and this is why he wants you to explain what are the benefits and problems of budgeting at Godel before considering switching to an alternative approach.

Required:

(a) Advise the CEO on the implications for performance management at Godel of analysing variances into the planning and operational elements as shown in Appendix 1. **(6 marks)**

(b) Evaluate the budgeting system at Godel. **(11 marks)**

(c) Evaluate the proposal to move to zero-based budgeting at Godel, giving a recommendation on whether to proceed. **(8 marks)**

(Total: 25 marks)

Appendix 1

Note: You may assume that all figures in this appendix are correct.

Operating statement for Godel

Period: May 2014

	$	$	
Budgeted profit		214,200	
Budget fixed production costs		264,180	Favourable
		———	
Budgeted contribution		478,380	
Sales variances volume	20,100		Adverse
price	8,960		Adverse
	———		
	29,060	Adverse	
		———	
Actual sales minus standard cost of sales		449,320	

		Favourable $	Adverse $	
Variable cost variance				
Material	price		4,200	
	usage	3,500		
Labour	rate	1,100		
	efficiency	24,480		
	idle time		5,600	
Variable overhead	expenditure		1,080	
	efficiency	3,060		
		———	———	
		32,140	10,880	

	$	
	21,260	Favourable
Actual contribution	470,580	

	$	$	
Budgeted fixed production overhead	271,728		
Expenditure variance	18,696		Adverse
	———		
Actual fixed production overhead		290,424	
		———	
Actual profit		180,156	

Detailed variances

		$	
Total variable cost variances			
	Planning	20,680	Favourable
	Operational	580	Favourable
Sales price variances			
	Planning	15,600	Adverse
	Operational	6,640	Favourable

18 DIBBLE (MAR/JUN 16)

Dibble is formed of two autonomous divisions, Timber and Steel, and manufactures components for use in the construction industry. Dibble has always absorbed production overheads to the cost of each product on the basis of machine hours.

Timber Division

Timber Division manufactures timber frames used to support the roofs of new houses. The timber, which is purchased pre-cut to the correct length, is assembled into the finished frame by a factory worker who fastens the components together. Timber Division manufactures six standard sizes of frame which is sufficient for use in most newly built houses.

Steel Division

Steel Division manufactures steel frames and roof supports for use in small commercial buildings such as shops and restaurants. There is a large range of products, and many customers also specify bespoke designs for short production runs or one-off building projects. Steel is cut and drilled using the division's own programmable computer aided manufacturing machinery (CAM), and is bolted together or welded by hand.

Steel Division's strategy is to produce novel bespoke products at a price comparable to the simpler and more conventional products offered by its competitors. For example, many of Steel Division's customers choose to have steel covered in one of a wide variety of coloured paints and other protective coatings at the end of the production process. This is performed off-site by a subcontractor, after which the product is returned to Steel Division for despatch to the customer. Customers are charged the subcontractor's cost plus a 10% mark up for choosing this option. The board of Steel Division has admitted that this pricing structure may be too simplistic, and that it is unsure of the overall profitability of sales of some groups of products or sectors of the market.

Recently, several customers have complained that incorrectly applied paint has flaked off the steel after only a few months' use. More seriously, a fast food restaurant has commenced litigation with Dibble after it had to close for a week while steel roof frames supplied by Steel Division were repainted. Following this, the production manager has proposed increasing the number of staff inspecting the quality of coating on the frames, and purchasing expensive imaging machinery to make inspection more efficient.

The chief executive officer (CEO) at Dibble has approached you as a performance management expert for your advice. 'At a conference recently', he told you, 'I watched a presentation by a CEO at a similar business to ours talking about the advantages and disadvantages of using activity based costing (ABC) and how over several years the adoption of activity based management (ABM) had helped them to improve both strategic and operational performance.'

'I don't want you to do any detailed calculations at this stage, but I'd like to know more about ABC and ABM, and know whether they would be useful for Dibble', he said.

You are provided with extracts of the most recent management accounts for Timber and Steel Divisions:

Division ($000)	Timber	Steel
Revenue	25,815	20,605
Materials	12,000	10,100
Direct labour	4,500	850
Subcontract costs	75	650

Analysis of production overheads ($000)

Set up time for CAM machinery	–	575
Machining time	–	2,777
Storage of goods awaiting or returned from subcontractors	120	395
Transfer of goods to and from subcontractors	50	300
Inspection and testing	35	425
Total production overheads	205	4,472
Gross profit	9,035	4,533

Required:

(a) (i) Advise the CEO how activity based costing could be implemented. **(4 marks)**

(ii) Assess whether it may be more appropriate to use activity based costing in Timber and Steel Divisions than the costing basis currently used. **(8 marks)**

(b) Advise the CEO how activity based management could be used to improve business performance in Dibble. **(13 marks)**

(Total: 25 marks)

19 HERMAN SWAN & CO (DEC 12 – AMENDED)

 Question debrief

Herman Swan & Co (HS) is a family-owned company that has made fashionable clothes and leather goods for men for over 100 years. The company has been successful in building a strong reputation for quality by sourcing from local textile and leather producers. It sells its goods across the world through a chain of owned shops and also franchised stalls inside large, well-known stores. The company is still owned and run by the family with no other shareholders. The main goal of the firm is to organically grow the business for the next generation of the Swan family.

Customers are attracted to HS products due to the history and the family story that goes behind the products. They are willing to pay the high prices demanded as they identify with the values of the firm, especially the high quality of manufacturing.

The competition for HS has been increasing for more than ten years. It is made up of other global luxury brands and also the rising national champions in some of the rapidly expanding developing countries. The competitors often try to leverage their brands into many different product types. However, the Swan family have stated their desire to focus on the menswear market after an unsuccessful purchase of a handbag manufacturer five years ago.

The company is divided into a number of strategic business units (SBU). Each production site is an SBU, while the whole retail operation is one SBU. The head office previously functioned as a centre for procurement, finance and other support activities. The company has recently invested in a new management information system (MIS) that has increased the data available to all managers in the business.

This has led to much of the procurement shifting to the production SBUs and the SBU managers taking more responsibility for budgeting. The SBU managers are delighted with their increased responsibilities and with the results from the new information system but feel there is still room for improvement in its use. The system has assisted in a project of flattening the organisation hierarchy by cutting out several layers of head office management.

You are the management accountant at HS and have been trying to persuade your boss, the finance director, that your role should change.

You have read about Burns and Scapens' report 'Accounting Change Project' and think that it suggests an interesting change from your current roles of preparing and reviewing budgets and overseeing the production of management and financial accounts. Your boss is sceptical but is willing to listen to your arguments. He has asked you to submit an explanation of the change that you propose and why it is necessary at HS.

Also, your boss has asked you for an example of how your role as an 'internal consultant' would be valuable at HS by looking at the ideas of brand loyalty and awareness. You should consider their impact on performance management at HS, both from the customer and the internal business process perspectives and how to measure them.

Required:

(a) **Describe the changes in the role of the management accountant based on Burns and Scapens' work. Explain what is driving these changes and justify why they are appropriate to HS.** **(13 marks)**

(b) **Using HS as an example, discuss the impact of brand loyalty and awareness on the business both from the customer and the internal business process perspectives.**
(8 marks)

(c) **Evaluate suitable measures for brand loyalty and awareness at HS.** **(4 marks)**

(Total: 25 marks)

 Calculate your allowed time, allocate the time to the separate parts..............

20 BOOXE (JUN 14)

Booxe is a furniture manufacturing company based in the large, developed country of Teeland. Booxe is the largest furniture manufacturer in Teeland supplying many of the major retail chains with their own-brand furniture and also, making furniture under its own brand (Meson). In a highly competitive market such as Teeland, Booxe has chosen a strategy of cost leadership.

Booxe has been in business for more than 70 years and there is a strong sense of tradition and appreciation of craft skills in the workforce. The average time which an employee has worked for the firm is 18 years. This has led to a bureaucratic culture; for example, the company's information systems are heavily paper based. In addition and in line with this traditional culture, the organisation is divided into a set of functional departments, such as production, warehousing, human resources and finance.

In order to drive down costs, the chief executive officer (CEO) decided to re-engineer the processes at Booxe. She decided that there should be a small pilot project to demonstrate the potential of business process re-engineering (BPR) to benefit Booxe and she selected the goods receiving activity in the company's warehousing operations for this.

The CEO has asked you as a performance management expert to complete the post-implementation review of the pilot project by assessing what it has delivered in financial terms. The project identified that 10 of the warehouse staff spend about half of their time matching goods delivered documents to purchase orders and dealing with subsequent problems. It was noted that 25% of all such matches failed and the staff then had to identify the issue and liaise with the purchasing department in order to get the goods returned to the supplier and a suitable credit note issued. The project introduced a new information system to replace the existing paper-based system. The new system allowed purchase orders to be entered by the purchasing department and then checked online to the goods delivered as they arrived at the warehouse. This allowed warehouse staff to reject incorrect deliveries immediately.

The following are further details provided in relation to the project:

Notes relating to old system:

1   Average staff wage in warehouse $25,000 p.a.

2   Purchasing staff time in handling delivery queries 8.5 days per week

3   Average staff wage in purchasing is $32,000 p.a. for working a 5-day week

Notes relating to new system:

New IT system costs:

		$
4	Hardware for warehouse and purchasing depts	220,000
5	Software total cost	275,000
6	On-going servicing cost (p.a.)	22,500

7   It is expected that the new system will last for eight years.

The CEO now plans to apply BPR across Booxe and as well as completing the post-implementation review, she also needs to know how BPR will change the accounting information systems and the culture at Booxe. Booxe's current accounting system is a traditional one of overhead absorption based on labour hours with variances to budget used as control indicators.

She has heard that an activity-based approach using enterprise resource planning (ERP) systems is fairly common and wants to know how these ideas might link to BPR at Booxe.

The CEO is concerned that middle management unrest may be a problem at Booxe. For example, the warehouse manager was uncomfortable with the cultural change required in the BPR project and decided to take early retirement before the project began. As a result, a temporary manager was put in place to run the warehouse during the project.

The CEO has also begun to reconsider the human resources system at Booxe and she wants your advice on how the staff appraisal process can improve performance in the company. The existing system of manager appraisal is for the staff member to have an annual meeting with their line superior to review the previous year's work and discuss generally how to improve their efforts. Over the years, it has become common for these meetings to be informal and held over lunch at the company's expense. The CEO wants to understand the purpose of a staff appraisal system and how the process can improve the performance of the company. She also wants comments on the appropriate balance between control and staff development as this impacts on staff appraisal at Booxe.

Required:

(a) Assess the financial impact of the pilot business process re-engineering (BPR) project in the warehousing operations. **(6 marks)**

(b) Assess the impact of BPR on the culture and management information systems at Booxe. **(11 marks)**

(c) Advise on the appraisal process at Booxe as instructed by the CEO. **(8 marks)**

(Total: 25 marks)

21 GANYMEDE UNIVERSITY (JUN 12 – AMENDED)

Ganymede University (GU) is one of the three largest universities in Teeland, which has eight universities in total. All of the universities are in the public sector. GU obtains the vast majority of its revenue through government contracts for academic research and payments per head for teaching students. The economy of Teeland has been in recession in the last year and this has caused the government to cut funding for all the universities in the country.

In order to try to improve efficiency, the chancellor of the university, who leads its executive board, has asked the head administrator to undertake an exercise to benchmark GU's administration departments against the other two large universities in the country, AU and BU. The government education ministry has supported this initiative and has required all three universities to cooperate by supplying information.

The following information has been collected regarding administrative costs for the most recent academic year:

	GU $000	AU $000	BU $000
Research:			
contract management	14,430	14,574	14,719
laboratory management	41,810	42,897	42,646
Teaching facilities management	26,993	27,263	26,723
Student support services	2,002	2,022	2,132
Teachers' support services	4,005	4,100	4,441
Accounting	1,614	1,571	1,611
Human resources	1,236	1,203	1,559
IT management	6,471	6,187	6,013
General services	17,049	16,095	18,644
Total	115,610	115,912	118,488

		GU $000	AU $000	BU $000
Drivers:				
Student numbers		28,394	22,783	29,061
Staff numbers		7,920	7,709	8,157
Research contract value	$m	185	167	152

The key drivers of costs and revenues have been assumed to be research contract values supported, student numbers and total staff numbers. The head administrator wants you to complete the benchmarking and make some preliminary comment on your results.

Required:

(a) Assess the progress of the benchmarking exercise to date, explaining the actions that have been undertaken and those that are still required. **(10 marks)**

(b) Evaluate, as far as possible, Ganymede University's benchmarked position.

(15 marks)

(Total: 25 marks)

22   MAXWELL (DEC 14 – AMENDED)

Maxwell Electricity Generation (Maxwell) is an electricity-generating firm producing power for industry and the general public in the country of Deeland. In the past, the company has been dominated by the need to make suitable returns on capital for its shareholders.

All power stations work in broadly the same way by taking in fuel (coal, gas or nuclear) and producing electricity and waste products.

Maxwell has the following mix of power stations:

Power station type		Details for each type of station			Totals for Maxwell		
		Maximum generating power (MW)	Operating cost of electricity ($/MWh)	Capital cost ($m)	Number of stations	Total capital invested ($m)	Total CO_2 emissions (million tonnes)
Coal	(small)	300	25	1,320	4	5,280	3.15
	(large)	600	25	2,640	4	10,560	12.61
Gas	(small)	300	50	300	8	2,400	3.15
	(large)	900	50	900	2	1,800	7.10
Nuclear		1,200	20	6,000	2	12,000	0.50
						32,040	26.51

Notes:

1   Maximum generating power is the output of the station measured in megawatts (MW) at 100% operating capacity. The electricity produced by a station is measured in megawatt hours (MWh).

2   It is assumed that the same load factor applies across all the different types of station, i.e. they are working at the same percentage of capacity throughout the year.

3   Operating cost of electricity is the cost before the cost of financing the capital invested in a station.

4   The CO_2 (carbon dioxide) emissions are estimated based on industry standard figures for similar stations.

5   Capital costs and CO_2 emission figures are current best estimates.

The business has two alternative plans (plans 1a and 1b) to maintain current generating capacity while plan 2 will grow the business.

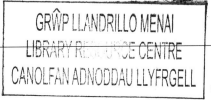

Plan 1a

Build a new nuclear power station (the same as the existing nuclear type) to replace one of the 300 MW coal stations, one of the 600 MW coal stations and, also, one of the 300 MW gas stations. The stations being replaced are all reaching the end of their useful lives.

Plan 1b

Replace the gas and coal stations mentioned in plan 1a with equivalent gas and coal stations, thus maintaining the current generating mix.

Plan 2

In order to grow the business, a new nuclear station is being considered in combination with one of plan 1a or 1b. This new nuclear station would be the same as the existing stations.

Maxwell is trying to raise finance for either plan 1a or plan 1b and, in addition to one of these plans, plan 2. A nuclear plant takes about five years to build (assuming no regulatory difficulties or problems over the design choice). It has a working life of 40 years and costs about $1bn at current prices to decommission although this estimate is uncertain as each site is unique in the decommissioning difficulties which it presents.

The government of Deeland has joined the international community in pledging to have greater concern for the environment. Initially, it has stated that there is a national goal to reduce carbon dioxide emissions by 20% in the next five years. The government is aware that electricity demand is estimated to rise by around 10% over the next five years; nevertheless, it is strongly encouraging businesses to help achieve this reduction in CO_2 emissions. There is a proposal to raise a carbon tax on CO_2 emissions in order to encourage reductions. The government is also concerned that there are other pollutants emitted by power stations but has decided to focus efforts on CO_2 initially, as it is a key cause of climate change.

In order to join the wider community in achieving these aims and as one of the major electricity generators in Deeland, Maxwell has stated its own environmental goal as:

'to help reach national targets for reduction in CO_2 emissions while maintaining our ability to contribute to the electricity needs of the people of Deeland.'

The finance director is interested in broadening environmental reporting within the company and has asked you as his performance measurement expert to explain some of the limitations of traditional accounting systems in dealing with environmental costs and to look at introducing environmental lifecycle costing.

Required:

(a) Using Maxwell's stated environmental goal, assess the proposed investment plans 1a and 2. **(10 marks)**

(b) Explain, giving examples, how traditional accounting systems are unable to deal adequately with environmental costs. **(8 marks)**

(c) Discuss the lifecycle costing issues associated with Plan 2. **(7 marks)**

(Total: 25 marks)

23   ENT ENTERTAINMENT CO (JUN 11 – AMENDED)

ENT Entertainment Co (ENT) is a large, diversified entertainment business based in Teeland. The company's objective is the maximisation of shareholder wealth for its family owners. It has four divisions:

1   Restaurants

2   Cafes

3   Bars

4   Dance clubs

Recently, ENT's board have identified that there are problems in managing such a diversified company. They have employed consultants who have recommended that they should perform a Boston Consulting Group (BCG) analysis to understand whether they have the right mix of businesses. The chief executive officer (CEO) has questioned whether using this analysis is helpful in managing the group's performance. A business analyst has prepared information on each division in the table below.

Revenue ($m)	Actual 2010	Actual 2011	Forecast 2012	Forecast 2013
Restaurants				
ENT	54	56	59	62
Market sector	10,752	10,860	10,968	10,968
Cafes				
ENT	31	34	41	47
Market sector	3,072	3,348	3,717	4,051
Bars				
ENT	349	342	336	336
Market sector	9,984	9,784	9,491	9,206
Dance clubs				
ENT	197	209	219	241
Market sector	1,792	1,900	2,013	2,195

In Teeland, the economy is generally growing at about 2% per annum. The restaurant, cafe and bar sectors are all highly fragmented with many small operators. Consequently, a market share of more than 3.0% is considered large as that is comparable to the share of the largest operators in each sector. There are fewer small late night dance club operators and the market leader currently holds a 15.0% market share. There have not been many new developments within the divisions except for a new wine bar format launched by the bars division which has surprised the board by its success.

Each of the division's performance is measured by economic value-added (EVA™). The divisional managers have a remuneration package that is made up in two equal parts by a salary set according to industry norms and a bonus element which is based on achieving the cost budget numbers set by the company board. The chairman of the board has been examining the consistency of the overall objective of the business, the divisional performance measure and the remuneration packages at divisional level. He has expressed the worry that these are not properly aligned and that this might lead to dysfunctional behaviour by the divisional management.

Required:

(a) Perform an analysis of ENT's business in terms of relative market share and market growth. **(6 marks)**

(b) Using your answer to (a) and the resulting BCG analysis, evaluate the company's performance. **(5 marks)**

(c) Critically evaluate this BCG analysis as a performance management system at ENT. **(8 marks)**

(d) Evaluate the divisional managers' remuneration package in light of the divisional performance system and your BCG analysis. **(6 marks)**

(Total: 25 marks)

24 PLX REFINERY CO (PILOT 10 – AMENDED)

PLX Refinery Co is a large oil refinery business in Kayland. Kayland is a developing country with a large and growing oil exploration and production business which supplies PLX with crude oil. Currently, the refinery has the capacity to process 200,000 barrels of crude oil per day and makes profits of $146m per year. It employs about 2,000 staff and contractors. The staff are paid $60,000 each per year on average (about twice the national average in Kayland). PLX has had a fairly good compliance record in Kayland with only two major fines being levied in the last eight years for safety breaches and river pollution ($1 m each).

The government of Kayland has been focussed on delivering rapid economic growth over the last 15 years. However, there are increasing signs that the environment is paying a large price for this growth with public health suffering. There is now a growing environmental pressure group, Green Kayland (GK), which is organising protests against the companies that they see as being the major polluters.

Kayland's government wishes to react to the concerns of the public and the pressure groups. It has requested that companies involved in heavy industry contribute to a general improvement in the treatment of the environment in Kayland.

As a major participant in the oil industry with ties to the nationalised oil exploration company (Kayex), PLX believes it will be strategically important to be at the forefront of the environmental developments. It is working with other companies in the oil industry to improve environmental reporting since there is a belief that this will lead to improved public perception and economic efficiency of the industry. PLX has had a fairly good compliance record in Kayland with only two major fines being levied in the last eight years for safety breaches and river pollution ($1m each).

The existing information systems within PLX focus on financial performance. They support financial reporting obligations and allow monitoring of key performance metrics such as earnings per share and operating margins. Recent publications on environmental accounting have suggested there are a number of techniques (such as activity-based costing (ABC), a lifecycle view and flow cost accounting) that may be relevant in implementing improvements to these systems.

PLX is considering a major capital expenditure programme to enhance capacity, safety and efficiency at the refinery. This will involve demolishing certain older sections of the refinery and building on newly acquired land adjacent to the site. Overall, the refinery will increase its land area by 20%.

Part of the refinery extension will also manufacture a new plastic, Kayplas. Kayplas is expected to have a limited market life of five years when it will be replaced by Kayplas2.

The refinery accounting team have forecast the following data associated with this product and calculated PLX's traditional performance measure of product profit for the new product:

All figures are $m's

	2012	2013	2014	2015	2016
Revenue generated	25.0	27.5	30.1	33.2	33.6
Costs					
Production costs	13.8	15.1	16.6	18.3	18.5
Marketing costs	5.0	4.0	3.0	3.0	2.0
Development costs	5.6	3.0	0.0	0.0	0.0
Product profit	0.6	5.4	10.5	11.9	13.1

Subsequently, the following environmental costs have been identified from PLX's general overheads as associated with Kayplas production.

	2012	2013	2014	2015	2016
Waste filtration	1.2	1.4	1.5	1.9	2.1
Carbon dioxide exhaust extraction	0.8	0.9	0.9	1.2	1.5

Additionally, other costs associated with closing down and recycling the equipment in Kayplas production are estimated at $18m in 2016.

The board wishes to consider how it can contribute to the oil industry's performance in environmental accounting, how it can implement the changes that this might require and how these changes can benefit the company.

Required:

Write to the board of PLX to:

(a) Discuss and illustrate four different cost categories that would aid transparency in environmental reporting both internally and externally at PLX. **(8 marks)**

(b) Explain and evaluate how the three management accounting techniques mentioned can assist in managing the environmental and strategic performance of PLX. **(9 marks)**

(c) Evaluate the costing approach used for Kayplas's performance compared to a lifecycle costing approach, performing appropriate calculations. **(8 marks)**

(Total: 25 marks)

25 FGH TELECOM (FGH) (DEC 10 – AMENDED)

FGH Telecom (FGH) is one of the largest providers of mobile and fixed line telecommunications in Ostland. The company has recently been reviewing its corporate objectives in the light of its changed business environment. The major new addition to the strategic objectives is under the heading: 'Building a more environmentally friendly business for the future'. It has been recognised that the company needs to make a contribution to ensuring sustainable development in Ostland and reducing its environmental footprint. Consequently, it adopted a goal that, by 2017, it would have reduced its environmental impact by 60% (compared to year 2001).

The reasons for the board's concern are that the telecommunications sector is competitive and the economic environment is increasingly harsh with the markets for debt and equities being particularly poor. On environmental issues, the government and public are calling for change from the business community. It appears that increased regulation and legislation will appear to encourage business towards better performance. The board have recognised that there are threats and opportunities from these trends. It wants to ensure that it is monitoring these factors and so it has asked for an analysis of the business environment with suggestions for performance measurement.

Additionally, the company has a large number of employees working across its network. Therefore, there are large demands for business travel. FGH runs a large fleet of commercial vehicles in order to service its network along with a company car scheme for its managers. The manager in charge of the company's travel budget is reviewing data on carbon dioxide emissions to assess FGH's recent performance.

Recent initiatives within the company to reduce emissions have included:

(a) the introduction in 2010 of a homeworking scheme for employees in order to reduce the amount of commuting to and from their offices and

(b) a drive to increase the use of teleconferencing facilities by employees.

Data on FGH Telecom:

Carbon Dioxide emissions	Base year		
Measured in millions of kgs	2001	2009	2010
Commercial Fleet Diesel	105.4	77.7	70.1
Commercial Fleet Petrol	11.6	0.4	0.0
Company Car Diesel	15.1	14.5	12.0
Company Car Petrol	10.3	3.8	2.2
Other road travel (Diesel)	0.5	1.6	1.1
Other road travel (Petrol)	3.1	0.5	0.3
Rail travel	9.2	9.6	3.4
Air Travel (short haul)	5.0	4.4	3.1
Air Travel (long haul)	5.1	7.1	5.4
Hire Cars (Diesel)	0.6	1.8	2.9
Hire Cars (Petrol)	6.7	6.1	6.1
	———	———	———
Total	172.6	127.5	106.6
	———	———	———

Required:

(a) Perform an analysis of FGH's business environment to identify factors which will affect its environmental strategy. For each of these factors, suggest performance indicators which will allow FGH to monitor its progress. **(9 marks)**

(b) Evaluate the data given on carbon dioxide emissions using suitable indicators. Identify trends from within the data and comment on whether the company's behaviour is consistent with meeting its targets. **(12 marks)**

(c) Suggest further data that the company could collect in order to improve its analysis and explain how this data could be used to measure the effectiveness of the reduction initiatives mentioned. **(4 marks)**

(Total: 25 marks)

26 GMB CO (DEC 07 – AMENDED) *Online question assistance*

GMB Co designs, produces and sells a number of products. Functions are recognised from design through to the distribution of products. Within each function, a number of activities may be distinguished and a principal driver identified for each activity.

Each sales order will normally comprise a number of batches of any one of a range of products. The company is active in promoting, where possible, a product focus for design, dedicated production lines and product marketing. It also recognises that a considerable level of expenditure will relate to supporting the overall business operation.

It is known that many costs may initially be recognised at the unit, batch, product sustaining (order) or business/facility sustaining (overall) levels. A list of expense items relating to Order Number 377 of product Zeta is shown below.

The methods of calculating the values for Order Number 377 shown below are given in brackets alongside each expense item. These methods also indicate whether the expense items should be regarded as product unit, batch, product sustaining (order) or business/facility sustaining (overall) level costs. The expense items are not listed in any particular sequence. Each expense item should be adjusted to reflect its total cost for Order Number 377.

Order Number 377 comprises 5,000 units of product Zeta. The order will be provided in batches of 1,000 product units.

Order Number 377

	$
Production scheduling (rate per hour × hours per batch)	60,000
Direct material cost (per unit material specification)	180
Selling – batch expediting (at rate per batch)	60,000
Engineering design & support (rate per hour × hours per order)	350,000
Direct labour cost (rate per hour × hours per unit)	150
Machine set-up (rate per set-up × number of set-ups per batch)	34,000
Production line maintenance (rate per hour × hours per order)	1,100,000
Business/facility sustaining cost (at 30% of all other costs)	1,500,000
Marketing (rate per visit to client × number of visits per order)	200,000
Distribution (tonne miles × rate per tonne mile per batch)	12,000
Power cost (rate per Kilowatt hour × Kilowatts per unit)	120
Design work (rate per hour × hours per batch)	30,000
Administration – invoicing and accounting (at rate per batch)	24,000

Required:

(a)   Explain what is meant by Activity Based Management (ABM).   **(5 marks)**

(b)   Prepare a statement of total cost for Order Number 377, which analyses the expense items into sections for each of four levels, with sub-totals for each level where appropriate. The four levels are:

(i)   Unit-based costs

(ii)   Batch-related costs

(iii) Product sustaining (order level) costs; and

(iv) Business/facility sustaining (overall level) costs.   **(5 marks)**

(c) **Identify and discuss the appropriateness of the cost drivers of any TWO expense values in EACH of levels (i) to (iii) above and ONE value that relates to level (iv).**

In addition, suggest a likely cause of the cost driver for any ONE value in EACH of levels (i) to (iii), and comment on possible benefits from the identification of the cause of each cost driver. **(10 marks)**

(d) **Discuss the practical problems that may be encountered in the implementation of an activity-based system of product cost management.** **(5 marks)**

(Total: 25 marks)

 Online question assistance

27 FILM PRODUCTIONS CO (FP) (DEC 10 – AMENDED)

Film Productions Co (FP) is a small international company producing films for cinema release and also for sale on DVD or to television companies. FP deals with all areas of the production from casting, directing and managing the artists to negotiating distribution deals with cinema chains and TV channels. The industry is driven by the tastes of its films' audience, which when accurately predicted can lead to high levels of profitability on a successful film.

The company's stated mission is to 'produce fantastic films that have mass appeal'. The company makes around $200 million of sales each year equally split between a share of cinema takings, DVD sales and TV rights. FP has released 32 films in the past five years. Each film costs an average of $18 million and takes 12 months to produce from initial commissioning through to the final version. Production control is important in order to hit certain key holiday periods for releasing films at the cinema or on DVD.

The company's films have been moderately successful in winning industry awards although FP has never won any major award. Its aims have been primarily commercial with artistic considerations secondary.

The company uses a top-down approach to strategy development with objectives leading to critical success factors (CSFs) which must then be measured using performance indicators. Currently, the company has identified a number of critical success factors. The two most important of these are viewed as:

(i) improve audience satisfaction

(ii) strengthen profitability in operations

At the request of the board, the chief executive officer (CEO) has been reviewing this system in particular the role of CSFs. Generally, the CEO is worried that the ones chosen so far fail to capture all the factors affecting the business and wants to understand all possible sources for CSFs and what it means to categorise them into monitoring and building factors.

These CSFs will need to be measured and there must be systems in place to perform that role. The existing information system of the company is based on a fairly basic accounting package.

However, the CEO has been considering greater investment in these systems and making more use of the company's website in both driving forward the business' links to its audience and in collecting data on them.

The CEO is planning a report to the board of Film Productions and has asked you to help by drafting certain sections of this report.

Required:

(a)   **Identify information that FP could use to set its CSFs and explain how it could be used giving two examples that would be appropriate to FP.**   **(6 marks)**

(b)   **For each of the two critical success factors given in the question, identify two performance indicators (PIs) that could support measurement of their achievement and explain why each PI is relevant to the CSF.**   **(10 marks)**

(c)   **Discuss the implications of your chosen PIs for the design and use of the company's website, its management information system and its executive information system.**   **(9 marks)**

(Total: 25 marks)

B – IMPACT OF RISK AND UNCERTAINTY ON ORGANISATIONAL PERFORMANCE

28   SWEET CICELY (SC) (SEPT/DEC 17)

Sweet Cicely (SC) manufactures sweets and confectionery and has delivered stable but modest increases to the shareholder wealth for many years. Following a change in ownership, the new shareholders are keen to increase the long-term performance of the business and are prepared to accept a high level of risk to achieve this.

SC is considering setting up a factory to manufacture chocolate bars. There are three options (1, 2 and 3) for the size and output capacity of the new chocolate factory. SC must choose a size most suited to the expected demand for its products. As well as the impact of the quality, branding and pricing of its products, demand for SC chocolate bars will   be influenced by external factors such as consumer tastes for chocolate over other sweets, and even the suggested health benefits of certain types of chocolate.

A high-cost ingredient in chocolate bars is cocoa, a commodity traded on international markets. The market price of cocoa fluctuates with worldwide demand. Due to economic growth, chocolate consumption is rising in many countries, where it was once considered a luxury. In some countries, however, governments are considering introducing additional taxes on products containing sugar in order to reduce the consumption of chocolate and confectionery products. Being derived from an agricultural crop, the availability and price of cocoa is also influenced by climatic conditions, soil erosion, and disease. Conflicts and political instability in cocoa growing regions can also restrict its availability. Recent technological advances in the production of cocoa, such as the use of genetically modified crops, promise higher yields from cocoa plants in the near future.

You have been asked to help SC choose one of the three options for the new chocolate factory. One board member told you: 'The board proposed expanding into cake manufacturing several years ago. With hindsight, our planning on that proposal was poor. We sold only slightly fewer cakes than expected, but hadn't realised how sensitive our operating profit would be to a small change in demand. The previous shareholders thought problems in the cake business would put their dividends at risk, so SC stopped manufacturing cakes, barely a year after it started. The board does not want to repeat these mistakes. We want to minimise the opportunity cost of making the wrong decision about the size of the new chocolate factory.'

Appendix 1 shows the net present values for the three options discounted at SC's current cost of capital. Appendix 2 shows the expected operating profit generated by the three options in the first year of the project, according to the market price of cocoa, and assuming an annual demand of 70 million chocolate bars.

Required:

(a) Advise SC why decisions, such as what size of chocolate factory to build, must include consideration of risk and uncertainty, and evaluate the use of PEST analysis in managing the risk and uncertainty surrounding the project. **(14 marks)**

(b) Using the data in Appendix 1, explain which of the three options for the new chocolate factory would be preferred by the board and the new shareholders according to their respective risk appetites. **(6 marks)**

(c) Using the data in Appendix 2, recommend which of the three options for the new chocolate factory a risk neutral investor would choose, and explain any problems with the approach used to make the choice. **(5 marks)**

(Total: 25 marks)

Appendix 1

Net present values for the three options discounted at SC's current cost of capital ($m)

	Option 1	Option 2	Option 3
Annual demand for chocolate bars			
50 million	4.0	(8.0)	(32.0)
60 million	6.0	16.0	(24.0)
70 million			
	6.0	16.0	17.0

Appendix 2

Expected operating profit generated by the three options in the first year of the project, assuming an annual demand of 70 million chocolate bars ($m)

	Market price of cocoa			
Probability	**($ per ton)**	**Option 1**	**Option 2**	**Option 3**
0.3	2,500	3.0	5.0	7.0
0.4	3,000	0.5	2.0	1.5
0.3	3,500	(2.0)	(1.0)	(2.0)

29 TURING (JUN 14)

Turing Aerodynamics (Turing) has formed a joint venture (JV) with Riemann Generators (Riemann) in order to design and manufacture high-performance wind turbines which generate electricity. The joint venture is called TandR with each party owning 50%. Turing will design and build the pylons, housing and turbine blades while Riemann will supply the generators to be fitted inside the housing.

Turing is a medium sized firm known for its blade design skills. It is owned by three venture capital firms (VCs) (each holding 30% of the shares), with the remaining 10% being given to management to motivate them. The VCs each have a large portfolio of business investments and accept that some of these investments may fail provided that some of their investments show large gains. Management is an ambitious group who enjoys the business and technical challenges of introducing new products.

On the other hand, Riemann is a large, family-owned company working in the highly competitive electricity generator sector. The shareholders of Riemann see the business as mature and want it to offer a stable, long-term return on capital. However, recently, Riemann had to seek emergency refinancing (debt and equity) due to its thin profit margins and tough competition, both of which are forecast to continue. As a result, Riemann's shareholders and management are concerned for the survival of the business and see TandR as a way to generate some additional cash flow. Unlike at Turing, the management of Riemann does not own significant shareholdings in the company which has preferred to pay fixed salaries.

TandR is run by a group of managers made up from each of the JV partners. They are currently faced with a decision about the design of the product. There are three design choices depending on the power which the wind turbines can generate (measured in megawatts [MW]):

Design type	Description
8 MW	a large 8 MW unit
3 MW	a 3 MW unit
1 MW	a basic 1 MW unit

The engineering for the 1 MW and 3 MW units is well understood and so design is much simpler than for the 8 MW unit which would be world leading if completed.

The demand for the different types of units will depend on government subsidies of the electricity price charged by the electricity generating companies who will buy the wind turbines and the planning regulations for building such large structures. It is believed that there will be orders for either 1,000 or 1,500 or 2,000 units but there is no clear picture yet of which demand level is more likely than the others.

The estimated costs and prices for the units are:

Type	Variable cost per unit $m	Fixed costs $m	Price per unit $m
8 MW	10.4	7,500.0	20.8
3 MW	4.8	820.0	9.6
1 MW	1.15	360.0	4.6

Notes:

1   The fixed costs cover the initial design, development and testing of the units.

2   The costs and prices are in real terms with the 8 MW unit likely to take two more years to develop than the others.

Required:

(a)   **Assess the risk appetites of the two firms in the joint venture and provide a justified recommendation for each firm of an appropriate method of decision-making under uncertainty to assess the different types of wind turbines.**

(9 marks)

(b)   **Evaluate the choice of turbine design types using your recommended methods from part (a) above.** **(8 marks)**

(c)   **Discuss the problems encountered in managing performance in a joint venture such as TandR.** **(8 marks)**

(Total: 25 marks)

30 FRANCHISING FOR YOU LTD (F4U) (JUN 09)

Franchising For You Ltd (F4U) markets a range of franchises which it makes available to its customers, the franchisees. F4U supplies the franchisee with information of the mode of operation, detailed operation schedules and back-up advice (by telephone, internet) and undertakes national advertising. Each franchisee must arrange for its own premises, equipment and undertake local marketing.

F4U is considering the introduction of a Dance and Drama franchise which would have an expected life of six years. From this project, the only income F4U will receive from franchisees comes from the initial franchise fee.

The following estimates have been made relating to the cash outflows and inflows for F4U in order that F4U can evaluate the financial viability of the Dance and Drama franchise proposal:

1   Initial investment of $6m. This will include a substantial element relating to the 'intellectual capital' requirement of the proposal.

2   Development/improvement costs of $1m per year at the end of each of years two and three.

3   300 franchises will be sold each year at a fee of $20,000 per franchisee.

4   Variable costs, payable in full on the issue of each franchise, are estimated at $6,000 per franchise.

5   Directly attributable fixed costs of $0.6m per year in each of years one to six. No further fixed costs will be payable by F4U after this period.

6   Corporation tax at the rate of 30%, payable in the year in which cash flow occurs. Tax allowances are not available on the initial investment or development/improvement costs payable by F4U.

7   All cash flows are stated in current prices and with the exception of the initial investment will occur at the end of each year.

8   The money cost of capital is 15.44%. Annual inflation during the period is estimated at 4%.

Required:

(a)   **Calculate the net present value (NPV) of the Dance and Drama franchise proposal and recommend whether it should be undertaken by F4U.**   **(6 marks)**

(b)   **Discuss the elements to be considered as 'intellectual capital' and issues associated with its valuation for inclusion in the initial investment of $6m.**   **(6 marks)**

(c)   **Discuss ways in which reliance solely on financial performance measures can detract from the effectiveness of the performance management system within an organisation.**   **(6 marks)**

F4U has identified key variables as follows:

1   The number of franchises taken up each year. It is estimated that a flexible pricing policy will result in the following outcomes:

Fee per franchise $	Number of franchises sold each year
22,000	270
20,000	300
18,000	355

2   The variable cost per franchise may be $7,000, $6,000 or $5,000.

The NINE possible outcomes of a spreadsheet model used in calculating the NPV and incorporating the variables 1 and 2 above, have been identified as follows:

Payoff Matrix: NPV values

Fee per franchise ($000)

		18	20	22
Variable cost	5	4,348,226	4,007,630	4,274,183
Per franchise	6	3,296,822	3,119,120	3,474,524
($000)	7	2,245,419	2,230,610	2,674,865

Required:

(d)   State the franchise fee pricing strategy ($ per franchise) which will result from the operation of each of the following decision rules:

(i)   Maximax

(ii)   Maximin

(iii)   Minimax regret.

Your answer should explain the basis of operation of each of the three decision rules.   **(7 marks)**

(Total: 25 marks)

31   THE EQUINE MANAGEMENT ACADEMY (EMA) (JUN 10)

The Equine Management Academy (EMA) which was founded in 1990 is a privately owned organisation located in Hartland, a developing country which has a large agricultural sector and where much transportation is provided by horses. EMA operates an Equine College which provides a range of undergraduate and postgraduate courses for students who wish to pursue a career in one of the following disciplines:

*   Equine (Horse) Surgery

*   Equine Dentistry, and

*   Equine Business Management.

The Equine College which has a maximum capacity of 1,200 students per annum is currently the only equine college in Hartland.

The following information is available:

1   A total of 1,200 students attended the Equine College during the year ended 31 May 2010. Student mix and fees paid were as per the following table:

Student category	% of total number of students	Fee ($) per student, per annum
Surgery	30	12,000
Dentistry	25	10,000
Business Management	45	6,000

2   Total operating costs (all fixed) during the year amounted to $6,500,000.

3   Operating costs of the Equine College are expected to increase by 4% during the year ending 31 May 2011. This led to a decision by the management to increase the fees of all students by 5% with effect from 1 June 2010. The management expect the number of students and the mix of students during the year ending 31 May 2011 to remain unchanged from those of the year ended 31 May 2010.

4   EMA also operates a Riding School at which 240 horses are stabled. The Riding School is open for business on 360 days per annum. Each horse is available for four horse-riding lessons per day other than on the 40 days per annum that each horse is rested, i.e. not available for the provision of riding lessons. During the year ended 31 May 2010, the Riding School operated at 80% of full capacity.

5   Horse-riding lessons are provided for riders in three different skill categories. These are 'Beginner', 'Competent' and 'Advanced'.

During the year ended 31 May 2010, the fee per riding lesson was as follows:

Skill category of horse rider	Lesson mix	Fee ($) per lesson
Beginner	50%	15
Competent	25%	30
Advanced	25%	50

6   Total operating costs of the Riding School (all fixed) amounted to $5,750,000 during the year ended 31 May 2010.

7   It is anticipated that the operating costs of the Riding School will increase by 6% in the year ending 31 May 2011. The management have decided to increase the charge per lesson, in respect of 'Competent' and 'Advanced' riders by 10% with effect from 1 June 2010. There will be no increase in the charge per lesson for 'Beginner' riders.

(8)   The lesson mix and capacity utilisation of the Riding School will remain the same during the year ending 31 May 2011.

Required:

(a)   Prepare a statement showing the budgeted net profit or loss for the year ending 31 May 2011.

(7 marks)

Some time ago the government of Hartland, which actively promotes environmental initiatives, announced its intention to open an academy comprising an equine college and riding school. The management of EMA are uncertain of the impact that this will have on the budgeted number of students and riders during the year ending 31 May 2011, although they consider that due to the excellent reputation of the instructors at the riding school capacity utilisation could remain unchanged, or even increase, in spite of the opening of the government funded academy. Current estimates of the number of students entering the academy and the average capacity utilisation of the riding school are as follows:

Equine College		*Riding School*	
Student fees	*Probability*	*Capacity utilisation*	*Probability*
No change	0.20	90%	0.10
Decrease by 10%	0.60	80%	0.60
Decrease by 20%	0.20	70%	0.30

Required:

(b) **(i)** **Prepare a summary table which shows the possible net profit or loss outcomes, and the combined probability of each potential outcome for the year ending 31 May 2011. The table should also show the expected value of net profit or loss for the year.** **(9 marks)**

(ii) **Comment briefly on the use of expected values by the management of EMA.** **(3 marks)**

(iii) **Suggest three reasons why the government of Hartland might have decided to open an academy comprising an equine college and a riding school.** **(6 marks)**

(Total: 25 marks)

32 STOKENESS ENGINEERING (JUN 13)(SPECIMEN 18)

Company information and mission

Stokeness Engineering's (Stokeness) mission is to provide world-leading, reduced-emission, fuel-efficient products for the motor industry in order to optimise shareholder returns.

Stokeness has existed for only five years and is owned by its management and venture capitalists (VCs). The management were all engineers who had been working on the basic research associated with new fuel technologies and saw the opportunity to commercialise their expertise. Stokeness is highly regarded in the industry for its advanced, efficient fuel cell designs. As a result, the VCs were eager to invest in Stokeness and have assisted by placing experienced managers into the business to aid the original engineering team.

New product development

Stokeness is developing hydrogen fuel cells for use in powering large motor vehicles such as buses and trucks. They will replace standard petrol/diesel engines. The fuel cells have a clear advantage over these older technologies in having lower carbon dioxide (a greenhouse gas) emissions. The governments of many developed countries are keen to see cuts in such emissions and are supportive of a variety of possible technological solutions to this issue (such as fuel cells, electrical batteries and compressed natural gas).

External business environment

It takes five to ten years to develop a viable product for sale in this motor market. There are a number of companies developing fuel cells but Stokeness is believed to have a two-year lead over them and to be only three years away from commercial launch.

Alternative power technologies like the hydrogen fuel cells would be fitted by the major international vehicle manufacturers into their vehicles for sale to their customers. The vehicle manufacturers will need to form a close partnership with any engine producer in order to make their technologies compatible and this has already begun to happen, with two of the major manufacturers signing deals with other engine makers recently.

A major problem which needs to be overcome with any of these new technologies is that there must be an infrastructure accessible to the end users for refuelling their vehicles (as the petrol station chains do for petrol engine vehicles at present).

Governments have indicated their desire to support the development of such technologies to address environmental issues and to try to establish new, high-value industries in their jurisdiction. They may do this through tax breaks and investment to support the development of the refuelling infrastructure.

Production of Stokeness' fuel cells uses a special membrane which requires rare and expensive elements. Also, it has partnered with two other engineering firms to subcontract the production of certain components in the fuel cell. Stokeness has had to share much of its fuel cell design with these firms in order to overcome certain engineering difficulties.

Also, there are a number of start-up companies developing the other technologies mentioned above, as well as large, existing diesel and petrol engine manufacturers who are constantly reducing the emissions from their existing engines.

The VCs have stressed the need to analyse competition and competitive advantage in order to understand how to make the business profitable in the long term. The chief executive officer (CEO) of Stokeness wants to understand the external business environment and its effect on performance management.

Required:

(a) Using Porter's five forces model, assess the impact of the external business environment on the performance management of Stokeness and give a justified recommendation of one new performance measure for each of the five force areas at Stokeness. **(16 marks)**

(b) Discuss how the problems of defining the market in measuring a market share apply for Stokeness. **(4 marks)**

(c) Assess the risk appetite of the venture capitalists and discuss how this might impact on performance measurement at Stokeness. **(5 marks)**

(Total: 25 marks)

C – PERFORMANCE MEASUREMENT SYSTEMS AND DESIGN

33   NELSON, JODY AND NIGEL (NJN) (MAR/JUN 17)

Nelson, Jody and Nigel (NJN) operates a warehouse and distribution centre, storing and distributing 5,000 product lines on behalf of its client, an overseas sports equipment manufacturer.

NJN receives goods in shipping containers, which should include a packing list of the items they contain. Sometimes, packing lists are lost in transit and the manufacturer is asked for duplicates. Packing lists are manually input into NJN's warehouse information system (WIS) in batches, usually within 48 hours of the goods being received. Goods are first unpacked into a sorting area, and later moved to wherever there is available warehouse space once the packing list has been input. The WIS records the location within the warehouse where each item is located. The client's customers, who are retail stores, place orders by email, and do not currently have access to real-time inventory levels in NJN's warehouse.

Each morning picking lists are printed in the warehouse office. These lists show the quantities of items to be picked   and the items' 12 digit product codes. Staff use these codes to retrieve items from the warehouse locations for despatch to retailers. In 8% of picking lists, at least one item is not in the location or does not have the quantity specified by the WIS. As a result, the item is not despatched, or the wrong item is picked. A small team investigates these discrepancies, using special reports which the warehouse manager extracts from the WIS. The team manually reconciles quantities of missing items in the warehouse to the sports equipment manufacturer's own records of the items which should be in inventory. If missing items cannot be found, the customer is informed via an email that they are unavailable.

The sports equipment manufacturer has a service level agreement with NJN, covering the accuracy of picking and the proportion of customers' orders successfully fulfilled. NJN's performance on these has deteriorated, especially when there is increased seasonal demand for certain products. At these times staff are under increased pressure to pick items quickly, and so picking accuracy deteriorates and absenteeism increases. There have also been accidents where goods have not been safely placed or safely picked from warehouse locations at busy times. These accidents have resulted in minor injuries to some employees.

The sports equipment manufacturer has threatened to end NJN's contract if performance does not improve. In response, NJN has recruited more staff to investigate discrepancies between items physically in warehouse locations, and those shown on the WIS at busy periods. It has also begun a series of cyclical inventory counts where every   product line is counted every month to correct the quantities and locations shown on the WIS. NJN has rented an additional nearby warehouse in which to sort incoming items before they are put away.

NJN has hired a management consultant who is an expert in 'lean' principles and the application of these to management information systems. She believes that the WIS is wasteful, not adding value to the business or to its customers, and has suggested that NJN would benefit from the application of lean principles to this system.

She has suggested three proposals:

- that NJN reorganise the warehouse by storing high volume items close to the despatch area,

- shut down the additional warehouse, and

- discontinue the cyclical inventory counts.

To help with the adoption of lean principles in the warehouse reorganisation, the management consultant recommends NJN apply the '5Ss'* of lean principles, and she has suggested performance metrics which can be used to evaluate NJN's progress towards adopting these (Appendix 1).

*Structurise, Systemise, Sanitise, Standardise, Self-discipline.

Required:

(a) **Assess whether NJN's existing warehouse information system (WIS) is effective in reducing waste and adding value to NJN's workflow.** **(10 marks)**

(b) **Advise whether the three proposals suggested by the management consultant will help to eliminate the different types of waste identified under lean principles.** **(6 marks)**

(c) **Evaluate whether the application of each of the 5Ss following the warehouse reorganisation at NJN is adequately measured by the performance metrics in Appendix 1.** **(9 marks)**

(Total: 25 marks)

Appendix 1 – Performance measures for 5Ss relating to warehouse reorganisation

1   Warehouse manager's daily assessment of the tidiness of the warehouse on a scale of 1–10.

2   The proportion of inventory not stored in order of its alphabetical description with products with names beginning with 'A' nearest the despatch area and 'Z' furthest away.

3   The number of accidents caused by goods being incorrectly stored or picked.

34   INTEGRATED REPORTING

TRE is a listed high street retailer that sells a range of goods such as food, drink, clothing, electrical goods, CDs, DVS and garden equipment.

At a recent board meeting the topic of Integrated Reporting (IR) was raised with very mixed views in the discussion.

The Marketing Director argued that IR was simply a mixture of the sustainability report and the financial report into a single communication intended mainly for investors. As such it had very little new to offer and was just another compliance requirement.

The Finance Director replied that, in his view, IR would give a greater emphasis on the different types of 'capital' within the firm and would assist in more focussed performance management.

Required:

(a) Briefly explain what is meant by an 'Integrated Report' and comment on the views of the Marketing Director. (5 marks)

(b) Identify and describe the SIX different types of 'capital' described within the IR Framework. (9 marks)

(c) Explain FOUR objectives of integrated reporting. (6 marks)

(d) Explain how an emphasis on the six types of capital above could result in more focussed performance management. (5 marks)

(Total: 25 marks)

35 BLUEFIN SCHOOL (DEC 11 – AMENDED)

Bluefin School (Bluefin) is a school for 12 to 17-year-old pupils. It currently has 1,000 pupils attending drawn from its local area. The school is run by an executive group comprising the head of school and two deputy head teachers. This group reports to a board of governors who are part-time and selected from the local community and parents. The school is wholly funded by the government.

The school's ethos is 'to promote learning, citizenship and self-confidence among the pupils. This is developed from a consensus, led by the board of governors and the head of school and informed by the views of the pupils' parents.'

The school information systems are highly decentralised. Each department keeps its own records on a stand-alone PC using basic word processing and spreadsheet packages. The school's administrative department has a small network in its own offices with compatible applications and also a database and financial recording and reporting package for use in schools (provided by the government).

The school is broken down into 11 academic departments such as mathematics, science and history. Each department head must prepare information for reporting to the board by inputting and processing the data. They obtain some help from an administrator who visits each department to spend a few hours per week helping in the recording and preparation of the departmental information. The department heads have different approaches to reporting their performance, with some using average marks in the annual exams for each class and some using pass rates of the annual exams. Some department heads present graphs of their data while most use tables of figures.

The information is passed from each department to the school administration office on a memory stick (USB flash drive). The school administration office prints out the information for each department and adds it to a financial report creating a governors' pack of usually about 13 pages for the annual review board meeting. The financial report is a detailed income and expenditure statement for the period under review (usually a two page print-out from the reporting package). An example of one of the 11 departments' report is given in the Appendix.

The board of governors meets every quarter and reviews the governors' pack once a year. The board are concerned that the information that they are receiving is not meeting their needs and that there are a number of problems with the control and security of some of the data.

It has been suggested that the school should consider improving its information systems by installing a network across the school to link the departmental computers and the administration department. A single database would be created to store all the performance information. The computers would then be linked to the internet in order to facilitate data transfer to other schools in the region and to the government.

Appendix: Bluefin School: Mathematics department

Year 2010/2011		Average marks	
		Current yr	Previous yr
	Class	%	%
Year 1	A	63	59
	B	60	61
	C	51	55
	D	47	44
Year 2	A	61	70
	B	58	62
	C	49	47
	D	45	43
Year 3	A	67	67
	B	61	57
	C	50	50
	D	42	41
Year 4	A	62	58
	B	59	59
	C	50	54
	D	46	47
Year 5	A	57	58
	B	51	49
	C	47	48
Year 6		54	53

Notes:

Each year contains pupils of the same age.

Annual national exams are set in years 4, 5 and 6.

Each year group is divided into different classes in order to ensure that classes do not exceed 35 pupils. (Not all pupils take every subject each year.)

Average marks are for the annual examinations.

Required:

(a)   With reference to the current situation at Bluefin School, discuss the controls and security procedures that are necessary for management information.   **(9 marks)**

(b)   Using the limited information available, evaluate the usefulness of the pack that is provided to the board of governors.   **(6 marks)**

(c)   Evaluate the improvements suggested to the information systems at Bluefin.

   (5 marks)

(d)   Discuss how Bluefin could use benchmarking for performance management purposes.   **(5 marks)**

(Total: 25 marks)

36 QUARK HEALTHCARE (DEC 13)

Quark Healthcare (Quark) runs a number of large hospitals which provide general medical care for the people of Veeland. Veeland is an advanced economy and healthcare is considered to be a high skill, high technology and high status industry. It is compulsory for the people of Veeland to purchase health insurance and then the insurance companies reimburse the healthcare providers for services delivered. The insurance companies audit the healthcare providers and grade them for value for money. As there are a number of hospital chains (such as Quark), the insurers will encourage their insured customers to use those which are most efficient. The ultimate sanction for a healthcare provider is for an insurance company to remove them from the list of acceptable providers.

Quark has large amounts of capital tied up in expensive medical equipment and a drug inventory. The existing systems for accounting for these items are traditional ones aimed at avoiding theft and obsolescence. Quark has an inventory system which requires regular (weekly) physical checks of the drugs in inventory in order to update it. It is important that the right drugs must be in easily accessible stores (located throughout the hospital) in order to act quickly in case of a medical emergency. Also, the accounting staff at Quark maintain a non-current asset register (NCAR) which logs the location of all major assets including medical equipment. The problem with the non-current asset register is that it is often out-of-date as doctors will take equipment in time of emergency and not properly log its new location. This often leads to equipment lying unused in one area of the hospital while being searched for in another area, to the detriment of patient care.

Quark has recently instituted a tagging project where radio-frequency identification devices (RFID) will be attached to the most valuable pieces of equipment used in treatment and also to batches of high-value drugs. The hospitals are fitted with WiFi networks which can pick up the RFID signal so that the RFID tags will be detectable throughout a hospital. The tags will identify the object which they are attached to by a unique identification number and will give its location. The identifier number will link to the inventory system which will identify the product, the quantity initially delivered in that batch and the date of delivery. The RFID information will be accessible through the computer terminals throughout the hospitals.

The chief financial officer (CFO) of Quark has asked you to advise him on the impact of this new system on performance management at Quark. He has suggested that you look at the costs and benefits which will be associated with producing the information from the RFID system, the impact of the nature of the information supplied, the changes to performance management reporting and how the new information could be used for improved control at the hospital. He is keen to be seen to be at the forefront of accounting and management developments and has been reading about cost control techniques. Recently, he has heard about 'lean' systems, so wants to know how the RFID system and its impact on the hospital fit with this concept. Given the importance of the medical staff in running the hospital, he also wants to know how their behaviour will be affected by the control information from the RFID system. There is a very strict social order among these staff (in increasing order of skills: nurses, general doctors and specialist doctors) which regularly causes friction when one group feels it is not given its due status. For example, recently, the general doctors agreed to a new method for nurses to record drugs administered to patients but this new system has not been fully implemented due to complaints by the nurses and specialist doctors who were not consulted on the change.

Required:

(a) Assess the impact of the radio-frequency identification devices (RFID) system on the performance management at Quark as suggested by the CFO. **(12 marks)**

(b) Evaluate whether the overall management of the hospital can be considered to be 'leaner' as a result of the RFID information system. **(7 marks)**

(c) Evaluate how the medical staff's attitudes will influence the design and implementation of the RFID system and how it might be used to promote responsibility and accountability at the hospital. **(6 marks)**

(Total: 25 marks)

37 FORION ELECTRONICS (JUN 15)

Forion Electronics (Forion) manufactures a range of electronic goods. Its business has grown rapidly over the last ten years and is now complex and international. Forion manufactures over 100 different products, selling into 25 different countries. There is a supplier base of over 200 companies from which Forion sources. As the business has become more complex, the board has found it difficult to pull together all the information that they require in order to make decisions.

The current information systems are developed in-house and are based in the functional departments (such as purchasing, manufacturing, warehousing and delivery, selling and marketing). The organisation uses the financial system as a means of bringing together information for an overview of corporate performance.

There have been a number of examples of problems encountered with information in Forion:

- there are inefficiencies arising from ordering the wrong amount of subcomponents

- there are often stock-outs or obsolescence of unsold goods in the warehouses, although the marketing department prepares good sales forecasts; and

- sometimes, there are insufficient delivery vehicles available to meet customer deadlines.

The board of Forion believes the problems arise from poor information sharing within the company. They are considering the purchase of an enterprise resource planning system (ERPS) to be the single information system for the whole organisation.

Also, Forion is planning to launch a smartphone. However, in order to make it competitive they need to have high-visibility, durable screens. As the cost of screen development is considerable, it has been decided to form a strategic alliance with a well-known screen manufacturer to provide this key component for the new smartphone. Bon Accord Screens (BAS) has been chosen as the strategic ally, as they have a strong reputation for their quality of manufacturing and new product development. BAS has been trying to break into the smartphone market for several years.

The alliance agreement has stipulated three critical areas of performance for BAS' supply to Forion:

1 quality of manufacturing, measured by fault rates of screens supplied being within agreed tolerances (so that they fit Forion's phone-bodies)

2 time of delivery, measured by the number of times a shipment is more than one day overdue; and

3 the ability to provide technical upgrades to the screens as the market demands.

The service level agreement (SLA) will be based on these three points and there will be financial penalties built into the agreement if BAS fails to meet these.

Required:

(a) Discuss the integration of information systems in an ERPS and how the ERPS may impact on performance management issues at Forion. **(10 marks)**

(b) Evaluate, from Forion's viewpoint, the usefulness of the three critical areas in the alliance agreement for measuring the performance of BAS. **(8 marks)**

(c) Evaluate the relative reliability of financial and non-financial data from internal and external sources in the context of the alliance between Forion and BAS. **(7 marks)**

(Total: 25 marks)

38 ALBACORE (PILOT 10)

Albacore Chess Stores (Albacore) is a chain of twelve shops specialising in selling items associated with the game of chess: boards, pieces, clocks, software and books. Three years ago, the company was the subject of a venture capital buyout from a larger group. A new senior management team was put in place after the buyout. They have the aim of running the business in order to maximise profits.

The Chief Financial Officer (CFO) along with the other members of senior management sets the annual budget and uses a standard costing approach with variance analysis in order to control individual shop performance. The head office handles all capital purchases and brand marketing. All inventory purchasing is done centrally and the shop opening times are set as standard across the company. As an illustration of senior management attitude, the CFO had set the budget for 2011 staff costs at $7 per hour for part-time staff and this was rigorously observed in the period.

Each shop is run by a manager who reports their financial results to the operational director at head office. The shop managers recruit and manage the staffing of their shop. They have some autonomy in setting prices locally and have been given authority to vary prices by up to 10% from a master list produced by the CFO. They also have a local marketing budget agreed each year by the shop's manager and the marketing director as part of the annual appraisal process.

The shop managers have approached the Chairman of Albacore to complain about the way that they are managed and their remuneration. They feel that their efforts are unrecognised by senior management. One manager commented 'I have had a successful year in hard economic circumstances. I have run a number of promotions in the shop that have been well received by the customers. However, the budgets that are set are impossible to achieve and as a result I have not been paid any bonus although I feel that I have done everything in my power to bring in good profits.'

The shop managers at Albacore are paid a basic salary of $27,000 with bonuses of up to 30% of basic salary dependent on two factors: performance above budget and the operational director's assessment of the manager's performance. The budget for the next year is prepared by the CFO and presented by the operational director at the shop manager's annual appraisal.

The Chairman has come to you to ask if you can consider the system of performance assessment for the shop managers and give an independent perspective on the reward systems at Albacore. She has heard of variance analysis but is unsure as what would be relevant in this situation. She has provided the following illustrative branch report from the previous year for one shop:

Albacore Chess Stores

Tunny Branch Year to Sept 2011

		Budget	Actual	Variance
		$	$	$
Sales		266,000	237,100	−28,900
Cost of sales		106,400	94,840	11,560
Gross profit		159,600	142,260	−17,340
Marketing		12,000	11,500	500
Staff costs	Manager	27,000	27,000	0
	Part-time staff	38,000	34,000	4,000
Property costs		26,600	26,600	0
Shop profit		56,000	43,160	−12,840

Notes:

Property costs includes heating, lighting and rental.

Positive variances are favourable.

End of report

The manager of this shop commented at the appraisal meeting that she felt that the assessment was unfair since her failure to make budget was due to general economic conditions. The industry as a whole saw a 12% fall in revenues during the period and the budget for the period was set to be the same as the previous period. She was not paid a bonus for the period.

Required:

(a) Evaluate the suitability of the existing branch report as a means of assessing the shop manager's performance and draft an improved branch report with justifications for changes. **(13 marks)**

(b) Analyse the performance management style and evaluate the performance appraisal system at Albacore. Suggest suitable improvements to its reward system for the shop managers. **(12 marks)**

(Total: 25 marks)

D – STRATEGIC PERFORMANCE MEASUREMENT

39   CHICORY (SEPT/DEC 17)

Chicory operates a chain of depots in Deeland, supplying and fitting tyres and other vehicle parts to lorries, buses and agricultural vehicles. Chicory's objective is to maximise shareholder wealth. Due to a slowdown in the Deeland economy, Chicory's recent performance has been weak. An unsuccessful acquisition has also caused cash flow problems and a write-off of goodwill of $23.7m in the year to 30 June 2017.

The board has commissioned a benchmarking exercise to help improve Chicory's performance. This exercise will involve comparison of a range of financial and other operational performance indicators against Fennel, a similar business in Veeland. Fennel has agreed to share some recently available performance data with Chicory as they operate in different countries. The reason Fennel was chosen as a benchmark is that as well as supplying and fitting tyres and parts to heavy vehicles, a large part of Fennel's business involves supplying electricity to charging points to recharge electric cars. Fennel installs and operates the charging points in public places, and users pay Fennel for the electricity they use. The board of Chicory intends to follow a similar business model as the use of electric cars is increasing in Deeland.

The Veeland economy is growing strongly. Electric car use there has increased rapidly in the last two years, encouraged by tax incentives for businesses, like Fennel, to install and operate charging points. The Veeland government has also underwritten loans taken out by businesses to finance this technology, which has enabled Fennel to borrow funds   for the significant capital investment required. The cost of components used in the charging points is falling rapidly. Capitalisation of development costs related to this technology is permitted in Veeland, but not in Deeland. In 2015, Fennel invested heavily in IT systems which significantly improved performance by increasing the availability of parts in its depots, and reducing inventories.

Chicory uses return on average capital employed (ROCE) as its main financial performance indicator, and this is to be benchmarked against Fennel. One board member suggested that, though it may have some disadvantages, EBITDA (earnings before interest, tax, depreciation and amortisation) could have advantages as a performance measure over the existing measure, and should also be included in the benchmarking exercise.

You have been given the most recently available financial data for both businesses in Appendix 1, with the data for Fennel being converted into $ from its home currency.

Required:

(a) Evaluate the relative financial performance of Chicory against Fennel using the two financial performance measures identified in the benchmarking exercise and evaluate their use as performance measures in this situation.

  (i)   ROCE   **(6 marks)**

  (ii) EBITDA   **(10 marks)**

(b) Advise Chicory on the problems of using the benchmarking exercise with Fennel as a way to improve performance.   **(9 marks)**

(Total: 25 marks)

Appendix 1

Benchmark data ($m)

Extract from statement of financial position

End of year	30 June 17 Chicory	31 December 15 Fennel[1]
Total assets	140.0	296.0
Current liabilities	(81.0)	(120.0)

Beginning of year[1]	Chicory	Fennel
Total assets	138.0	290.0
Current liabilities	(60.0)	(120.0)

Income statement

	30 June 17 Chicory	31 December 15 Fennel
Revenue	175.1	350.0
Cost of sales	(130.1)	(299.0)
Gross profit	45.0	51.0
Administrative expenses	(11.0)	(25.0)
Write off of goodwill	(24.7)	-
Operating profit[2]	9.3	26.0
Interest payable	(1.8)	(8.0)
Profit before tax	7.5	18.0
Tax	(3.0)	(1.0)
Net profit	4.5	17.0

Notes

[1] $6m of new capital was introduced into Fennel on 31 March 2015. Normally, new net investment is spread evenly over the year.

[2] Operating profit is after charging depreciation of non-current assets of $18m in Chicory, and $25m in Fennel.

40 TOSEMARY AND RHYME HOSPITAL (TRH) (SEPT/DEC 17)

Tosemary and Rhyme Hospital (TRH) is a small hospital for the treatment of patients with only minor injuries. Patients arriving at TRH with more serious injuries are referred to a larger hospital nearby. Those with minor injuries are admitted into TRH and wait to be seen by a doctor. After treatment, most patients leave the hospital and need not return. If their treatment has failed, however, they are re-admitted for additional treatment.

Patients do not have to pay for treatment at TRH, which is a not-for-profit, public sector hospital. It is funded entirely by the government from taxation and a fixed level of funding is received from the government each year. It is up to TRH to allocate its funding to different areas, such as doctors' salaries, medicines and all other costs required to run a hospital.

TRH's objectives are:

- to give prompt access to high quality medical treatment for patients

- to provide value for money for the taxpayer, as measured by the '3Es' framework of economy, efficiency and effectiveness

- to contribute to medical science by developing innovative ways to deliver treatment to patients.

It has been suggested to TRH that the hospital has inadequate performance measurement systems in place to assess whether it is achieving its objectives, and that insufficient attention is given to the importance of non-financial performance indicators. You have been asked for your advice, and have met with some of the doctors to get their opinions.

One senior doctor has told you, 'I think TRH always delivers value for money. We've always achieved our total financial budgets. Doctors here work much longer hours than colleagues in other hospitals, often without being paid for working overtime. There is not enough government funding to recruit more doctors. At busy times, we've started referring more patients arriving at TRH to the larger hospital nearby. This has helped reduce average waiting times. Patients arriving at TRH are now seen by a doctor within 3 hours 50 minutes rather than 4 hours as was previously the case. So, we're already doing all we can. I don't know how much time we spend developing innovative ways to deliver treatment to patients though, as most of the performance data we doctors receive relates to financial targets.'

Recent performance data for TRH and national average information has been provided in Appendix 1. This is indicative of the data which the doctors at TRH receive.

Required:

(a) Explain why non-financial performance indicators are particularly important to measure the performance of not-for-profit organisations such as TRH. **(5 marks)**

(b) Justify one performance measure for each of the components of the value for money framework used at TRH and, using that measure evaluate whether TRH is delivering value for money. **(10 marks)**

(c) Evaluate the extent to which the management style at TRH can be said to be budget constrained and advise on the implications of this approach for managing TRH's performance. **(10 marks)**

(Total: 25 marks)

Appendix 1

Data for the year ended 31 August 2017

	TRH	National average[1]
Number of doctors	25	24
Total doctors' salaries including overtime	$3.75m	$4.20m
Total doctors' salaries budget including overtime	$3.75m	$3.20m
Number of patients treated	24,375	20,000
Average staff satisfaction rating[2]	9%	89%
Number of patients re-admitted	1,830	300

Notes

[1] National average for other public sector minor injuries hospitals.

[2] Staff satisfaction rating was obtained by conducting a survey of all 25 doctors. A survey score of 100% represents 'totally satisfied', and a score of 0% represents totally unsatisfied.

41 PITLANE (MAR/JUN 17)

Pitlane Electronic Components (Pitlane) manufactures components for use in the electricity distribution network in Deeland. Demand from Pitlane's biggest customer, to replace identical but worn out components, has been constant for many years. Pitlane has recently renewed an exclusive long-term supply agreement with this customer, who has always agreed to buy the components for their total standard cost plus a fixed profit margin of 15%. Variances between standard and actual costs of the components are negligible. Pitlane runs several production lines in two factories located in different areas of Deeland. The factories' layout is poorly designed and the production process requires components to be transported around and between the factories.

The Deeland government wants to encourage renewable electricity generation. It is offering a three-year subsidy scheme, beginning in 2018, for consumers to have solar panels installed on the roofs of their homes. As an added incentive, businesses will be exempt from tax on profits made on the sale of solar panels and related components.

To take advantage of this scheme, Pitlane has built a prototype of a new electrical component, known as the 'Booster', which increases the output from domestic solar panels. The Booster will be sold to installers of solar panels and not directly to consumers. Pitlane's marketing department has estimated market data for the duration of the scheme based on a similar scheme in Veeland (Appendix 1). As a result of its products being unchanged for many years, Pitlane has little recent experience of developing new products and estimating costs and potential revenues from them. It is expected that many competitor products will be launched during the scheme, at the end of which demand is expected to fall greatly, and production of the Booster will discontinue.

Pitlane's shareholders insist that for the Booster project to go ahead, it must meet the financial performance objective of achieving a 15% net profit margin, after all costs, for the duration of the scheme.

The Booster's total fixed costs during the scheme are estimated to be $10m, including $2.8m upfront development costs to enable the Booster to communicate the amount of solar energy generated directly to consumers' smartphones via an app. The product development team at Pitlane believes this feature, and the use of highest quality packaging, will allow it to charge 10% more that the average price of its competitors. The marketing team, however, has questioned the overall value of these two features and whether customers would be prepared to pay extra for them, as most of the Deeland population do not yet own smartphones.

Pitlane has estimated the direct costs for the Booster (Appendix 2). The largest direct cost is for the four main sub-components. These are bought in bulk from six different suppliers in Deeland, though all are readily available from suppliers worldwide. The sub-components are fragile. During production of the Booster prototype, many sub-components were found to be damaged during the production process by workers incorrectly assembling them. This resulted in the completed prototype Boosters being scrapped after testing by the quality control department. The manufacturing director is concerned that the incorrect assembly of sub-components by workers may mean that it may not be profitable for Pitlane to start full scale production of Boosters. To counteract these quality problems, Pitlane will employ more highly skilled workers, who are paid around 30% more than most other workers in the business which is accounted for in the cost estimate given in Appendix 2. Pitlane staff have never been encouraged to suggest any ways to improve the manufacturing process.

Pitlane's directors are concerned that the Booster project will not meet the shareholders' financial performance objective. They have asked you, as a consultant experienced in target costing, Kaizen costing and other Japanese business practices, for your advice.

Required:

(a) **Calculate the cost gap per unit in each of the three years of the Booster's life, taking into account all estimated costs.** **(6 marks)**

(b) **Advise on the extent to which target costing would help Pitlane to achieve the financial performance objective set by the shareholders.** **(12 marks)**

(c) **Advise Pitlane how Kaizen costing may be used to help the Booster project achieve the financial performance objective set by the shareholders.** **(7 marks)**

(Total: 25 marks)

Appendix 1 – Estimated market data for Booster

	2018	*2019*	*2020*
Total market size (units)	600,000	500,000	460,000
Average price of competitors products ($/unit)	180	170	160
Booster market share of total market	10%	15%	20%

Appendix 2 – Estimated unit direct cost of Booster

	$
Sub-components	94
Assembly labour	21
Packaging	10
Distribution	2
Internal transport and handling	7
Total	134

42 JENSON, LEWIS AND WEBB (JLW) (MAR/JUN 17)

Jenson, Lewis and Webb (JLW) manufactures tubes of acrylic paint for sale to artists and craft shops in Kayland and Seeland. JLW has two divisions, Domestic division and Export division, both based in Kayland. All costs are incurred in Kayland Dollars ($KL). Domestic division is an investment centre and sells only to customers in Kayland. Export division is a profit centre and exports all its products to Seeland, where customers are invoiced in Seeland Pounds (£SL), at prices fixed at the start of the year. The objective of JLW is to maximise shareholder wealth.

At the beginning of the year ended 31 December 2016, the head office at JLW purchased new production machinery for Export division for $KL2.5m, which significantly increased the production efficiency of the division. Managers at Domestic division were considering purchasing a similar machine, but decided to delay the purchase until the beginning of the following financial year. On 30 June 2016 the $KL weakened by 15% against the £SL, after which the exchange rate between the two currencies has remained unchanged.

The managers of the two divisions are currently appraised on the performance of their own divisions, and are awarded a large bonus if the net profit margin of their division exceeds 8% for the year. Extracts from the management accounts for the year ended 31 December 2016 for both divisions are given in Appendix 1. On being told that she would not be receiving a bonus for the financial year, the manager of Export division has commented that she has had difficulty in understanding the bonus calculations for her division as it is not based on traceable profit, which would consider only items which relate directly to the division. She also does not believe it is appropriate that the net profit margin used to appraise her performance is the same as 'that which is used to evaluate the performance of Export division itself'. She has asked for a meeting with the directors to discuss this further.

JLW's directors intend to award divisional managers' bonuses on the basis of net profit margin achieved in 2016 as planned, but have asked you as a performance management consultant for your advice on the comments of the Export division manager in advance of their meeting with her. One director has also suggested that, in future, economic value added (EVA^{TM}) may be a good way to evaluate and compare the performance of the two divisions. You are asked for your advice on this too, but you have been specifically asked not to attempt a calculation of EVA^{TM}.

Required:

(a) **Evaluate the comments of the Export division manager that the net profit margin used to appraise her own performance should be different from that used to appraise the performance of the Export division itself.**   **(7 marks)**

(b) **Recommend, using appropriate calculations, whether the manager of the Export division should receive her bonus for the year.**   **(8 marks)**

(c) **Advise whether the use of economic value added (EVA^{TM}) is an appropriate measure of performance of the two divisions. You are not required to perform and EVA^{TM} calculation.**   **(10 marks)**

(Total: 25 marks)

Appendix 1 – Extracts from management accounts for year ended 31 December 2016

$KL000	Export division	Domestic division
Revenue **(1)**	8,000	12,000
Cost of sales	(4,800)	(7,800)
Gross profit	3,200	4,200
Depreciation	(395)	(45)
Allocated head office costs	(360)	(540)
Other overheads **(2)**	(1,900)	2,300
Net profit	545	1,315
Net profit margin on revenue	6.8 %	11.0 %
Capital employed **(3)**	6,500	8,500

(1)   Revenue accrues evenly over the financial year.

(2)   Other overheads for Domestic division include the creation of a bad debt provision equivalent to $KL75,000 for a wholesale customer who had financial difficulties during the year, and $KL90,000 for advertising a new range of paints launched at the end of the year.

(3)   JLW is financed in equal proportions by debt and equity. The cost of equity is 8% and the after tax cost of debt is 5%.

43   THE BETTER ELECTRICALS GROUP (BEG) (JUN 10 – AMENDED)

The Better Electricals Group (BEG), which commenced trading during 2002, manufactures a range of high quality electrical appliances such as kettles, toasters and steam irons for domestic use which it sells to electrical stores in Voltland.

The directors consider that the existing product range could be extended to include industrial sized products such as high volume water boilers, high volume toasters and large steam irons for the hotel and catering industry.

They recently commissioned a highly reputable market research organisation to undertake a market analysis including the use of strategic models such as PEST and Porter's Five Forces. Their analysis identified a number of significant competitors within the hotel and catering industry.

At a recent meeting of the board of directors, the marketing director proposed that BEG should make an application to gain 'platinum status' quality certification in respect of their industrial products from the Hotel and Catering Institute of Voltland in order to gain a strong competitive position. He then stressed the need to focus on increasing the effectiveness of all operations from product design to the provision of after sales services.

An analysis of financial and non-financial data relating to the application for 'platinum status' for each of the years 2011, 2012 and 2013 is contained in the appendix.

The managing director of BEG recently returned from a seminar, the subject of which was 'The Use of Cost Targets'. She then requested the management accountant of BEG to prepare a statement of total costs for the application for platinum status for each of years 2011, 2012 and 2013. She further asked that the statement detailed manufacturing cost targets and the costs of quality.

The management accountant produced the following statement of manufacturing cost targets and the costs of quality:

	2011 Forecast $m	2012 Forecast $m	2013 Forecast $m
Variable manufacturing costs	8,400	10,500	12,600
Fixed manufacturing costs	3,000	3,400	3,400
Prevention costs	4,200	2,100	1,320
Appraisal costs	800	700	700
Internal failure costs	2,500	1,800	1,200
External failure costs	3,100	2,000	980
Total costs	22,000	20,500	20,200

APPENDIX

'Platinum Status' Quality Certification Application – Relevant Statistics

	2011 Forecast	2012 Forecast	2013 Forecast
Total market size ($m)	300	320	340
BEG – sales ($m)	24	30	36
BEG – total costs ($m)	22	20.5	20.2
BEG – sundry statistics:			
% of products achieving design quality standards and accepted without further rectification	92	95	99
Rectification claims from customers ($m)	0.96	0.75	0.1
Cost of after sales rectification service ($m)	1.8	1.05	0.8
% of sales meeting planned delivery dates	88.5	95.5	99.5
Average cycle time:			
(Customer enquiry to product delivery) (days)	49	45	40
Product enquiries not taken up by customers (% of enquiries)	10.5	6	3
Idle capacity of manufacturing staff (%)	12	6	1.5

Required:

(a) Briefly explain how strategic models such as PEST and/or Porter's Five Forces can assist with strategic performance management. **(5 marks)**

(b) Explain how the use of cost targets could be of assistance to BEG with regard to their application for platinum status. Your answer must include commentary on the items contained in the statement of manufacturing cost targets and the costs of quality prepared by the management accountant. **(8 marks)**

(c) Assess the forecasted performance of BEG for the period 2011 to 2013 with reference to the application for 'platinum status' quality certification under the following headings:

(i) Financial performance and marketing

(ii) External effectiveness; and

(iii) Internal efficiency. **(12 marks)**

(Total: 25 marks)

44 ESSLAND POLICE FORCE (DEC 13)

You are a performance management expert brought in by the Chief Executive Officer (CEO) of the Department of the Interior for the country of Essland. The department is a branch of the Essland government which handles security, policing, immigration and border control. The CEO is a civil servant and he reports to the Minister for the Interior. The Minister for the Interior is an elected politician selected by the Prime Minister of Essland, who leads its government.

The newly-elected Minister for the Interior has instructed the CEO to implement his policy for improving the regional police forces' performance by copying the method used for schools.

In a recent initiative by the School's Ministry, a league table for the hundreds of schools in Essland was created, showing the best and worst in terms of examination performance only, in order to motivate senior school managers to improve. The league table was used to create targets for assessing the schools' and their managers' performance. Additionally, parents in Essland have the right to choose which school their children attend and so often base their selection on league table performance. Therefore, the Minister has had a policy review body draw up a method of creating a league table for the police forces.

The CEO has requested your help to clarify his own thinking on this new policy for the four regional police forces in Essland (Cashire (C), Dashire (D), Eshire (E) and Fashire (F)). The CEO needs you to assess the use of the league table using the policy review body's suggested method and has collected the data and calculation of the league table given in Appendix 1 to assist you. He also wants to assess whether the table will help in meeting the Department's aim and goals for the police. The overall aim of the Department (and its police forces) is 'to provide a value-for-money service to ensure that the community can live in safety with confidence in their physical and legal security'.

The detailed goals of the Department are to:

- Tackle the underlying causes of crime and achieve long-term sustainable solutions
- Bring perpetrators to justice
- Provide protection and support for individuals and communities at risk of harm
- Respond to community needs by being accessible and engaging with their concerns.

The CEO warned you, 'I'm not interested in the performance of the forces. I'm interested in the method of assessment, so don't waste time with your ideas on how to improve actual policing.'

The CEO also wishes to understand the strengths and weaknesses of the use of a league table, its link to targets and the likely reaction of employees to this system of performance management, especially as there is a strong union representing the police. He is worried about the employees' attitude to the introduction of the system and its effects on their behaviour and their sense of accountability. He is also concerned about importing the use of a league table from the schools sector, as it might not be appropriate here.

Required:

(a) **Evaluate the method of calculating and measuring the Force Scores for use in the league table in achieving the Department of the Interior's aims and goals.**

(14 marks)

(b) **Discuss the merits of league tables in performance management and address the CEO's concerns over their use in managing the performance of Essland's police forces.** (11 marks)

(Total: 25 marks)

Appendix 1

The appendix defines the policy review body's method for scoring each force, provides the basic data for each force and then calculates the current force score placing the forces into a league table:

Force score = Rank 1 × 0.25 + Rank 2 × 0.25 + Rank 3 × 0.25 + Rank 4 × 0.25

where each Rank is the ranking from 4 to 1 which each force gets for each of the following variables (4 is best, 1 is worst):

- Rank 1 is based on the number of crimes per 10,000 of population

- Rank 2 is based on the solution rate for crimes reported in the year

- Rank 3 is based on the user satisfaction score (based on a survey of the population)

- Rank 4 is based on the percentage of calls to police answered within 10 seconds

For example, a force which was top ranked in each of the Ranks would get a Force Score of 4 (= 4 × 0.25 + 4 × 0.25 + 4 × 0.25 + 4 × 0.25).

Data by region: For the calendar year 2012

	C	*D*	*E*	*F*
Population	1,250,000	900,000	1,700,000	1,500,000
Number of crimes reported in year	62,500	47,250	83,300	63,000
Number of crimes solved in year	31,250	22,680	45,815	33,390
User satisfaction score	71%	80%	73%	68%
Percentage of calls to police answered within 10 seconds	92%	93%	91%	94%
Number of police force employees	6,200	4,400	8,500	7,900
Cost of police force for year ($m)	404	298	572	510

Calculation of Force Score:

	C	*D*	*E*	*F*
Number of reported crimes per 10,000 of population	500	525	490	420
Rank 1	2	1	3	4
Solution rate for crimes reported in year	50%	48%	55%	53%
Rank 2	2	1	4	3
Rank 3 (user satisfaction)	2	4	3	1
Rank 4 (call handling)	2	3	1	4
Force score	2	2.25	2.75	3

The league table for 2012 is:

	Force	*Score*
1	F	3.00
2	E	2.75
3	D	2.25
4	C	2.00

Note: You should assume that the calculations in Appendix 1 are accurate.

45 TELECOMS AT WORK (TAW) (JUN 08 – AMENDED)

 *Question debrief*

Telecoms At Work (TAW) manufactures and markets office communications systems. During the year ended 31 May 2008 TAW made an operating profit of $30 million on sales of $360 million. However, the directors are concerned that products do not conform to the required level of quality and TAW is therefore not fulfilling its full potential in terms of turnover and profits achieved.

The following information is available in respect of the year ended 31 May 2008:

1   Production data:

Units manufactured and sold	18,000
Units requiring rework	2,100
Units requiring warranty repair service	2,700
Design engineering hours	48,000
Process engineering hours	54,000
Inspection hours (manufacturing)	288,000

2   Cost data:

	$
Design engineering per hour	96
Process engineering per hour	70
Inspection per hour (manufacturing)	50
Rework per communication system reworked (manufacturing)	4,800
Customer support per repaired unit (marketing)	240
Transportation costs per repaired unit (distribution)	280
Warranty repairs per repaired unit (customer service)	4,600

3   Staff training costs amounted to $180,000 and additional product testing costs of $72,000.

(4)   The marketing director has estimated that sales of 1,800 units were lost as a result of public knowledge of poor quality at TAW. The average contribution per communication system is estimated at $7,200.

Required:

(a)   **Prepare a cost analysis which shows actual prevention costs, appraisal costs, internal failure costs, and external failure costs for the year ended 31 May 2008. Your statement should show each cost heading as a % of turnover and clearly show the total cost of quality. Comment briefly on the inclusion of opportunity costs in such an analysis.** **(11 marks)**

(b)   A detailed analysis has revealed that the casings in which the communications systems are housed are often subject to mishandling in transit to TAW's manufacturing premises.

The directors are considering two alternative solutions proposed by the design engineering team which are aimed at reducing the quality problems that are currently being experienced. These are as follows:

Option 1 – Increase the number of immediate physical inspections of the casings when they are received from the supplier. This will require an additional 10,000 inspection hours.

Option 2 – Redesign and strengthen the casings and the containers used to transport them to better withstand mishandling during transportation. Redesign will require an additional 2,000 hours of design engineering and an additional 5,000 hours of process engineering.

Internal failure costs of rework for each reworked communication system are as follows:

	$
Variable costs	
(including direct materials, direct labour rework and supplies)	1,920
Allocated fixed costs	
(equipment, space and allocated overhead)	2,880
	———
Total costs (as per note 2 on cost data)	4,800
	———

The directors of TAW believe that, even if it is able to achieve improvements in quality, it will be unable to save any of the fixed costs of internal and external failure.

If TAW chooses to inspect the casings more carefully, it expects to eliminate re-work on 720 communication systems whereas if it redesigns the casings it expects to eliminate rework on 960 communication systems.

If incoming casings are inspected more carefully, TAW estimates that 600 fewer communication systems will require warranty repair and that it will be able to sell an additional 300 communication systems. If the casing is redesigned, the directors estimate that 840 fewer communication systems will require warranty repair and that an additional 360 communication systems will be sold.

External failure costs of repair for each repaired communication system are as follows:

	Variable costs	Fixed costs	Total costs
	$	$	$
Customer support costs	96	144	240
Transportation costs	210	70	280
Warranty repair costs	1,700	2,900	4,600

Required:

Prepare an estimate of the financial consequences of each option and advise the directors of TAW which option should be chosen. **(9 marks)**

(c) **Explain how the four quality categories used in part (a) can be adapted for use as part of an environmental costing exercise.** **(5 marks)**

(Total: 25 marks)

46 WESTAMBER (PILOT 07 – AMENDED)

The Westamber Hospital ('Westamber'), which is partially government-funded, specialises in the provision of ear, nose and throat operations for patients in Zonderland.

Its mission statement states that the hospital 'is committed to providing high quality healthcare to all patients'.

Westamber provides treatment to private fee-paying patients as well as to patients who are funded by the government.

Relevant operating data for Westamber for the year ended 30 June 20X6 is as follows:

Income statement for the year ended 30 June 20X6

	Budget	Actual
Revenue:	$000	$000
Private patients:		
Ear	5,256	3,066
Nose	7,008	3,504
Throat	11,680	5,110
	23,944	11,680
Government patients:		
Ear	3,504	6,132
Nose	5,256	7,884
Throat	9,344	12,264
	18,104	26,280
Total revenue	**42,048**	**37,960**
Variable costs:		
Surgery	7,080	8,284
Nursing	1,920	2,224
Sundry	920	1,116
Total variable costs	9,920	11,624
Contribution	**32,128**	**26,336**
Fixed costs:		
Surgery	26,550	26,550
Nursing	5,600	5,600
Depreciation	1,700	1,700
Administration	3,250	3,412
Sundry	4,600	4,912
Total fixed costs	41,700	42,174
Net loss	**(9,572)**	**(15,838)**

A recently qualified accountant employed by Westamber has stated that 'it is obvious that the mix of government to private patients mix is the key determinant of profitability. Next year it looks as if demand for total operations will exceed our available capacity and therefore we should give priority to private fee-paying patients as we receive more fees from them for each type of operation. It is as simple as that since there aren't any ethical issues to be considered'.

Further information

1   Fees (budget and actual) payable to Westamber in respect of each patient who received treatment from the hospital are as follows:

Type of operation:	Fee payable by private patients ($)	Fee payable by government ($)
Ear	3,000	2,000
Nose	4,000	3,000
Throat	5,000	4,000

2   Budgeted variable surgical costs include a total amount of $1,000,000 in respect of operations undertaken on an emergency basis. The actual costs of emergency operations was $800,000.

3   Westamber had no loan finance during the year.

4   Other statistics relating to Westamber:

	Budget	Actual
Total number of operations	11,680	11,680

	Budget	Actual
Patient mix (%):		
Government-funded patients	50%	75%
Privately-funded patients	50%	25%

Eastgreen Hospital ('Eastgreen'), is a privately owned hospital which also specialises in the provision of ear, nose and throat operations. All of its patients are responsible for the payment of their own fees. Eastgreen does not undertake operations on an emergency basis.

The summary income statement for Eastgreen on an actual basis was as follows:

	$000
Fee income	36,000
Costs:	
Surgery & nursing	25,000
Depreciation	3,400
Loan interest	500
Administration and sundry	5,100
Total costs	34,000
Net profit	2,000

(i)   Eastgreen operates comparable accounting policies to those of Westamber.

(ii)   The income of Eastgreen is derived from the provision of an annual healthcare scheme. Each patient pays $100 per month under a fixed term contract of three years. All contracts were renewed on 1 July 20X5. There were 30,000 contracts in existence throughout the year.

Note: Contracts can only be entered into on 1 July in each year.

Each hospital is comprised of 15 wards, each of which can accommodate eight patients. The average patient stay in both hospitals was three days. Each hospital is open for 365 days per annum.

Required:

(a) Explain FOUR reasons why it may be inappropriate to make a direct comparison of the financial performance of the Westamber and Eastgreen hospitals on the basis of the information provided. **(6 marks)**

(b) Using only the information contained in the question make THREE adjustments to the income statements that you consider would assist in the development of a more appropriate comparison of the financial performance of Westamber and Eastgreen hospitals. **(6 marks)**

(c) Discuss the statement of Westamber's recently qualified accountant including comments on the ethical implications of the statement. **(4 marks)**

(d) Excluding the number of complaints by patients, state SIX performance measures that may be used in order to assess the surgical quality provided by a hospital indicating how each measure may be assessed. **(9 marks)**

(Total: 25 marks)

47 ALPHA DIVISION (DEC 07)

Alpha Division, which is part of the Delta Group, is considering an investment opportunity to which the following estimated information relates:

1   An initial investment of $45m in equipment at the beginning of year 1 will be depreciated on a straight-line basis over a three-year period with a nil residual value at the end of year 3.

2   Net operating cash inflows in each of years 1 to 3 will be $12.5m, $18.5m and $27m respectively.

3   The management accountant of Alpha Division has estimated that the NPV of the investment would be $1.937m using a cost of capital of 10%.

4   A bonus scheme which is based on short-term performance evaluation is in operation in all divisions within the Delta Group.

Required:

(a)   **(i)**   Calculate the residual income of the proposed investment and comment briefly (using ONLY the above information) on the values obtained in reconciling the short-term and long-term decision views likely to be adopted by divisional management regarding the viability of the proposed investment. **(6 marks)**

   (ii)   A possible analysis of divisional profit measurement at Alpha Division might be as follows:

	$m
Sales revenue	xxx
Less: variable costs	xxx
1 Variable short run contribution margin	xxx
Less: controllable fixed costs	xxx
2 Controllable profit	xxx
Less: non-controllable avoidable costs	xxx
3 Divisional profit	xxx

Required:

Discuss the relevance of each of the divisional profit measures 1, 2 and 3 in the above analysis as an acceptable measure of divisional management performance and/or divisional economic performance at Alpha Division.

You should use appropriate items from the following list relating to Alpha Division in order to illustrate your discussion:

(i)   Sales to customers external to the Delta Group

(ii)   Inter-divisional transfers to other divisions within the Delta Group at adjusted market price

(iii) Labour costs or equipment rental costs that are fixed in the short term

(iv)   Depreciation of non-current assets at Alpha Division

(v)   Head office finance and legal staff costs for services provided to Alpha Division.   (8 marks)

(b) Summary financial information for the Gamma Group (which is not connected with the Delta Group) is as follows:

Income statements/financial information:

	2006 $m	2007 $m
Revenue	400	450
Profit before tax	96	117
Income tax expense	(29)	(35)
Profit for the period	67	82
Dividends	(23)	(27)
Retained earnings	44	55

Statements of financial position (Balance Sheets):

	2006 $m	2007 $m
Non-current assets	160	180
Current assets	180	215
	340	395
Financed by:		
Total equity	270	325
Long-term debt	70	70
	340	395

Other information is as follows:

1   Capital employed at the end of 2005 amounted to $279m.

2   The Gamma Group had non-capitalised leases valued at $16m in each of the years 2005 to 2007 which were not subject to amortisation.

3   Amortisation of goodwill amounted to $5m per year in both 2006 and 2007. The amount of goodwill written off against reserves on acquisitions in years prior to 2006 amounted to $45m.

4   The Group's pre-tax cost of debt was estimated to be 10%.

5   The Group's cost of equity was estimated to be 16% in 2006 and 18% in 2007.

6   The target capital structure is 50% equity, 50% debt.

7   The rate of taxation is 30% in both 2006 and 2007.

8   Economic depreciation amounted to $40m in 2006 and $45m in 2007. These amounts were equal to the depreciation used for tax purposes and depreciation charged in the income statements.

9   Interest payable amounted to $6m per year in both 2006 and 2007.

10   Other non-cash expenses amounted to $12m per year in both 2006 and 2007.

Required:

(i)   **Stating clearly any assumptions that you make, estimate the Economic Value Added (EVA™) of the Gamma Group for both 2006 and 2007 and comment briefly on the performance of the Group.**   **(8 marks)**

(ii)   **Briefly discuss THREE disadvantages of using EVA™ in the measurement of financial performance.**   **(3 marks)**

                                                                        (Total: 25 marks)

48   BEESHIRE LOCAL AUTHORITY (BLA) (DEC 14)

Beeshire Local Authority (BLA) is a local government body which provides a range of services for the area of Beeshire within the country of Seeland. Beeshire is a wealthy area within the country with many tourist attractions. One of BLA's tasks is to ensure that waste is collected from the homes and businesses in Beeshire. The goal for BLA's waste management department is 'to maintain Beeshire as a safe, clean and environmentally friendly place where people and businesses want to both stay in and return to.' The need for waste collection is linked to public health concerns, the desire to keep the streets clean and attractive and the desire to increase the amount of rubbish which is recycled.

BLA is funded through a single local tax and does not charge its residents or businesses separately for most of its services, including waste collection. There is no public or political appetite for outsourcing services such as waste management.

Waste collection is performed by the workforce using a fleet of vehicles. The waste is either taken to recycling plants or else to landfill sites for burying. BLA obtains revenues from all the recycled waste but this only just covers the cost of running the recycling facilities.

Against a background estimate that waste will increase by 1% p.a. in the future, the national government has ordered local authorities, such as BLA, to promote the recycling of waste and has set a target of 40% of all waste to be recycled by 2015. In order to discourage the creation of non-recyclable waste, the government has imposed a levy per tonne of waste buried in landfill sites and has stated that this levy will rise over the next five years in order to encourage continuing improvement in the amount of recycled waste.

Currently, Seeland is in a long recession and so local authority revenues have fallen as tax revenues reflect the poor state of the economy. Along with other local authorities, BLA has tried to cut costs and so has focused on financial measures of performance. In a recent, private meeting, the chief executive of BLA was heard to say 'keep costs under control and we will worry about quality of service only when complaint levels build to an unacceptable level.' As one of the area's largest employers, cutting staff numbers has been very difficult for BLA due to the impact on the local economy and the reaction of the residents.

The current performance indicators used at BLA are drawn from the existing information systems with national figures given for comparison. Those relating to waste collection for the year ending 31 March 2014 are:

			BLA	National total
Total cost	($m)		250	2,850
Volume of waste				
	landfilled	(tonnes)	1,250,000	13,750,000
	recycled	(tonnes)	950,000	9,500,000
	total	(tonnes)	2,200,000	23,250,000
No. of staff			3,500	39,900
Staff cost	($m)		110	1,190
No. of households			2,380,952	26,190,476
No. of complaints about waste uncollected			18,250	200,750

	BLA	National average
Frequency of waste collections (days)	14	12

Notes on BLA data:

1   Cost data and no. of households comes from BLA's financial systems.

2   Waste data comes from weighing lorries at the landfill sites and recycling facilities.

3   Staff data is collected from BLA's HR system.

4   Complaints data is based on numbers of letters and phone calls to the waste management department.

5   Frequency of collection data is obtained from the department's vehicle schedules.

Required:

(a)   Explain why non-financial indicators are particularly useful for public sector organisations, illustrating your answer with brief examples relevant to BLA.

(6 marks)

(b)   Explain how the value for money provision of waste services by BLA should be assessed by suggesting and calculating justified performance indicators using the information in the scenario.
(12 marks)

(c)   Discuss the difficulties of measuring qualitative factors of performance, suggesting appropriate solutions for BLA.
(7 marks)

(Total: 25 marks)

49   SSA GROUP (DEC 09 – AMENDED)

You are the management accountant of the SSA Group which manufactures an innovative range of products to provide support for injuries to various joints in the body. The group has adopted a divisional structure. Each division is encouraged to maximise its reported profit.

Division A, which is based in a country called Nearland, manufactures joint-support appliances which incorporate a 'one size fits all people' feature. A different appliance is manufactured for each of knee, ankle, elbow and wrist joints.

Budget information in respect of Division A for the year ended 31 December 2010 is as follows:

Support appliance	Knee	Ankle	Elbow	Wrist
Sales units (000s)	20	50	20	60
Selling price per unit ($)	24	15	18	9
Total variable cost of sales ($000)	200	350	160	240

Each of the four support products uses the same quantity of manufacturing capacity. This gives Division A management the flexibility to alter the product mix as desired. During the year to 31 December 2010 it is estimated that a maximum of 160,000 support products could be manufactured.

The following information relates to Division B which is also part of the SSA group and is based in Distantland:

1   Division B purchases products from various sources, including from other divisions in SSA group, for subsequent resale to customers.

2   The management of Division B has requested two alternative quotations from Division A in respect of the year ended 31 December 2010 as follows:

Quotation 1 – Purchase of 10,000 ankle supports.

Quotation 2 – Purchase of 18,000 ankle supports.

The management of the SSA Group has decided that a minimum of 50,000 ankle supports must be reserved for customers in Nearland in order to ensure that customer demand can be satisfied and the product's competitive position is maintained in the Nearland market.

The management of the SSA Group is willing, if necessary, to reduce the budgeted sales quantities of other types of joint support in order to satisfy the requirements of Division B for ankle supports. They wish, however, to minimise the loss of contribution to the Group.

The management of Division B is aware of another joint support product, which is produced in Distantland, that competes with the Division A version of the ankle support and which could be purchased at a local currency price that is equivalent to $9 per support.

SSA Group policy is that all divisions are allowed autonomy to set transfer prices and purchase from whatever sources they choose. The management of Division A intends to use market price less 30% as the basis for each of quotations 1 and 2.

Required:

(a) Outline the key objectives of a transfer pricing system. **(5 marks)**

(b) (i) The management of the SSA Group have asked you to advise them regarding the appropriateness of the decision by the management of Division A to use an adjusted market price as the basis for the preparation of each quotation and the implications of the likely sourcing decision by the management of Division B.

Your answer should cite relevant quantitative data and incorporate your recommendation of the prices that should be quoted by Division A for the ankle supports in respect of quotations 1 and 2, that will ensure that the profitability of SSA Group as a whole is not adversely affected by the decision of the management of Division B. **(8 marks)**

(ii) Advise the management of Divisions A and B regarding the basis of transfer pricing which should be employed in order to ensure that the profit of the SSA Group is maximised. **(4 marks)**

(c) After considerable internal discussion concerning Quotation 2 by the management of SSA Group, Division A is not prepared to supply 18,000 ankle supports to Division B at any price lower than 30% below market price. All profits in Distantland are subject to taxation at a rate of 20%. Division A pays tax in Nearland at a rate of 40% on all profits.

Advise the management of SSA Group whether the management of Division B should be directed to purchase the ankle supports from Division A, or to purchase a similar product from a local supplier in Distantland. Supporting calculations should be provided. **(8 marks)**

(Total: 25 marks)

50 LOCAL GOVERNMENT HOUSING DEPARTMENT (JUN 10 – AMENDED)

Norchester City Council has stated its mission as 'Caring for the community'.

Norchester City Council's housing department (NCCHD) has funds which it is proposing to spend on the upgrading of air conditioning systems in its housing inventory.

It is intended that the upgrading should enhance the quality of living for the occupants of the houses.

Preferred contractors will be identified to carry out the work involved in the upgrading of the air conditioning systems, with each contractor being responsible for upgrading of the systems in a proportion of the houses.

Contractors will also be required to provide a maintenance and operational advice service during the first two years of operation of the upgraded systems.

Prior to a decision to implement the proposal, NCCHD has decided that it should carry out a value for money (VFM) audit.

You have been given the task of preparing a report for NCCHD, to help ensure that it can make an informed decision concerning the proposal.

Required:

(a) Critically evaluate Norchester City Council's stated mission in terms of its usefulness for performance management purposes. **(5 marks)**

(b) Prepare a detailed analysis which will form the basis for the preparation of the final report for the NCHD. The analysis should include a clear explanation of the meaning and relevance of each of (i) to (iii) below:

(i) Value for Money (VFM) audit (including references to the roles of principal and agent). **(6 marks)**

(ii) Economy, efficiency and effectiveness as part of the VFM audit. **(6 marks)**

(iii) The extent (if any) to which each of intangibility, heterogeneity, simultaneity and perishability may be seen to relate to the decision concerning the proposal, and any problems that may occur. **(8 marks)**

Note: Your analysis should incorporate specific references to examples relating to the upgrading proposal.

(Total: 25 marks)

51 TENCH CARS (DEC 11 – AMENDED)

Tench Cars (Tench) is large national car manufacturing business. It is based in Essland, a country that has recently turned from state communism to democratic capitalism. The car industry had been heavily supported and controlled by the bureaucracy of the old regime. The government had stipulated production and employment targets for the business but had ignored profit as a performance measure. Tench is now run by a new generation of capitalist business people intent on rejuvenating the company's fortunes.

The company has a strong position within Essland, which has a population of 200 million and forms the majority of Tench's market. However, the company has also traditionally achieved a good market share in six neighbouring countries due to historic links and shared culture between them and Essland. All of these markets are experiencing growing car ownership as political and market reforms lead to greater wealth in a large proportion of the population. Additionally, the new government in Essland is deregulating markets and opening the country to imports of foreign vehicles.

Tench's management recognises that it needs to make fundamental changes to its production approach in order to combat increased competition from foreign manufacturers. Tench's cars are now being seen as ugly, pollutive and with poor safety features in comparison to the foreign competition. Management plans to address this by improving the quality of its cars through the use of quality management techniques. It plans to improve financial performance through the use of Kaizen costing and just-in-time purchasing and production. Tench's existing performance reporting system uses standard costing and budgetary variance analysis in order to monitor and control production activities.

The Chief Financial Officer (CFO) of Tench has commented that he is confused by the terminology associated with quality management and needs a clearer understanding of the different costs associated with quality management. The CFO also wants to know the impact of including quality costs and using the Kaizen costing approach on the traditional standard costing approach at Tench.

Required:

Write to the CFO to:

(a) Discuss the impact of collection and use of quality costs on the current costing systems at Tench. **(6 marks)**

(b) Discuss and evaluate the impact of the Kaizen costing approach on the costing systems and employee management at Tench. **(8 marks)**

(c) Briefly evaluate the effect of moving to just-in-time purchasing and production, noting the impact on performance measures at Tench. **(6 marks)**

(d) Briefly discuss any problems that the existing performance reporting system may cause for Tench. **(5 marks)**

(Total: 25 marks)

52 THEBE TELECOM (JUN 12 – AMENDED)

Thebe Telecom is a large national telephone business in Fayland. Thebe provides telephone service to more than 11 million customers through its fixed line and mobile services. Thebe has three strategic business units: mobile; fixed line telephone (incorporating broadband); and corporate services (serving other businesses' telephone needs). It has become the largest mobile operator in Fayland through a series of acquisitions of competitors and operating licences.

Thebe's CEO has won many awards for being an innovative businessman who recognises the rapid changes in technology, regulation and competitor action that occur in the sector. Thebe's major competitor in Fayland is the original nationalised telephone company, FayTel, which was privatised 20 years ago but which retains many of the features of a monopoly supplier including a massive infrastructure. As a result, Thebe's CEO realised long ago that competition on the basis of price and volume would not work against such a large competitor and so he has focused on customer service as the key to growing the business.

In order to improve the company's competitive position, the CEO decided that the company should consider a Six Sigma initiative to give an immediate step change improvement to the service quality at Thebe. The initiative involved a number of projects including one to improve the quality of customers' bills. FayTel was publicly criticised by the government's consumer advocate who pointed to occasional misallocations of call minutes to the wrong numbers and also, more frequently, the application of incorrect tariffs in calculating the costs of calls. Thebe's CEO is aware that all telephone businesses (including Thebe) have these problems but this is an area in which Thebe can gain a competitive advantage and has taken a special interest in this project by championing it himself.

The project is focused on improving the accuracy of customers' bills and the handling of complaints. Within the billing department, the company divided activities into normal money collection, credit control on overdue payments and managing complaints. Process diagrams were created for each of these areas and then data was sourced from customer feedback at the various points of interaction with Thebe employees (such as complaint handling) and internal measurables created. The project team was formed from line managers from all three strategic business units and the billing department.

Required:

(a) **Explain how the general way in which Six Sigma is implemented helps improve the quality of performance illustrating your answer with reference to Thebe.**

(8 marks)

(b) **Explain and illustrate how the DMAIC method for the implementation of Six Sigma could be applied at Thebe.**

(9 marks)

(c) **Evaluate the appropriateness of introducing other quality practices at Thebe.**

(8 marks)

(Total: 25 marks)

53 LINCOLN & LINCOLN ADVERTISING (DEC 12 – AMENDED)

Lincoln & Lincoln Advertising (LLA) is an advertising agency based in Veeland, which is a large well-developed country considered to be one of the wealthiest in the world. LLA operates out of three regional offices (North, East and West) with its head office functions based in the East offices. The business offers a wide range of advertising services:

Strategic: Advising on an overall advertising campaign (mix of advertising channels and overall themes)

Buying: Advising and buying advertising space (on television, radio, websites and in newspapers and magazines); and

Creative: Designing and producing specific adverts for the customers' use.

The company is one of the three largest agencies in Veeland with many years of experience and many awards won. Competition in advertising is fierce, as advertising spending by businesses has suffered recently during a general economic downturn. Most new business is won in tender competitions between different advertising agencies.

Veeland is a large country with considerable diversity of markets, economic conditions and fashions across its regions. As a result, the regional offices have developed with a considerable amount of decision-making autonomy. This also reflects the temperament of the key creative employees of the firm who have a strong attachment to their campaign ideas and take great personal pride in their success. The individualism of the key employees also comes from the way that LLA has grown. The business has been built through acquisition of small, local businesses in each of the three regions. Each of these acquisitions has been consolidated into the appropriate regional office.

You have been recruited in to LLA in order to take up the newly created post of senior management accountant. Your recruitment caused some concern amongst the board but was championed by the chief executive officer (CEO) as 'necessary to stay ahead of the game'. The board have asked that you prove yourself and also give a fresh perspective on LLA by providing them with a report. Initially, you have been asked to provide an assessment of the current financial position of the three regional offices. The most recent management accounts are in Appendix 1. The basic assessment calculations have already been accurately completed by one of the junior staff and the results are in Appendix 2.

As part of the briefing for this exercise, you attended part of a recent board meeting where you were told that the board want your views on the choice of net income as the performance measure for each of the regional offices. They want you to suggest other measures and why they are appropriate for each office. The CEO has advised you that you may want to use different key measures for each office, rather than have a 'one-size fits all policy'. During the board's discussion, issues around controllability and responsibility accounting appear to be the main concerns of the board. The CEO also stated that the board would not be interested in a long list of which numbers have gone up and which have gone down. They will want to be given a coherent picture of what is going on at each of the regional offices.

Finally, the CEO said, 'Well, if you are not completely tired out at the end of this little project then I'd also like you to comment on our remuneration policy at the regional offices including ideas based on your assessment of performance measures.' Later, the CEO gave you a note (see Appendix 3) describing these policies at LLA.

Required:

(a)   Assess the recent performance of the three regional offices by interpreting the data given in Appendices 1 and 2.   **(10 marks)**

(b)   Evaluate the choice of net income as the performance measure for the regional offices and suggest other measures and why they are appropriate for each office.
                                                                                      (8 marks)

(c)   Using the information provided, evaluate LLA's remuneration policy suggesting changes as appropriate.   **(7 marks)**

Note: The Appendices follow on the next two pages.

                                                                                (Total: 25 marks)

Appendix 1: LLA financial data

The figures are drawn from the regional offices' management accounts for year to September 2012.

	North	East	West
	$m	$m	$m
Revenue	151	523	467
Cost of sales	45	147	159
Staff costs	53	194	145
Other costs	27	86	67
Operating profit	26	96	96
Allocated head office costs	6	31	16
Net income	20	65	80
Net cash flow in year	24	86	46
Current assets	22	82	119
Current liabilities	10	35	31
Capital expenditure	3	10.2	23.8
Capital employed	39	121	112

Notes:

1 East office data is for the regional office only. It excludes any costs of the head office function based there other than the allocated costs listed.

2 Notional cost of capital at LLA is 9%.

3 Current assets contains only accounts receivable for each office.

Appendix 2: Basic calculations

[These can be assumed to be calculated correctly.]

		Change on year		Margins		
		Sep–12	Sep–11	Sep–12	Sep–11	Sep–10
Revenue						
	North	−1.9%	−1.3%			
	East	1.0%	1.0%			
	West	8.9%	8.1%			
Cost of sales						
	North			29.8%	29.9%	30.1%
	East			28.1%	29.0%	30.0%
	West			34.0%	31.9%	30.0%
Staff costs						
	North			35.1%	35.1%	35.3%
	East			37.1%	37.1%	37.0%
	West			31.0%	31.0%	31.0%
Operating profit						
	North	−7.1%	0.0%	17.2%	18.2%	17.9%
	East	7.9%	8.5%	18.4%	17.2%	16.0%
	West	5.5%	4.6%	20.6%	21.2%	21.9%
Net Income						
	North	−4.8%	−4.5%	13.2%	13.6%	14.1%
	East	12.1%	13.7%	12.4%	11.2%	9.9%
	West	6.7%	5.6%	17.1%	17.5%	17.9%

Notes:

1 Other costs and allocated head office costs are fixed.

2 Margins are calculated as a percentage of revenue.

		Sep-12	Sep-11	Sep-10
Current ratio				
	North	2.2	2.3	2.1
	East	2.3	2.3	2.4
	West	3.8	2.9	2.4
Receivable days				
	North	53	55	54
	East	57	58	59
	West	93	68	55

ROCE	based on operating profit	*Sep-12*	*Sep-11*	*Sep-10*
	North	67%	88%	117%
	East	79%	90%	103%
	West	86%	106%	140%
	based on net income			
	North	51%	66%	92%
	East	54%	59%	64%
	West	71%	87%	115%
Residual income ($m's)	based on operating profit			
	North	22.5	25.1	25.8
	East	85.1	80.1	74.8
	West	85.9	83.3	81.4
	based on net income			
	North	16.5	18.1	19.8
	East	54.1	49.1	43.8
	West	69.9	67.3	65.4

Appendix 3: Note on remuneration from the CEO:

There are broadly five grades of staff at each regional office. The following is an outline of their remuneration packages. (The head office staff are treated separately and are not part of this exercise.)

Senior management

All staff at this level are paid a basic fixed salary, which reflects industry norms over the last few years, plus a bonus dependent on the net income of their office.

Creative staff

The 'creatives' are on individual packages which reflect the market rates in order to recruit them at the time that they were recruited. Some are fixed salary and some have a fixed element plus a bonus based on their office's revenues.

Buying staff

The buyers are paid a fixed salary plus a bonus based on the prices for advertising space that they negotiate compared to the budgeted cost of space. The budget is set by the finance team at head office based on previous years' experience and their forecast for supply and demand in the year in question.

Account management staff

Account management handles relationships with clients and also develops new clients. They are paid a fixed market-based salary.

Administration staff

These staff are paid the market rate for their jobs as a fixed salary based on hours worked.

(**Note:** The scenario in this question is longer than you would expect to see under the current style of the examiner and therefore additional time may be required to read and absorb the information. However, it is a very useful question for revision purposes.)

54 LANDUAL LAMPS (JUN 13)

Landual Lamps (Landual) manufactures and delivers floor and table lamps for homes and offices in Beeland. The company sells through its website and uses commercial logistics firms to deliver their products. The markets for its products are highly competitive. The company has traditionally relied on the high quality of its designs to drive demand for its products.

The company is divided into two divisions (components and assembly), plus a head office that provides design, administrative and marketing support.

The manufacturing process involves:

1   the components division making the housing components and electrical components for the lamp. This is an intricate process as it depends on the specific design of the lamp and so serves as a significant source of competitive advantage for Landual

2   the assembly division assembling the various components into a finished lamp ready for shipment. This is a simple process.

The finance director (FD) of Landual is currently overloaded with work due to changes in financial accounting policies that are being considered at board level. As a result, she has been unable to look at certain management accounting aspects of the business and has asked you to do a review of the transfer pricing policy between the components and assembly divisions.

The current transfer pricing policy at Landual is as follows:

(a)   market prices for electrical components are used as these are generic components for which there is a competitive external market; and

(b)   prices for housing components based on total actual production costs to the components division are used as there is no external market for these components since they are specially designed for Landual's products.

Currently, the components division produces only for the assembly division in order to meet overall demand without the use of external suppliers for housing and electrical components. If the components division were to sell its electrical components externally, then additional costs of $269,000 would arise for transport, marketing and bad debts.

The FD is considering two separate changes within Landual: one to the transfer pricing policy and a second one to the divisional structure.

First, the transfer pricing policy for housing components would change to use variable cost to the components division. The FD wants to know the impact of the change in transfer pricing policy on the existing results of the two divisions and the company. (No change is proposed to the transfer price of the electrical components.)

Second, as can be seen from the divisional performance report below, the two divisions are currently treated as profit centres. The FD is considering splitting the components division into two further separate divisions: an electrical components division and a housing components division. If the board agrees to this proposal, then the housing components division will be treated as a cost centre only, charging its total production cost to the assembly division. The electrical components and assembly divisions will remain as profit centres.

The FD needs to understand the impact of this proposed new divisional structure on divisional performance assessment and on the company as a whole. She has asked that, in order to keep the discussion on the new divisional structure simple, you use the existing transfer pricing policy to do illustrative calculations. She stated that she would reallocate head office costs to the two new components divisions in proportion to their cost of sales.

You are provided with the following financial and other information for Landual Lamps.

Actual data for Landual Lamps for the year ended 31 March 2013

	Components division $000	Assembly division $000	Landual Lamps $000
Sales Electrical	1,557		
Housing	8,204		
sub-total	9,761	15,794	15,794
Cost of sales			
Electrical	804	1,557	
Housing	6,902	8,204	
sub-total	7,706	9,761	7,706
Fixed production costs			
Electrical	370		
Housing	1,302		
sub-total	1,672	1,268	2,940
Allocated head office costs	461	2,046	2,507
Profit	(78)	2,719	2,641

Note:

1   The components division has had problems meeting budgets recently, with an adverse variance of $575,000 in the last year. This variance arises in relation to the cost of sales for housing component production.

Required:

(a)   Evaluate the current system of transfer pricing at Landual, using illustrative calculations as appropriate.   **(10 marks)**

(b)   Advise the finance director (FD) on the impact of changing the transfer pricing policy for housing components as suggested by the FD and comment on your results, using illustrative calculations as appropriate.   **(6 marks)**

(c)   Evaluate the impact of the change in proposed divisional structure on the profit in the divisions and the company as directed by the FD.   **(9 marks)**

(Total: 25 marks)

55   BEACH FOODS (JUN 15)

Beach Foods (Beach) is a family-owned business which has grown strongly over its 100 year history. The objective of the business is to maximise the family's wealth through their shareholdings. Beach has three divisions. It manufactures a variety of foods in two of the divisions: Beach Baby Foods (Baby) and Beach Chocolate Foods (Chocolate). Each of these divisions knows its own market and sets prices accordingly. The third division (R&D) researches new products on the instructions of the other divisions and is considered to be vital to the survival and growth of Beach. The board of Beach has been considering the impact of using a divisional structure and has come to you as a performance management consultant to ask for your advice.

There is disagreement at board level about the correct choice of divisional performance measure to be used in the two manufacturing divisions. Currently, the business uses EVA^{TM} but two directors have been questioning its value, complaining that it is complicated to understand. These directors have been promoting the use of either residual income (RI) or return on investment (ROI) as alternatives. The board wants to use the same measure for each division. As well as qualitatively evaluating these different measures, the board needs an assessment of the impact of a change in performance measure on their perception of these divisions' performance. Therefore, as an example, they require you to calculate and discuss the use of ROI and RI at Baby division, given the data in Appendix 1.

The chief executive officer (CEO) of Beach has engaged a business analyst to perform a study of the portfolio of manufacturing businesses which make up Beach. This has been completed in Appendix 2. The CEO wants your comments (based on the categorisation given in Appendix 2) on how this work will impact on the performance management of the divisions. Specifically, the CEO has asked for your recommendations on how to control each division; that is, whether each division should be treated as a cost/profit/investment centre and also, the appropriate management style to use for handling staff in each division. The CEO commented to you:

'I have heard of different approaches to the use of budget information in assessing performance: budget-constrained, profit-conscious and also a non-accounting style. I need to know how these approaches might apply to each division given your other comments.'

All of this work has been partly prompted by complaints from the divisional managers. The Chocolate divisional managers complain that they had to wait for a year to get approval to upgrade their main production line. This production line upgrade has reduced wastage and boosted Chocolate's profit margin by 10 percentage points. The Baby division has been very successful in using the ideas of the R&D division, although Baby's managers do complain about the recharging of R&D costs to their division. Head office managers are worried about Chocolate as it has seemed to be drifting recently with a lack of strategic direction. Chocolate's managers are considered to be good but possibly not sufficiently focused on what benefits Beach as a whole.

Required:

(a)   Assess the use of EVA^{TM} as a divisional performance measure for the manufacturing divisions at Beach.   **(8 marks)**

(b)   Using Appendix 1, calculate the ROI and RI for Baby and assess the impact of the assumptions made when calculating these metrics on the evaluation of the performance of this division and its management.   **(7 marks)**

(c)   Provide justified recommendations for each division's control and management style as requested by the CEO.   **(10 marks)**

(Total: 25 marks)

Appendix 1

Figures from Beach management accounts for year ended 31 March:

Baby division	2015
	$m
Revenue	220
Costs	
Divisional operating costs	121
R&D costs recharged	11
Allocated head office management fees	28
Profit before tax	60
Capital employed	424

Notes:

1 Baby launched a new product with a large publicity campaign during the year.

2 The notional cost of capital for Baby is estimated by the chief financial officer at 11%. WACC for Beach is 7.5%.

3 ROI for similar entities is 20%.

4 EVA™ for Baby is calculated as $35m.

Appendix 2

Star		Problem child
Baby:		
Market growth	18%	
Relative market share	105%	
Cash cow		**Dog**
Chocolate:		
Market growth	3%	
Relative market share	120%	

Relative market share is the market share of the division compared to that of the market leader. If an organisation is a market leader, then its market share is compared to the next largest competitor.

Note: You may assume that the calculations and this categorisation are accurate.

56 POSIE FURNITURE (SEPT/DEC 15)

Posie is a large business which manufactures furniture. It is made up of two autonomous divisions in Deeland. The manufacturing division purchases raw materials from external suppliers, and performs all manufacturing and packaging operations. All sales are made through the retail division which has 95 retail stores in Deeland, as well as through Posie's own well-developed website. Posie has retail operations in eight other countries as well as in Deeland. These overseas businesses operate as independent subsidiaries within the Retail Division, each with their own IT and accounting functions.

The furniture is sold in boxes for customers to assemble themselves. About 10% of the products sold by Posie are purchased already packaged from other manufacturers. All deliveries are outsourced through a third party distribution company.

Posie's corporate objective is to maximise shareholder wealth by producing 'attractive, functional furniture at low prices'. This is how customers generally perceive the Posie brand. The CEO of Posie is concerned about increasing levels of returns made by customers and increasing numbers of consumers complaining on online forums about products purchased from Posie.

Concerned about the impact on the Posie brand and the cost-leadership strategy, the CEO has asked you as a performance management expert to help Posie implement the six sigma technique to reduce the number of products returned and in particular to define customers' requirements and measure Posie's existing performance. The production director has been appointed to sponsor the project and you will be supported by a small team of managers who have recently received training in six sigma. The board member responsible for manufacturing quality recently resigned because she thought it was unfair that the manufacturing division was being held responsible for the increased level of customer returns.

You have been given access to some information concerning the reasons why customers return goods to help you measure existing performance in this area (Appendix 1). This is an extract from the management reporting pack presented to the board at their monthly meetings. The returns data, however, are only compiled every six months due to the lengthy analysis required of data from Posie's overseas retail operations. It is included twice a year in the board report along with the KPIs for customer satisfaction. The last time this information was produced 93% of customers indicated they were satisfied with the quality of the manufacture of Posie's products.

The CEO has heard that six sigma requires 'large amounts of facts and data'. He suggested that the returns data contain insufficient detail and that as part of your project you may need to do more analysis, for example, on why customers are not satisfied with the manufacturing quality.

He also added, 'I'm not sure that our current IT systems are capable of generating the data we need to identify which responsibility centres within the manufacturing division are the root causes of the problem of customer returns. We are planning to change the designation of the overseas retail businesses from profit centres to revenue centres, but again we need to know first how this will affect the information requirements of the business and any potential problems with doing so.'

Appendix 1

Reasons given by customers for returning goods

Category	Reason for return of goods	% Responses
1	Difficult to assemble or pieces missing	48%
2	Goods arrived damaged	14%
3	Goods were not as described or were defective	25%
4	Goods were of poor quality or no longer wanted	11%
5	Arrived late	2%
Total		100%

Required:

(a) Advise the board how the six sigma project at Posie to reduce returns from customers could be implemented using DMAIC methodology. **(15 marks)**

(b) Evaluate the impact on Posie's information requirements arising from:

    (i) The need to identify and improve on the level of customer returns. **(6 marks)**

    (ii) The proposed re-designation of the overseas subsidiaries from profit centres to revenue centres. **(4 marks)**

(Total: 25 marks)

57 UNIVERSITIES IN TEELAND (MAR/JUN 16)

Universities in Teeland have three stated objectives:

1   To improve the overall standard of education of citizens in Teeland.

2   To engage in high quality academic research.

3   To provide well-qualified university graduates to meet the needs of the graduate jobs market in Teeland.

Each university is funded by a fixed sum of money from the Teeland government according to the number of students studying there. In addition, universities receive extra funds from the government and also from other organisations, such as large businesses and charities. These funds are used to support academic research.

Following the onset of an economic recession, the Teeland government has stated its intention to reduce spending on publicly funded services such as the universities. One senior politician, following his recent visit to neighbouring Veeland, was controversially quoted as saying:

'The universities in Veeland offer much better value for money for the citizens there compared to our universities here in Teeland. There are 25 students for each member of academic staff in Veeland, whereas in Teeland, the average number is 16, and yet, the standard of education of citizens is much higher in Veeland. The Veeland government sets targets for many aspects of the services delivered by all the universities in Veeland. Furthermore, league tables of the performance of individual universities are published on the internet, and university leaders are given bonuses if their university falls within the top quarter of the league table. In Veeland, the system of performance measurement of the universities is considered so important that there is a special government department of 150 staff just to measure it.'

He went on to add, 'I want to see a similar system of league tables, targets and bonuses for university leaders being introduced here in Teeland. To appear near the top of the league tables, I think we should expect each university to increase the number of graduates entering graduate jobs by at least 5% each year. I would also like to see other steps taken to increase value for money, such as reducing the number of academic staff in each university and reducing the salary of newly recruited academic staff.'

You have been asked to advise the Teeland government on the measurement of value for money of the universities and the proposed introduction of league tables for comparing their performance. Appendix A contains details and existing performance data relating to four of the best known universities in Teeland.

Northcity University is famous for its high teaching standards and outstanding academic research in all subjects. As such, it attracts the most able students from all parts of the world to study there.

Southcity University is a large university in the capital city of Teeland and offers courses in a wide range of subjects, though most of the funding it receives for academic research is for science and technology in which it is particularly successful.

Eastcity University is a small university specialising in the teaching of arts and humanities subjects such as history and geography.

Westcity University currently offers less strict entry standards to students to attract students from more diverse backgrounds, who may not normally have the opportunity of a university education.

Appendix A

Existing university performance data

	North	South	East	West
Number of students	17,600	30,400	5,200	11,200
Number of academic staff	1,750	2,400	485	625
Entry requirements[1]	100	77	72	48
Total annual payroll cost of academic staff	$109m	$149m	$20m	$37m
Graduate jobs filled each year[2]	4,180	6,555	1,154	1,750
Funds received for academic research	$491m	$474m	$26m	$14m
TSOR survey rating[3]	84%	76%	73%	90%
Position in league table[4]	1	11	14	21

Key to performance data

[1] – Entry requirements represent students' average attainment in examinations prior to entering university. The entry requirement of the highest ranking university is scored as 100, with the score of all other universities being in proportion to that score.

[2] – The number of graduates each year who go on to further study or who begin jobs normally undertaken by university graduates. In Teeland, students attend university for an average of 3.2 years.

[3] – The TSOR (Teeland students overall satisfaction rating) survey is undertaken by the Teeland government to assess students' overall satisfaction with the standard of teaching, the social and support aspects of university life and their optimism for their own future job prospects.

[4] – The education department of the Teeland government has produced a provisional league table ranking the overall performance of each of the 45 universities in Teeland, with 1 being the highest ranking university. This has been compiled using a number of performance measures, weighted according to what the government believes are the most important of these measures.

Required:

(a)   Advise the Teeland government how it could assess the value for money of the universities in Teeland, using the performance data in Appendix A.   (12 marks)

(b)   Assess the potential benefits of league tables for improving the performance of universities in Teeland and discuss the problems of implementing the proposal to introduce league tables.   (13 marks)

(Total: 25 marks)

58 LAUDAN ADVERTISING AGENCY (LLA) (SEPT/DEC 16)

Laudan Advertising Agency (LAA) is based in Geeland and has three autonomous subsidiaries: A, B and C. All three subsidiaries are profit centres and LAA seeks to maximise the long-term wealth of its shareholders. A is based in Geeland, while both B and C are located in other parts of the world. LAA is a highly respected advertising agency, which in the last five years has created advertising campaigns for 25 of the world's top 100 most recognised brands. LAA's four key objectives published on its website are:

- To delight our clients by the quality of our work

- Provide excellent value for money to our clients

- Give our clients access to specialist and local knowledge

- Ensure our clients return to us time after time

There are three main functions within LAA:

1 Campaign management, which involves researching and understanding clients' requirements and budgets and designing a suitable advertising campaign for them.

2 Creative design, which is where the visual appearance of the advert and graphics are created.

3 Media buying, which negotiates prices with, and buys advertising time and space from, magazine and newspaper publishers, internet search engines and TV companies.

Each subsidiary has its own department for campaign management and for media buying. Only A, however, has a creative design department.

The directors at LAA believe that without visually appealing design, any advertising campaign is unlikely to be successful and meet the expectations of the client. They identified the importance of being able to produce high quality creative design as a critical success factor for the business. Two years ago, they decided to concentrate all of LAA's creative design at a 'centre of design excellence' within A. The intention was to improve the quality of creative design within the business by giving staff access to the latest design technology, and by attracting the most talented designers to work there.

To encourage the three subsidiaries to use the internal creative design department within A, instead of external third party design agencies, the directors created a new additional key performance indicator on which to appraise the performance of all subsidiaries and of subsidiary managers:

- All subsidiaries, including A, must purchase at least 90% of creative design work internally from A.

Prior to the introduction of this performance indicator, 40% of creative design work in each of the three subsidiaries was purchased from external design agencies.

The directors of LAA have become concerned that the introduction of the new key performance indicator may be causing managers to operate in ways which are not helping to meet LAA's stated objectives. They have asked for comments from subsidiary managers (Appendix 1) about whether they have met the 90% target in the most recent period and if not, to explain why this is.

Appendix 1

Subsidiary managers' comments on achievement of KPI for 90% creative design work purchased internally

Subsidiary A

'A purchased 86% of design work from our internal design department in the period. It would have been almost 100%, but we won a large order for a new client who operates in a specialised industry of which we have no experience. As a result, we had to use the services of a specialised external design agency, which was much more expensive than using our in-house team.'

Subsidiary B

'B purchased 62% of design work internally in the period. Though the quality of the designs is very good, they were more appealing to consumers in Geeland than here in Veeland, where B operates. The internal design department did not seem to understand consumer preferences in Veeland, and many of their designs were rejected by a key client of ours. As a result, an important advertising campaign missed key deadlines, by which time the internal design department had insufficient capacity to finish the work and we had to use an external agency.

'As there is no formal transfer pricing policy in place at LAA, the basis of the transfer price charged by the internal design department is also unclear to us. It appears to be based on full cost of the design work, including apportioned overheads and an allowance for bad debts and marketing expenses, plus a very substantial mark up. We have spent a long time trying to negotiate this price with A, which is much more expensive than external designers. Furthermore, we are currently being investigated by the tax authorities here in Veeland who have indicated that the prices charged by A for design do seem well in excess of market rates.'

Subsidiary C

'C purchased 91% of design work from the internal design department in the period, as well as achieving all our other performance targets. A key client of ours ran a major advertising campaign during the period. We used the internal design department for the first time for this campaign, instead of the usual external agency that we have used in the past for work for this client. The client was very unhappy with the extra cost that this incurred, as the number of design hours and the hourly rate was much higher than for previous campaigns. The internal design department refused to reduce the price after long negotiations and we had to give a large discount to the client before they would settle our invoice. As a result, our gross profit margin for the period was significantly reduced.

'It would be much fairer if the transfer price charged by A was based on the market price of the services provided.

Required:

(a) Evaluate how the following help LAA to manage performance in order to achieve its stated objectives:

    (i) identifying the critical success factor of producing high quality creative design, and

    (ii) setting the key performance indicator for the requirement to purchase 90% of design work internally. **(8 marks)**

(b) Assess the need for a formal transfer pricing policy at LAA. **(9 marks)**

(c) Advise the directors whether LAA should use a market value transfer price as suggested by the manager of subsidiary C. **(8 marks)**

                                   (Total: 25 marks)

59 THE HEALTH AND FITNESS GROUP (HFG) (JUN 08 – AMENDED)

 Question debrief

The Health and Fitness Group (HFG), which is privately owned, operates three centres in the country of Mayland. Each centre offers dietary plans and fitness programmes to clients under the supervision of dieticians and fitness trainers. Residential accommodation is also available at each centre. The centres are located in the towns of Ayetown, Beetown and Ceetown. The following information is available:

1   Summary financial data for HFG in respect of the year ended 31 May 2008.

	Ayetown	Beetown	Ceetown	Total
	$000	$000	$000	$000
Revenue:				
Fees received	1,800	2,100	4,500	8,400
Variable costs	(468)	(567)	(1,395)	(2,430)
Contribution	1,332	1,533	3,105	5,970
Fixed costs	(936)	(1,092)	(2,402)	(4,430)
Operating profit	396	441	703	1,540
Interest costs on long-term debt at 10%				(180)
Profit before tax				1,360
Income tax expense				(408)
Profit for the year				952

	Ayetown	Beetown	Ceetown	Total
	$000	$000	$000	$000
Average book values for 2008:				
Assets				
Non-current assets	1,000	2,500	3,300	6,800
Current assets	800	900	1,000	2,700
Total assets	1,800	3,400	4,300	9,500
Equity and liabilities:				
Share capital				2,500
Retained earnings				4,400
Total equity				6,900
Non-current liabilities				
Long-term borrowings				1,800
Total non-current liabilities				1,800
Current liabilities	80	240	480	800
Total current liabilities	80	240	480	800
Total liabilities				2,600
Total equity and liabilities				9,500

2   HFG defines Residual Income (RI) for each centre as operating profit minus a required rate of return of 12% of the total assets of each centre.

3   At present HFG does not allocate the long-term borrowings of the group to the three separate centres.

4   Each centre faces similar risks.

5   Tax is payable at a rate of 30%.

6   The market value of the equity capital of HFG is $9 million. The cost of equity of HFG is 15%.

7   The market value of the long-term borrowings of HFG is equal to the book value.

8   The directors are concerned about the return on investment (ROI) generated by the Beetown centre and they are considering using sensitivity analysis in order to show how a target ROI of 20% might be achieved.

9   The marketing director stated at a recent board meeting that 'The Group's success depends on the quality of service provided to our clients. In my opinion, we need only to concern ourselves with the number of complaints received from clients during each period as this is the most important performance measure for our business. The number of complaints received from clients is a perfect performance measure. As long as the number of complaints received from clients is not increasing from period to period, then we can be confident about our future prospects'.

Required:

(a)   Discuss which of the three centres is the most 'successful'? Your answer should include a commentary on return on investment (ROI), residual income (RI), and economic value added (EVA) as measures of financial performance. Detailed calculations regarding each of these three measures must be included as part of your report.

Note: A maximum of seven marks is available for detailed calculations.   **(14 marks)**

(b)   Calculate the percentage change in revenue, total costs and net assets during the year ended 31 May 20X8 that would have been required in order to have achieved a target ROI of 20% by the Beetown centre.

Your answer should consider each of these three variables in isolation.

State any assumptions that you make.   **(6 marks)**

(c)   Discuss whether or not you agree with the statement of the marketing director in note (9) above.   **(5 marks)**

(Total: 25 marks)

 Calculate your allowed time, allocate the time to the separate parts...............

E – PERFORMANCE EVALUATION AND CORPORATE FAILURE

60   ROYAL BOTANICAL GARDENS

The Royal Botanical Gardens has been established for more than 120 years and has the following mission statement:

'The Royal Botanical Gardens belongs to the Nation. Our mission is to increase knowledge and appreciation of plants, their importance and their conservation, by managing and displaying living and preserved collections and through botanical and horticultural research.'

Located toward the edge of the city, the Gardens are regularly visited throughout the year by many local families and are an internationally well-known tourist attraction. Despite charging admission it is one the top five visitor attractions in the country. Every year it answers many thousands of enquiries from Universities and research establishments, including pharmaceutical companies from all over the world and charges for advice and access to its collection. Enquiries can range from access to the plant collection for horticultural work, seeds for propagation or samples for chemical analysis to seek novel pharmaceutical compounds for commercial exploitation. It receives an annual grant in aid from Central Government, which is fixed once every five years. The grant in aid is due for review in three years' time.

The Finance Director has decided that, to strengthen its case when meeting the Government representatives to negotiate the grant, the Management Board should be able to present a balanced scorecard demonstrating the performance of the Gardens. He has asked you, the Senior Management Accountant, to assist him in taking this idea forward. Many members of the board, which consists of eminent scientists, are unfamiliar with the concept of a balanced scorecard.

Required:

(a) **Prepare a briefing For the benefit of the Management Board, on the concept of a balanced scorecard, which also analyses its usefulness for The Royal Botanical Gardens.** (10 marks)

(b) **Discuss the process you would employ to develop a suitable balanced scorecard for The Royal Botanical Gardens and give examples of measures that would be incorporated within it.** (15 marks)

(Total: 25 marks)

61 BLA (DEC 03 – AMENDED)

Assume that the date is December 20X3.

BLA is a design consultancy that provides advice to clients regarding property maintenance and improvements. Three types of consultant are employed by BLA. These are:

1   Architectural consultants who provide advice with regard to exterior building improvements

2   Interior design consultants who provide advice regarding interior design, and

3   Landscape consultants who provide advice regarding landscaping of properties and garden design improvements.

BLA does not undertake building work on behalf of its clients and will only recommend contractors that undertake the three types of work when requested to do so by its clients. The following information is relevant:

(i)   Each consultation, other than those detailed in notes (iv) and (v), is charged at a rate of $150 per consultation.

(ii)   The consultants are each paid a fixed annual salary of $45,000. In addition they receive a bonus of 40% of the fee income generated in excess of budget. The bonus is shared equally among the consultants employed by BLA on 31 October in the year to which the bonus relates.

(iii)   Other operating expenses (excluding the salaries of the consultants) were budgeted at $2,550,000 for the year to 31 October 20X3. The actual amount incurred in respect of the year to 31 October 20X3 was $2,805,000, which excludes payments to subcontractors per note (vii) below.

(iv)   In an attempt to gain new business, consultants may undertake consultations on a 'no-fee' basis. Such consultations are regarded as Business Development Activity by the management of BLA.

(v)   Consultants will sometimes undertake remedial consultations with clients who experience problems at the time when work commences on each client's site. Remedial consultations are also provided on a non-chargeable, i.e. 'no fee' basis.

(vi)   In November 20X2, BLA purchased 'state of the art' business software for use by its consultants in simulating design improvements. The software was used throughout the year by consultants who specialise in landscape and garden design. It is now planned to introduce the use of the software by the other categories of consultant within BLA.

(vii)   BLA has a policy of maintaining staff at a level of 45 consultants on an ongoing basis, irrespective of fluctuations in the level of demand. Also, BLA has retained links with retired consultants and will occasionally subcontract work to them at a cost of $150 per consultation, if current full-time consultants within a particular category are fully utilised. During the year ended 31 October 20X3 subcontractors only undertook non-chargeable client consultations.

BLA

Sundry statistics for year ended 31 October 20X3

	Budget	Actual
Number of consultants by category:		
Exterior design	18	15
Interior design	18	18
Landscape and garden design	9	12
Total client enquiries:		
New business	67,500	84,000
Repeat business	32,400	28,000
Number of chargeable client consultations:		
New business	24,300	22,400
Repeat business	16,200	19,600
Mix of chargeable client consultations:		
Exterior design	16,200	13,830
Interior design	16,200	17,226
Landscape and garden design	8,100	10,944
	Budget	Actual
Number of non-chargeable client consultations undertaken by BLA consultants		
Number of business development consultations	1,035	1,200
Number of remedial consultation	45	405
Number of non-chargeable client consultations undertaken by subcontractors		120
Other statistics:		
Number of complaints	324	630

Required:

(a)   Briefly describe Fitzgerald and Moon's building block model of performance management. **(4 marks)**

(b)   Evaluate the performance of BLA using the building block model using the six dimensions of the building block model. **(15 marks)**

(c)   Briefly discuss THREE factors that should be considered in the determination of expected standards in a performance measurement system. **(6 marks)**

(Total: 25 marks)

62 CULAM (DEC 14) (SPECIMEN 18)

Company and industry background

Culam Mining (Culam) is a mineral ore mining business in the country of Teeland. It owns and operates four mines. A mine takes on average two years to develop before it can produce ore and the revenue from the mine is split (25:75) between selling the ore under fixed price contracts over five years and selling on the spot market. The bulk of the business's production is exported. A mine has an average working life of about 20 years before all the profitable ore is extracted. It then takes a year to decommission the site and return the land to a useable form for agriculture or other developments.

Recent events

One of Culam's foreign competitors surprised the market by becoming insolvent as a result of paying too much to acquire a competitor when the selling price of their minerals dipped as the world economy went into recession. As a result, the chief executive officer (CEO) wanted to know if this was likely to happen to Culam. She had read about the Altman Z-score as a way of predicting corporate failure and had a business analyst prepare a report calculating the Z-score for Culam. The report is summarised in Appendix 1.

The analyst had done what was asked and calculated the score but had not explained what it meant or what action should be taken as a result. Therefore, the CEO has turned to you to help her to make sense of this work and for advice about how to use the information and how Culam should proceed into the future.

Required:

(a) Evaluate both the result of the analyst's calculations and the appropriateness of these two models for Culam. **(10 marks)**

(b) Explain the potential effects of a mine's lifecycle on Culam's Z-score and the company's probability of failure. Note: You should ignore its effect on the Q-score. **(7 marks)**

(c) Give four detailed recommendations to reduce the probability of failure of Culam, providing suitable justifications for your advice. **(8 marks)**

(Total: 25 marks)

Appendix 1

Analyst's Report (extract)

The Altman Z-score model is:

$Z = 1.2X1 + 1.4X2 + 3.3X3 + 0.6X4 + X5$

Another quantitative model (Q-score model) has been produced by academics working at Teeland's main university based on recent data from listed companies on the small Teeland stock exchange. It is:

$Q = 1.4X1 + 3.3X3 + 0.5X4 + 1.1X5 + 1.7X6$ Where for both models:

X1 is working capital/total assets
X2 is retained earnings reserve/total assets
X3 is profit before interest and tax/total assets
X4 is market value of equity/total long-term debt (MVe/total long-term debt)
X5 is revenue/total assets

and

X6 is current assets/current liabilities.

Using the most recent figures from Culam's financial statements (year ending September 20X4), Culam's Altman Z-score is 3.5 and its score from the other model (Q) is 3.1.

For both models, a score of more than 3 (for Z or Q) is considered safe and at below 1.8, the company is at risk of failure in the next two years.

63 PERFORMANCE PYRAMID (JUN 06 – AMENDED)

(a)   'EAJ', which commenced trading on 1 June 20X3, is a business services group whose consultants implement three types of application software packages designed to meet the accounting, distribution and manufacturing requirements of its clients. Each consultant specialises in the implementation of one type of application software i.e. accounting, distribution or manufacturing. EAJ does not sell application software packages. EAJ implements application software packages but clients are responsible for purchasing the packages.

At a recent CPD course the Finance Director learnt about the performance pyramid and wishes to use the perspectives as part of the performance management system within IAJ.

The following information relates to the year ended 31 May 20X6:

1   Each consultation, other than those detailed in notes (4) and (5), is charged at a rate of $700 per day for new clients and $550 per day for existing clients. Consultants are budgeted to work for 240 days per year.

2   The consultants are each paid a fixed annual salary of $50,000. In addition they receive a bonus of 40% of the net value of the fee income generated in excess of budget minus the revenue foregone as a consequence of undertaking remedial consultations (per notes 5 and 8) based on a 'notional' rate of $700 per consultant day. The bonus is shared equally among the consultants employed by EAJ on 31 May in the year to which the bonus relates.

3   Other operating expenses (excluding the salaries of the consultants) were budgeted at $3,600,000. The actual amount incurred was $4,500,000.

4   In an attempt to gain new business, consultants may undertake consultations on a 'no-fee' basis. Such consultations are regarded as business development activity by the management of EAJ. Each of these consultations is budgeted to take one consultant day.

5   Consultants will sometimes undertake remedial consultations with new clients who experience problems with regard to implementation.

Remedial consultations are also provided on a non-chargeable, i.e. 'no fee' basis. Each of these consultations requires two consultant days.

6   Since its formation EAJ has had a policy of maintaining staff at a level of 100 consultants on an ongoing basis, irrespective of fluctuations in the level of demand.

7   EAJ has a help desk which provides support to its client base.

8   Sundry statistics for the year ended 31 May 20X6 together with other statistics for the previous two years are as follows:

	Budget	Actual
Number of consultants by category:		
Accounting	40	40
Distribution	30	25
Manufacturing	30	35
Total client enquiries (in days):		
New clients	12,000	15,000
Existing clients	25,200	24,500
*Number of **chargeable** client days:*		
New clients	4,200	4,500
Existing clients	12,600	14,700
*Mix of **chargeable** client days:*		
Accounting	6,720	8,480
Distribution	5,040	4,000
Manufacturing	5,040	6,720

Other statistics (all stated on an ACTUAL basis) relating to the years ended 31 May 20X4–20X6 are as follows:

	2004	2005	2006
Number of clients	320	500	700
Number of client complaints:	160	225	280
Number of on-time implementations (%)	92%	96%	99%
Implementation time per application (days)	3.0	2.5	2.0
Number of accounts in dispute	20	15	10
% of support desk calls resolved	85%	95%	99%
Chargeable client days	16,800	18,000	19,200
Number of business development consultations	100	200	300
Number of remedial consultations (New clients)	310	380	450
Turnover ($000)	4,000	7,500	?
Net profit ($000)	600	900	?

Required:

Using the above information, analyse and discuss the performance of EAJ for the year ended 31 May 20X6 under the following headings:

(i)   financial performance and competitiveness

(ii)   external effectiveness

(iii)   internal efficiency.   **(15 marks)**

(b)   Discuss the limitations of performance management which is based purely on quantitative information. Identify issues which an organisation needs to consider when working with qualitative information.   **(10 marks)**

(Total: 25 marks)

64   BPC (DEC 07 – AMENDED)

The directors of Blaina Packaging Co (BPC), a well-established manufacturer of cardboard boxes, are currently considering whether to enter the cardboard tube market. Cardboard tubes are purchased by customers whose products are wound around tubes of various sizes ranging from large tubes on which carpets are wound, to small tubes around which films and paper products are wound. The cardboard tubes are usually purchased in very large quantities by customers. On average, the cardboard tubes comprise between 1% and 2% of the total cost of the customers' finished product.

The directors have gathered the following information:

1   The cardboard tubes are manufactured on machines which vary in size and speed. The lowest cost machine is priced at $30,000 and requires only one operative for its operation. A one-day training course is required in order that an unskilled person can then operate such a machine in an efficient and effective manner.

2   The cardboard tubes are made from specially formulated paper which, at times during recent years, has been in short supply.

3   At present, four major manufacturers of cardboard tubes have an aggregate market share of 80%. The current market leader has a 26% market share. The market shares of the other three major manufacturers, one of which is JOL Co, are equal in size. The product ranges offered by the four major manufacturers are similar in terms of size and quality. The market has grown by 2% per annum during recent years.

4   A recent report on the activities of a foreign-based multinational company revealed that consideration was being given to expanding operations in their packaging division overseas. The division possesses large-scale automated machinery for the manufacture of cardboard tubes of any size.

5   Another company, Plastic Tubes Co (PTC) produces a narrow, but increasing, range of plastic tubes which are capable of housing small products such as film and paper-based products. At present, these tubes are on average 30% more expensive than the equivalent sized cardboard tubes sold in the marketplace.

Required:

(a)   **Using Porter's five forces model, assess the attractiveness of the option to enter the market for cardboard tubes as a performance improvement strategy for BPC.**

(10 marks)

JOL Co was the market leader with a share of 30% three years ago. The managing director of JOL Co stated at a recent meeting of the board of directors that: 'our loss of market share during the last three years might lead to the end of JOL Co as an organisation and therefore we must address this issue immediately'.

Required:

(b)   **Discuss the statement of the managing director of JOL Co and discuss six performance indicators, other than decreasing market share, which might indicate that JOL Co might fail as a corporate entity.**   (10 marks)

(c)   **Discuss how performance management systems may need to change if a company starts exhibiting signs of financial distress and even potential corporate failure.**

(5 marks)

(Total: 25 marks)

65   THE SENTINEL COMPANY (TSC) (DEC 08 – AMENDED)

 Question debrief

The Sentinel Company (TSC) offers a range of door-to-door express delivery services. The company operates using a network of depots and distribution centres throughout the country of Nickland. The following information is available:

1   Each depot is solely responsible for all customers within a specified area. It collects goods from customers within its own area for delivery both within the specific area covered by the depot and elsewhere in Nickland.

2   Collections made by a depot for delivery outside its own area are forwarded to the depots from which the deliveries will be made to the customers.

3   Each depot must therefore integrate its deliveries to customers to include:

(i)   goods that it has collected within its own area; and

(ii)   goods that are transferred to it from depots within other areas for delivery to customers in its area.

4   Each depot earns revenue based on the invoiced value of all consignments collected from customers in its area, regardless of the location of the ultimate distribution depot.

5   Depot costs comprise all of its own operating costs plus an allocated share of all company costs including centralised administration services and distribution centre costs.

6   Bonuses for the management team and all employees at each depot are payable quarterly. The bonus is based on the achievement of a series of target values by each depot.

7   Internal benchmarking is used at TSC in order to provide sets of absolute standards that all depots are expected to attain.

8   (a)   The Appendix shows the target values and the actual values achieved for each of a sample group of four depots situated in Donatellotown (D), Leonardotown (L), Michaelangelotown (M), and Raphaeltown (R).

(b)   The target values focus on three areas:

(i)   depot revenue and profitability

(ii)   customer care and service delivery; and

(iii)   credit control and administrative efficiency.

(c)   The bonus is based on a points system, which is also used as a guide to the operational effectiveness at each depot. One point is allocated where the target value for each item in the Appendix is either achieved or exceeded, and a zero score where the target is not achieved.

Appendix:

Target and actual value statistics for Donatellotown (D), Leonardotown (L), Michaelangelotown (M), and Raphaeltown (R) for the Year ended 31 October 2008

Revenue and profit statistics:

	Revenue (1)		Profit (2)	
	Target	Actual	Target	Actual
	$m	$m	$m	$m
Company overall	200	240	30	32
Selected depots:				
D	16	15	2.4	2.3
L	14	18	2.1	2.4
M	12	14	1.8	2.2
R	18	22	2.7	2.8

Note: For the purpose of calculation of each depot's points it is essential that actual profit as a percentage of actual revenue must exceed the target profit (%).

Customer care and service delivery statistics:

			Actual		
Selected depots:	Target	D	L	M	R
	%	%	%	%	%
Measure (% of total):					
(3) Late collection of consignments	2.0	1.9	2.1	1.8	2.4
(4) Misdirected consignments	4.0	4.2	3.9	3.3	5.1
(5) Delayed response to complaints	1.0	0.7	0.9	0.8	1.2
(6) Delays due to vehicle breakdown	1.0	1.1	1.4	0.3	2.0
Measure (% of revenue):	Target	D	L	M	R
(7) Lost items	1.0	0.6	0.9	0.8	1.9
(8) Damaged items	2.0	1.5	2.4	1.5	1.8

Credit control and administration efficiency statistics:

			Actual		
	Target	D	L	M	R
(9) Average debtor weeks	5.5	5.8	4.9	5.1	6.2
(10) Debtors in excess of 60 days (% of total)	5%	3.1	3.7	2.9	2.7
(11) Invoice queries (% of total)	5%	1.1%	1.4%	0.8%	2.7%
(12) Credit notes as a % of revenue	0.5%	0.3%	0.2%	0.2%	0.6%

Note: TSC operates all year round.

Required:

(a) Produce a summary table that shows the points gained (or forfeited) by each depot. The points table should facilitate the ranking of each depot against the others for each of the 12 measures provided in the Appendix. **(6 marks)**

(b) Evaluates the relative performance of the four depots as indicated by the analysis in the summary table prepared in (a). **(5 marks)**

(c)   Assess TSC in terms of financial performance, competitiveness, service quality, resource utilisation, flexibility and innovation and discusses the interrelationships between these terms, incorporating examples from within TSC; and   **(9 marks)**

(d)   Critique the performance measurement system at TSC.   **(5 marks)**

(Total: 25 marks)

 Calculate your allowed time, allocate the time to the separate parts...............

66   THE SPARE FOR SHIPS COMPANY (SFS) (JUN 10 – AMENDED)

The Spare for Ships Company (SFS) has a specialist machining facility which serves the shipbuilding components market. The current job-costing system has two categories of direct cost (direct materials and direct manufacturing labour) and a single indirect cost pool (manufacturing overhead which is allocated on the basis of direct labour hours). The indirect cost allocation rate of the existing job-costing system is $120 per direct manufacturing labour-hour.

Recently, the Visibility Consultancy Partnership (VCP) proposed the use of an activity-based approach to redefine the job-costing system of SFS. VCP made a recommendation to retain the two direct cost categories. However, VCP further recommended the replacement of the single indirect-cost pool with five indirect-cost pools.

Each of the five indirect-cost pools represents an activity area at the manufacturing premises of SFS. Each activity area has its own supervisor who is responsible for his/her operating budget.

Relevant data are as follows:

Activity area	Cost driver used as allocation base	Cost allocation rate ($)
Materials handling	Number of components	0.50
Lathe work	Number of cuts	0.70
Milling	Number of machine hours	24.00
Grinding	Number of components	1.50
Inspection	Number of units inspected	20.00

SFS has recently invested in 'state of the art' IT systems which have the capability to automatically collate all of the data necessary for budgeting in each of the five activity areas.

The management accountant of SFS calculated the manufacturing cost per unit of two representative jobs under the two costing systems as follows:

	Job order 973	Job order 974
	$	$
Current costing system	1,172.00	620.00
Activity-based costing system	1,612.00	588.89

Required:

(a) **(i)** Compare the cost figures per unit for Job order 973 and Job order 974 calculated by the management accountant and explain the reasons for, and potential consequences of, the differences in the job cost estimates produced under the two costing systems. **(8 marks)**

(ii) Explain two potential problems that SFS might have experienced in the successful implementation of an activity-based costing system using its recently acquired 'state of the art' IT systems. **(4 marks)**

(b) The application of Activity Based Management (ABM) requires that the management of SFS focus on each of the following:

(i) Operational ABM

(ii) Strategic ABM

(iii) The implicit value of an activity'.

Required:

Critically appraise the above statement and explain the risks attaching to the use of ABM. **(8 marks)**

(c) Briefly discuss how ABM can assist other performance improvement strategies, such as Total Quality Management, Six Sigma and Business Process Reengineering. **(5 marks)**

(Total: 25 marks)

67 THE SUPERIOR BUSINESS CONSULTANCY (SBC) (JUN 10 – AMENDED)

The Superior Business Consultancy (SBC) which is based in Jayland provides clients with consultancy services in Advertising, Recruitment and IT Support. SBC commenced trading on 1 July 2003 and has grown steadily since then.

The following information, together with that contained in the appendix, is available:

1 Three types of consultants are employed by SBC on a full-time basis. These are:

Advertising consultants who provide advice regarding advertising and promotional activities

Recruitment consultants who provide advice regarding recruitment and selection of staff, and

IT consultants who provide advice regarding the selection of business software and technical support.

2 During the year ended 31 May 2010, each full-time consultant was budgeted to work on 200 days. All consultations undertaken by consultants of SBC had a duration of one day.

3 During their 200 working days per annum, full-time consultants undertake some consultations on a 'no-fee' basis. Such consultations are regarded as Business Development Activity (BDA) by the management of SBC.

4 SBC also engages the services of subcontract consultants who provide clients with consultancy services in the categories of Advertising, Recruitment and IT Support. All of the subcontract consultants have worked for SBC for at least three years.

5   During recent years the directors of SBC have become increasingly concerned that SBC's systems are inadequate for the measurement of performance. This concern was further increased after they each read a book entitled 'How *to improve business performance* measurement' which was written by Ino Itall, a business analyst of worldwide repute.

Appendix:

SBC – Relevant actual and forecast statistics

	2010 Actual	2011 Forecast	2012 Forecast
Number of full-time consultants by category:			
Advertising	20	20	20
Recruitment	30	25	20
IT Support	50	50	50
Salaries per full-time consultant ($):			
Advertising	40,000	40,800	40,800
Recruitment	35,000	35,700	35,700
IT Support	30,000	30,600	30,600
Number of chargeable consultations (total demand):			
Advertising	4,200	4,100	4,000
Recruitment	6,250	5,750	5,000
IT Support	10,250	10,500	10,000
Per cent of chargeable days spent on Business Development Activity (%):			
Advertising	7	8	10
Recruitment	22	22	25
IT Support	12	13	14
Cost per consultation undertaken by subcontract consultants ($):			
Advertising	300		
Recruitment	220		
IT Support	200		
Other operating costs ($000):			
Full-time consultants	1,075	1,050	1,270
Subcontract consultants	125	270	182

Required:

(a)   Discuss the importance of non-financial performance indicators (NFPIs) and evaluates, giving examples, how a 'balanced scorecard' approach may be used to improve performance within SBC.   **(13 marks)**

(b)   Calculate the actual average cost per chargeable consultation for both full-time consultants and separately for subcontract consultants in respect of each of the three categories of consultancy services during the year ended 31 May 2010.

                                                                                                                    (7 marks)

(c)   Suggest reasons for the trends shown by the figures contained in the appendix.

                                                                                                                    (5 marks)

                                                                                                       (Total: 25 marks)

68   LOL CO (DEC 10 – AMENDED)

LOL Co is a chain of shops selling cards and gifts throughout its country. It has been listed on the stock exchange for 10 years and enjoys a fairly high profile in the retail sector of the national economy. You have been asked by the chief executive officer (CEO) to advise the company on value-based management (VBM), as a different approach to performance management. The CEO has read about this method as a way of focusing on shareholder interests and in the current tough economic climate, she thinks that it may be a useful development for LOL.

The company has traditionally used earnings per share (EPS) growth and share price in order to assess performance. The changes being proposed are considered significant and the CEO wants to be briefed on the implications of the new analysis and also how to convince both the board and the major investors of the benefits.

Financial data for LOL

	2009 $m	2010 $m
Profit before interest and tax	50.7	43.5
Interest paid	4.0	7.8
Profit after interest and tax	35.0	26.8
Average number of shares in issue (millions)	160	160
Capital employed at the end of the year was	(in $m)	

2008	99.2	
2009	104.1	
2010	97.8	

LOL aims for a capital structure of 50:50 debt to equity.

Costs of capital were	2009	2010
Equity	12.70%	15.30%
Debt (post-tax cost)	4.20%	3.90%

Corporation tax is at the rate of 25%.

Stock market information

Stock market all-share index	2,225.4	1,448.9
Retailing sector index	1,225.6	907.1
LOL (average share price) ($)	12.20	10.70

Required:

(a)   Explain to the CEO what value-based management involves and how it can be used to focus the company on shareholder interests.   **(4 marks)**

(b)   Perform an assessment of the financial performance of LOL using Economic Value Added (EVA™) and evaluate your results compared with those of earnings per share (EPS) growth and share price performance. You should state any assumptions made.   **(12 marks)**

(c)   Evaluate VBM measures against traditional profit based measures of performance.   **(4 marks)**

(d)   The CEO has also read how the use of net present values (NPV) can focus a company on increasing shareholder value. Discuss the relationship between EVA™ and NPV.   **(5 marks)**

(Total: 25 marks)

69 RM BATTERIES CO (DEC 10)

RM Batteries Co (RMB) is a manufacturer of battery packs. It has expanded rapidly in the last few years under the leadership of its autocratic chairman and chief executive officer, John Smith. Smith is relentlessly optimistic. He likes to get his own way and demands absolute loyalty from all his colleagues.

The company has developed a major new product over the last three years which has necessitated a large investment in new equipment. Smith has stated that this more efficient battery is critical to the future of the business as the company operates in a sector where customers expect constant innovation from their suppliers.

However, the recent share price performance has caused concern at board level and there has been comment in the financial press about the increased gearing and the strain that this expansion is putting on the company. The average share price has been $1.56 (2008), $1.67 (2009) and $1.34 (2010). There are 450 million shares in issue.

A relevant Z-score model for the industry sector is:

$$Z = 1.2X1 + 1.4X2 + 3.3X3 + 0.6X4 + X5$$

Where

X1 is working capital/total assets (WC/TA)

X2 is retained earnings reserve/total assets (RE/TA)

X3 is Profit before interest and tax/total assets (PBIT/TA)

X4 is market value of equity/total long-term debt (Mve/total long-term debt); and

X5 is Revenue/total assets (Revenue/TA).

A score of more than 3 is considered safe and at below 1.8, the company is at risk of failure in the next two years.

The company's recent financial performance is summarised below:

Summary income statements

	2008 $m	2009 $m	2010 $m
Revenue	1,460	1,560	1,915
Operating costs	1,153	1,279	1,724
Operating profit	307	281	191
Interest	35	74	95
Profit before tax	272	207	96
Tax	87	66	31
Profit for the period	185	141	65

Statements of Financial Position

	2008 $m	2009 $m	2010 $m
Assets			
Non-current assets	1,120	1,778	2,115
Current assets	235	285	341
Total assets	1,355	2,063	2,456
Equity and liabilities			
Share capital	230	230	230
Retained earnings reserve	204	344	410
Long-term borrowings	465	991	1,261
Current liabilities	456	498	555
Total equity and liabilities	1,355	2,063	2,456

Required:

(a) Discuss the strengths and weaknesses of quantitative and qualitative models for predicting corporate failure. **(6 marks)**

(b) Calculate the following for each of the three years given: the market capitalisation, the Z score and the gearing level [debt/equity]. **(5 marks)**

(c) Comment on your figures calculated in part (b). **(5 marks)**

(d) Identify the qualitative problems that are apparent in the company's structure and performance and explain why these are relevant to possible failure. **(5 marks)**

(e) Critically assess the results of your analysis in parts (c) and (d) alongside details of RMB's recent financial performance and suggest additional data that should be acquired and how it could be used to assess RMB's financial health. **(4 marks)**

(Total: 25 marks)

70   APX ACCOUNTANCY (JUN 11 – AMENDED)

APX Accountancy (APX) is an accountancy partnership with 12 branches covering each of the main cities of Emland. The business is well established, having organically grown over the last 40 years to become the second largest non-international practice in Emland. The accountancy market is mature and expands and contracts along with the general economic performance of Emland.

APX offers accountancy, audit, tax and business advisory services. The current business environment in Emland is dominated by a recession and the associated insolvency work is covered within the business advisory area of APX.

At present, the practice collects the following information for strategic performance evaluation:

	Audit	Tax	Business Advisory	Total
Revenue ($m)				
APX	69.1	89.2	64.7	223.0
Accounting industry	557.0	573.0	462.0	1,592.0
Change in revenue on previous year				
APX	3.0%	8.0%	22.0%	10.0%
Accounting industry	2.5%	4.5%	16.0%	6.8%
Profit margin at APX	6.4%	7.8%	10.5%	8.1%
Customer service score (1 to 5 with 5 being excellent)				
APX	3.4	3.9	4.1	

The above figures are for the most recent financial year and illustrate the metrics used by APX. Equivalent monthly figures are produced for each of the monthly partner meetings which review practice performance.

The staff are remunerated based on their grade, with non-partners obtaining a bonus of up to 10% of basic salary based on their line managers' annual review. The partners receive a fixed salary with a share of profit which depends on their contractual responsibilities within the partnership.

The managing partner of APX is dissatisfied with the existing performance management system, as she is not convinced that it is helping to achieve the long-term goal of expanding and ultimately floating the business on the national stock exchange. Therefore, she has asked you to consider the impact of applying Fitzgerald and Moon's building block approach to performance management in the practice.

Required:

(a)   Briefly describe Fitzgerald and Moon's building block model.   **(4 marks)**

(b)   Evaluate the existing performance management system at APX by applying the building block model.   **(9 marks)**

(c)   Explain the main improvements the introduction of a building block approach to performance management could provide, and suggest specific improvements to the existing system of performance measures at APX in light of the introduction of the building block model.   **(12 marks)**

(Total: 25 marks)

71   COD ELECTRICAL MOTORS (DEC 11 – AMENDED)

Cod Electrical Motors (Cod) manufactures electrical motors for some of the 24 different European domestic appliance manufacturers. Their motors are used in appliances such as washing machines and refrigerators. Cod has been in business for over 50 years and has obtained a reputation for producing reliable, low cost motors.

Cod has recently rewritten its mission statement, which now reads:

'Cod Electrical Motors is committed to providing competitively priced, high quality products, with service exceeding customer expectations. We will add value to our business relationships by investing in product development and highly trained personnel.'

The board have recognised that their existing key performance indicators (KPIs) do not capture the features of the corporate mission. They are worried that the staff see the mission statement as a public relations exercise rather than the communication of Cod's vision.

The monthly board papers contain a simple performance summary which is used as the key performance measurement system at that level.

Example of board papers for November 2011:

Cod Electrical Motors – key performance indicators for November 2011

	This month	YTD	Comparative
Profit ($m)	2.1	25.6	1.9
Free cash flow ($m)	3.4	17.6	1.6
Return on capital employed (%)	12.4	11.7	11.8

Notes:

(a)   The year end is 31 December.

(b)   The comparative figure is for the same month in the previous year.

(c)   ROCE is an annualised figure.

(d)   YTD means year to date.

There are additional performance indicators not available to the board that line management use for a more detailed picture.

Additional performance information:

	Note 1	2011	2010
Activity			
No of orders		2,560	2,449
No of deliveries		1,588	1,660
Staff			
No of staff (FTE basis)	2	1,229	1,226
No of staff training days		2,286	1,762
No of vacant posts	3	11	17
Customers			
No of orders with a complaint	4		
late delivery		26	25
product quality		39	31
customer service		21	24
other		52	43
Preferential supplier status	5	14	12
Production			
New products			
begun in year to date		2	1
in development at month end		4	3
launched in year to date		1	1
Quality			
internal failure costs ($000)		3,480	2,766
external failure costs ($000)		872	693

Notes:

1   Figures are year to date with comparatives from the previous year quoted on the same basis.

2   FTE = Full-time equivalent staff numbers.

3   Post is considered vacant if unfilled for more than four months.

4   Complaints are logged and classified into the four categories given when received.

5   Number of customers where Cod holds preferred supplier status.

Required:

(a)   Assess whether the current key performance indicators (KPIs) meet the expected features of a modern performance measurement system.   **(7 marks)**

(b)   Explain how the performance pyramid (Lynch and Cross) can help Cod's board to reach its goal of a coherent set of performance measures.   **(6 marks)**

(c)   Evaluate the current system using the performance pyramid and apply the performance pyramid to Cod in order to suggest additional KPIs and a set of operational performance measures for Cod.   **(12 marks)**

(Total: 25 marks)

72   CALLISTO (JUN 12 – AMENDED)

Callisto Retail (Callisto) is an on-line reseller of local craft products related to the historic culture of the country of Callistan. The business started ten years ago as a hobby of two brothers, Jeff and George. The brothers produced humorous, short video clips about Callistan which were posted on their website and became highly popular. They decided to use the website to try to sell Callistan merchandise and good initial sales made them believe that they had a viable business idea.

Callisto has gone from strength to strength and now boasts sales of $120m per annum, selling anything related to Callistan. Callisto is still very much the brothers' family business. They have gathered around themselves a number of strategic partners into what Jeff describes as a virtual company. Callisto has the core functions of video clip production, finance and supplier relationship management. The rest of the functions of the organisation (warehousing, delivery and website development) are outsourced to strategic partners.

The brothers work from their family home in the rural North of Callistan while other Callisto employees work from their homes in the surrounding villages and towns. These employees are involved in video editing, system maintenance, handling customer complaints and communication with suppliers and outsourcers regarding inventory. The employees log in to Callisto's systems via the national internet infrastructure. The outsourced functions are handled by multinational companies of good reputation who are based around the world. The brothers have always been fascinated by information technology and so they depend on email and electronic data interchange to communicate with their product suppliers and outsourcing partners.

Recently, there have been emails from regular customers of the Callisto website complaining about slow or non-delivery of orders that they have placed. George has commented that this represents a major threat to Callisto as the company operates on small profit margins, relying on volume to drive the business. He believes that sales growth will drive the profitability of the business due to its cost structure.

Jeff handles the management of outsourcing and has been reviewing the contracts that exist between Callisto and its strategic partner for warehousing and delivery, RLR Logistics. The current contract for warehousing and delivery is due for renewal in two months and currently, has the following service level agreements (SLAs):

1   RLR agree to receive and hold inventory from Callisto's product suppliers.

2   RLR agree to hold 14 days inventory of Callisto's products.

3   RLR agree to despatch from their warehouse any order passed from Callisto within three working days, inventory allowing.

4   RLR agree to deliver to customers anywhere in Callistan within two days of despatch.

Breaches in these SLAs incur financial penalties on a sliding scale depending on the number and severity of the problems. Each party to the contract collects their own data on performance and this has led to disagreements in the past over whether service levels have been achieved although no penalties have been triggered to date. The most common disagreement arises over inventory levels held by RLR with RLR claiming that it cannot be expected to deliver products that are late in arriving to inventory due to the product suppliers' production and delivery issues.

Required:

(a)   **Assess the difficulties of performance measurement and performance management in complex business structures such as Callisto, especially in respect of the performance of their employees and strategic partners.**   **(17 marks)**

(b)   **Evaluate appropriate measures that Callisto could use to assess the performance of its employees and strategic partners. Suggest suitable methods for collecting the data required to make this assessment.**   **(8 marks)**

(Total: 25 marks)

73   COAL CREEK NURSING HOMES (DEC 12 – AMENDED)

Coal Creek Nursing Homes (CCNH) is a company operating residential care homes for the elderly in Geeland. Residents are those elderly people who can no longer care for themselves at home and whose family are unable to look after them. There are 784 homes with about 30,000 residents under the care of the company. There are about 42,500 staff, who range from head office staff through the home managers to the care staff and cleaners and caterers. The company is a private company which aims to make a suitable return to its shareholders. It had revenues of $938m in the last year and is one of the largest providers of residential care places in Geeland.

The company is split into two divisions: General Care (GC) which handles ordinary elderly residents and Special Care (SC), which is a newer operation that handles residents who need intensive care and attention due to physical or mental ailments.

The company does not own its homes but rents these from a number of large commercial landlords.

It has taken on a large number of new homes recently in order to cope with the expansion of SC, which has proved successful with 24% pa revenue growth over the last two years. GC is a mature business with little growth in a sector that is now fully supplied. GC has seen volumes and margins falling as price pressure comes from its main customers (public sector health organisations who contract out this part of their care provision).

A new chief executive officer (CEO) has just taken over at CCNH. She was appointed because the board of CCNH believed that the company was in difficulty. The previous CEO had been forced to leave following a scandal involving a number of the homes where residents' money had gone missing and their families had called in the police. The finance director and the operations director had also resigned, leaving the company without any experienced senior management.

The board have tasked the new CEO with ascertaining the current position of the business and identifying a strategy to address the issues that arise. The CEO wants to address the strategy, deciding whether to divest or retain elements of the business.

The CEO has come to you, as the most senior member of finance staff, for assistance with this task. The first area that she wants help on is the problem that the business is having with its landlords. The company struggled to meet its most recent rental payment, which the bank eventually agreed to cover through an increase to the overdraft, as CCNH had no ready cash. She is upset that the chosen strategic measures of performance (earnings per share growth and operating profit margin) did not identify the difficulties that the firm is now facing. One of the other directors had mentioned gearing problems but she did not follow what this meant.

Also, she has heard of qualitative models for predicting corporate failure and wants to apply one at CCNH. Obviously, she wants to know if CCNH exhibits any symptoms of failure.

You have been given the outline financial statements to help with this task (see Appendix below).

Required:

(a)   **Discuss why indicators of liquidity and gearing need to be considered in conjunction with profitability at CCNH. Illustrate your answer with suitable calculations.**

(14 marks)

(b)   **Explain one qualitative model for predicting corporate failure (such as Argenti) and comment on CCNH's position utilising this model. You are not expected to give scores, only to comment on the areas of weakness at CCNH.**   **(11 marks)**

(Total: 25 marks)

Appendix: Outline financial statements for CCNH for the year just ended

Summary Income Statements

	General care $m	Special care $m	Total $m
Revenue	685	253	938
Operating costs			
Homes payroll	397	139	536
running	86	24	110
Rents	193	64	257
Central costs	27	3	30
Operating profit	(18)	23	5
Interest			5
Profit before tax			0
Tax			0
Profit for the period			0

Statement of Financial Position

	General care $m	Special care $m	Total $m
Assets			
Non-current assets	244	87	331
Current assets	17	47	64
Total assets	261	134	395
Equity and liabilities			
Share capital			165
Retained earnings reserve			24
Long-term borrowings			102
Current liabilities	76	28	104
Total equity and liabilities			395

Note: A breakdown of the long-term financing into the two divisions has not been possible.

74   GRAVITON CLOTHING (DEC 13)

Graviton Clothing (Graviton) is a listed manufacturer of clothing with a strong reputation for producing desirable, fashionable products which can attract high selling prices. The company's objective is to maximise shareholder wealth. Graviton's products are sold through its own chain of stores. Graviton's markets demand designs which are in tune with current fashion trends which can alter every few weeks. Therefore, the business's stated aim is to focus production on these changing market trends by maintaining flexibility to adapt to that market demand through close control of all stages of the supply chain (design, manufacture and distribution).

The chief executive officer (CEO) is unhappy with the current performance measurement system at Graviton. The system was created about five years ago by the finance director who has subsequently retired. The aim of the system was to provide the company with a list of measures which would cover performance at the strategic, tactical and operational levels of management. An example of the most recent performance report is given in Table 1.

Table 1: Graviton Performance Dashboard Report for the year to Sep 2013

	2013	2012	2011	Change 2013/2012
Financial				
Revenue ($m)	1,723	1,570	1,413	9.7%
Operating profit ($m)	320	314	308	1.9%
ROCE	15.8%	15.9%	15.9%	
Design				
Design awards won	3	2	3	50.0%
Manufacture				
Average time to market (days)	22.2	22.3	22.1	−0.4%
Distribution				
Deliveries on time	87.0%	86.8%	87.3%	0.2%

Commentary:

- The revenue growth of the business remains strong in a difficult market.

- Return on capital employed matches the industry average of about 16%.

- Time to market for new designs has been maintained at 22 days by paying overtime to designers in order to meet production schedules.

Recent press reports about Graviton have been mixed, with positive comments about the innovative new designs and much admiration over the growth of sales which the business has achieved. However, there has been some criticism from customers of the durability of Graviton's clothes and from institutional investors that the dividend growth is not strong.

The CEO believes that there are major gaps in the current list of key metrics used by Graviton. She wants an evaluation of the current system and suggestions for improvements. However, she has warned you that the board wants a reasoned argument for each measure to be included in the list in order to avoid overloading each level of management with too much data.

Although rapidly growing, Graviton has had some problems in the last few years which have appeared on recent internal audit reports. It was found that a senior manager at factory site 1 has been delaying invoicing for completed orders in order to ensure that profit targets are met in both the current and the next accounting period. At factory site 2, there has been excellent return on a low capital employed figure although there is a significant adverse variance in the equipment repairs account.

The board is dominated by long-serving executives who are sceptical of change, given Graviton's growth over the past three years. At a recent board meeting, they have shared the CEO's concern about data overload and also have pointed out a variety of problems with the use of performance measures. They presented the CEO with a list of three common problems (myopia, gaming, ossification) and argued that the current good performance of the business did not justify changing the performance measurement system. The CEO needs to know if these problems apply to Graviton and if they do, then what can be done to manage them.

Required:

(a) **Evaluate the current performance measurement system using the Performance Pyramid of Lynch and Cross.** **(15 marks)**

(b) **Assess whether the three problems listed by the board apply to Graviton and suggest appropriate performance management solutions to them.** **(10 marks)**

(Total: 25 marks)

75   VICTORIA-YEELAND LOGISTICS (JUN 15)

Victoria-Yeeland Logistics (Victoria) is a logistics support business, which operates a fleet of lorries to deliver packages of goods on behalf of its customers within the country of Yeeland. Victoria collects packages from its customers' manufacturing sites or from the customers' port of importation and delivers to the final user of the goods. The lorries are run and maintained from a set of depots spread throughout Yeeland.

The overall objective of Victoria is to maximise shareholder wealth. The delivery business in Yeeland is dominated by two international companies and one other domestic business and profit margins are extremely tight. The market is saturated by these large operators and a number of smaller operators. The cost base of Victoria is dominated by staff and fuel, with fuel prices being highly volatile in the last few years.

In order to improve performance measurement and management at Victoria, the chief financial officer (CFO) plans to use the balanced scorecard (BSC). However, she has been pulled away from this project in order to deal with an issue with refinancing the business' principal lending facility. The CFO has already identified some suitable metrics but needs you, as her assistant, to complete her work and address any potential questions which might arise when she makes her presentation on the BSC to the board. The CFO has completed the identification of metrics for three of the perspectives (Appendix 1) but has yet to complete the work on the metrics for the customer perspective. This should be done using the data given in Appendix 2.

Additionally, two issues have arisen in the reward management system at Victoria, one in relation to senior management and the other for operational managers. Currently, senior management gets a fixed salary supplemented by an annual bonus awarded by the board. Shareholders have been complaining that these bonuses are not suitable. The operational managers also get bonuses based on their performance as assessed by their management superiors. The operational managers are unhappy with the system. In order to address this, it has been suggested that they should be involved in bonus target setting as otherwise there is a sense of demotivation from such a system. The CFO wants an evaluation of this system of rewards in light of the introduction of the BSC and best practice.

Required:

(a)   Discuss how Victoria's success in the customer perspective may impact on the metrics given in the financial perspective.   (5 marks)

(b)   Recommend, with justification, and calculate a suitable performance metric for each customer perspective success factor. Comment on the problems of using customer complaints to measure whether packages are delivered safely and on time.   (11 marks)

(c)   Advise Victoria on the reward management issues outlined by the CFO.   (9 marks)

(Total: 25 marks)

Appendix 1

Financial perspective

(How do we appear to our shareholders?)

Return on capital employed

Profit margin

Revenue growth

Customer perspective

(How do we appear to our customers?)

Success factors:

Ability to meet customers' transport needs

Ability to deliver packages quickly

Ability to deliver packages on time

Ability to deliver packages safely

Internal process perspective

(What business processes must excel?)

Time taken to load and unload

Lorry capacity utilisation

Learning and growth perspective

(How do we sustain and improve our ability to grow?)

Leadership competence (qualitative judgement)

Training days per employee

Appendix 2

The process: A customer makes a transport request for a package to be collected and delivered to a given destination. The customer is supplied with a time window in which the delivery will occur. Packages are then loaded onto lorries and delivered according to a route specified by the depot's routing manager.

Total number of customer transport requests	610,000
Total number of packages transported	548,000
Total number of lorry journeys	73,000
Total package kilometres	65,760,000
Total package minutes	131,520,000
Number of delivery complaints from customers:	
from damaged packages	8,220
from late delivery (outside agreed time window)	21,920

Notes:

1   All figures are for the last financial year.

2   A package kilometre is defined as a kilometre travelled by one package.

3   A package minute is defined as a minute spent in transit by one package.

76   SOUP RAIL SERVICES (SEPT/DEC 15)

Soup operates passenger rail services in Deeland, a technologically advanced country, with high demand for fast reliable rail travel from business and leisure passengers. Many passengers choose train travel because they see it as less harmful to the environment than other forms of transport.

Soup's main objective is to maximise shareholder wealth. Since becoming licensed to operate routes in Regions A and B by the Deeland government five years ago, Soup has consistently delivered increased dividends and share prices for investors. In its initial appraisal of the licensing opportunity, Soup expected to operate the routes for at least 15 years, however, their licence may not be renewed when it expires in three years' time. The government has warned Soup it 'is unhappy about high returns to shareholders while there are many reports of poor passenger service, overcrowded trains and unreliable services on certain routes and at busy times'.

Soup owns its fleet of diesel powered trains. Each train in Region A has seven coaches with 70 passenger seats available per coach. In the less busy Region B, each train has six coaches each with 70 seats. As a condition of the licence, Soup runs a set number of services at both busy and quieter times in both regions. Soup has two larger rivals, both operating electric trains, which cause less harm to the environment than diesel powered trains. They run on the same routes in both regions.

The government regulates fares charged to passengers, which are the same per distance travelled for every operator in that region. The railway track, stations and other infrastructure are managed by the government which charges the operators a fee. There are several stations along the route which are only used by Soup trains and others where Soup trains do not stop at all.

Soup's trains are 25 years old, originally purchased cheaply from an operator whose licence was withdrawn by the government. Soup believes the low price it paid is a key competitive advantage enabling them to steadily increase their return on capital employed, the company's main performance measure, to a level well in excess of their rivals. The shareholders are pleased with the growth in passenger numbers over the last five years, which is the other performance measure Soup uses.

Soup's ageing trains spend increasing time undergoing preventative maintenance, safety checks or repairs. A recent television documentary also showed apparently poor conditions on board, such as defective heating and washroom facilities and dirty, torn seating. Passengers complained in the programme of difficulties finding a seat, the unreliability of accessing wireless internet services and even that the menu in the on-board cafe had not changed for five years.

Soup's CEO responded that unreliable internet access arose from the rapid growth in passengers expecting to access the internet on trains. She said Soup had never received any formal complaints about the lack of choice in the on-board cafe, nor had she heard of a recent press report that Soup's trains were badly maintained, so causing harm to the environment.

The CEO has asked you, as chief management accountant, for your advice. 'In view of the government's warning, we must develop performance measures balancing the needs of passengers with the requirements of the shareholders', she has said. 'I don't want to know how to improve the actual performance of the business; that is the job of the operational managers, nor do I just want a list of suggested performance measures. Instead I need to know why these performance measures will help to improve the performance of Soup.'

The following data applies to Soup:

	Region A	Region B
Number of services per day		
Peak times	4	4
Other times	6	8
Number of passengers per day		
Peak times	2,500	1,400
Other times	2,450	1,850

Required:

(a)   Advise the CEO on how the use of the balanced scorecard could improve the performance management system of Soup.   (10 marks)

(b)   Using the performance data given, evaluate the comments of the Deeland government that Soups trains are overcrowded.   (7 marks)

(c)   Assess the problems Soup may encounter in selecting and interpreting performance measures when applying the balanced scorecard to its performance management system.   (8 marks)

(Total: 25 marks)

77   PHARMACEUTICAL TECHNOLOGIES CO (PILOT 10)

Pharmaceutical Technologies Co (PT) is a developer and manufacturer of pharmaceuticals medical drugs in Beeland. It is one of the 100 largest listed companies on the national stock exchange. The company focuses on buying prospective products drugs from small bio-engineering companies that have shown initial promise in testing from small bioengineering companies. PT then leads these through three regulatory stages to launch in the general medical market. The three stages are:

1   to confirm that the safety of the drug product (does it harm humans?), with small scale trials

2   to test the efficacy of the product (does it help cure?), again in small scale trials; and

3   finally, large scale trials to definitively decide on the safety and efficacy of the product.

The drugs are then marketed through the company's large sales force to health care providers and end users (patients). The health care providers are paid by either health insurance companies or the national government dependent on the financial status of the patient.

The Beeland Drug Regulator (BDR) oversees this testing process and makes the final judgement about whether a product can be sold in the country.

Its objectives are to protect, promote and improve public health by ensuring that:

●   medicines have an acceptable balance of benefit and risk

●   the users of these medicines understand this risk-benefit profile; and

●   new beneficial product development is encouraged.

The regulator is governed by a board of trustees appointed by the government. It is funded directly by the government and also, through fees charged to drug companies when granting licences to sell their products in Beeland.

PT has used share price and earnings per share as its principal measures of performance to date. However, the share price has underperformed the market and the health sector in the last 2 two years. The chief executive officer (CEO) has identified that these measures are too narrow and is considering implementing a balanced scorecard approach to address this problem.

A working group has drawn up a suggested balanced scorecard. It began by identifying the objectives from the board's medium term strategy:

- Create shareholder value by bringing commercially viable drugs to market

- Improve the efficiency of drug development

- Increase shareholder value by innovation in the drug approval process.

The working group then considered the stakeholder perspectives:

- Shareholders want a competitive return on their investment

- Payers Purchasers (governments, insurers and patients) want to pay a reasonable price for the drugs

- Regulators want an efficient process for the validation of drugs

- Doctors want safe and effective drug products

- Patients want to be cured.

Finally, this leads to the proposed scorecard of performance measures:

- Financial – share price and earnings per share

- Customer – number of patients using TTPT products

- Internal business process – above exceed industry-standard quality of on design and testing; time to regulatory approval of a product

- Learning and growth – training days undertaken by staff; time to market of new product; percentage of drugs bought by TTPT that gain final approval.

This balanced scorecard now needs to be reviewed to ensure that it will address the company's objectives and the issues that it faces in its business environment.

Required:

(a) **Evaluate the performance measures proposed for PT's balanced scorecard.**

(10 marks)

(b) **Briefly describe a method of analysing stakeholder influence and analyse the influence of four different external stakeholders on the regulator (BDR).** **(8 marks)**

(c) **Using your answer from part (b), describe how the application of the balanced scorecard approach at BDR would differ from the approach within PT.** **(7 marks)**

(Total: 25 marks)

78 BETTASERVE (PILOT 07)

Bettaserve Limited has identified and defined a market in which it wishes to operate. This will provide a 'gold standard' focus for an existing range of services. Bettaserve plc has identified a number of key competitors and intends to focus on close co-operation with its customers in providing services to meet their specific design and quality requirements. Efforts will be made to improve the effectiveness of all aspects of the cycle from service design to after-sales service to customers. This will require inputs from a number of departments in the achievement of the specific goals of the 'gold standard' range of services. Efforts will be made to improve productivity in conjunction with increased flexibility of methods.

An analysis of financial and non-financial data relating to the 'gold standard' proposal for each of the years 2007, 2008 and 2009 is shown below.

Required:

(a)   Prepare an analysis (both quantitative and discursive) of the 'gold standard' proposal for the period 2007 to 2009. You should use the information provided in the question, together with the data in Schedule 1 below. Your analysis should include the following:

(i)   A definition of corporate 'vision or mission' and consideration of how the proposal may be seen as identifying and illustrating a specific sub-set of this 'vision or mission'.   **(5 marks)**

(ii)   Discussion and, where possible, quantification of the proposal in both marketing and financial terms.   **(5 marks)**

(iii)   Discussion of the external effectiveness of the proposal in the context of ways in which each of Quality and Delivery are expected to affect customer satisfaction and hence the marketing of the product.   **(5 marks)**

(iv)   Discussion of the internal efficiency of the proposal in the context of ways in which the management of each of Cycle Time and Waste are expected to affect productivity and hence the financial aspects of the proposal.
                                                                                   (5 marks)

Schedule 1: 'Gold Standard' proposal – estimated statistics

	2007	2008	2009
Total market size ($m)	240	250	260
Bettaserve plc – sales ($m)	30	36	40
Bettaserve plc – total costs ($m)	28.2	25.448	25.1
Bettaserve plc – sundry statistics:			
Services achieving design quality standards (%) and accepted without further rectification	95	97	98
Rectification claims from customers ($m)	0.9	0.54	0.2
Cost of after sales rectification service ($m)	3	2.5	2
Sales meeting planned completion dates (%)	90	95	99
Average cycle time: (customer enquiry to service finalisation) (weeks)	6	5.5	5
Service enquiries not taken up by customers (% of enquiries)	7.50	5.00	2.50
Idle capacity of service personnel (%)	10	6	2
Analysis of total cost:	$000	$000	$000
target cost – variable	12,000	14,400	16,000
target cost – fixed	4,000	4,000	5,000
internal failure costs	3,200	1,840	1,050
external failure costs	4,000	2,208	1,050
appraisal costs	1,000	1,000	1,000
prevention costs	4,000	2,000	1,000
Total cost	28,200	25,448	25,100

(b) Discuss the links, both vertical and horizontal, of the performance measures investigated in (a). The discussion should include comment on the hierarchy and inter-relationships between the measures, including internal and external aspects of the expected trends in performance.

(Note: A diagram may be used to illustrate the links, together with relevant discussion). (5 marks)

(Total: 25 marks)

Section 3

ANSWERS TO PRACTICE QUESTIONS – SECTION A

1 THYME (SEPT/DEC 17)

Key answer tips

This question is consistent with previous sittings in terms of the content and structure of the scenario, the standard of the requirements, the breadth of syllabus examined and the discursive marks available.

Requirement (i) asks for an evaluation of the given performance dashboard. This is a commonly examined area but in this requirement you are expected to focus on the positive (rather than the negative) aspects of the report.

Requirement (ii) directly examines the syllabus requirement on integrated reporting. Previously unexamined but, as part of the syllabus, its inclusion as a requirement should have been anticipated.

In requirement (iii) 6 marks are available for calculations; a clear and logical layout is required here. Another 6 marks are available for linking the target cost with TQM. Linking different syllabus areas will be expected in the exam.

In requirement (iv) be careful to answer all parts of the requirement. This is broken down into three parts.

Report

To: CEO of Thyme

From: A. Accountant

Date: September 2016

Subject: Reporting performance and quality issues at Thyme Engine Products

This report analyses the positive features of the award winning dashboard identifying some areas which specifically apply to Thyme. The role of the management accountant in providing information for integrated reporting is explained. Then, the target cost gap for the new engine is calculated and an evaluation is provided of the use of this target cost within the TQM approach. Finally, issues associated with the costs of quality at Thyme are addressed.

(i) **Positive features** of award winning dashboard

The following are features of the dashboard which will have weighed in the assessors' minds when making the award. They are placed in a priority order of most important first and then there are a few specific comments about the possible use of such a template at Thyme.

Achievement of the objectives and strategies of the business

The critical measure of whether the dashboard is fit for its purpose is whether it answers the question: has the business achieved its key objectives?

The dashboard measures all of the key objectives of the business growth of the firm:

1   shareholder wealth and returns through EVA™ and TSR; and

2   growth through revenue and market share growth.

It also measures the strategies used to achieve these results:

1   world-class engineering to design engines through the class leading design specifications;

2   high quality production through fault rates in manufacturing and delivery; and

3   customer service through those same fault rates and market share (an indirect indicator).

Balanced view

The report presents a balanced view of the business's performance. It deals with various perspectives (shareholders (TSR), customers (market share), internal business (fault rates) and innovation (design position)) which are used in the balanced scorecard approach. This is also achieved using both internal and external data (fault rates and average sector growth). It presents both the results and the determinants of those results by giving financial and non-financial indicators. For example, revenue growth will be driven by the customers' view of product and service, so design and manufacturing quality measures are important. Short and longer term measures are given such as profit margin and economic value added.

Planning and control

The dashboard should allow the board to perform both its vital functions in planning and controlling the business. The forecasts for next year (budgets) are given and also, as noted above, there are non-financial determinants of performance such as design and customer service which will drive the future short-term competitive position of the business.

The control activities of the board are served by providing historic trends and also current budget variances. The major headings are provided for under the financial headings with activity measured by revenue, profit by the margin and shareholder wealth by economic value added.

Presentation

The dashboard is kept brief as the board will have an opportunity prior to the board meeting to use it to identify issues requiring further analysis at the meeting. There is a short narrative commentary which deals with the major commercial points arising from the dashboard and also, gives further external market data as context for the figures (e.g. average sector growth). It is also worth noting that the narrative picks up on strategic issues of risk and opportunity which can more difficult to capture in numerical form. Hence, the commentary appears appropriate to assist in an annual review of the business.

Specific issues at Thyme

There are certain issues particular to Thyme which may be added to the example dashboard, though if these are deemed short term, then they may not necessarily appear on this main dashboard view. The example dashboard does not show measures of cash flow performance (such as free cash flow generated) nor gearing ratio, both of which would be important for future fund raising. There are no measures associated with governance and ethics which in the light of the bribery scandal may have a higher priority at Thyme. Ethical training costs may give a measure of this area.

(ii)   Integrated reporting

There is no standard format for integrated reporting. However, there are changes in focus of the company's reporting which will require the input of the management accountants of that business. Integrated reporting has a focus on opportunities and risk, how resources are allocated and performance both recent historic and expected in the future. There are six capitals involved in value creation including traditional tangible and financial assets but also including human, intellectual, environmental and social assets.

For the management accountant, these newer forms of capital will require information systems capable of capturing and processing such non-financial measures. The forward-looking nature of such reporting will require more information of a forecast nature (with the accompanying requirement to understand their estimating assumptions). The more strategic view which integrated reporting intends to give also requires reporting on factors which drive long-term performance. A key part of the integrated report is linking performance to strategic goals and the ability to create value. This will require a less structured and more contingent approach to reporting. In other words, proforma reporting must be better tailored to the specific business's situation. However, it is considered a key requirement of such reporting that it is concise and so the management accountant must help to ensure that only the key information is reported. It can be seen that the dashboard discussed in the above section of this report achieves many of these requirements.

(iii) **New jet engine: target costing and TQM**

Workings:

	$000
Target cost	2,125
Production costs	1,825
Design and development	100
Sales and marketing	500
Current cost	2,425

Target cost gap	300 (12% of current cost)

The target cost for the new engine is $2·125m and the current estimated cost is $2·425m. Therefore, there is a need to cut costs by 12% to achieve the target profit margin. It is common for the initial costs to be higher than the target cost and for cost savings to be achieved as the product reaches maturity in its lifecycle. It should be noted that even at this higher initial cost, the engine will be making a small $0·075m profit per unit (a 3% margin).

Target costing involves setting a selling price based on what will be competitive in the market then deducting a target profit margin to obtain the target cost. An estimate is made of the cost of the engine based on the current design specification. The gap between this cost and the target cost is the target cost gap and opportunities to bridge this gap are sought by amending the product design or cutting costs in production.

Total quality management (TQM) is a management approach which seeks to have no defects in resource or relationship management. It aims to have a culture of continuous improvement in the organisation.

In this new engine project, the TQM philosophy will fit well with the need to cut a relatively small amount of costs in order to meet the target. By small but frequent improvements as the production team climb the learning curve associated with such a new product, it would be expected that such cost savings would be made.

Given the size of the cost gap, it does not seem that a major redesign of the engine is required.

(iv) **Quality costs**

There are four categories of quality costs:

– Prevention costs are costs to prevent the production of engines which fail to meet specifications;

– Appraisal costs are costs incurred in inspecting products to ensure that they meet specifications;

– Cost of internal failure are costs associated with making good products which are identified as sub-standard before delivery to the customer; and

– Cost of external failure are costs associated with making good products which are identified as sub-standard after delivery to the customer.

Working:

	$m
Prevention	139 (= 11 + 92 + 36)
Appraisal	138 (= 110 + 28)
Cost of internal failure	95
Cost of external failure	279 (= 223 + 56)
Total	651

Comments of results

The total quality costs are 5.7% of revenue which seems surprisingly low for an organisation which recognises this as a key competitive advantage; notable is the large size of the external failure costs of 2.4%.

Possible other relevant costs

Overall, there are likely to be administrative costs associated with many of these categories and some attribution of overhead should be undertaken beyond the customer complaint handling mentioned.

Appraisal costs include performance testing of final assembly and performance testing of subcomponents from suppliers. There may also be costs associated with inspection of raw materials inward since these make a difference to quality (shown by the higher purchase costs).

Internal failure costs include costs of re-inspection after repairs after final assembly testing. There must also be costs associated with repairing faulty goods identified at final testing and possibly also scrapping failed products. It is possible that there is idle time costs due to work held up by internal identification of faulty products.

External failure costs include customer complaint handling and replacements under warranties. There is also the cost of damage done to Thyme's brand by such problems although many customers will accept that these are inevitable and provided they are infrequent and covered by warranty, they need not be important.

New products such as the new jet engine will likely generate additional failure costs while production methods are optimised.

Relative importance of categories

Given the high cost of external failure and the importance of reputation for Thyme, the most important category is prevention. It would be appropriate for Thyme with a TQM approach to be spending heavily in this area. This will still need to be combined with warranty spending in order to protect the reputation of Thyme when problems do occur. As prevention succeeds, so the importance of the other categories will decline. It is worrying that external failure costs are more than twice internal failure costs, which suggests that final testing is not identifying a significant number of the faults in production.

Marking scheme

			Marks
(i)	1 mark per point with additional marks for development of these issues		
	Specific issues at Thyme not measured – up to 3 marks		
		Maximum	15
(ii)	Description of IR – up to 3 marks		
	Impact on management accountant – up to 6 marks		
		Maximum	6
(iii)	Calculations: 1 mark for each of the following ($000)		
	Target cost 2,125		
	Production costs 1,825		
	Design and development 100		
	Sales and marketing 500		
	Target cost gap 300 (12% current cost)		
	Current profit margin $0.075m or 3%		
	Discussion of cost savings – 1 mark		
	Definition of target costing – 1 mark		
	Definition of TQM – up to 2 marks		
	Fit of TQM with target costing approach – up to 6 marks		
		Maximum	12
(iv)	Definition of quality costs – up to 2 marks		
	Calculations: 1 mark for absolute ($m) or as a % of revenue		
	Prevention 139 (1.21%)		
	Appraisal 138 (1.20%)		
	Cost of internal failure 95 (0.83%)		
	Costs of external failure 279 (2.43%)		
	Total 651 (5.66%)		
	Discussion of results – up to 2 marks		
	Identification of other quality costs omitted which are appropriate for Thyme – up to 6 marks		
	Relative importance of the categories – up to 4 marks		
		Maximum	13
Professional marks			
		Maximum	4
Total			50

Examiner's comments

This 50-mark question was based around a manufacturing company and required candidates to consider the use of a dashboard, costing and quality methods, and the role of the management accountant.

Part (i) asked for an evaluation of a company's performance dashboard. Similar questions to this have been examined in previous diets and as such candidates tended to score relatively well here. It is worth noting though that a significant number of candidates provided very superficial answers. For example, stating that there is not a lot of detail could be an advantage or a disadvantage depending on the users of the information, so it is essential to explain why something is good or bad. Candidates should clearly explain their logic behind such statements. Also, this particular question required candidates to detail the elements that were particularly good, and as such, parts of answers that discussed negative aspects scored little credit.

Part (ii) asked for an explanation of the role of the management accountant in providing information for integrated reporting. It was essential here for candidates to relate their answers to integrated reporting. Many candidates did not seem familiar with this type of report and simply discussed the role of a management accountant generally and how that role has changed in recent years. The marking team would like to point out that technical articles are made available on the ACCA website to assist students in their studies and these are an invaluable source of information. Several of the topics that have been examined in recent diets, including this one, have been discussed via these articles.

Part (iii) was about costing and quality methods. The calculations in this section were performed particularly well by most candidates. Care should be taken to present calculations in a logical order to allow the marking team to award marks for method even if the final answer is incorrect. Good candidates also went on to discuss the results well.

Part (iv) was based around quality aspects of manufacturing. Similar to part (iii), many candidates performed well on the calculations, although some candidates were not able to correctly categorise the costs. Also, candidates should pay close attention to all the verbs within a requirement – this part of Question 1 specifically asked for four things (categorise, calculate, suggest and evaluate) and therefore candidates' performance would be improved if answers addressed each of these separately.

As has become common, those candidates who had practised writing professional answers prior to the examination performed admirably in the presentation area (4 marks). The marker team was looking for suitable report headings, an introduction, a logical structure, signposted by the good use of subheadings in the answer, and a clear, concise style. A conclusion was not required for the 4 marks but if a suitable and substantive one was offered then it was given credit. However, it may be worth noting that introductions of the form 'I am writing this report at the request of the directors', are inadequate. A more substantive description of the contents of the report isrequired.

2 DARGEBOARD SERVICES (MAR/JUN 17)

Key answer tips

This is a clear question with no surprises and is comparable to other recent Section A questions in terms of difficulty and scope. Do be careful not to write too much. Use the mark allocation when deciding how much time to spend on each requirement.

Report

To: **The board of DS**

From: **An Accountant**

Date: **March 2017**

Subject: **Strategic performance reporting and reward systems at DS**

This report assesses the coherence of the choice of key performance indicators (KPIs) with the mission of DS followed by the assumptions used in their calculation. Other aspects of the presentation of the dashboard report are then evaluated. Finally, an overview of the operation of the building block model and an assessment of two proposed reward schemes are provided.

(i) **Linking the mission to the current KPIs**

The mission statement can be broken into several parts. The principal aim is maintainable, profitable growth which is supported by three further goals: developing the best talent; providing world-class services; and being efficient.

The KPIs are linked to elements of this statement as follows:

- Operating profit margin shows that the organisation is profitable and also as a margin, it indicates efficiency in cost control.

- Secured revenue indicates the amount of revenue which is contracted and so has greater likelihood of being earned. Contracts give an indication of maintainability though here only in the short term.

- Management retention links to the need for best talent though it does not measure the developing of that talent.

- Order book shows the maintainability into the future of the business though it does not show the average length of the contracts.

- Organic revenue growth shows historic growth and may indicate what the management are capable of into the future.

- ROCE demonstrates the efficiency of profit-generation from the capital base of DS.

None of the measures are external, looking at the competitive environment and so it is not possible to indicate if DS has 'world-class services'.

Tutorial note

This is a highly examinable area. Review each KPI in turn and examine whether it helps to achieve all aspects of the mission.

(ii) **Assumptions underlying the current KPI calculations**

Every KPI will involve some assumptions in its calculations. The aim of this section is to highlight how each indicator could be manipulated to show a better picture so that the business can avoid this in the future and the subsequent bad image portrayed in the investing community.

Operating profit margin is a standard performance measure and the only area which can be questioned is the categorisation of costs below this line, for example, the movement of operating costs into 'exceptional costs' below this line in order to artificially inflate this indicator. If the $55m reorganisation cost was included in overall operating profit which was $91m (=5·9% of $1,542m) then the business would show an operating margin of 2·3%. The catering business would show a loss of $39m.

Secured revenue represents long-term recurring revenue streams. A good picture will show a high percentage of secured revenue but will be below 100% so that management can indicate that budget targets are being exceeded. It is worrying that the budget is completed well after the year start as this may indicate such manipulation. If the original budgeted revenue figure is used then the secured revenue for 2016 was 82%.

Management retention only includes retention of employees on full-time contracts which at 65% of all managers excludes a material number. Poor treatment (and thus retention) of part-time managers is therefore ignored. This may be a particular issue for managers with young children who often take advantage of such contracts.

Order book is a 'total 'value' figure but is this the cash or present value figure? By choosing cash value of the contract, this will give a much larger figure than the discounted present value, especially where some revenues will not be received for 10 years.

Organic revenue growth is calculated by using the total revenue figure as reported in the accounts. The main purpose of   stating organic is that it is growth from within the organisation as it stands and so acquisitions should be ignored. The current figure would fall from 7·2% overall to a less impressive 3·9%.

Return on capital employed (ROCE). Capital employed is being calculated using the statement of financial position figures   which may exclude many intangible assets. As such it may overemphasise the tangible capital base which is not as important   in a service business such as DS. The focus on this measure can lead to suboptimal decisions.

Tutorial note

A clear layout is required. Look at each KPI in turn and assess how the assumptions and definitions may serve to artificially boost the measure (and hence DS's share price).

(iii) **Evaluation of the strategic performance dashboard**

The current information used by the board is both financial and non-financial allowing different elements of the mission to be measured. However, none of the measures are external, looking at the competitive environment and so it is not possible to indicate if DS has 'world-class services'. Also, the measures do not focus on shareholder concerns although the mission statement indicates that they are the principal stakeholders. Other measures beyond ROCE might have been expected given that priority, such as EPS or dividend per share. No breakdown of ROCE is provided for each business unit, this may be due to the lack of availability of capital employed figures for the units but it does seem an odd inconsistency since ROCE is the best KPI provided for shareholder use.

No revenue figures are given and as most figures are ratios it is not possible to gauge the absolute scale of the business. It is particularly surprising that an absolute profit measure is not included on the dashboard given the importance of profitable growth to shareholders.

Generally, there is a lack of external figures to allow benchmarking or the assessment of the competitive position of DS.

The breakdown of results into business sectors will help in the judgement of performance of the managers of those units but they may not be comparable, for example, comparing building services and security, it seems that building services is growing more rapidly but with weaker margins. Also, it may be that the employment market is different between each sector and so no comparison of management retention figures is sensible. Again, it may be helpful to provide either an external benchmark through industry averages or an internal one through a historic trend for these sector specific indicators.

The report does have good qualities as it is brief and clearly presented. The use of ratios makes for easy understanding.

(iv) The building block model

The model takes the important step of distinguishing within the dimensions of performance between what is the desired outcome (results) and what are the drivers of those results (determinants). It then highlights the need to measure both within the performance reporting systems of an organisation.

The standards are the target level for the specific measures chosen for each dimension appropriate to an employee's performance. Employees must take ownership so they need to be persuaded to accept the target and be motivated by the targets. Targets must be achievable and so challenge the employee without being viewed as impossible to achieve and so be demotivating. For example, they must take account of external market conditions which will be beyond the control of the employee, but this can be managed by benchmarking against an industry average. Targets must be fair, for example, different businesses within DS must be measured against their sector (catering, security, etc).

(v) Assessment of the proposed reward scheme

As the board is already considering using the building block model, it is appropriate to outline the main criteria in the model for reward schemes.

Rewards must be

–   clear, that is, understood by the managers

–   motivating, that is, of value to the employee; and

–   controllable, that is, related to their area of responsibility.

Scheme 1

The scheme has the benefit that it continues with the successful policy of offering an equity share in DS. It continues to utilise the knowledge of the line manager in performing the appraisal. It attempts to address a problem of the current scheme which is that the breadth of the categories gives the line manager scope to continue to show favouritism to specific employees. This is addressed as the bonus for line management will be affected by their appraisal according to performance on this new scheme and it will be helped practically by giving them an expectation of the distribution of bonus shares. This will also mean that forecasting staff costs will be simpler.

However, this scheme does not address the problem that the appraisal categories are vague and do not reflect the KPIs of DS. It also could create a problem as line managers will give bonuses according to the stated expectation, for example, even where all staff are, in absolute terms, performing brilliantly only 20% will get the maximum. Also, there is no mention of the scale of the scheme bonuses as there is for Scheme 2, where the maximum is stated as 50% of basic salary.

Scheme 2

Scheme 2 loses a key benefit of the current scheme in not rewarding in shares but cash is an acceptable alternative. Cash may well be a preferred option for the managers as it offers a certain value to them. This form of benefit also reduces the desire to manipulate share prices. It sets standards based on the KPIs and so should lead to greater focus by each employee on the goals of DS. Involvement of both strategic and line management in this process should lead to a better set of measures being used.

It is not clear, however, why five targets are being chosen. This seems an arbitrary figure and it may be more sensible to suggest a range from three to six (the number of strategic KPIs) to be decided by the managers in consultation. The size of the maximum reward seems likely to motivate but the equal weighting for each heading may not be effective. It requires that, say, operating profit margin has the same importance as management retention.

Tutorial note

You are expected to recognise that there are drawbacks, as well as attributes, to each of the two reward schemes.

			Marks
Marking scheme			
(i)	Breaking down the mission – up to 2 marks 1 mark per point	**Maximum**	8
(ii)	Up to 3 marks for comments on each indicator Operating profit margin Secured revenue Management retention Order book Organic revenue growth ROCE	**Maximum**	12
(iii)	1 mark per point	**Maximum**	8
(iv)	Results and determinants Standards: ownership, achievable targets, fair	**Maximum**	6
(v)	1 mark per point Up to 2 marks for general assessment of reward scheme 6 marks per scheme	**Maximum**	12
Professional marks		**Maximum**	4
Total			50

Examiner's comments

This question required the candidates to consider the performance reporting system of a service company and its proposed reward schemes.

The first three parts of the question asked a set of questions around the current indicators used at a strategic level by the company.

Part (i) requested an evaluation of the links between the mission and the indicators. This required a common APM task of identifying the mission from the scenario. Candidates were good at repeating the mission statement from the question but few showed appreciation of the structure of the mission and how certain goals were subsidiary to an overall aim. However, most scored reasonably well as they linked the indicators given to the parts of the mission.

Part (ii) required a detailed consideration of how performance measures are put together. The responses, here, were limited with many candidates only scoring a single mark per indicator but with 6 indicators and 12 marks on offer, they failed to develop their answers. For example, it was often clear that a candidate had correctly identified that there was a problem with the calculation of a particular indicator but very few attempted to quantify the impact of this problem. Many candidates showed that they did not understand how to calculate return on capital employed, which is an important financial indicator and one that they should be very familiar with.

Part (iii) required a general evaluation of the presentation of the business' dashboard of indicators. Candidates often scored some marks by making general points but then missed out by not expanding their answers using the specifics of the scenario.

The last parts of the question surrounded the reward schemes of the business.

Part (iv) required an explanation of certain detailed parts of the Building Block model. Responses to this question were generally poor as many candidates ignored the detailed requirements of the CEO and provided a rote-learned answer that irrelevantly described the whole model. This illustrates the importance of reading the requirement which stated 'explain…as required by the CEO' which was intended as an indicator for candidates to look at what the CEO had said in the scenario.

Part (v) required two proposed reward schemes to be evaluated and was generally well done with many candidates using the Building Block model concepts to good effect by illustrating how the two schemes demonstrated the ideal features from the model.

As has become common, those candidates who had practised writing professional answers prior to the examination performed admirably in the presentation area (4 marks). The markers were looking for suitable report headings, an introduction, a logical structure, signposted by the good use of subheadings in the answer, and a clear, concise style.

3   FLACK (MAR/JUN 16)

Key answer tips

This is a typical Section A question – it requires you to write a report to the Board on a number of performance management issues. Make sure that you score the four professional marks that are available in Section A:

- Who is the report to and from? Insert the date and give the report a heading.

- Include a short introduction explaining what will be covered in the report.

- Use plenty of headings, sub-headings and short paragraphs.

- Use language and tone that is appropriate for the reader.

- Include any detailed calculations in an appendix.

- Apply your knowledge to the particulars of the scenario.

In part (i), as with previous past exam questions of this nature, make sure that you evaluate (i.e. examine the good and bad parts of the report in detail) the performance report and not the performance.

In parts (ii)-(iv) you are expected to discuss the appropriateness of different performance measures. This is a commonly examined area and is core to APM. Remember, 'what gets measured gets done'.

Part (v) is typical of how information systems (IS) may be examined – the end part of the scenario commonly introduces a change to an IS or a new IS.

Report

To: **Board of Flack**

From: **A. Accountant**

Date: **June 2016**

Subject: **Performance reporting and management issues at Flack**

Introduction

This report evaluates the current performance report for Flack and the introduction of two new performance measures. Then, the effect of a proposed change in divisional performance measure is assessed. Next, the use of expected ROCE for new store proposals is evaluated. Finally, the report explains how the proposed new information system can help to improve business performance at Flack.

(i)   Performance reporting at Flack

The current report has a number of strengths and weaknesses. These will be discussed according to whether the report:

- addresses the mission,

- contains appropriate information for decision-making,

- shows signs of being short term and

- is well presented.

The current mission can be broken down into two parts:

– to be the first choice for customers and

– to provide the right balance of quality, service and price.

There are three strategies for achieving this mission, reflecting stakeholder concerns:

– earning customer loyalty,

– utilising all resources and

– serving shareholders' interests.

The report does not address the first part of the mission. This can only be measured using external data but the report is utilising only Flack's internal data. This part of the mission relates to the first strategy to gain customer loyalty. Customer loyalty could be gauged through repeat purchases or market share information but neither is supplied. This is clearly important to a retailer and may be more easily gathered once the data from the new information system are available for inclusion in this report.

The report provides no measures of the balance of quality, service and price other than through the historic growth in revenue. It would only be through comparison with competitors or customer survey data that a picture of the mix of these qualities could be gained.

The second strategy of utilising resources requires that the key resources be identified. Clearly, the stores themselves (and thus the capital invested) are an important resource and the introduction of the revenue and profit per square metre and comparison with competitors will indicate the efficiency of their use. However, there are likely to be other important resources such as staff and no measure of their performance is offered. Staff costs are not shown in the trading account although a more sophisticated measure such as revenue per employee is a commonly used metric and would address this.

The report is much better on the third strategy of serving shareholder interests as it supplies two helpful measures: total shareholder return and return on capital employed. However, most shareholders will want comparison with benchmark returns within the retail sector and the market more widely, since these represent their alternatives.

The criticism of the company's management as being short term is reflected in the performance reporting. The report only contains for comparison budget information and the previous year's figures. There are no longer term forecasts or information on future capital investment. Also, there are few indicators which would be described as determinants of performance. These are often non-financial and focused on the external business environment (behaviour of customers and competitors).

As already noted, there is a significant gap in the information in the report as it contains no external information. Also, although revenue is broken down into broad product categories, no further information about growth within these categories nor the margins being earned is supplied. As a result, it could be questioned whether this break-down is worthwhile.

In terms of presentation, the data is clear and in a form which would be easily recognisable to those used to reading accounts. However, no narrative commentary is provided which would highlight the key features in the report such as major deviations from the budget or performance well outside industry norms. There should be a comment on each of the five areas within the mission and strategies as well as comments about specific, material issues arising in the period covered. The report could be made easier to read by reducing the volume of numbers present both by cutting out unnecessary measures (see earlier discussion of product categories) and also by rounding all figures to millions.

(ii)   New asset utilisation indicators

Revenue and operating profit per square metre reflect the utilisation of the key capital asset used in their generation (the store). Therefore, they are directly addressing a major part of the aim of utilising all resources; however, they do not address all resources which the business uses. There are likely to be significant staff costs and so similar measures of revenue and operating profit per employee could also be introduced in order to reflect these human resources.

	Metro	*Hyper*	*Flack*
Revenue per sq. metre	13,702	13,165	13,251
Operating profit ($000s)	159,058	498,791	657,849
Operating profit per sq. metre	987	592	656

These measures reflect the importance of the use of the store's space which is an area which the business does not give sufficient attention as is reflected in the problems with divisional performance measures. Focus on these measures will require addressing issues of volume of sales and the profitability of those sales. The two types of store at Flack will have different impacts on these measures. For example, the smaller Metro stores may be capable of earning higher margins as they are convenient to customers while selling lower volumes. The Hyper stores may concentrate on selling in volume to customers who come to buy in bulk. However, in terms of the overall performance of the business it is essential that Flack sells in high volumes as it is a low margin business but it must not sacrifice profitability, in effect buying customers' revenue by selling at or near a loss.

(iii)   Divisional performance assessment

The current measure of divisional operating profit reflects the trading in the period under consideration. Profit will link to the whole business's operating profit which is the correct level to reflect the efforts of the divisional managers. However, this measure only indirectly addresses the capital being used by the divisions (depreciation charged to operating profit). This is distorting the behaviour of the divisional managers.

The managers are not investing in refurbishing their stores which is causing the press (and presumably customers) to notice their run-down appearance. This may reduce the depreciation charge against operating profit. They are prioritising new store capital expenditure over the refurbishment since they are not being charged for the use of that capital (financing charges are deducted after operating profit is calculated). This may not be optimal since small spending on existing capital assets often yields higher returns than new spending (which may be subject to greater risks).

The proposal to change the divisional performance measure addresses the issue of not reflecting the capital used since residual income (RI) deducts an imputed interest charge. Divisions can then be set targets in terms of their RI. The difficulties in calculating RI lie in correctly setting the imputed interest rate and calculating the capital being employed by the division. However, since both divisions are types of stores they will have similar assets and so the same rules can be applied to each to fairly calculate the capital used. An advantage of RI is that the imputed interest rate can be changed to reflect the different risks of the divisions. The two divisions here do not seem to have significant risk differences unless the geographical locations introduce these (city centres and city edges). However, it is worth noting that using RI can discourage investment. As net book values of assets fall over time, RI automatically increases and 'do not invest' could become an attractive option to the managers.

Overall, the proposed change addresses existing problems and would be considered a normal solution to measuring divisional performance in this industry.

(iv) Use of expected ROCE in new store appraisal

The expected ROCE is calculated as:

Demand scenarios	Low	Medium	High
Revenue ($m)	12.5	13	13.5
Probability (%)	20	50	30
Forecast operating margin (%)	4.1	4.3	4.4
Forecast operating profit ($m)	0.5125	0.559	0.594
Expected operating profit ($m)	0.5602		
Expected ROCE	13.34%		

The expected ROCE is above 13% which is Flack's required ROCE, so this should be an acceptable investment.

The use of expected values in the calculation of ROCE is appropriate if the probabilities used can be reasonably estimated and the decision is likely to be one which is made a number of times. Since Flack has opened many stores, it is likely to be able to predict volumes and margins with reasonable accuracy. Since Flack is going to continue to open stores, this decision will occur a number of times which makes using a probabilistic approach viable. In general, ROCE is neither considered as accurate nor as direct a measure of shareholder wealth as, for example, net present value (NPV).

(v) Loyalty card system

The proposed new information system will collect data from customers' purchases and store it for data mining purposes in a data warehouse. The capital required will be significant at $100m (the equivalent of about 24 new stores at $4.2m each). There will also be considerable annual running costs. However, the benefits could be significant although quantifying them will be difficult as they depend on influencing customer behaviour and so are not simply cutting costs.

The new system will help to address the mission of Flack as it will help the board to understand customers better and so improve their loyalty to the business. By focusing offers on those things which customers enjoy Flack can enhance the brand and also take the opportunity to sell greater volumes alongside the offered products.

The data warehouse will allow data mining for relationships, for example, geographical preferences for products; links between price offers and volumes sold; products which are often bought together; seasonality of product purchases. These relationships can then be used to address the CEO's three target areas of advertising, product range choices and price offers.

Potentially, there will be cost savings by more efficient advertising. The data on each individual customer can be searched to profile customers and identify their individual preferences. Marketing can then be targeted to groups of customers using products which they commonly buy. Data mining will also identify associated products (those often bought together) so that offers can be grouped, for example, with a price reduction on buying a linked pair of products.

A problem in most retail businesses is the size of the product portfolio which they offer since more products (and potentially more suppliers) require more effort to manage. The new system may allow a Pareto-style analysis where the least profitable non-essential products are identified and can be cut from the product range.

Marking scheme		
		Marks
(i)	Performance report	
	Breaking down the mission – up to 3 marks	
	Two main aims, three CSFs/strategies, noting how these are logically connected	
	Comments on how report addresses mission and strategies – up to 6 marks	
	Missing information – up to 3 marks	
	Lack of external info; margins by product category	
	Report is 'short-termist' – up to 3 marks	
	Comments on presentation – up to 3 marks	
	Lack of narrative; data overload; rounding	
	Maximum	**14**
(ii)	New asset utilisation indicators	
	Addressing the mission – up to 3 marks	
	Calculations – 3 marks	
	Use in managing business performance – up to 5 marks	
	Maximum	**8**
(iii)	Divisional performance	
	Discussion of existing behaviour and measure – up to 5 marks	
	Discussion of new measure – up to 5 marks	
	Maximum	**8**
(iv)	Decision-making under risk	
	Calculations:	
	1 mark for method	
	1 mark for correct profit under each scenario	
	1 mark for expected operating profit	
	1 mark for expected ROCE	
	Comments – 1 mark per point; up to 4 marks	
	Maximum	**8**
(v)	New information system	
	Description and costs – up to 2 marks	
	Benefits – 1 mark per point up to 8 marks	
	Maximum	**8**
Professional marks		
	Maximum	**4**
Total		**50**

Examiner's comments

This 50-mark question was based around a supermarket chain with two divisions, one of smaller, city-centre stores and one of large supermarkets on the edge of cities.

Part (i) required an evaluation of the board's performance report, including how it fit the mission and strategy of the business. This part was generally well done. Candidates performed well when they used the signposts given in the scenario for specific issues to look for within the report.

Part (ii) required an evaluation of two new performance indicators again with regard to specific needs for the CEO. This part was often not done well as many candidates could not identify how the new measures fit with the specific strategy point that they were seeking to address. Also, candidates often did not pick up simple calculation marks by failing to recognise that they were working in $000s.

Part (iii) called for an assessment of a change to the divisional performance indicator. This was usually reasonably well done with candidates structuring their comments into criticism of the existing measure and then, analysis of how the proposed new measure would address these issues. Unfortunately, a number of candidates decided to focus their answer on a different new performance indicator of their own choosing and so they missed many marks.

Part (iv) required a calculation of the expected return of capital employed of a new store proposal and comment on this method of appraisal of such a project. This was often well done with many candidates scoring all marks available for the calculations although the commentary on the method was often lacking an appreciation of the circumstances in which 'expected' values are appropriate.

Also, many candidates ignored the advice to focus their answer on the concept of an 'expected' value for the indicator rather than offering a general discussion of the indicator.

Part (v) needed an explanation of how a new information system supporting a loyalty card would benefit the business' performance. This part was generally well done with most candidates showing an understanding of the information that such a system could provide and how that information could be used to improve performance.

As has become common, those candidates who had practised writing professional answers prior to the examination performed admirably in the presentation area (4 marks). The markers were looking for suitable report headings, an introduction, a logical structure, signposted by the good use of subheadings in the answer, and a clear, concise style.

4   MONZA (SEPT/DEC 16)

Key answer tips

A typical Section A question containing five clear requirements covering a range of syllabus areas. You have the common role of a performance management expert and have been asked to produce a report for the Board.

In part (i) to score a good mark you need to include examples relevant to Monza.

In part (ii) you should have identified that the proposed system was limited and deviated little from the current system.

Part (iii) was a more difficult requirement. Make sure that you plan your answer so that you have enough relevant points. Do not focus too much on the calculations.

A well prepared candidate should have scored well in part (iv), correctly analysing the costs into the four categories and discussing how TQM would impact each category.

(v) – Remember the importance of reviewing the technical articles on the ACCA website. An article was released a short time before the exam on this area.

Report

To: **The board of Monza**

From: **A. Accountant**

Date: **September 2016**

Subject: **Performance measurement and management issues at Monza**

This report addresses the problems of using the balanced scorecard within Monza. The current and proposed performance measures are evaluated and the main current measure is discussed in detail. Quality costs and the new quality programme at the manufacturing division are analysed. Finally, the lean philosophy is applied to the new information system for the drug development division.

(i)   Problems with using the balanced scorecard

The balanced scorecard (BSC) provides no aggregate or single summary measure of performance unlike the value-based approach. Also, there is no simple, direct link between shareholder value, the main objective of Monza, and the balanced scorecard measures.

The measures in the scorecard can conflict, for example, cost controls (financial perspective) can obstruct the investment needed in order to speed up manufacturing processes (internal business perspective). Overall, the measures should seek to align with the fundamental need to create shareholder value.

It can be difficult to select measures. In particular, there is the danger of losing sight of key information in a plethora of indicators. This may be an issue for Monza as it has only had three indicators in the past and this will now increase significantly (a potential of 12, if there is one for each level of management in the four perspectives).

There must be management commitment to the change to the scorecard. In particular, there must not be a return to a focus on the financial measures which have been used in the past at Monza. Management should acquire the expertise for understanding non-financial measures through training.

There are potentially significant costs in collecting the additional information which will be needed for the new performance measures. Many of the measures will be non-financial and so new information systems will be required to collect and record the data.

(ii)   **Choice of current and proposed performance measures**

Current measures

The current measures are all historic, financial ones and so the BSC approach will bring a longer term view by using non-financial measures which consider those factors which might drive future growth, for example, those in the learning and growth perspective. The current measures do not directly link to shareholder value which appears to be the overall aim of the company. A measure such as economic value added would do this more effectively.

The three measures do give a broad view of financial performance. ROCE is a widely-used measure which it should be possible to benchmark against competitors. As far as the divisions are concerned, there is a measure of success in selling through revenue growth, though this may not be due to only the sales division but also the drugs brought to market by the development division. Average cost to develop a new drug is a financial measure of the development division's performance but this does not measure its aim of innovation in development. Indeed, this measure may conflict with that aim as cost control of development may hinder innovative thinking. It would appear more appropriate to have a cost control measure associated with manufacturing as its goal is to be more efficient. The performance of the manufacturing division is only measured indirectly through its effect on the financial performance of the company as a whole.

Consultants' proposed measures

The suggested measures do not seem to deviate much from the existing measures, though there may be an advantage in this as the new system would be using existing information systems and known measures in that case. However, this advantage is secondary to the need to find measures which will drive useful performance in the four perspectives.

The proposed measures from the consultants' interim report mostly fit within the standard four perspectives of the BSC, although revenue growth is more appropriate as a measure from the financial perspective. Customer perspective measures should focus on the strategies which will achieve success in the eyes of the customers rather than just measuring the results of those strategies. Examples of this would be measuring the efficacy of the drugs which are developed by Monza or the reputation of Monza's medicines among the medical community.

Taking the others in turn, ROCE does not seem to be directly linked to shareholder value as, for example, economic value added or net present value would be. ROCE considers the performance over the whole capital base while the shareholders will be more directly concerned with returns on their equity investment. As a profit-based measure, ROCE may also be failing to target cash-generation which is ultimately driving dividend payments and value creation for shareholders.

As already indicated, cost control in business processes is important but other measures of success such as time to market for the development of new products and quality initiatives should also be considered.

The fourth perspective is particularly relevant to a high-technology firm such as Monza. There will be considerable competitive advantage in having a highly skilled workforce; however, the measure proposed is imprecise as it values all training days, whether for knowledge workers or unskilled labourers, as equally valuable. Measures of the number of innovations within each division may be appropriate as these will be qualitatively different (new compounds developed, manufacturing quality improvements and sales techniques/initiatives developed).

Overall, the initial proposed set of measures does appear limited and does not address the overall aim of Monza or the problem of the narrowness of the existing set of measures.

(iii) **Variation in calculating return on capital**

	ROCE	ROE
Using operating profit	18%	
Using operating profit before restructuring	23%	
Using profit after tax		97%

Return on capital employed is normally calculated by dividing operating profit by capital employed (debt and equity). The calculations above illustrate the possibilities using the different return (profit) and capital figures available.

The ROCE figure should not use gross profit as this ignores the operating costs not directly attached to sales and at Monza these will include significant overheads from the drug development and manufacturing divisions which are relevant to overall performance. The return figure should match with the capital used to generate that return. As ROCE is calculated based on the return on total capital, it should not include financing costs and so profit before and after tax are not consistent with this view. The one area that could be argued is whether to include the one-off costs of restructuring in performance. It would probably be best to disclose both figures to the company's stakeholders and to identify how any competitor would perform such a calculation for benchmarking.

A suitable approach for Monza

Return on equity (ROE) may be a more suitable measure given Monza's focus on shareholder (not debt provider) performance. In this case, the relevant return figure is the profit after tax as this is the return available to shareholders after the debt providers have been paid. The figure here (97%) is very large. This is due partly to the fact that the capital figures used in these calculations are from the financial statements and are not market values. (Market values of equity and debt would give a more accurate measure of performance both for ROCE and ROE.) Another reason why the ROE is large compared to ROCE is that Monza is highly geared (88%). ROE, therefore, demonstrates the benefit of the chosen capital structure of Monza.

Overall, therefore, ROE is a better measure than ROCE as it fits with the prioritisation of shareholders as opposed to all capital providers.

(iv)   Quality costs and total quality management at manufacturing division

Quality costs are usually broken into four categories:

- Prevention costs which relate to avoiding producing defective items in the first place

- Appraisal costs which relate to ensuring that the products produced meet an acceptable standard

- Costs of internal failure which relate to products which fail appraisal and how these are handled; and

- Costs of external failure which relate to products which fail the standard but are still shipped to customers.

At Monza, for the most recent period, the following quality costs have been identified:

Prevention costs – $8m (training)

Appraisal costs – $12m (product testing)

Costs of internal failure – $13m (batches rejected)

Costs of external failure – $27m = $5m (fines) + $22m (discounts for late delivery)

Total raw material costs might hide relevant quality costs if the company is buying higher quality material to prevent problems of quality, however, this cannot be quantified in this scenario.

It can be seen that there were $40m of failure costs in the period but only $8m was spent on prevention. A 10% improvement in the failures could generate $4m in cost savings and the budget for improvements to production which prevent such failures could be significantly expanded in light of this. The analysis of quality costs should help to emphasise the importance of prevention by showing its financial value and this is vital to motivate a total quality management (TQM) approach.

Impact of TQM on manufacturing division

Total quality management focuses on the customer perspective and the need for each part of the organisation to avoid defects in the chain of production. Prevention is the key to improvement and so management should focus on avoiding defects through training and improved process design rather than appraisal. All employees must accept personal responsibility for their work and act to remove defects from production. Quality certification programmes are often instituted in order to encourage the focus on 'zero defects'. Quality circles may be formed as small, autonomous groups aimed at devising solutions to quality problems.

(v)   Making the new information system 'lean' in drug development division

Lean systems aim to get the right thing to the right place at the right time, first time. They aim to reduce waste while being flexible. The need for flexibility will be important for the drug development division as it is constantly working in a changing environment.

The information in the system should be organised so that it can be retrieved with minimum difficulty. The information will also have to be accurate so that time is not wasted in making errors. The information should be presented clearly and, in particular, should not be excessive given the needs of the users. The information should be able to be exchanged easily. This will be important in a collaborative environment such as a research group in the development division.

Tutorial note

The 5Ss (Structurise, Systemise, Sanitise, Standardise, Self-discipline) could also be used to structure an acceptable answer.

	Marking scheme		
			Marks
(i)	Problems with using the balanced scorecard		
	Up to 2 marks per point if made relevant to Monza		
		Maximum	8
(ii)	Choice of current and proposed performance measures		
	Current measures – up to 6 marks		
	Proposed measures – up to 9 marks		
		Maximum	12
(iii)	Variation in calculating return on capital		
	Calculations – 3 marks for profit calculation of appropriate ROCE figures; 1 for doing ROE calculation; 1 for gearing		
	Maximum 5 marks		
	Discussion of ROCE – up to 5 marks		
	Discussion of ROE – up to 3 marks		
	Justified recommendation – 1 mark		
		Maximum	11
(iv)	Quality costs and TQM at manufacturing division		
	Discussion of categories of quality cost – up to 2 marks		
	Calculation/identification of quality costs – up to 3 marks		
	Discussion of results – up to 3 marks		
	Effect of TQM – up to 5 marks		
		Maximum	10
(v)	New information system		
	Aims of lean approach – up to 2 marks		
	Ways of achieving a lean system – up to 5 marks		
		Maximum	5
	Professional marks		4
			——
Total			50
			——

Examiner's comments

This 50-mark compulsory question was based around performance management and the potential introduction of new techniques and systems in a manufacturing company.

(i) asked for an assessment of the problems of using a particular management accounting technique. In questions of this nature, candidates should focus on the theoretical areas where they believe the problems lie and then try to exemplify or illustrate these problems by reference to the entity. What many candidates do – and unfortunately this is poor examination practice – is to address the question by discussing another technique that they have spent more of their time revising. Making a suggestion as to an alternative may be worth merit but nevertheless does not address the fundamental question asked, which is for an overall assessment of a specific technique. It is a fundamental requirement of any APM exam that candidates should know about performance management and control techniques and the challenges that may arise from their implementation.

(ii) asked for an evaluation of both the current measurements that the company was using and other measures suggested by consultants. This is an area where most candidates addressed the question asked though it is worthwhile emphasising as part of good examination practice in this paper that assessment of current measures in the light of their suitability as KPIs of the company's strategic direction is very different to asking for an assessment of performance. This is why it is always beneficial to spend time reading the question to ensure that the requirements are fully understood. It is also good practice to ensure that suggestions are justified and supported: it is very common for candidates to highlight, for example, that 'more non-financial indicators are needed' or 'they should measure liquidity' in a question of this type. Such comments are not worth merit unless supported by reference to such aspects as achievement of some of the company's specific objectives. A key focus of any analysis is the justification behind the points that are being made and it would be good examination practice for candidates to consider this in their revision and ask questions such as: why is that relevant?; how/why would it benefit the company? Candidates should also be aware of some of the language used in their analysis of techniques: of course financial figures are the result of accounting standards which can be interpreted in different ways but this does not mean that results are being deliberately 'manipulated.' Candidates should reserve their use of this word to instances where they feel there is intentioned malpractice.

(iii) asked for an evaluation of the usefulness of specific financial metrics. This question was poorly done as candidates did not demonstrate the technical knowledge that is expected at this level with regard to the composition of the measures of performance. As such, this is a very clear example of the difference between APM and PM and candidates have to be able to interpret the results that measures are producing. Too many candidates gave descriptions of measurements rather than an evaluation of usefulness. For future diets, candidates would be best suited to consider and reflect upon what the metrics and ratios they have learned might mean and consider how they might differ from each other. When might it be more appropriate to use one than the other? Which costs, for example, might some include and why might that be significant in terms of measurement and management? It is also, as with question (i) above, always best as a matter of good examination practice to respond about the metrics that the question asked candidates to consider. Justified alternatives, as with (i), may be of some merit but answers should always be directed to the question that was asked.

(iv) asked for an analysis of cost and the potential implementation of a new technique. Some basic technical knowledge was lacking in the analysis of costs and the marks awarded here were ones that should have been gained by most candidates. The implementation of a new technique was a part of the question that was generally well done as most candidates focused on specific areas around implementation and tried to relate these to the entity.

(v) asked for a consideration of the effect on a new information system on a method of production. This question was generally badly done as, again, most candidates did not apply the operation of the system to the production method. Most answers mentioned and explained only either the production method or the system when the requirement of the question was clear in that the two had to be considered in the light of the effect of one on the other. This is another example of application that candidates should consider in future diets and reinforces the fact that rote learned definitions, etc, do not address the demands of the learning outcomes of APM.

5 BOLTZMAN (DEC 14 – AMENDED)

Key answer tips

The scenario in this question is reasonably succinct with clear explanations of exactly what is and what is not required.

(i) This requirement is a test of knowledge (the detail of the Performance Pyramid must be known) but you are also expected to relate these back to the information in the scenario.

(ii) You should use Mendelow's matrix to analyse the company's stakeholders. In the second part of the requirement you are asked to evaluate the performance measures – therefore a balanced answer is required with both pros and cons.

(iii) An easy five calculation marks are available here. An evaluation of the approach to benchmarking is required, so again you would be expected to discuss pros and cons.

(iv) You should feel relatively comfortable with JIT but make sure that you come up with enough separate points and/ or add the required depth to your points.

To: **The board of Boltzman**

From: **A Accountant**

Date: **December 2014**

Subject: **A coherent approach to performance management at Boltzman**

This report brings the different initiatives together using the performance pyramid framework. The suggested performance measures are evaluated and then used in a benchmarking exercise of Boltzman compared to General Machines. Finally, the quality improvement initiative is commented upon.

(i) **Performance pyramid**

The performance pyramid shown below indicates how strategies to assist in the achievement of corporate vision may be cascaded down through four levels.

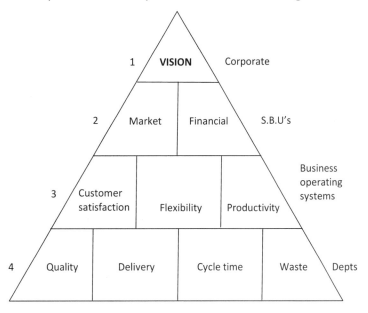

Level 1: At the top of the organisation is the corporate vision through which the organisation describes how it will achieve long-term success and competitive advantage.

Level 2: This focuses on the achievement of an organisation's CSFs in terms of market-related measures and financial measures. The marketing and financial success of a proposal is the initial focus for the achievement of corporate vision.

Level 3: The marketing and financial strategies set at level 2 must be linked to the achievement of customer satisfaction, increased flexibility and high productivity at the next level. These are the guiding forces that drive the strategic objectives of the organisation.

Level 4: The status of the level 3 driving forces can be monitored using the lower level departmental indicators of quality, delivery, cycle time and waste.

The left hand side of the pyramid contains measures which have an external focus and which are predominantly non-financial. Those on the right are focused on the internal efficiency of the organisation and are predominantly financial.

The analysis of stakeholder power will provide ideas on how the stakeholders can contribute to the success of Boltzman. For example, the relatively weak position of suppliers may lead Boltzman to be able to push them to make improvements to the quality of their components while maintaining the same selling prices. This impacts objectives for competitive strategy in level and will cascade down to quality measures in level 4.

The benchmarking exercise will help in setting strategies with which the business aims to achieve stakeholder satisfaction. It may identify strategies for improvement although here the data used will only give a strategic view, relevant for setting objectives and targets for level 2. However, as it is not operationally detailed, it is unlikely to supply much information for levels 3 and 4.

The quality initiative will impact primarily on level 3 – business operating systems. There will be a need to redesign processes in order to meet stricter quality standards. There will be a need to increase the capabilities of the organisation to manufacture with lower fault rates and at finer tolerances and this may come through greater emphasis on staff training to improve their capabilities or alternatively, through investment in the automation of processes to improve speed and accuracy of production. Each of these may impact objectives and KPIs set at levels 3 and 4.

(ii) **Stakeholder analysis**

The matrix suggests different management approaches are appropriate for each group of stakeholders, depending on their likelihood of engagement in decision-making and their ability to influence that decision-making.

Shareholders have considerable power but do not wish active involvement in decision-making (this is what they pay the management to handle). Therefore, they must be kept satisfied by ensuring their financial targets are met.

Employees have little power generally and so need to be kept informed. However, there is a sub-group of key employees with skills who the company must retain and this sub-group should be kept satisfied by the provision of opportunity to develop their skills through training and work on new technologies.

Customers are key players given the importance of our components to their business and the lost revenue if one were to drop us as a supplier. Therefore, they should be managed closely by having staff dedicated to liaising with them and involving them in product development. This type of close cooperation is likely to be necessary in high-technology industries such as ours.

Suppliers have little power and Boltzman should be in a position of strength in negotiation over the price and quality of their goods. They should require minimal effort and they would be expected to be doing the work to meet our needs as a major customer. However, suppliers are a common source of innovation, so keeping them informed of developments would be sensible. In particular, good supplier relations will be important for a move to JIT manufacturing.

Evaluation of suggested performance indicators

Performance measures should be focused on the influential stakeholders identified above.

It is appropriate that most of the indicators are directed towards the key players identified above. Return on capital employed, economic value added, revenue growth and net profit margin are all suitable measures for the shareholders as these measure financial returns across the organisation – its efficiency in deploying capital, its ability to grow sales and its efficiency in turning sales into returns for shareholders.

There are no indicators directed at customers who are key players. This is a major omission in the list of indicators suggested. It would be helpful to have indicators covering the price/quality mix of Boltzman's products and their innovative nature in such high-technology industry sectors. Also, there are no external measures of competitive advantage given in the list of indicators.

Average pay per employee is a poor indicator as this does not focus on the sub-group of key employees. It is appropriate to have an indicator for this group and it would be their average pay (possibly as a percentage of an industry benchmark) which would be valuable.

Suppliers do not have significant power or importance to Boltzman, being easily interchangeable. Therefore, it is appropriate that there is no indicator directed at them, although this will have to change as JIT is introduced.

(iii) **Benchmarking against General Machines**

Benchmarking method

The benchmarking exercise is an external one where comparison is drawn with a major competitor. This is valuable in identifying areas of the competitor's competitive advantage and also areas for improvement with a similar business. However, although this method can suggest areas where Boltzman can catch up with its major competitor, it will not identify how to gain advantage over General Machines.

Another fault in this method of benchmarking is that it will only indicate strategic improvements not operational ones, as such detailed information is unlikely to be in the public domain. It may be sensible to consider functional benchmarking with a world-class company from another business sector. Boltzman could share detailed operational data without the worry of loss of confidential information directly to a competitor. This is commonly done where quality initiatives, such as at Boltzman, are being introduced. Boltzman may find that its customers are already collecting process quality data and would be willing to share with a top tier supplier.

Benchmarking results

	Boltzman	General Machines
Return on capital employed	15.5%	9.2%
Economic value added ($m)		
Operating profit	2,907	1,882
Less tax charge	(663)	(718)
Less tax benefit of interest	(81)	(88)
	———	———
NOPAT	2,163	1,076
WACC	11%	11%
Capital employed	18,785	20,373
Economic value added (= NOPAT – rC)	97	(1,165)
Revenue growth	6.4%	1.0%
Average pay per employee ($ p.a.)	54,618	52,299
Net profit margin	8.2%	3.3%
Other indicators:		
Product development cost/Revenue	11.2%	10.2%
Top tier supplier status (out of possible 20)	13	14

Tutorial note

ROCE figures are based on year opening figures although year closing figures are acceptable. Credit was also given if adjustment of EVA for product development costs was considered.

Two new indicators have been suggested based on the previous analysis of stakeholders. It was identified that there was a major omission of measures associated with customers and so the level of product development spending and the company's status as a main supplier to large customers are considered. The product development indicator will demonstrate the potential for innovation in products and possible growth of the business. The supplier status gives a measure of the customers' perception of quality of the business's products.

The results suggest that Boltzman is doing better than General Machines financially (ROCE, economic value added and profit margin) and has better current and possibly future growth prospects (revenue growth being driven by higher product development spending). The one area of weakness identified relates to size where General Machines has a higher revenue and more top customer accounts but with the higher growth of Boltzman, this may not last long.

(iv)   JIT initiative

The JIT initiative will bring great benefits to Boltzman but will also place new demands on management in the business. It will fit well with the move to lean manufacturing.

The difficulties involved in introducing just-in-time manufacturing begin with the need to forecast demand accurately in order to time manufacture as required. This requires close links to our customers which should be possible given our status as a top tier supplier.

If we are only producing to order, then we can suffer if our own suppliers fail to make deliveries of sufficient quality and on time. The suppliers used at present are bulk suppliers and may not be used to the level of quality and ability to deliver on time which JIT requires. We will need to perform a detailed review of our supply chain in order to identify those suppliers who can meet our needs now, or else be brought up to that standard. We may then partner with a few suppliers in order to help them to improve their standards of service and quality of components.

By restricting the number of suppliers, we will be more open to disruption of our supply chain. We may wish to keep our suppliers local to the manufacturing sites but, of course, this restricts further our choice of supplier and so increases their bargaining power with us.

A further challenge will be the change in mind set which will come from moving to JIT where the focus of effort is no longer just on cost reduction but also on appreciation of the value of non-financial factors associated with quality. This change will have to occur throughout the organisation and is often most difficult at the operational level, where, for example, the basic layout of the factory must be redesigned and the workforce need to be flexible on working patterns and multi-skilled to avoid bottlenecks.

Marking scheme		
		Marks
(i)	4 marks for the general description of the pyramid levels. (**Note:** Diagram not essential) Up to 3 marks for the discussion of each initiative and how it fits within the pyramid	
	Maximum	9
(ii)	Up to 2 marks for analysis of each of the four stakeholders Up to 10 marks for evaluation of the five indicators suggested	
	Maximum	14
(iii)	Up to 6 marks for evaluating the method of benchmarking Calculations: 1 mark for each indicator calculated (up to 6 marks) except economic value added 3 marks for calculation of economic value added 1 mark for the justification of each of the two new indicators suggested Up to 3 marks for a reasonable conclusion	
	Maximum	16
(iv)	1 mark for identifying each difficulty of implementing JIT – additional marks where this is developed for Boltzman's situation.	
	Maximum	7
Professional presentation: up to 4 marks		4
Total		50

6   CANTOR (JUN 14)

Key answer tips

This question is broken down into five requirements testing a number of syllabus areas. The examiner is very clear about what he wants.

(i)   A common requirement asking you to evaluate the performance report. Be careful – you are expected to discuss the pros and cons of the report and not to evaluate the company's performance.

(ii)   Not a commonly examined syllabus area but you should be able to come up with a handful of relevant points here. Review the answer in detail if you are unsure of this requirement.

(iii) A typical EVA question – a reasonably straightforward calculation with only a handful of adjustments. Make sure you discuss your result and any assumptions.

(iv)   This requirement asks for an explanation and evaluation of VBM. You need to have your knowledge in place but be careful to tailor your answer to the question rather than simply writing down everything that you know about VBM.

(v)   In this requirement you are expected to work through the calculations quickly and focus on the difficulties in measuring the treatment of employees and in interpreting the results.

To: CEO

From: A Accountant

Date: June 2014

Subject: Performance reporting and value-based management at Cantor

This report evaluates the current performance reporting and cost structures of Cantor. It evaluates the impact of value-based management at Cantor calculating its current economic value added. Finally, recommendations for new performance measures for the new ethical area in the company's amended mission are made.

(i)   Current performance report

The current report has a number of strengths and weaknesses. These will be discussed according to whether the report:

- addresses the overall aims of the group

- assists the individual subsidiaries

- is well-presented

- contains appropriate information for decision-making.

The current mission of the group can be broken down into three parts:

- to maximise shareholder value

- supplying good value food and drink; and

- providing appealing environments for our customers.

The report does not directly measure shareholder value which could be done through considering net present value or economic value added (EVA™) or share price and dividends. This problem has been recognised and is addressed in a later section of this report. The current report uses period profits as its main measure of performance. This can suffer from being short term unlike the shareholder value measures mentioned. The report does compare budget and actual performance which gives an indication of whether plans are being followed and is helpful in controlling the organisation.

There is an indirect measure of the customer value being offered by the group through the gross profit which, when compared to the industry average, gives a partial measure of value but without data on the price/quality mix compared to competitors, it is difficult to be conclusive about this. Revenue growth compared to industry growth would aid in giving an impression of the attractiveness of our offering to the customer. However, no historic information is given which would allow trends to be calculated.

Measuring the appeal of the sites to customers will be difficult and involve subjective non-financial measurements. Customer loyalty and price elasticity of demand will give some indication of the appeal but it will be difficult without directly surveying customers to untie this from the issues of price/quality mentioned above.

The main board would probably find it easier if less detailed figures were given and a clear statement of the key measures of subsidiary performance provided.

The report seems to treat the subsidiaries in the same way as the group, using profit and comparison to industry average margins and budgets as the main assessment tools. As already mentioned, the reporting of performance against budget is a helpful control tool. However, as the subsidiaries will have more detailed issues than the group, it does not seem appropriate to be using the same high-level overview as for the group board. For the subsidiaries, it would be expected that there would be a more detailed breakdown of revenues and gross margins by product line. Marketing, which is a significant cost, is not attributed to specific sites/products which would help to explain the changes in these categories. The subsidiary managers would probably benefit from the inclusion of a breakdown of profit by geographical region as well. It would seem that the measure being used to assess subsidiary performance would be the operating profit, which is appropriate as it contains the elements of performance controllable by the subsidiaries' managers. The annual reporting period would also appear to be too lengthy to allow the detailed control of operations required by the subsidiary boards.

In terms of presentation, the data is clear and in a form which would be easily recognisable to those used to reading accounts. However, it is common to provide a narrative commentary with such a report in order to highlight the key features in the report, such as major deviations from the budget or performance well outside industry norms. The report could be made easier to read by rounding all figures to thousands and thus removing unnecessary detail.

To summarise, additional information which could be supplied in the report also includes:

- historic information to demonstrate trends (especially important at Juicey with its fast growth)

- greater detail by product or site to aid the managers of the subsidiaries

- competitor information relating to their performance in the three areas of Cantor's mission (shareholder value, product value, site appeal).

(ii) Cost structures

The costs at Cafes and Juicey are a mix of fixed and variable. Fixed costs represent a risk to Cantor since if there is a fall in the general economy, these must still be covered by revenues. So, a breakeven analysis would be helpful in this situation. The difficulty with such an analysis is that some costs are partly fixed and partly variable.

Staff costs are likely to be part-fixed and part-variable. As these represent a significant part of the cost base, it will be necessary to establish what element is fixed (how many staff are the minimum required to run a site?) and what element is variable (how many staff can be used as needed when the sites are busy?). This cost area will be managed through decisions over the balance of the numbers of permanent and casual staff with casual staff being used to manage fluctuations in business.

Rent costs affect each subsidiary differently. At Cafes, rent is fixed and this is appropriate for a mature, established business where revenues ought to be predictable and so the fixed nature of the cost should not threaten the survival of the operation. At Juicey, the rent is a percentage of revenue and in a new operation this is appropriate as the rent will grow with the business.

However, the percentage demanded will reflect the risk which the landlord is taking on the success of Juicey and so will be higher than a fixed rent such as negotiated by Cafes. As Juicey becomes established, it may be worth considering beginning to move to negotiating fixed rental deals for Juicey in order to cut this cost.

This last point illustrates the dilemma which many businesses face in thinking about the balance of fixed and variable costs. Variable costs are more desirable as they do not threaten the survival of the business but they are often higher than a fixed cost deal.

(iii) Economic value added

	$
Operating profit	10,852,970
Add back	
Marketing capitalised	3,819,000
Less	
Tax paid	2,100,000
Lost tax relief on interest	200,250
	—————
NOPAT	12,371,720
Capital employed	
At 2014 year start	53,400,000
Marketing spend capitalised	3,819,000
	—————
Adjusted capital employed	57,219,000

WACC $= (1/1.3 \times 15.7\%) + (0.3/1.3 \times 6.5\% \times (1 - 25\%))$

$= 13.2\%$

EVA™ $= $ NOPAT $- $ (WACC $\times$ Capital employed)

$= 4,818,812$

The EVA™ of Cantor for 2014 was $4.82m, showing this was added to shareholder value over the period by the group. The result reflects the fact that the group is comfortably exceeding its cost of capital.

This calculation is limited by the information available and a number of approximations and assumptions have had to be made. One approximation is that the accounting depreciation charge represents the economic depreciation suffered by the company. A more detailed examination would be required in order to check this against the full version of the EVA™ calculation. The marketing spend is partially capitalised to the extent that it represents a long-term investment in the brand name of Cantor. Further work should be done to identify if this long-term marketing spending requires to be amortised and so charged back against NOPAT; the capital employed calculation gives an illustration of how the year start figure might be affected but all prior years with their related amortisation would need to be considered for a full answer.

It may prove useful for the subsidiaries' performance management to collect data and calculate their individual EVA™s.

Tutorial note

Credit would be given for narrative comment or illustrative adjustment for marketing spend on capital employed. The calculation of EVA™s is discussed in a two-part article entitled 'Economic value added versus profit-based measures of performance'.

(iv)   Value-based management

VBM begins from the view that the value of a company is measured by its discounted future cash flows. The idea being that value is only created when companies generate returns which beat their cost of that capital. VBM then focuses the management of the company on those areas which create value. A key to this process is the identification of the drivers of value and then a concentration of effort at all levels (strategic, tactical and operational) on these drivers in order to increase the value of the firm.

The implementation will broadly involve four steps:

1   A strategy is developed to maximise value.

2   Key value drivers must be identified and then performance targets (for both the short and long term) are defined for those value drivers.

3   A plan is developed to achieve the targets.

4   Performance metrics and reward systems measurement and incentive systems are created compatible with these targets.

At Cantor, these steps might include a strategy of acquisition and disposal to go alongside the organic growth of Juicey. The key value drivers for each operating subsidiary would have to be identified from strategic to operational levels and these could include gross margins (strategic) and site service levels (operational). Targets must then be developed from these measures – possibly by benchmarking against competitors.

The impact for Cantor would be the introduction of new performance measures based on the drivers and a reward system to motivate staff. There will be the need to develop such measures, targets and reward at the group level, then at the subsidiary level and, finally, at the individual site level in order to ensure full coordination of the system across Cantor. In order to align the interests of employees and management with shareholder value, a feature of the new reward system is often a share-based payment scheme.

The key benefits of VBM are the focus on value as opposed to profit, so reducing the tendency to make decisions which have positive short-term impact but may be detrimental in the long term. VBM thus will help to make Cantor more forward looking.

A danger of the VBM exercise is that it becomes an exercise in valuing everything but changing nothing. It is important that the detailed operational issues of the organisation are addressed through the new measures/targets. A further difficulty in implementation is that the measurement of the key value drivers can often involve non-financial indicators and these can represent a significant change for accounting-based management information systems.

(v)   Measurement of treatment of employees

The measurement of treatment of employees is difficult due to its subjective nature. The organisation will constantly be in negotiation with the employees as they have conflicting aims, for example, over pay rates and workloads. The information in the appendices allows a number of measures to be calculated which could provide some indication of employee satisfaction and treatment.

	Cafes	Juicey	Group
Average employee numbers	1,498	106	1,624
Employee turnover rates	9.7%	14.2%	9.9%

Using staff costs and employee numbers, the average pay at Cantor is $13,143 (= 21.345m/1,624) and this could be compared to competitors. The comparative information is not given in the reports at present, although an indication is given through the staff cost margin which shows Cantor paying a slightly higher proportion of revenue than the industry average. However, caution must be taken with such a measure as it is an average and does not necessarily reflect the position of many individual employees.

The staff numbers data also allows calculation of staff turnover rates as 9.9% (= 161/1,624) at the group as a whole and 9.7% at Cafes and 14.2% at Juicey. This indicates staff satisfaction and the variation between Cafes and Juicey should be investigated. It may be due to the learning curve which managers are experiencing in the fast growing and newer operation.

Tutorial note

Using year-end figures is acceptable too in this case.

	Marking scheme		
			Marks

(i)	1 mark per point – must be based on the scenario information
	For example:
	    Assessment of whether report meets mission
	    Appropriateness of the level of detail for the three boards
	    Use of budgets
	    Use of industry averages		

		Maximum	15
(ii)	1 mark per point		
		Maximum	6
(iii)	EVA Calculation:		
	Marketing		1
	Tax		2
	Capital employed – marketing		1
	WACC		1
	EVA result		1
	Comments:		
	Result		1
	Assumptions	up to	3
			—
		Maximum	9
			—
(iv)	VBM General description of VBM up to 2 marks Description and impact of implementation of VBM up to 10 marks		
		Maximum	10

(v)	Calculations – up to 3 marks
	1 mark per point on areas such as
	    difficulty of measuring
	    pay rates
	    staff turnover		

		Maximum	6
Professional marks:			
Introduction and report headings			1
Use of suitable subheadings in report			1
Clarity and language use			2
Conclusion (not required here but given if reasonably attempted)			1
			—
		Maximum	4
			—
Total			50
			—

Examiner's comments

This 50-mark question was based around a national, listed food and drink retailer, Cantor. Cantor had two operating subsidiaries.

In part (i), most candidates performed reasonably well. There were a number of candidates who provided an irrelevant evaluation of the performance of Cantor. Those who attempted the question asked scored most of the marks associated with such reports in general but few scored marks that were present in appreciating the scenario surrounding Cantor.

In part (ii) most candidates knew what fixed and variable costs were and had some ability in applying these to the scenario information. However, very few showed sensitivity to the performance management aspects of operational gearing.

Part (iii) was generally well done. Two areas that demonstrated weak performance though were calculations of WACC and in selecting the capital employed. Finally, many candidates stated the assumptions rather than 'justifying' them.

In part (iv) the problem for the majority of candidates was lack of knowledge with many vaguely talking of value without an understanding of it in the context of the scenario.

In part (v) a number of points were not understood; firstly, comments about the existing mission statement were irrelevant. Secondly, the requirement asked for justified performance measures and so a list of points was of limited value. Finally, the requirement stated the answer should use the 'information in the appendices'.

7 JHK COFFEE MACHINES CO (JUN 11 – AMENDED)

Key answer tips

In part (a) make sure you focus on *divisional* performance measures and their relative strengths and weaknesses. Try to include a discussion of the different profit figures that could be used and issues such as controllable v uncontrollable costs.

In parts (b) and (c) ensure you back up your commentary with adequate supporting calculations.

In part (d) make sure you focus on making comments about the impact of the new system on performance management not the specific difficulties in initial implementation of the system.

(a) To: **Finance Director**

     From: **A Accountant**

     Date: **June 2011**

     Subject: **Divisional performance issues at JHK and the introduction of a new information system**

This report examines recent divisional performance issues. It begins by evaluating the performance of each division and offering a general consideration of the different measures of divisional performance.

The nature of transfer prices and suitable methods of transfer pricing the work of the service division back into the main manufacturing and sales division are reviewed. Finally, the impact of a unified corporate database and improved information systems are considered.

Divisional performance evaluation

	Manufacturing & Sales	Service
Controllable return on investment	30%	16%
(Operating profit/Capital employed)		
Residual income ($m)	270	3
(Operating profit less notional interest charge)		
Non-controllable return on investment	23%	13%
(PBT/Capital employed)		
EVA™ ($m)	158	1.1
NOPAT – WACC*Capital employed		
Operating profit	386	6.0
Add: other non-cash expenses	4	0.3
Less: Tax	116	1.8
NOPAT	274	4.5

WACC – used notional interest rate

Both divisions are performing well. They make a healthy return on investment although we have no target rate with which to compare them. Also, both divisions make a positive residual income and economic value added which again implies healthy returns.

Divisional performance measures

The appropriate return on investment (controllable ROI) is calculated on profit before interest and tax divided by capital employed at the division. The profit figure excludes allocated head office costs as these are not controllable at divisional level. The residual income takes the same profit figure but subtracts a notional interest charge based on the capital employed by the division. Both divisions are offering good returns with positive RI and high controllable ROI, although there would normally be a target ROI set in order to compare to actual performance. The target would have to exceed the 9% cost of capital as it does not take account of necessary head office costs.

ROI is a simple, commonly used measure of divisional performance. However, it can encourage divisions to delay investment in new assets since this measure improves as assets are depreciated with age. RI offers the possibility of applying different costs of capital to divisions with different risk profiles. However, RI does not allow a clear comparison of performance between divisions since it is an absolute measure of performance.

Both ROI and RI have the disadvantage of being based on profit measures of performance rather than cash. Measures such as NPV use cash flows which are less subject to the interpretation of accounting rules and are more directly aligned with shareholder interests.

It is unclear that either of these measures will align with the overall performance measure of TSR, since it depends on share price and dividends paid.

EVA™ is an absolute performance measure like RI. It involves a more complex calculation than RI with many adjustments to the accounting figures of profit and net assets, such as the use of replacement costs for asset values and economic depreciation rather than accounting depreciation. (Here, the calculated figures are an estimate using the available information.)

Many of the EVA™ adjustments are intended to avoid distortion of results by accounting policies that are present in ROI and RI. Thus, EVA™ is more directly aligned with the objective of increasing shareholder wealth and so should help to ensure that there is congruence between the divisional and corporate goals. EVA™, like RI, has the advantage that by treating certain costs as investments it encourages appropriate capital expenditure.

However, EVA™ depends on historical data while shareholders will be focused on future performance. Unlike ROI, EVA™ and RI would not help to judge relative divisional performance at JHK as the divisions are not of similar size and so an absolute measure is not comparable.

(b)   Transfer pricing

The transfer price is the price that the service division would charge to the manufacturing and sales division for its warranty servicing for which it would otherwise not receive any income. The objective of a transfer pricing system is to allow divisional management to be assessed on the basis of divisional profit and so provide them with motivation while retaining their autonomy.

The transfer price should be set so that the decisions of the divisions individually are beneficial to the company as a whole but still represent a fair position for both divisions. If divisions are in different tax regimes then the transfer price should minimise the overall company tax liability within the law.

The general rule for goal congruent decision-making is that transfer prices should be set with reference to the opportunity cost of sale to the selling division (service division) and the opportunity cost to the buying division (manufacturing and sales division). There are different situations if there is surplus capacity or a capacity constraint in the service division or if there is an external market for the service, since these affect the opportunities available to the divisions.

(c)   The two different methods of pricing the service division's work are now considered.

Market based pricing

The service division could consider an external market price since there is the opportunity to outsource and therefore, its managers would charge $200. This would generate a reduced divisional profit to the company of $0.59m from the warranty work as opposed to the profit from the current agreement of $2.67m (see appendix for working). Thus it would still provide motivation for the service division to take the warranty work.

However, there would be savings if the work were kept internal to JHK, such as the overhead of negotiating and managing the contract with the local engineering firm. Doing the work internally would save these costs and so, a market price adjusted down for these savings would be appropriate. There is also the danger of outsourcing the service function in that the company loses control of a strategically important part of its offering to customers. It is clear that the warranty is a key selling point for JHK and it may not be able to control the quality of the repair work if this is outsourced.

A market price will guide the service division to the right decision on whether to continue to do the warranty work in-house or whether to outsource it and free capacity for other opportunities. If external work offers a better contribution than warranty work, the service division will automatically do external work. It will also measure profits at market-based prices. Thus, this method will provide motivation without a price being imposed by head office.

The volume and profitability of external work that may be available to the service division should also be investigated. If this were more profitable than internal work then this would suggest that the service division should prioritise this work and outsource if there is a lack of capacity to cover the internal work. It should be noted that the current quote from the outsourcer demands a minimum volume of work and so their work may need to be repriced.

Cost based pricing

The work could also be charged on the basis of the cost to the service division. The variable cost is $135 on average per repair and so the $10m contract represents a contribution for the division of $4,654k (based on the expected 39,600 repairs per year). This represents a divisional profit of $2,674k (see appendix for working).

The work could be charged at variable cost but then there would be no contribution to the service division's profits and so no incentive for the service division to do this work. It would, therefore, prioritise external sales over internal ones.

If a breakeven divisional profit was desired then a price of $185 per repair should be charged as this covers fixed overheads in the division. Although it would not contribute to head office costs, service division managers would still be motivated to perform the warranty work. M/S division managers would accept any cost below the alternative of $200 per repair for outsourcing the work.

It may be worth comparing a cost plus approach with the existing agreement. The service division would have to charge $253 per repair in order to make the same divisional profit as it enjoys under the current agreement.

Current pricing method

The current fixed price charge provides a contribution to the division's fixed costs which will incentivise the service division. However, this may cause problems in quality since it is not related to the volume of work done by service and if there were a much higher number of repairs than expected then the service division might compromise quality in order to control costs.

(d) **New information system**

The executive information system (EIS) will bring a number of benefits in decision-making at the strategic level at JHK but at certain costs and with certain problems.

The benefits relate to improved decision-making as the EIS should allow drill-down access to the more detailed operational records but the initial presentation of data should be based on the key performance indicators for the company. This system should also be linked to external data sources so that senior management do not fall into the trap of only looking inwards in the organisation at the risk of ignoring wider issues in the business environment (for example, the demand for external servicing work and market prices of this work).

The new system will increase the amount of information and analysis that it will be possible for senior managers to perform. It will present opportunities for better decision-making using the more up-to-date information. However, it may present the problem of information overload for managers. Therefore, the system will need to be designed to give access to only those areas that it is appropriate for any given manager to see.

The data used in decision-making will be more robust as a single database will reduce the problem of redundancy where multiple copies of the same data are held on different systems. This will remove the danger of inconsistencies and reduce the storage required by the company.

The EIS would allow access to decision support systems such as large spreadsheet models built in order to pull data out of the database for use in forecasting and appraising projects (for example, warranty repairs forecasting is important for the current fixed fee contract between the sales and service divisions).

The EIS will also give access to tactical information such as budgets in order to help the executive control the business.

In order to gain the maximum benefit from the new system, executive managers will need to be trained and this training should occur just before the new system is available so that they are in a position to use it immediately.

Overall, the new system should provide valuable information if used correctly but the cost of the system must be weighed against the benefits of the system which will be mostly intangible and so difficult to measure (e.g. improved decision-making).

(e) It is important that the new Executive Information system captures both internal and external information in order to allow appropriate business decisions. The types of external information may include details on competitor offerings such as machine features as well as information about the service provided, for example extended warranties.

It would also be useful to collate customer feedback about the products and services offered by JHK and incorporate this information into the system to track any changes in customer requirements. This would enable JHK to modify their machines if necessary.

As JHK is looking into providing warranty repair services for other companies, they should also collect information on other service providers in this area. It would be particularly important at this stage to understand the industry pricing to ensure the price offered by the local engineering company remains competitive. This would need to be combined with information regarding the cost of performing this service.

In conclusion of the report, the two suggested divisional performance measures do not align with the overall corporate strategy and it is recommended that the company use EVA™ as a more appropriate measure of performance. The current method of transfer pricing gives a good contribution to fixed costs in the service division but may not encourage both divisions to perform optimally from the perspective of the whole company. Further work needs to be undertaken to investigate the possibility of obtaining an additional stream of outside revenue for the service division.

Appendix:

	$
Labour (per repair)	36
Variable divisional overhead (per repair)	24
Fixed divisional overhead (per repair)	50
Parts	75
So	
Variable cost (per repair)	135
Total cost (per repair)	185

Number of repairs per year

440,000 units where 9% need repairing every three years. Given continuous production, this means in total 39,600 will need warranty repairs each year.

	Current recharge agreement $000	Market pricing $000
Revenue	10,000	7,920
Variable costs	5,346	5,346
Contribution	4,654	2,574
Fixed costs	1,980	1,980
Divisional profit (before head office costs)	2,674	594

Cost plus prices

To give equivalent contribution to current recharge agreement	10m/39,600 = $252.53
To cover variable costs	5.346m/39,600 = $135.00
To give breakeven contribution to the division	(10m – 2.674m)/39,600 = $185.00

	Marking scheme		Marks

<table>
<tr><td>(a)</td><td colspan="2">7 marks for calculation of ROI, RI and EVA.
4 marks for ROI and RI: 1 for use of controllable profit; 1.5 for ROI and 1.5 for RI.
3 marks for EVA:</td><td></td></tr>
<tr><td></td><td colspan="2">Other non-cash expenses</td><td>0.5</td></tr>
<tr><td></td><td colspan="2">Tax</td><td>0.5</td></tr>
<tr><td></td><td colspan="2">Depreciation treatment</td><td>0.5</td></tr>
<tr><td></td><td colspan="2">NOPAT</td><td>0.5</td></tr>
<tr><td></td><td colspan="2">WACC used</td><td>0.5</td></tr>
<tr><td></td><td colspan="2">EVA</td><td>0.5</td></tr>
<tr><td></td><td colspan="2">Up to 2 marks for assessment of performance from the calculated numbers.
Up to 3 marks for comments on each measure.</td><td>____</td></tr>
<tr><td></td><td></td><td>Maximum</td><td>15</td></tr>
<tr><td>(b)</td><td colspan="2">Transfer pricing system
Up to 5 marks on transfer pricing system, 1 mark per point.</td><td>5</td></tr>
<tr><td>(c)</td><td colspan="2">Calculations</td><td></td></tr>
<tr><td></td><td colspan="2">Number of warranty repairs pa</td><td>1</td></tr>
<tr><td></td><td colspan="2">Costs per repair</td><td>2</td></tr>
<tr><td></td><td colspan="2">Contribution under current agreement</td><td>1</td></tr>
<tr><td></td><td colspan="2">Contribution with market price</td><td>1</td></tr>
<tr><td></td><td colspan="2">Prices for breakeven under cost plus</td><td>3</td></tr>
<tr><td></td><td></td><td></td><td>____</td></tr>
<tr><td></td><td></td><td>Maximum</td><td>8</td></tr>
<tr><td></td><td></td><td></td><td>____</td></tr>
<tr><td></td><td colspan="2">Transfer pricing commentary
Up to 5 marks on evaluating transfer pricing at JHK.</td><td></td></tr>
<tr><td></td><td></td><td>Maximum for (c)</td><td>12</td></tr>
<tr><td></td><td></td><td></td><td>____</td></tr>
<tr><td>(d)</td><td colspan="2">Up to 5 marks for benefits. Up to 6 marks for problems.</td><td></td></tr>
<tr><td></td><td></td><td>Maximum</td><td>10</td></tr>
<tr><td>(e)</td><td colspan="2">1 mark per point</td><td>4</td></tr>
<tr><td></td><td colspan="2">Up to 4 professional marks</td><td>4</td></tr>
<tr><td></td><td></td><td></td><td>____</td></tr>
<tr><td>Total</td><td></td><td></td><td>50</td></tr>
<tr><td></td><td></td><td></td><td>____</td></tr>
</table>

8   METIS RESTAURANTS (JUN 12 – AMENDED)

Key answer tips

This question, concerning the performance reporting and management at a restaurant, looks at the core APM issues of assessing and improving existing performance reporting, calculating and evaluating the use of certain performance measures and considering how measurement and reporting impact on management.

In Part (a) make sure you answer the question set- you were asked to assess and suggest improvements to the existing (poor) board report in terms of its content and presentation. The question did not ask you to 'critically assess the performance of Metis'!

Part (b) is a strong reminder of the need to be able to perform key calculations from material covered in PM.

In part (c) the key was to relate your points back to the specific issues mentioned in the scenario.

To: J Sum

From: A Accountant

Date: 8 June 2012

Subject: Performance reporting and management at Metis

This report assesses the existing performance reporting at Metis and suggests improvements and new measures of performance in the business. Additionally, it considers the impact that performance measurement has on management activity.

(a) Current performance report

The existing performance report has some good elements and many weaknesses. The current report shows clearly the calculation of profit and the profit margin from the business and shows how this has changed over the past three years along with a forecast of the next year. There is also a breakdown of the performance in the last two quarters which gives a snapshot of more immediate performance. The report breaks revenue and costs into product categories and so might allow a review of selling and procurement activities.

However, there are a number of weaknesses with the existing report. Firstly, the report only clearly answers the question 'what was the profit?' The owners have indicated that their aim is to 'make money' and it is possible that making money and profit may not be entirely compatible in the short term. For example, there are no cash measures of performance on the report. These are likely to assume greater importance given the planned improvements and any long-term expansion of the business. The owners might wish to consider refining their long-term goal in order to make it a more precise statement.

The current report does not present its information clearly. There is too much unnecessary information (e.g. the detail on operating costs). The style of presentation could easily be confusing to a non-accountant as it shows a large table of numbers with few clear highlights. The use of more percentage figures rather than absolute numbers may help (e.g. gross margins, change on comparative period percentages). Also, the numbers are given to the last $ where it would probably be sufficient to work in thousands of dollars.

The current report does not break down conveniently according to the functional areas over which each owner-manager has control. It summarises the overall build-up of profit but, for example, it cannot be easily used to identify performance of the service staff except indirectly through growth in total revenue. In order to improve this aspect of the report, the critical success factors associated with each functional area will need to be identified and then suitable performance measures chosen. For example, Sheila's area is customer-facing and so a measure of customer satisfaction based on number of complaints received or changes over time in average scores in customer surveys would be helpful. Bert's area is kitchen management and so staff efficiency (measured by number of meals produced per staff hour) and wastage control (measured by gross margin) may be critical factors. In your own financial and legal areas, costs are mostly fixed and so absolute measures such as the cost of capital may be helpful. In the area of procurement, purchasing the appropriate quality of food and drink for the lowest price is critical and so a gross margin for each product category would aid management.

The timescales reported in the current format are possibly not helpful for quarterly meetings. The existing report shows evidence of seasonality in the large change between Q3 and Q4 performance (42% fall in revenue).

The figures for two years ago may not be particularly relevant to current market conditions and will not reflect recent management initiatives. It may be useful to consider reporting the last quarter's monthly performance giving comparative figures from the previous year and drop the use of the detailed 2010 and 2011 figures in favour of just supplying net profit figures for those years in order to give an overview of long-term performance.

The current report does not give much benchmark data to allow comparisons in order to better understand the results. It would be helpful to have budget figures for internal comparison and competitor figures for an external comparison of performance. Such external data is often difficult to obtain although membership of the local trade association may give access to a suitably anonymised database provided Metis is willing to share its data on the same basis.

Finally, the current document only reports financial performance. I have already indicated that this may not be sufficient to capture the critical factors that drive the business. A restaurant will be judged on the service and quality of its products as well as its pricing. It would be an improvement to include this style of reporting although gathering reliable data on these non-financial areas is more demanding.

(b) Revenue has grown significantly over the last three years which is to be expected for a relatively new business. Overall growth is 58% since the first year and this has been consistently achieved across all revenue sources.

A rather more conservative 9% growth has been forecast for the coming year which is in line with the slower progress made between 2011 to 2012. As Metis begins to measure both quality and service as well as financial performance it may identify areas where further improvements can be made.

Metis has achieved a healthy gross margin of 66% in each of its first three years. Although this can be commended, it may now be appropriate for the company to investigate ways of improving the margin further. As the business is growing in size it may be possible to secure greater volume discounts on many of its supplies which would serve to improve the gross profit.

It would be particularly beneficial to obtain better prices for the food supplies as this represents approximately 60% of the total cost of sales each year.

A significant amount of money was spent in the first year on marketing. This is to be expected in the first year of a business as the company tries to create awareness of its presence. This naturally fell in the following two years but another significant amount is forecast for next year. It is important that the company is clear what this money will be spent on as it is concerning that the additional marketing is not reflected in a larger increase in sales. Other costs have risen broadly in line with inflation which is to be expected although again the company could investigate whether there is any scope for savings to be made.

(c) **Summary of results:**

Net profit after tax (2012)	$163,046
EVA™ (2012)	$108,626
Return on capital employed (2012)	44%
Return on Equity (2012)	65%
NPV over the three years of the business	$(78,987)
MIRR over the three years of the business	6.75%

The business is currently performing well generating healthy after tax profit for the owners and a positive EVA™, which implies the business is adding value for the shareholders.

The NPV and MIRR measures do not look healthy as normally a business would seek only investments that returned positive NPV values or a MIRR above the cost of capital (12.5% for Metis). However, these are measures that take account of the first three years trading and so include the understandably weak opening year's performance when the business was building up. They may provide a long-term view of historic performance but are less helpful in judging the current state of the business. You may want to view the goal of reaching nil NPV as a long-term target for the business so at least meeting its cost of capital (in fact it looks like the business will achieve this in the next year).

(d) **'What gets measured, gets done'**

The idea behind the quote, 'What gets measured, gets done' is that the staff and management will only react to the performance measures chosen by the owners. In other words, poor performance reporting can lead to inefficient management. If an area is not measured then there is a danger that it is not efficiently managed and equally, if an area is measured then there is the danger that it is over-managed. For example, the current report has annual revenue and the previous two quarters' revenues reported, therefore, it might promote the idea that quarterly growth is critical. However, it is likely that the business is seasonal and so it would be more helpful to have a comparison of each quarter with the equivalent quarter in the previous year. Otherwise, the owners may react to a fall in revenue shown when this is not controllable.

Further examples of the quote are given in the areas that the owners are complaining about in their meetings. Sheila has complained that the staff are not smiling enough but there is no measure of customer satisfaction available in the current report and so no way to quantify or substantiate this concern. This has resulted in Bert's dismissive comment.

However, the control of electricity costs can be seen in the slowing growth of the utilities cost on the current report (the annual increase has fallen from 3% to 0.5% pa in the last two years) and so the effectiveness of Sheila's actions can be demonstrated although the use of monetary totals and lack of these trend figures would mean that this is not immediately obvious. Bert's criticism of her work can at least be partially answered and so she can be encouraged to continue with these ideas.

Bert has complained that there is too much wastage of food and that he is devoting considerable staff time on instinct without solid information. The problem is additionally complicated as it may be caused by purchasing lower cost but poor quality produce or it could be caused by how the produce is handled and stored in the kitchen. The first cause is an issue for procurement, which is not Bert's area of responsibility, and so any actions of his are unlikely to address the problem. The report needs to identify changes in gross margin which might indicate changes in procurement policy and it should also have a measure of wastage such as the average actual cost of food per dish served compared to a budgeted cost of food per dish.

The quote may not be entirely applicable as management may still take action out of other motivations such as the results from training or personal motivation to demonstrate their own skills.

However, the quote is intended to bring into focus the fact that many people will tend to focus effort on the explicit measures of their performance.

In conclusion, as Metis grows it will need to refine its performance reporting so that management become more efficient in focusing their work on areas which will achieve the business' objectives.

Workings:

	Year to 31 March		
	2010	*2011*	*2012*
	Actual	*Actual*	*Actual*
PBIT	31,200	199,579	262,322
Interest	29,400	29,400	29,400
PBT	1,800	170,179	232,922
Tax	540	51,054	69,877
PAT	1,260	119,125	163,046
Cash flows			
PBIT	31,200	199,579	262,322
Tax on operating cash flows	9,360	59,874	78,697
Depreciation	120,000	120,000	120,000
Free cash flows	141,840	259,705	303,626

NPV

Consider the business as a three-year project to date based on an initial investment of $600,000

	2010	*2011*	*2012*
PV as at 2012 at 12.5%	179,516	292,169	303,626
			gives a total of $775,310

PV of initial investment at 2012 $600,000 \times (1 + 12.5\%)^3 = \$854,297$

Hence NPV at 2012 = $–78,987

Tutorial note

The NPV calculation if done for the start of project, would read –

Consider the business as a three-year project to date based on an initial investment of $600,000.

	2010	2011	2012
PV as at start of project at 12.5%	*126,080*	*205,199*	*213,246*

gives a total of $544,525

Hence NPV at start of project = $–55,475.

This yields similar comments as in the model solution.

MIRR

PV of investment at start of business $600,000

Terminal values of returns from the project to date (2012)

	2010	2011	2012	Total
At 4.5%	154,892	271,392	303,626	729,910

MIRR is discount rate at which the terminal value of the return phase equates to the present value of the investment phase. So 600,000 = 729,910 × 1/(1 + MIRR)^3

MIRR = 6.75%

EVA

EVA™ = NOPAT – Capital employed × WACC = $108,626

Where NOPAT = $183,626

ROCE 43.72%

ROE 65.22% (PAT/Equity invested)

Notes:

- Accounting depreciation has been assumed to be equal to economic depreciation in the calculation of NOPAT.

- Although marketing expenditure can generate a long-term intangible asset and so could be considered capital rather than revenue expenditure in the EVA™ calculation and adjusted for accordingly. However, a more prudent approach has been taken to treat it as a period cost in these calculations since it is stated to be only for short- term purposes.

- The NPV is taken to be for the present value (2012). It could be taken as at the start of the project (then a previous value is calculated as at the start of the project).

			Marks
Marking scheme			
(a)	Strengths of current reporting: 1 mark per point	up to	3
	Weaknesses of current reporting: 1 mark per point	up to a maximum of	12
	Measuring overall objective		
	Data overload		
	Use of absolute numbers		
	Breakdown by functional area		
	Timescales used in report		
	Use of NFPIs		
	Other acceptable points		
		Maximum	**15**
(b)	Calculation of ratios and trends: 1 mark per pair	up to	2
	Comments on performance: 1 mark per point	up to a maximum of	6
	Revenue growth		
	Margin analysis		
	Other cost analysis		
		Maximum	**6**
(c)	Calculations		
	NPV		
	Deriving free cash flows		3
	Calculating NPV		2
	EVA™		
	NOPAT		1
	EVA™ answer		1
	MIRR		
	PV of investment		0.5
	TV of returns		1.5
	MIRR answer		1
	ROCE		1
	ROE		
	Tax/PAT		1
	ROE		1
	Commentary: 1 mark per point up to maximum of 5 marks		5
		Maximum	**15**
(d)	General comment on the meaning of the quote	up to	2
	Specific examples appropriate to Metis up to 3 marks per example	up to	10
	(Examples can be illustrations of how management responds to measures or the problems that arise from the lack of measures in the performance report.)		
		Maximum	**10**
	Professional marks for the format, style and structure of the discussion of the answer.		4
Total			**50**

9 KOLMOG HOTELS (JUN 13)

Key answer tips

Make sure you relate your comments to the particular circumstances of Kolmog throughout this question. It is very easy to give a generic answer and then score badly.

Report

To: CEO

From: A. Accountant

Date: June 2013

Subject: Balanced scorecard and targets at Kolmog Hotels

Introduction

This report explains the differences between service and manufacturing industries and evaluates the current board performance information. Next, it evaluates the proposed balanced scorecard and describes the difficulties in implementing and using it. Finally, the purpose of setting challenging targets is explained and the hotel managers' standards and rewards are evaluated using the building block model.

(i) Characteristics differentiating service from manufacturing businesses

The service nature of the hotel business can be analysed as:

- simultaneous in that the service is created as it is consumed during the customer's stay

- heterogeneous (variable) in that it is hard to standardise the service since each hotel and city stayed in is different

- intangible in that there is no physical product, only nights' stay in the hotel. This is a cause of the low cost of sales at 12% of revenue

- perishable in that hotel nights cannot be stored as they are used that night. Thus, in the hotel industry room occupancy is often a key performance measure; and

- there is no transfer of ownership as the guest's stay only gives them right of access to use the hotel facilities for a limited period.

(ii) Current strategic performance information

The current information used by the board is purely financial in nature and, as a result, it omits to measure many of the elements mentioned in the mission. It covers the shareholder value aspects through EPS growth, share price performance and ROCE, although there are arguably better measures of shareholder value in total shareholder return and economic value added. However, it does not quantify customer and employee loyalty nor product innovation, which are the routes by which the primary mission is to be achieved.

Most strikingly, there is also no attempt to measure the goal of being the No. 1 hotel chain in Ostland. An obvious way to measure this would be market share but there is no external data given in the report. The use of ratios comparing to revenue is a helpful communication tool in showing how resources/costs generate sales but, again, no external comparators are given which would aid in judging competitive position.

The breakdown of results into geographical areas is only helpful if these are comparable. A breakdown of the results by hotel type may be a more useful management tool, as luxury hotels will use a higher staff to guest ratio than budget ones and the geographical results will be distorted unless each geographical area has the same mix of these different product types. Year on year growth figures are given but no inflation figure is given which might explain growth as a non-management achievement.

There is limited information on fixed and variable costs in the report which is relevant to Kolmog, as hotels naturally have high operational gearing since many costs (financing, property, staff and administration) are fixed and so profit is sensitive to small changes in revenues. There are a number of traditional measures of hotel performance that would improve the report by helping to capture this issue, such as occupancy rates and revenue per available room.

Finally, the report does not link to the budget which appears to be the main operational control tool. Summary budget figures and variances may aid the board in their role of overseeing performance.

(iii)   BSC proposal

Generally, the BSC will aid in communicating, implementing and controlling the strategy of the company. It aims to help achieve coherence between the stated goals and the measures used at Kolmog.

The proposed scorecard has the advantage of using only a limited number of measures and so should avoid the danger of information overload. Taking each perspective in turn:

The financial perspective is covered by the measures of strategic financial performance (share price and ROCE). This fits with the objective of maximising shareholder value. It is also common to use dividend per share as well as share price to reflect total shareholder return. Return on capital employed is a standard measure of overall performance but this may now have less value for Kolmog. The change in strategy in no longer owning the hotels that it operates will reduce the capital dependence of the business. It may be more appropriate to use a measure such as operational gearing (fixed costs/total costs) that reflects the returns against fixed costs (especially rental payments). Revenue growth will also be an important measure of the achievement of being the leading hotel chain in Ostland.

The customer perspective is addressed by the customer survey scores. This addresses the objective of delighting customers. However, there is no direct attempt to measure the objective of improving brand loyalty. The customers are a major stakeholder whose loyalty Kolmog will want to improve. Growth in returning customers (i.e. repeat business) would be better measured, for example, through growth in customer account revenues.

The internal process perspective is addressed through the hotel budget variance analysis. This analysis will need to be broken down into detailed areas for each hotel. It may be necessary to have different areas of emphasis depending on the hotel type, for example, country house hotels will have different occupancy levels from city centre ones due to the seasonality of this trade. Benchmarking performance against these internal comparators should assist in spreading best practice within the chain. This communication of best practice may help to instil brand loyalty among employees if they feel that other members of the chain are helping to improve their own hotel's performance.

The learning and growth perspective would appear to be an obvious area to address, given the objective on product innovation. Yet there is no measure given for this. A possible metric would be percentage of revenue generated from new hotel types or hotel services. Hotels are a fairly mature business and so this may be a difficult objective to realise.

Instead, the objective of employee loyalty is addressed by measuring staff turnover. The happiness and motivation of staff is likely to be a key driver of the customer experience and so it has been highly prioritised. This can be measured through surveys of staff attitudes.

In relation to all the measures proposed, Kolmog should benchmark their performance against their competitors. This will measure whether they are achieving the 'No. 1' status that is the primary objective.

(iv)   Difficulties of implementing and using the BSC

The first difficulty is in selecting the metrics for use in the scorecard. It is important that the BSC does not become a long list of metrics that obscure the truth with information overload. It is important to measure what is needed to be measured, not just what can be measured. There is often difficulty with measuring the innovation and learning perspective and other qualitative/non-financial areas. There is also the need to translate the strategic measures down to the operational level, for example, breaking down general customer satisfaction into specific areas of customer interaction such as reception and room service.

The second difficulty is that some of the perspectives and their metrics will naturally conflict with each other. For example, reducing employee turnover may require increasing their pay but this will conflict with profit targets. These conflicts may be required to be resolved at board level by looking at what will achieve the overall mission of the company.

The third difficulty is that the use of many metrics requires managers to be capable of interpreting each metric and also handling the volume of metrics presented. This expertise is less common among non-financial staff.

The final difficulty is the need for senior management to be committed to use of the BSC, otherwise staff will fall back on the traditional financial performance measures. The use of the BSC can be emphasised by tying the individual's performance appraisal into measures derived from the BSC.

(v)   Hotel manager targets

Challenging targets

Target setting is a difficult task. The targets must be challenging enough to push employees, in order to motivate them to maximum effort, without being perceived to be so improbable to achieve that they demotivate the employees. The proposal here is to use so-called stretch targets that aim beyond the easily achievable but fall short of the improbable.

At Kolmog, there is a history of setting targets that have been too difficult to achieve, so that many employees will never expect a bonus and so make no effort beyond the minimum acceptable to keep their job. The new targets will need to be perceived as more difficult but achievable in order to motivate employees.

Standards

Standards are the measures of employee performance. Employees must take ownership so they need to participate, accept and be motivated by the targets. Targets must be achievable and so challenge the manager without being demotivating. They must take account of expected market conditions that will be beyond the control of the hotel manager. Targets must be fair, for example, different types of hotels must be measured against similar standards (e.g. city centre hotels v other city centre ones and not country houses).

Rewards

Rewards must be

●   clear, that is, understood by the managers

●   motivating, that is, of value to the employee; and

●   controllable, that is, related to their area of responsibility.

The system proposed at Kolmog suffers from a number of potential problems. The basic measures are considered acceptable by the CEO but the detailed system conflicts with the building block principles given above.

●   The performance against budgeted profit may fail to be participative since the finance department at head office sets the budget. Hotel managers will need to be involved in budget setting.

●   The use of an industry wide standard for staff turnover would not be fair if staff wages are not controllable by the manager and set at a level that is not reasonably attractive in the industry. It may be better to compare staff turnover to the company average (or even the average within the company's product range) in order to get a fair comparison between hotel managers.

●   The use of company average customer satisfaction does not stretch staff to meet competitor performance. This area is much more in the control of the hotel manager and should be externally compared in order to generate competitive advantage.

●   The reward offered is valuable at up to 30% of salary. It would need to be compared to competitor offerings in order to judge the effect in retaining employees. It may not be clearly understood, as the precise level is based on the regional manager's assessment but this should be dealt with by explanation at the annual appraisal.

The company is already collecting data about the number of staff receiving different levels of bonus and this should be continued as it represents a way of quantifying the achievability of the targets.

Marking scheme		
		Marks
(i)	Service industry characteristics 1 mark per point which must be illustrated for the hotel industry **Maximum**	5
(ii)	Current performance reporting Comments on measuring objectives of Kolmog – up to 6 marks Other comments – 1 mark per point made up to 6 marks **Maximum**	8
(iii)	Proposed BSC Up to 4 marks for each perspective Other comments 1 mark per point **Maximum**	12
(iv)	Difficulties with BSC 1 mark per point up to 7 marks **Maximum**	7
(v)	Targets Explain the purpose of challenging targets – up to 3 marks To get all 3, must make answer relevant to Kolmog Standards 3 marks for explaining criteria (ownership, achievability, fairness) Rewards 3 marks for explaining criteria (clarity, motivation, controllability) Commenting on Kolmog system – 1 mark per point up to 7 **Maximum**	14
Professional marks 0.5 for report headings 1 for introduction 0.5 for use of suitable subheadings in report 2 for clarity and language use 1 for conclusion (not required here but give if reasonably attempted) **Maximum**		4
Total		50

Examiner's comments

In part (i) most candidates scored reasonably well in explaining the characteristics of a service business. The better candidates used examples that directly related to Kolmog or at least to a hotel business. Weaker candidates listed rote-learned jargon terms such as simultaneity, heterogeneity, intangibility and perishability with a simple general definition. Such answers scored poorly as they did not address Kolmog specifically or even compare service to manufacturing businesses.

Part (ii) required an evaluation of current performance reporting at Kolmog. Generally, this part was done reasonably well but most candidates still fail to apply a logical approach to such a question by firstly, considering what such reports aim to achieve and so relate the report to the achievement of the mission of the company being examined. There also were too many answers that ended up by listing many areas of information that could be added to the report with little thought to the danger of over-loading the board (as the current report did in a different way).

Future candidates may be able to avoid such a problem by reminding themselves of whom the report addresses (the board) and what their information needs are (strategic level).

Part (iii) requested an evaluation of a proposed balanced scorecard (BSC) with suggestions for improvement. The proposed BSC represented a simplified version of what candidates will see in the real world – a tailored BSC where the standard four perspectives were indirectly being covered. It was pleasing to see most candidates handle this aspect of the question well. However, as in part (ii), candidates would have scored more efficiently had they attended to the mission of the company and how the scorecard would aid its achievement.

In part (iv) candidates often drifted away from the question requirement for the difficulties (not improvements required) in implementing and using the BSC at Kolmog. The examining team were surprised at the poor answers to this question part as they considered that it would be a common practice in revision of a method in APM to consider its advantages, disadvantages and the likely difficulties encountered in using it. Those candidates that illustrated each of their difficulties with an example for Kolmog scored well.

Part (v) considered issues around the reward system at Kolmog. It was worth 14 marks for an explanation of the purpose of setting challenging targets and then an evaluation of standards and rewards at the company. Most candidates demonstrated good understanding of the use of 'stretch' targets and the reward system implications at Kolmog. However, there was weaker understanding of the 'standards' element from Fitzgerald and Moon's building block model. It was pleasing to see that most candidates knew at least some of the key criteria for judging standards and rewards (ownership, achievability, fairness/equity; clarity, motivation, controllability) but the illustration of these points with relevant comments for Kolmog was weaker.

Future candidates would be advised to use the mission and aims of the company in question in assessing their current and future plans for performance reporting and management.

10   LOPTEN INDUSTRIES (DEC 13 – AMENDED)

Key answer tips

Make sure that you answer the question set (e.g. discussing KPIs in part (c) not CSFs) and ensure that you can complete basic calculations quickly and accurately.

Also be prepared you argue your case – in particular, justifying each indicator under consideration in the question requirement.

To:	**Board of Lopten**
From:	**A. Accountant**
Date:	**December 2013**
Subject:	**KPIs for Lopten in Beeland**

Introduction

This report calculates the KPIs suggested by the board and evaluates their effectiveness in addressing identified external environmental issues, their ability to cover the CSFs chosen for the Beeland operations and how they address the key functions of senior management to plan and control Lopten. Finally, the report evaluates whether the two suggested marketing strategies enable Beeland to achieve its target profit.

(i)   Summary of KPIs

	Cheerful	*Posh*
Profit for each product ($m)	42	45
Average price per unit ($)	400	700
Contribution per unit ($)	145	375
Market share	12%	33%
Margin of safety	26%	27%
ROCE	13%	18%
Total quality costs ($m)	28	19
Consumer awards	1	4

Details of calculations are given in Appendix 1.

(ii)   Issues in the external environment

The issues in the external environment can be identified using the PEST acronym, which stands for political, economic, socio-cultural and technological.

The political environment is characterised by government actions which here included the giving of grants to a competitor to set up manufacturing operations in Beeland. This is not Lopten's mode of operation which is to manufacture outside Beeland and only create a selling operation within the country. None of the KPIs directly address this issue which could lead to increased profit available to develop the competitor's products or government action against Lopten by, say, increasing import tariffs.

The economic environment is characterised by growth as the populace of Beeland becomes wealthier. There is no measure of this included in the KPIs. There is no measure of competitor activity, although market share does provide some measure of the relative strength of Lopten and its competitors. It is notable that none of the KPIs measure current rates of growth in their area. Also, the given KPIs do not reflect the foreign exchange risk which Lopten could encounter in repatriating profits from Beeland.

The socio-cultural factors include demographic trends and changes in customers' tastes. The increasing wealth mentioned earlier will be a factor in driving the consumers' taste towards the more expensive Posh products. These would justify the large potential growth indicated in marketing Plan B. There are several measures which will bear on this area but, as noted above, all will require trends to be given, for example, the inflation of average price per unit and consequent improvement in profit and contribution indicators.

Technology can impact on Lopten in two ways. First, the development of new features for the products themselves will require continued product development at Lopten as a whole, although it will be less relevant to the operation in Beeland which may not have the market for cutting-edge technology yet. Therefore, it is appropriate that this area is not covered by the existing KPIs. Second, new technology in manufacturing could improve further the contribution per unit as costs are cut from the manufacturing process by, for example, increased automation in production. The use of contribution to measure this impact is indirect as it is also influenced by the selling price, so a measure of manufacturing cost per unit would better capture the change.

(iii) Linking the KPIs and CSFs

The first CSF is to obtain a dominant market presence. This will be measured by the market share and it can be seen that Posh has obtained about a third of the market and so can be said to be a major presence. In order to judge whether this is dominant, Lopten will need to have its competitors' market share. Other KPIs (average price per unit, ROCE, consumer awards) can be used in measuring market position but again, only if comparable data for the competition is supplied. In trying to achieve dominant market position, Lopten could chose to cut prices in order to drive up volumes and the contribution per unit shows how far the selling price can be cut before breakeven is reached (= average price – contribution).

The second CSF is the maximisation of profit within the risk appetite of the business. The absolute level of profit is given as a KPI and so a trend analysis of this will indicate optimisation. The trends in average price per unit and cost per unit (not a KPI but indirectly indicated through the contribution) will show the effectiveness of the marketing and production activities in contributing to profit. ROCE will provide an indication of the efficient use of capital in generating profit. The risk taken is measured by the margin of safety which shows how far current sales would have to fall to result in a breakeven profit situation.

The third CSF looks at maintenance of brand through product quality. The most direct measure of brand can be gained through the consumer awards as they show the impression being made on the customers by the products. The total quality costs figure gives an indication of the spend on quality but without an internal trend and external benchmarking, this figure is difficult to interpret. There is no KPI on the marketing spending which would be a common support for the brand.

(iv)   Planning and control at Lopten

Planning is carried out at Lopten where there is a top-down structure to the mission, objectives and CSFs leading to the KPIs. The KPIs which will be reflected in this activity are those which are forward looking. Margin of safety addresses the risk of making a loss going forward and the size of the margin will give the board comfort that they can afford to take strategic risks without risking the survival of the Beeland operation. Another forward looking indicator would be the awards won which should give the company ability to build volume and also margins in the future. The other indicators are of general financial health which will provide the capital base for future plans.

The control activity measures actual results against plan and then takes necessary action to correct activities back to plan. In order to be used in this way, the KPIs calculated above will need their benchmark comparators to be given. Most of the indicators given would be used in this way if benchmarks were provided.

At board level, much of the decision-making is planning while at the operational level, there is more control than planning activity. Therefore, the balance among the suggested KPIs is unusually towards control. This issue could be addressed by including measures such as revenue and market share growth which establish trends useful for financial projections.

(v)   Target operating profit

Using the calculations for profit already completed in Appendix 1, we have the following projected profits for the two plans:

PLAN A	*Most recent*	*Yr 1*	*Yr 2*
Contribution	$m	$m	$m
Cheerful	162	169	176
Posh	165	172	178
Fixed costs	240	240	240
Profit	87	100	114
PLAN B	*Most recent*	*Yr 1*	*Yr 2*
Contribution	$m	$m	$m
Cheerful	162	162	162
Posh	165	190	218
Fixed costs	240	240	240
Profit	87	112	141

Therefore, we can see that if we continue with the current marketing strategy and so maintain our product mix (Plan A), then Beeland will fall short of the target profit in two years' time by $21m.

However, if Lopten adopts Plan B, then the company can achieve its target profit in two years. The success of Plan B depends on the achievement of a high growth rate of 15% p.a. This growth rate will depend on the continued improvement of the general economy, as this will create the wealth to generate the demand for the higher contribution Posh product. It will also depend on the success of the increased marketing spend on promoting Posh. It would be wise to consider whether the increased marketing spend will be effective, as the current spend of $80m may be saturating the market at present and so additional spending will not generate proportionately more sales.

Tutorial note

Minor rounding differences in the calculations will not be penalised.

Conclusions

The current KPIs do not cover many of the external factors in Lopten's business environment and link weakly to the CSFs. The balance of the KPIs is towards control when the balance of the board's work will be forward looking towards planning the future of the business. A revision of the KPIs used should be undertaken in order to address these concerns.

The current marketing plan for Beeland will fall short of the target profit and so it should shift to emphasising the higher margin Posh products (Plan B) which will achieve the target provided the growth assumptions are realistic.

Appendix 1

	Cheerful	*Posh*
Units (millions)	1.12	0.44
	$m	$m
Revenue	448	308
Variable costs:		
Labour	67	35
Variable overheads	45	22
Materials	101	53
Distribution	50	20
Quality	22	13
Contribution	162	165
Fixed costs:		
Administration	18	18
Distribution	16	16
Quality	6	6
Marketing	80	80
Total fixed costs	120	120
Profit	42	45
Breakeven sales units (millions)	0.83	0.32

(= total fixed costs/contribution per unit)

				Marks
(i)	Variable costs			2
	Fixed costs			1
	Profit			1
	Average sales price per unit			1
	Contribution per unit			1
	Market share			1
	Breakeven			1
	Margin of safety			1
	Return on capital employed (ROCE)			1
	Total quality costs			1
			Maximum	**11**
(ii)	Using the PEST headings:			
	Up to 2 marks for discussion of the relevant issue in the scenario and up to 2 marks for commenting on the relevance of the suggested KPIs to the issue			
			Maximum	**11**
(iii)	Up to 4 marks for comments on each CSF		**Maximum**	**10**
(iv)	1 mark per point made		**Maximum**	**5**
(v)	Calculations:			
	Plan A			
	Contribution			2
	Profit			1
	Plan B			
	Contribution			1
	Profit			1
	Shortfall			1
	Comments:			
	1 mark per point up to 4 marks			
			Maximum	**9**
	Professional marks will be awarded for the format, style and structure of the discussion of your answer.			4
Total				**50**

Marking scheme

Examiner's comments

In part (i) most candidates performed well. The main weaknesses shown in this work were in the basic profit calculations and the margin of safety calculation. For such a basic set of calculations, it was disappointing that more candidates did not take the opportunity to score all 11 marks. A relatively common error which appeared here and in part (v) of this question was the treatment of fixed costs as volume related. Future candidates should be aware that breakeven and the associated analysis is something that they will be considered to be expert in by the time they reach APM.

Part (ii) required the use of PEST analysis to identify issues in the external business environment and then an evaluation of how the suggested KPIs addressed those issues identified. Again, this question part was generally well done. Most candidates identified a number of issues in the external environment using PEST (a SBL model) but were notably weaker in the application of it to the KPIs suggested. Two issues became apparent in marking: firstly, a minority of candidates did not use the PEST model and so were only given some credit as the question was about application of this model and; secondly, many candidates discussed their own set of KPIs ignoring the ones under consideration by the board. The second fault was particularly notable in answers which offered lists of new indicators with scant justification of their relevance and their impact on the proposed KPI set to be used by Lopten.

Part (iii) requested an evaluation of the appropriateness of the suggested KPIs in the light of the stated CSFs at Lopten. This part was mostly well done. However, as in part (ii), candidates had a tendency to ignore the suggested KPIs and produce lists of new KPIs to address the issues which were not justified in context. There was also a tendency to discuss problems with the CSFs rather than the KPIs which was not requested by the question. For example, a suitable response to the concept of 'acceptable risk' was to look at how it could be measured within the existing KPIs rather than just comment that the target level of acceptable risk was not clearly specified in the scenario.

In part (iv), candidates often drifted away from the question requirement which was an assessment of the extent to which the suggested KPIs could be used for planning rather than controlling the business. The purpose of the question was to offer candidates the chance to show that they appreciated the difference in these activities. Sadly, this question was poorly done with answers discussing control activities to the exclusion of planning. Candidates should not be afraid to say that there is poor coverage in an existing system provided that this opinion is justified in their answer.

Many candidates seem to think incorrectly that setting and monitoring of targets is a planning activity. The distinctions were more that suitable KPIs had to be forward-looking and focussed on the external environment of Lopten. Again, in this part, there was insufficient focus on the suggested KPI list.

Part (v) considered issues around possible marketing strategies for Lopten. This part was worth 9 marks for an evaluation of operating profit targets. This part was either done well or badly with little in between. Where a candidate addressed the fixed costs correctly and realised that the target profit was given as the profit in two years' time thereby, producing calculations for the two plans, then they tended to easily score above pass marks. Therefore, there were two common and fundamental errors in the calculations. Firstly, already noted above, was the failure to recognise the 'fixed' costs in the estimate of future profits, e.g. by taking the previously calculated profit per product and multiplying it by 1.042 in Plan A. Secondly, many candidates attempted to answer the question by doing only a calculation of profit in one years' time or else not doing any calculation work at all. (For those candidates that cannot see how poor such an answer is, we would suggest that you imagine the response of your boss when, having requested a forecast for next year's profit, you come to the meeting with either a forecast of the first 6 month's profit only or else a statement that things look okay based on the fact that you made a profit last year.) Such answers scored some marks for the discussion of the assumptions in the strategies but did not tend to collect many marks.

As has become common, those candidates who had practised writing professional answers prior to the examination performed admirably in the presentation area (4 marks). The markers were looking for suitable report headings, an introduction, a logical structure, signposted by the good use of subheadings in the answer, and a clear, concise style. A conclusion was not required for the 4 marks but if a suitable and substantive one was offered then it was given additional credit.

11 MERKLAND SPORTSWEAR (JUN 15)

Key answer tips

Make sure that you answer the question set, particularly in parts (i) and (v). In part (i) assessing the metrics does not mean assessing the company's performance. Also ensure that you can complete basic calculations quickly and accurately and be prepared to argue your case – in particular, justifying each indicator under consideration in the question requirement.

To: **The Board of MS**

From: **A Accountant**

Date: **June 2015**

Subject: **Performance management at Merkland Sportswear (MS)**

This report addresses a variety of performance management issues at MS. The existing choice of performance metrics in the dashboard is assessed in the light of the strategy and SWOT analysis. The impact of the child labour scandal for MS is addressed. Specifically, the impact the proposed new factory will have on the metrics is considered. Finally, suggestions are made for the use of the value chain analysis in management of this factory.

(i)   **Existing performance dashboard**

In assessing the choice of metrics in the dashboard, it would be best to begin with a clear picture of the aims and broad strategy of MS. The main aims appear financial and this is appropriately reflected in the main heading of the dashboard and the fact that this heading has three metrics not just the two in the other areas. The first aim is growth, which is reflected in the change on previous year data given in the dashboard and most specifically in the revenue data given. The trend can be seen with three years of data reflecting the growing activities of MS. The second aim is to maximise shareholder wealth. This is measured indirectly through return on capital employed (ROCE). However, as ROCE does not take account of a number of issues (e.g. tax or financing costs), it does not directly measure shareholder wealth. It would be worth considering replacing ROCE with a value-based measure such as economic value-added which over the long term should more accurately reflect shareholder wealth.

The other elements contained in the broad strategy are seeking competitive advantage in two ways:

1   to create innovative products which reduce injuries and improve performance.

2   to be the leading marketing operation in Ceeland.

The current dashboard reflects these strategies in the design and brand headings. However, the metrics used in each seem to lack important aspects of the stated strategies.

The number of design awards won indirectly measures the quality of the products but it does not measure innovation. The number of new products or features on our products would more accurately do this. The design heading does not specifically address the key advantages mentioned of injury reduction and sporting performance. It will be difficult to provide two metrics which will cover all of these areas. However, if the criteria of the awards are injury reduction and performance and if a metric of number of new products launched is added, then the strategy is broadly covered by two measures.

The strategy of being a leading marketer is partially covered by the existing metrics of brand awareness, although without a comparator it is difficult to gauge whether this is a market leading figure. A more appropriate measure in the context of competitive advantage would be market share and in fact, looking at the data on footwear, we have 32% (= 2m/6.25m) of this important market which is 55% of our revenues (= $150m/$273m).

Also, brand awareness is only measuring the recognition of the brand, not whether there are positive sentiments towards the brand. Market share, however, gives a clearer picture of this as it reflects the purchasing choices of consumers.

The SWOT analysis suggests further possible areas for measurement such as supply chain management, but the board has ruled out new headings on the dashboard. This would have to be indirectly measured through the financial heading by using a metric such as gross or operating margin. Indeed, it may be worth replacing the absolute operating profit figure with the margin figure for this purpose.

The SWOT analysis also identifies two issues in marketing:

1   There is a linked pair of points – weak IT expertise and the threat of change in marketing channels. This would affect MS' marketing operations as they may lack the skill to exploit these new marketing opportunities. This issue falls under the brand heading and if it is felt that market share covers brand awareness, as previously mentioned, then the second measure under this heading should address MS' management of the changes in marketing channels by looking at the number of followers of MS on social media who either read or more actively respond to our social media messages.

2   The loss of a brand ambassador which, as the business has only got 10 of these, may be significant. In addition, the fact that the loss is tied to an injury which should not happen with MS' products is particularly problematic. This suggests measures under the brand heading of 'number of ambassadors' or else requires an injury reduction metric under the design heading – although we already have two metrics proposed under this heading (awards won and new products).

The board will need to prioritise between these issues to decide on a second metric within the brand heading.

(ii)   **Impact of response 1**

Change in operating profit due to response 1

	$m
Increased cost of sales 10% × 2m units at $21 =	4.2
Audit costs	0.5
Marketing campaign	0.8
Loss of operating profit	5.5
New contribution per unit =	51.9
Number of units to cover lost operating profit =	105,973

Quantitative impact:

The main stakeholders affected financially are the shareholders. The increased compliance costs, both variable and fixed, lead to a loss of operating profit of $5.5m and would need to be covered by additional sales of 106,000 pairs of shoes. If MS can be seen to respond rapidly and decisively to the problems, it will gain a reputational advantage which may generate those extra sales.

Qualitative impact:

There are three stakeholder groups (customers, regulator and employees) who will be affected by the scandal and MS' response. All three will be disappointed that the company may be involved with an unethical practice. The company must first establish if this is in fact the case. If it is, then the damage may occur through fines imposed by the regulator and lost sales due to the impact on MS' reputation.

For the employees, the damage may be a loss of motivation and trust as the organisation would have broken its own code of ethics. For all three groups, the key solution is a rapid and public addressing of the problem and both responses 1 and 2 appear to do this. A key tactic in dealing with such issues is to be first into the public domain by owning up to any breaches of the MS code alongside the announcement of solutions.

(iii)   **Expected profit from new factory**

	Bad	Medium	Good
Probability	30%	60%	10%
Units manufactured (000s)	1,800	2,000	2,200
($000s)			
Variable costs	37,800	44,000	50,600
Fixed costs	2,500	2,500	2,500
Revenue	135,000	150,000	165,000
Profit before interest and tax	94,700	103,500	111,900
Expected profit before interest and tax =	101,700		

The expected profit before interest and tax is $101.7m. This is calculated as an expected value which is dependent on debatable probability estimates. The benefit of using expected values is that it simplifies the various possibilities into one number. However, the underlying problem with this method is that the expected profit only makes sense if the project will be done a number of times, as then the use of probabilities makes sense as in the long run the expected return will be achieved. The probabilities are for the market's possible reactions to the change in sourcing policy but as MS is shifting all footwear production, this will be a one-off event. So, the outcome will be one of $94.7m, $103.5m or $111.9m – not $101.7m, though the variation among these is not fundamental in the context of an annual operating profit for MS of $71 m.

(iv) **Impact of new factory on performance dashboard**

MS performance dashboard

Report for the year to March 2015

	Current	With new factory %	Change
Financial			
Revenue ($m)	273	273	0.00%
Operating profit ($m)	71.0	66.0	− 7.04%
ROCE	41.7%	30.4%	− 27.15%
Design			
Design awards won	2	2	0.00%
Brand			
Awareness	64%	64%	0.00%

Workings:

Operating profit:	$
Third-party manufacturing cost	21 per unit
Revenue	75 per unit

Existing operating profit	108,000,000 on 2,000,000 sales
Assumed operating profit of new factory	103,000,000
Loss of operating profit	5,000,000
	18

ROCE:	$m
Current capital employed	170.3
New factory	47
New capital employed	217.3
New ROCE	30.4%

The impact is to reduce the operating profit as the factory in Ceeland is more expensive to run being in a higher cost environment. The basic variable cost per unit is about the same as the cost of purchasing from a third-party supplier, however, there are the additional fixed costs of the factory to be incurred as well. Consequently, the operating gearing of MS will increase.

As MS is a product development and marketing operation, it has little fixed capital. This results in a high ROCE. This is also a feature of operations which spend heavily to establish a brand in order to give them the pricing power to charge high margins.

The impact of setting up the factory is to reduce operating profit and increase capital employed. However, this might be offset by avoided costs such as regulators' fines and lost sales due to damaged reputation.

The introduction of a significant manufacturing operation introduces problems which the existing dashboard does not reflect. Financially, there is no mention of how the factory will be funded. If it involves debt, then this may increase the financial risk of the business and there is no measure of such risk (e.g. by gearing on the dashboard). Non-financially, product quality will now be a direct management concern for MS rather than something which procurement can handle through the supply chain. As this is a new area, it may be wise to introduce a metric for this until the organisational knowledge of the factory operation has been gained.

(v)   **Value chain**

Generally, the value chain is a model of business integration showing the way that business activities are organised. This model is based around activities rather than traditional functional departments (such as finance). A key idea is that it is activities which create value and incur costs. The activities are split into two groups: primary ones which the customer interacts with directly and can 'see' the value being created and secondary ones which are necessary to support the primary activities. By identifying how value is created, the organisation can then focus on improving those activities through its performance measurement system (the dashboard at MS).

Another feature of the value chain is the idea of a chain. This is the thought that value is built by linking activities and so there must be a flow of information between the different activities and across departmental boundaries.

In performance management terms, this will affect:

- information systems which will have to ensure good communication across functional boundaries and

- job descriptions and reporting hierarchies as these will have to reflect activities.

The chain does not stop at the organisation's boundaries. This is likely to be obvious to MS given the importance of supply chain management but the value chain will allow the organisation to focus on those relationships on which value most depends.

Specifically for MS, the value chain would emphasise the importance of supplier management and lead times for new product development within inbound logistics, showing how this fed through to the launch of new products and relationships with distributors in outbound logistics.

The sales and marketing activity of MS is clearly one of its primary areas of value enhancement and its relationship with outbound logistics and the distributors of the products should be notable.

Although the chain shows procurement and technology development as secondary activities, they will be vital for MS. As MS does not currently manufacture their own goods, control of the price/quality balance of supplier relationships will be important and linked to the importance of management of the supply chain noted for inbound logistics. As for sales and marketing, product (technology) development is one of the strategic areas of profit generation for MS and so should be treated as a key area for management activity and thus for performance measurement.

Tutorial note

This answer is lengthy as it tries to cover a large number of acceptable points which can be made in answering this part of the question.

Marking scheme		
		Marks
(i)	Up to 2 marks for breaking down and identifying the aims and broad strategies	
	Evaluating the dashboard for each aim and strategy in turn	
	Growth	1
	Shareholder wealth	2
	Innovation	3
	Marketing	3
	Other comments from SWOT:	
	Supply chain management	2
	Social media and IT expertise	3
	Brand ambassadors	3
	Showing sensitivity to constraint on number of metrics on dashboard	1
	Maximum	**16**
(ii)	Calculation:	
	Increased CoS	1
	Lost operating profit	1
	New contribution per unit	1
	Required sales	1
	Comments:	
	Up to 4 marks	
	Maximum	**8**
(iii)	Calculation:	
	Variable costs	1
	Revenue	1
	Profit	1
	Expected profit	1
	Comments:	
	Expected value method	2
	Maximum	**6**
(iv)	Calculation:	
	Operating profit under 3rd party manufacturing	1
	Loss of operating profit	1
	New capital employed	1
	New ROCE	1
	No change to other metrics	1
	Comments:	
	Up to 5 marks	
	Maximum	**10**
(v)	1 mark per point	
	Maximum	**6**
Professional presentation	up to	**4**
Total		**50**

Examiner's comments

Part (i) for 16 marks, required an assessment of the five existing performance metrics in light of the strategy of the organisation and issues noted in a recent SWOT analysis. This question was often reasonably done but as it is a fundamental question for APM candidates, further discussion of weaknesses in answers is warranted.

- A significant minority of candidates still continue to respond so such a question with an assessment of the performance of the company. It has been noted in numerous examination reports and in examiner's articles about APM that the assessment of the metrics is not the same as the assessment of the company's performance. Those candidates who did this wrote much but scored little and so wasted valuable time.

- The majority of candidates still do not appear to have prepared to answer this type of question. Few answers tried to firstly analyse the company's strategy and then use this to assess whether the dashboard metrics were actually measuring the achievement of this strategy.

- Justification of the choice of metric is key to scoring marks in this type of question and this means a reasoned justification. A common example of an unacceptable response was the candidate who wrote, 'I would keep this metric' on the choice of metrics for brand but then moved on to suggesting other metrics for brand. If the candidate had explained why they would keep this metric (e.g. by relating to how it addressed part of the strategy) they could have scored a mark.

- The best part of candidates' answers were on the issues arising from the SWOT analysis though there still seems to be a misunderstanding that APM is just examining the same areas as SBL. Answers often strayed into irrelevant discussion of how to use a SWOT analysis and which strategy MS should pursue.

- Finally, and most worryingly for a practical examination, the majority of candidates ignored the instructions from the CEO to limit the number of metrics suggested. Many answers contained lists of new metrics with no attempt to keep within the constraints clearly laid out in the scenario. Candidates who showed sensitivity to this issue were rewarded. (It should be noted that, in the real world of work, an employee who writes a report, which in section 1 ignores the clear instructions of their manager, will find that the report will probably remain mostly unread and therefore, their efforts will be considered valueless).

Part (ii) of the question, worth 8 marks, required the candidates to use given data to assess the qualitative and quantitative impact of a change of outsourcing partners for footwear manufacture in order to address potential breaches of ethics in the current outsourcing partners. This part was reasonably answered especially the commentary on qualitative impact. However, within the comments on quantitative impact, there was again a significant minority of candidates who appeared unable to perform the calculations. As APM is an examination of management accounting skills, this is an unacceptable deficiency. As mentioned earlier, candidates generally demonstrated a very poor grasp of a straight-forward breakeven calculation.

Part (iii) for 6 marks considered a second response to the footwear manufacturing issue by bringing production in-house. The question part requested a calculation of the expected profit of a proposed new factory and an evaluation of this as a method of decision-making. This part was generally well done with many candidates scoring full marks.

In part (iv) for 10 marks, candidates were asked to evaluate the impact of the new factory on the values and choices of metrics in the current performance dashboard. Candidate performance in this part was the poorest in question 1. Many candidates attempted to recalculate the dashboard metrics but ignored the fact that the new factory was bringing in-house an existing process and so the change in operating profit was the difference between the new factory's profit and that which was made from existing outsourced sales. However, even if no calculations were attempted a number of candidates put together passing answers by simply going through the metrics and discussing how the new factory impacted on them and what changes should be made now that MS was moving into that type of activity as it had no manufacturing operation prior to this change).

Part (v) of the question, worth 6 marks, required the candidates to consider the impact of using the value chain at MS. A lengthy description of the value chain was not requested though often offered. A good answer showed how the existing operations of MS and the proposed changes to footwear sourcing would affect performance measurement and management at MS. Answers were often weakened by not attempting to make the answer relevant to MS.

Future candidates should practice this question for future papers as it illustrates a number of common and fundamental questions that are faced by the advanced performance management advisor.

12   IRON CHICKEN (SEPT/DEC 15) (SPECIMEN 18)

Key answer tips

Make sure that you answer the question set (e.g. part (i) did not ask for pros and cons of EVA) and ensure that you can complete basic calculations quickly and accurately.

Also be prepared you argue your case – in particular, justifying each indicator under consideration in the question requirement.

Report

To: **Board of Iron Chicken (IC)**

From: **A. Accountant**

Date: **December 20X5**

Subject: **Performance management issues at IC**

Introduction

This report evaluates the accuracy and assumptions used in the calculation of EVA™. It then suggests new KPIs for the current CSFs at IC. Finally it considers the impact of three quality improvement projects on these CSFs and a proposed new information system.

(i)   **Economic value added (EVA™)**

There are a number of errors in the existing calculation of (EVA™). These are described below and then the corrected EVA™ is calculated.

Non-cash expenses are correctly added back to profit as such costs are treated as unacceptable accounting adjustments on a cash-based view. Marketing activities for long-term benefit are correctly added back as they generate future value for the business and so the prior year expenditure is also added in to capital employed. Research and development (R&D) expenditure should be treated as for the long-term marketing spending (note that there was no R&D expenditure in the prior year). The tax cost in the calculation should be the amount paid adjusted for lost tax on interest and not the adjusted amount of tax charged in the accounts. The WACC is incorrectly calculated as it should be based on the post-tax cost of debt. The capital employed figure should be based on the year start figure.

Economic value added	**Year ended 30 June 20X5**
	$m
Operating profit	551.4
Add back	
Non-cash expenses	15.1
Marketing capitalised	23.1
Research and development	10.0
Less	
Tax	130.0
Lost tax relief on interest	24.5
	———
NOPAT	445.1
Capital employed	
At 20X5 year start	2,282.0
Marketing spend capitalised from YE 30 June 20X4	23.1
	———
Adjusted capital employed at 20X5 year start	2,305.1
	———

WACC = $(1/2 \times 16\%) + (1/2 \times 6.8\% \times (1 - 30\%)) = 10.38\%$

EVA^{TM} = NOPAT – (WACC × Capital employed) = 206

The recalculated economic value added has increased from $154m to $206m which still indicates a positive position for the company as it adds to shareholder wealth.

In addition to the corrections above, the following assumptions in the calculation require comment:

1   There is an implicit assumption that accounting depreciation (included in operating profit) is equivalent to economic depreciation (which should be used for EVAT" calculations). This is questionable generally, although there is no information to allow a more accurate calculation. Also, there is additional marketing spending which will probably have a limited economic life in building the brand. No estimation of this life and the resulting additional economic depreciation has been attempted in the above calculation.

2   It has been assumed that no amortisation needs to be charged on the research and development costs since the product has not yet launched. This is in line with the accounting treatment of such items.

(ii)   Key performance indicators for the critical success factors

Greater staff productivity

The current measure of units produced per labour hour does not reflect the skill and effort which goes into producing different units. The products of IC range from complex to simple and so revenue per employee would better reflect the different skill levels involved in production.

Reduction of wastage

The weakness of the existing measure is that it only looks at one cost area of production (power consumption). Stock obsolescence will measure the wastage due to technological change which is present in the complex products produced by IC.

Greater innovation of products

The number of patents filed will reflect greater innovation at IC. Patents will legally protect groups of products. This will represent a stronger measure of innovation than new products launched since the patent gives legal exclusivity.

Tutorial note

There are many possible acceptable answers to this question, e.g.

Greater staff productivity

Actual staff hours as a percentage of standard hours for actual production as this would measure staff efficiency in producing a wide range of products.

Reduction of wastage

Input/output analysis of material which looks at the percentage of material purchased which goes into the final product.

Greater innovation of products

Percentage of income earned from products which did not exist last year. This will measure the ability of IC to develop successful products. (The existing measure would record unsuccessful products as innovation.)

(iii)   Lean manufacturing projects

The three projects link together as improvements to the quality of the manufacturing process at IC. There are common elements to these projects in the elimination of waste and empowerment of employees which will occur in the long term. In the short term, there may be increased costs due to these disruptive changes.

Just-in-time manufacturing (JIT)

JIT seeks to produce on a pull-basis to meet the customers' demands rather than to produce products for inventory, which then acts as a buffer between production levels and demand. The main impact of JIT is the reduction of inventory which is held. The main enablers for such a system are a need for close links to customers and suppliers in order to predict demand and to quickly supply that demand. In terms of IC's CSFs, this project will improve productivity as production lines must be made more flexible to meet changes in demand, although it should be noted that there could be a negative impact as constant changes in production lines will require more time to be spent setting up new production runs. It will also help to reduce wastage through losses in inventory as there will be less inventory. It also pushes some of the responsibility for improved quality of components (and reduced wastage) on to suppliers. However, it does not directly impact on product innovation.

The project will not necessarily immediately change any of the existing KPIs as it is about producing the right products at the right time not just more products for any given input and does not impact directly on new product launches.

Use kaizen costing

Kaizen costing aims to reduce current costs of production through continuous improvement. Each period, goals for lower costs are set and then performance monitored against these using variances. At the end of the period, a new lower cost goal is set for the next period. The process also often uses target costing to set the initial planned cost of a product thus incorporating the idea of only producing what the customer values. The purpose is to build into the control of the production process the idea of continuous improvement.

This project has the explicit aim of reducing waste and improving productivity and so is directly linked to the first two CSFs. As a result, it will have an impact on the KPIs which are related to productivity and resource consumption. The project will also require the empowerment of staff to make improvement decisions within their quality circles (teams) and so it may give scope for more innovative thinking. However, this thinking is not aimed at producing new products but at improving the production process, so new product innovation may only be affected indirectly.

Costs of quality and a 'zero defects' approach to manufacturing

Costs of quality can be broken down into four parts:

- prevention costs which occur before or during production and aim to prevent the production of defective products;

- appraisal costs which occur after production and aim to check that products meet quality standards;

- internal failure costs which occur when products are identified as defective before delivery to the customer and so are scrapped or reworked; and

- external failure costs which occur when defective products are delivered to the customer.

The 'zero defects' approach is also known as 'total quality management' (TQM). The TQM philosophy is that it is better to spend money on prevention, which involves challenging all aspects of the production process in order to improve and so avoid failure costs.

This project will affect the CSFs relating to improved productivity and waste by reducing defective products, provided that staff time is not adversely affected by aiming for perfection in production. In terms of the KPIs, it may lead to increased time in production but reduced wastage. It will not have a direct impact on power consumption. Again, this project is unlikely to affect the number of new products launched as it focuses on the production process not product development.

(iv) New information system

The move to a single database for the organisation will integrate the subsystems from different functions (such as production and sales). It will require existing systems to be networked and compatible or else be replaced. It will affect overall decision-making by improving the visibility of each function's operations to the others and to the strategic decision-makers. This shift is often achieved by using an enterprise resource planning system and a strategic enterprise management system.

The unified database will be critical in achieving the goal of JIT manufacturing as close links between production scheduling and demand forecasts will be required in order to match production runs with demand forecasts/orders. Also, the production schedules will need links to inventory levels in warehousing so that inventory is run down before new production is initiated. As closer communication with suppliers and customers will also be required, some change to existing information systems will be necessary in any case. It may be worthwhile to consider including electronic data interchange (EDI) in the specifications of the new system.

In using kaizen costing, cross-functional communication will be important. The design team will need to communicate with the production team so that the design is more easily streamlined for production. The financial systems will need to be frequently updated for information from the quality circles as improvements are made. This will affect the kaizen cost targets which need to be continually monitored and new targets set regularly. Quality circles often involve groups from across the business and so a common information system will facilitate communications amongst them.

The introduction of TQM will require clearer reporting of quality costs to assist in the on-going motivation of staff, which is often a problem in TQM. Informing the quality teams of the impact that increased prevention costs are having on lowering failure costs will be important in maintaining the push to zero defects. The quality improvements and changes to production processes will need to be communicated across IC's different sites which the new database can facilitate.

The nature of the data used in the current system is quantitative but with the new projects, there will be a need to communicate qualitative information, for example, relating to the nature of defects or the new production processes put in place. This will require a fundamental change to existing systems which again motivates the change to a new database.

	ACCA Marking scheme		
			Marks
(i)	Economic value added		
	Calculation:		
	1 mark for each of:		
	Research and development		
	Tax paid		
	Capital employed year start figure		
	Non-cash expenses		
	Marketing		
	WACC		
	Economic value added		
	Conclusion		
	Assumptions and corrections – up to 10 marks		
		Maximum	15
(ii)	KPIs for CSFs Up to		
	2 marks per CSF		
		Maximum	6
(iii)	Quality projects		
	Definitions and descriptions up to 2 marks		
	Analysis up to 6 marks per project		
		Maximum	15
(iv)	New unified database		
	Definition and general points up to 3 marks		
	Interaction with each project up to 3 marks each		
	Other comments up to 3 marks		
		Maximum	10
	Professional presentation: up to 4 marks		
			____
Total			**50**
			____

Examiner's comments

Part (i) required an evaluation of the accuracy of an EVA calculation that had been provided. EVA is an important metric and as such it is fundamental for an APM candidate to be able to identify errors in a calculation and correct them. This part of the question was generally well attempted, although several candidates failed to optimise their marks. Therefore a discussion of some of the weaknesses is needed:

- Many candidates spent time discussing the advantages and disadvantages of using EVA, such as 'closely related to cash flow' and 'is difficult to calculate in practice', but this was not asked for in the requirement. Candidates should ensure that they focus on the specifics of the requirement, and although a brief explanation of a model/technique may add some value, it is unlikely to warrant several paragraphs, and in some cases pages, when it was not asked for.

- Several candidates failed to recognise the correct treatment of depreciation on leases or that the opening capital employed figure should be used and not the closing figure.

- Some candidates failed to notice that that WACC had not been too adjusted for the tax relief and therefore did not make an adjustment. However, it should be noted that the majority of candidates that did notice this went on to correctly calculate a revised WACC figure.

- Most worryingly was that fact that several students incorrectly interpreted a Debt: Equity ratio of 100% as meaning that the company was financed entirely by debt and there was no equity. This is a fundamental error and one the marking team was surprised to see at this level.

- The responses from several candidates were too superficial, with some providing revised calculations with no explanation of the changes. This type of question, which requires an evaluation of whether or not something is accurate, demands candidates to state more than it is right or wrong. Candidates must be able to state what is inaccurate, explain what the correct treatment should be, AND explain why this is the case.

Part (ii) asked for a brief explanation of the weaknesses of the current KPIs and provide justified alternative KPIs for the critical success factors. This question was generally attempted well with many candidates scoring maximum marks. It is important when setting KPIs to understand the impact it may have on performance and also to consider whether or not it is suitable in relation to the CSF. The only major failing on this part of the question was regarding the recommendations of alternative KPIs. Several candidates seemed to misunderstand what a KPI is and make bland statements like the company should 'focus on training' or 'ensure that customers receive quality products' as opposed to suggesting measurable metrics.

Part (iii) asked for an explanation of how each of three improvement projects would help meet the CSFs and the impact they would each have on the KPIs. The responses from candidates were mixed on this part of the question, ranging from summary explanations of the improvement projects (just-in-time, kaizen costs and examining costs of quality) to comprehensive discussion that each would have on the CSFs and KPIs. With any new project, care should be taken to ensure that they will assist in helping an organisation achieve its objectives, and as such whether or not they will be beneficial to the CSFs. In addition, changes to current processes may also lead to a change in appropriate KPIs. For example, is a KPI focused on the number of units produced per hour applicable within a just-in-time manufacturing environment where the focus is on quality and based on a demand-pull framework?

The responses from many candidates were limited by the fact that detailed knowledge of kaizen costing and costs of quality were lacking. Again, this emphasises the need for candidates to ensure that they have a sound grasp of basic management accounting knowledge.

Part (iv) asked for an assessment of the impact of a new information system on the three improvement projects. Many candidates re-iterated the features of the new system that were detailed in the question but provided little in the way of developing this into an assessment of how it would impact on the improvement projects. Candidates need to be aware of the fact that to assess the impact of a new information system on a project, a good answer will identify what are the information requirements of each project and whether or not the new system will meet these requirements. For example, the implementation of initiatives such as just-in-time manufacturing is heavily reliant on an appropriate information system allowing for co-ordination of deliveries and manufacturing schedules in order to meet customer demands.

Section 4

ANSWERS TO PRACTICE QUESTIONS – SECTION B

A – STRATEGIC PLANNING AND CONTROL

13 CUTHBERT (MAR/JUN 16)

Key answer tips

A fantastic question for ensuring you have the depth of knowledge that is required on BPR.

In part (a) be sure to discuss the influence on operational performance rather than performance in general.

Part (b) demonstrates how the examiner views APM as an entire subject rather than a number of individual topics – in this case a link is being made between BPR and changes to the reward system.

(a) Business process reengineering (BPR) involves radical and fundamental changes in the way processes in organisations are designed. A focus on the needs of the customer, and customer satisfaction, are key to BPR. BPR aims to improve key performance measures such as reducing costs, improving quality, service delivery and customer satisfaction.

The proposal is to move away from the existing functional structure where staff are attached to only one stage of the production process, or even to one type of machine within each function, to team working. This is a radical change for Cuthbert and as such, is an example of BPR.

Reorganising into teams

Currently, there is very little multi-skilling of production staff at Cuthbert. This was seen where there were insufficient trained zip machinists available for the emergency order for the Ceeland army, even though there were enough machinists to sew buttons. This led to the emergency order failing to meet the customer's requirements as it was not delivered on time.

Furthermore, it seems that machinists also prefer to work on one particular type of machine. This is probably because they are currently rewarded according to the speed of production, rather than the quality of production, and can work faster when using just one machine.

A change to team working would imply job enlargement for machinists, who would need to be trained so that they were multi-skilled in different parts of the production process. They could then perform the roles of other members of their team, to ensure that there were no bottlenecks in production.

The cost of reorganisation and the costs of training the machinists should be outweighed by the resulting improved efficiency and flexibility of production. In this way, there is more focus on the outcome (goods of the correct quality produced on time) and less focus on the individual tasks within the process, which is a key principle of BPR.

Production teams are responsible for quality

Cuthbert's brand has a strong reputation, and the use of its products for protection in harsh environments and by the armed forces means that quality is a key element of customer satisfaction. Cuthbert must be able to manufacture goods which are free of defects, unlike the emergency order for the Ceeland army.

Reorganising the production into teams of machinists, sometimes known as production 'cells', would make machinists responsible for decisions about quality of a particular product type. This should lead to improvements in quality and therefore to meeting the needs of the customer.

Reducing the number of processes for checking is typical of a reengineered process, and the quality checking currently performed by the supervisors would no longer be necessary. The production teams will be managing themselves in this respect, and the distinction between supervisors and machinists will be removed, which is again typical of organisations which have undergone BPR.

Encouraging machinists in each team to suggest improvements in the production process should bring about improvements in both quality and efficiency, and hence a reduction in costs. It is the machinists who are closest to the production process and may be able to see how it can be improved. Cuthbert could also consider a more formal system of incremental continuous improvements such as Kaizen costing.

Tracking with RFIDs

Typically, organisations with reengineered processes end up having a flatter hierarchy. It seems that the supervisors' current roles will no longer be required if the proposal is adopted. Quality checks will no longer be undertaken by them, nor will recording of batches, which will become automated using RFID tags. This should save salary costs and improve lines of communication in the business.

The use of RFID tags would capture the information required to manage the production process at source, and there would be no distinction between the gathering of information and processing it. This is in contrast to the current system of inputting batch data into a spreadsheet, and is a feature in organisations which have undergone BPR.

Practical and cultural aspects of the proposal

New performance measures related to quality rather than just quantity produced will have to be developed and processes and systems developed in order to record and report these. New rewards systems will also have to be developed and introduced as a result of the changes proposed.

The proposal by definition represents a significant cultural change for Cuthbert, and may meet resistance by staff who may perceive it is a threat and a one-off cost cutting measure rather than a fundamental long-term change in the business. It will also impact the organisational hierarchy, relationships between employees and the roles within Cuthbert. There will be significant costs with training staff and with the disruption the transition may cause.

(b) **The current reward system**

The machinists are currently paid a basic hourly wage plus an amount depending on how many items they sew. This will encourage them to work quickly, which will reduce product costs. However, as they are not directly rewarded for the quality of the work which they produce, they may not be motivated to produce high quality work. Furthermore, in order to work quickly, machinists prefer to work on only one type of machine. This reduces Cuthbert's overall flexibility to respond to customer needs such as with failure to deliver the emergency order for the Ceeland army.

The production supervisors also receive a bonus according to how many items machinists in their team are able to sew. This too does not reward the production of high quality work, and supervisors may also neglect quality in order to increase the speed of production. The machinists in their teams could also see it as unfair that the supervisors obtain a bonus based on what they see as their efforts.

The production manager does not receive a bonus for production or quality. It seems that the he has currently no direct motivation to improve on either of these two aspects of the process.

At 5% of salary, the bonus related to Cuthbert's overall profits is relatively small and it is unclear whether it is a significant motivator to any of the employees. Furthermore, machinists in particular may perceive their own efforts as too remote from the company's overall profit for them to bother to achieve it. Even if they were to be motivated by this, it is unclear what proportion of the total costs are related to direct labour as Cuthbert incurs many other costs such as advertising to maintain the brand. If the costs of direct labour were relatively low, even a large improvement in production efficiency by the machinists may have little effect on overall profit.

Under the new proposal

The existing reward systems would likely need to change if the move to team-based production were to be adopted.

It may still be appropriate to reward machinists with volume related bonuses, but as they worked in teams, a team-based performance bonus would be more appropriate. In that way the rest of the team would ensure that any underperforming machinists would improve their performance.

Rewards based on other factors such as quality, innovation, on time delivery and the ability to work as part of a team would also be appropriate and consistent with the machinists' enlarged job role. This would be a significant change for Cuthbert, where machinists are now being encouraged for the first time to bring about improvements in the production process. Rewards based on direct costs of production, or for the number of suggestions made by each machinist may be appropriate here.

New performance measures would need to be developed against which to align rewards to ensure that employees work towards the overall objectives of the organisation. New reporting systems will need to be put in place to feedback information regarding quality to each cell. This may incur additional costs in the development of existing or new information technology systems.

The commitment of senior management to these changes would be required, as well as communication and training of employees at all levels. This may again incur additional costs and divert management time away from existing activities.

Marking scheme		
		Marks
(a) Explanation of BPR – up to 2 marks		
Each element of BPR proposal – up to 4 marks		
Other practical issues – up to 4 marks		
	Maximum	14
(b) Evaluation of current system – up to 8 marks		
Recommendations – up to 6 marks		
	Maximum	11
Total		25

Examiner's comments

This 25-mark question was in the context of the introduction of a business process re-engineering (BPR) project at a clothing manufacturer.

Part (a) required an assessment of the impact of the proposed BPR changes on operational performance. This part was generally well done, with those candidates that broke their answers down into a detailed discussion of the impact of each part of the BPR project scoring most highly.

Part (b) called for an evaluation of the existing reward system at the business and advice on improvements in the light of the BPR changes. This part was reasonably done, with those candidates that addressed the specific issues with each level of employees scoring most highly.

Answers to this question which used the detailed structure of the question (BPR proposals and existing employee hierarchy) generally made points that scored easily since they directly addressed relevant issues for the business that was seeking advice. APM is about specific application not just generic points that could apply to any business and those candidates that do this often shift their marks materially into the range of a good pass.

14 FRAMILTONE (SEPT/DEC 16)

Key answer tips

Part (a) was a slight deviation from the normal style of the examiner but was very manageable. Good candidates will have worked methodically through each line of the budget, setting up workings to show the changes expected.

In part (b), good candidates will have examined, in detail, the suitability criteria for each type of budgeting, supporting their discussion with reference to the scenario.

(a) **Recalculate the budget for Luxury division to the end of the current year**

C$000	Q1 (Actual)	Q2	Q3	Q4	Total
Revenue (W1)	10,400	12,240	11,388	7,247	41,275
Cost of sales (W2)	(6,240)	(7,020)	(6,370)	(4,654)	(24,284)
Gross profit	4,160	5,220	5,018	2,593	16,991
Distribution costs (W3)	(624)	(734)	(682)	(434)	(2,474)
Administration costs (W4)	(2,296)	(2,243)	(2,186)	(2,132)	(8,857)
Operating profit	1,240	2,243	2,150	27	5,660

Recalculating Luxury division's budget for the year to reflect current conditions gives a more realistic target for the division managers. For the coming year, the effect of this is very significant and represents a much more challenging target for managers as it increases the expected total annual operating profit by 42% (5,660/4,000) over the original budget.

Workings (C$000):

(W1) Revenue	Q1 (Actual)	Q2	Q3	Q4	Total
Original budget	10,400.0	12,000.0	11,000.0	7,000.0	40,400.0
2% sales volume		240.0	220.0	140.0	600.0
1.5% sales price			168.3	107.1	275.4
Total	10,400.0	12,240.0	11,388.3	7,247.1	41,275.4

(W2) Cost of sales	Q1 (Actual)	Q2	Q3	Q4	Total
Original budget	6,240.0	7,120.0	6,460.0	4,720.0	24,540.0
2% sales volume		142.4	129.2	94.4	366.0
6.67% Exchange rate*		(242.2)	(219.7)	(160.6)	(622.5)
Total	6,240.0	7,020.2	6,369.5	4,653.8	24,283.5

*6.67% = 1 –– (1.4/1.5), applied to 50% of COS.

(W3) Distribution costs

	Q1 (Actual)	Q2	Q3	Q4	Total
Original budget	624.0	720.0	660.0	420.0	2,424.0
2% sales volume		14.4	13.2	8.4	36.0
1.31% Fuel tax increase*			8.8	5.6	14.4
Total	624.0	734.4	682.0	434.0	2,474.40

* 1.31% = 70% × (3/160)

(W4) Administration costs

	Q1 (Actual)	Q2	Q3	Q4	Total
Original budget	2,296.0	2,300.0	2,300.0	2,300.0	9,196.0
2.5% compound savings		(57.5)	(113.6)	(168.3)	(339.4)
Total	2,296.0	2,242.5	2,186.4	2,131.7	8,856.6

Workings for savings in administration costs:

Q2 2,300.0 × 2.5% = 57.5

Q3 57.5 + (2,242.5 × 2.5%) = 113.6

Q4 113.6 + (2,186.40 × 2.5%) = 168.3

(b)   **Incremental budgeting**

Framiltone currently uses this type of budgeting, the starting point of which is usually the previous year's actual performance or budget. This is then updated for any known changes in costs, or for inflation. The budget would normally remain unchanged for the remainder of the year.

Incremental budgeting is suitable for use in organisations which are stable and not undergoing significant changes. This is the case for Dairy division, which operates in a saturated market and has little opportunity to grow.

Production volumes in Dairy division have only increased by 0.5% over a full five years, so it is a very stable business. Dairy division has stability of both revenues and costs. It has long-term fixed cost and volume supply agreements with its supermarket customers. It also has similar fixed contracts with its suppliers of milk, the most significant raw material ingredient used in its products.

Though the third party distribution company is able to pass on some increases in fuel costs to Dairy division, these are capped at only 0.5% per year. This is significantly less than the tax increases which will increase Luxury division's fuel costs after the start of Q3. It appears that Dairy division has relatively little exposure to rising fuel prices.

Furthermore, these increases are agreed prior to the setting of the current year budget, so there is no need to update these costs on an ongoing basis throughout the year.

As the dairy foods market is saturated and stable, there is little opportunity for the division to incur discretionary costs such as research and development of new products.

Incremental budgeting is only suitable for business where costs are already well controlled. This is because a big disadvantage of incremental budgeting is that it perpetuates inefficient activities by often simply building inflation into previous year results or budgets. It appears that Dairy division, having been in existence for a relatively long time, does have good cost control as it has modern production plant and is recognised as having the most efficient production processes in the industry.

Incremental budgeting may, however, build in budget slack. Managers may spend up to their budgeted amounts in one year, so that their budget is not cut the next, which may affect their appraisal and reward in the future. It is unclear whether this is occurring at Dairy division, though for many years (while Dairy division was the only division at Framiltone), the budgets set following consultation with divisional managers have just been achieved. This may be consistent with the stability of the division, but could also indicate that budgets were not set at a challenging enough level, even though Dairy division had the best performance of the two divisions last year.

It is not therefore advisable that rolling budgets are introduced in Dairy division, as the current incremental process appears satisfactory. This is especially so since divisional managers have little experience of setting their own budgets, and the time and cost of using rolling budgets would exceed the value of them to the division.

Rolling budgets

Rolling budgets are continually updated to reflect current conditions and are usually extended by budgeting for an additional period after the current period, for example, a quarter, has elapsed. That way, the budget always reflects the most up to date trading conditions and best estimates of future costs and revenues, usually for the next four quarters.

Rolling budgets are suitable for businesses which change rapidly or where it is difficult to estimate future revenues and costs.

Luxury division was only set up two years ago, and is therefore a relatively new business. It also operates in quite a different sector of the industry to that in which Dairy division operates and where Framiltone has most experience. There is likely to be considerable uncertainty as to future costs and revenues as Framiltone has little direct experience on which to base its forecasts.

Whereas Dairy division operates in a saturated and stable market, Luxury division uses rare ingredients which are subject to variations in availability and cost, for example, as a result of poor harvests. There is no indication that Luxury division has fixed price and volume contracts with its customers or suppliers and is therefore likely to suffer from instability of supply as well as demand resulting from changes in consumer tastes.

The frequent changes in the product range are also likely to make forecasting for a year ahead difficult. The fact that a large proportion of ingredients are imported from Veeland, makes costs susceptible to changes in the C$:V$ exchange rates which can quickly make an annual budget out of date, though managers may use methods such as forward contracts to reduce these movements. If managers are appraised on a budget which is out of date or unrealistic, they are likely to give up trying to achieve the budget, which will negatively affect the performance of Framiltone.

Rolling budgets will provide a more accurate basis on which to appraise managers at Luxury division as they incorporate the best known estimates of future costs and revenues. It can be seen by the recalculation following Q1 results that Luxury division's revised budgeted operating profit for the year has increased significantly by 42% (5,660/4,000), most of which is due to exchange rate changes. Where costs and revenues are likely to change during the period, rolling budgets give a much more realistic basis on which to appraise divisional performance and appraise and reward divisional managers. Budgets are likely to be achievable, which will motivate managers to try and achieve them.

Though the regular updating of the budget required in rolling budgeting is costly, time consuming and possibly a distraction for divisional managers, it does seems that rolling budgets are more suitable for Luxury division than the current incremental approach, particularly as being realistic and achievable, they will increase managers' motivation to achieve the budget and so improve the performance of the business.

Marking scheme		Marks
(a) Calculations:		
Use of Q1 actual as starting point –— 1 mark		
Sales volume increase on revenue – 1 mark		
Sales price change from Q3 – 1 mark		
Sales volume increase on COS – 1 mark		
Exchange rate percentage – 1 mark		
Application of exchange rate change – 1 mark		
Sales volume increase on distribution costs – 1 mark		
Fuel tax percentage – 1 mark		
Application of fuel tax change – 1 mark		
Administration savings – 1 mark		
Conclusion— up to 2 marks		
	Maximum	12
(b) Use of incremental budgeting in the divisions – up to 8 marks		
Use of rolling budgeting in the divisions – up to 8 marks		
	Maximum	13
Total		25

Examiner's comments

This 25-mark question covered the preparation of budgets and evaluating the relative benefits of introducing a new budgeting system in a food manufacturing business.

Part (a) was attempted well by many candidates, and the layout of the answers was generally excellent. Although some of the calculations in this part of the question were tricky, candidates at the Strategic Professional Level, who read the requirement carefully should have had few problems here. The examination team was disappointed to see how many candidates could not adjust forecasts by a set percentage, or struggled to compensate for a change in an exchange rate. As mentioned above, candidates must ensure that all relevant workings are shown. Too many incorrect answers were presented without supporting calculations, and thus marks for method were potentially lost.

Part (b) was generally well done and most candidates who attempted this question scored at least half marks on this part. It was pleasing to see many candidates adopting a sensible structure to their answers here – explaining the budgeting system, discussing advantages and disadvantages of the system with regards to each division, and then making a suitable recommendation. It is recommended that candidates identify a clear structure for their discursive answers to ensure that all areas of the requirement are covered, and relevant examples to the scenario are used.

15 BRIGGS

Key answer tips

The McKinsey 7S model is not a commonly examined area. However, it is important that you are comfortable with all of the syllabus areas – if it is in the syllabus it may be tested! Make sure you learn the different elements and are able to use the model to assess the degree of alignment between the 7 factors.

(a) The McKinsey 7S model describes an organisation as consisting of seven interrelated internal elements, split between 'hard' and 'soft' elements.

Hard

There are three hard elements of business behaviour

- Strategy – what will the company do?

- Structure – how should it be organised?

- Systems – what procedures need to be in place (few or many)?

Hard elements are easier to define or identify and management can directly influence them.

Soft

There are four soft elements

- Staff – what staff will we require?

- Style – what management style will work best?

- Shared values – what culture (attitudes) will be most suitable?

- Skills – what skills will our staff/company need?

Soft elements are more difficult to describe, less tangible and are more influenced by culture.

All seven elements must be aligned to ensure organisational success – a change in one element will have repercussions on the others and must be taken into account to ensure good integration.

(b) The McKinsey 7S model can be applied to Briggs as follows:

Strategy

The initial strategy of market penetration in the domestic market was appropriate to the start-up but is no longer relevant as a 50% share has been achieved and would be increasing difficult to improve upon. Instead a strategy of market development is now the case and Tom needs to ensure that the other elements of the 7S model are aligned with this.

Structure

The initial simple structure was appropriate to a start-up but needed changing as the company grew. The functional bureaucratic model currently in place will assist efficiency but may have contributed to a loss of trust and teamwork. To facilitate growth into new markets a switch to a more divisional or even matrix structure would be more appropriate.

Systems

The start-up could cope with few formal systems. Current systems are mainly concerned with service support but there are no or few strategic planning and new business generation systems. New systems are needed to ensure growth is focussed and controlled.

Staff

Few employees were needed at the start and most of those would have been experts delivering the service to customers. They were motivated by successful business growth and rewarded with business shares, of which market value was rising. As the firm grew there was a need for more support staff and a more conventional reward system introduced, ensuring alignment with the strategy in place. In terms of the new strategy, there will be a need to recruit further technical specialists who are familiar with the different lifestyles in each country, are fluent in the languages concerned and are familiar with relevant local laws and regulations. There may also be a need to reassess the best reward systems for each country based on local culture.

Style

Tom's 'democratic but chaotic management style' would have worked initially as the company was small enough for Tom to oversee and control everything. However, there is currently a lack of alignment as a chaotic style will clash with the structured bureaucracy.

Certainly going forwards the democratic aspect should be encouraged but divisional heads will need to be appointed.

Shared values

Initial values such as teamwork and trust have since been lost within a growing bureaucratic structure and will limit future growth unless this can be rectified. For full alignment with the new strategy, each country should have a team of people motivated to drive it forwards.

In some respects the values that Tom is encouraging of enthusiasm and excellence will help towards the new strategy. However, new shared values should be allowed to evolve as many people from new cultures come to the company and bring their own values, often, very different than the current ones.

Skills

Initially, apart from the counsellors and lifestyle coaches, there were few specialized skills with the rest of jobs are undertaken by management (the founders). As time went on more specialised skills were needed as the functional structure developed. To take the business forwards new skills, especially those relating to strategic planning, will be required. If Tom hasn't built up a team of management expertise yet, then this will also be required to ensure the company isn't limited by his own skill set and experience.

(c) Assuming each new country is set up as a division in its own right, in order to better align the 'structure' element of the 7S model, the following critical success factors and key performance indicators would be appropriate:

Consultant recruitment

It is vital that Briggs manages to recruit further technical specialists who are familiar with the different lifestyles in each country, are fluent in the languages concerned and are familiar with relevant local laws and regulations.

The success of this can be monitored by setting targets for appropriate qualifications and experience for new recruits and then measuring whether personnel gaps are filled within the timescales required.

Customer satisfaction

It is critical that customers are pleased with the service provided and that they feel it was useful and appropriate to their cultural backgrounds and needs.

This could be measured via the website using a customer satisfaction survey – in particular whether or not customers would recommend their service to a friend

16 ALFLONNSO (SEPT/DEC 16)

Tutorial note

There is a reasonably large amount of information to absorb in this question. You should anticipate this and practise a broad range of questions before the exam so that you feel comfortable in reading, interpreting and using the scenario.

Key answer tips

Part (a)(i) – there are only 5 marks available here so briefly explain why ABC allocates costs more accurately before focusing on the two costs in the scenario. A detailed explanation of ABC and its advantages is not needed and would waste time.

Part (a)(ii) – hopefully a straightforward 3 marks on core ABC calculations.

Part (b) – a methodical approach to the calculation is required here, working through each item in the scenario in turn. Good candidates will have identified the huge benefit of taking a lifecycle approach in terms of accuracy.

Part (c) – the key to scoring a good mark here is being able to relate your EMA knowledge to the particulars of the scenario.

(a) (i) **Activity based costing**

Activity based costing (ABC) allocates costs to products based on the activities which actually drive the cost to better allocate the costs.

At Alflonnso, the group accounting policy is to allocate waste treatment overhead costs on the basis of revenue, which is arbitrary. From the analyst's calculations, R&D costs do not seem to be allocated to specific product costs at all. This may be appropriate elsewhere in the group, where different products may consume similar levels of overheads, but the three new products being evaluated consume quite different amounts of R&D and waste treatment overheads.

It is therefore inappropriate to charge these costs to the products on the basis of revenue. Charging these costs on the basis of the activities which drive them, which are research hours and volume of waste by-products for R&D costs and waste treatment costs respectively, will give a more accurate costing. This will provide a better basis on which to evaluate the new products and set appropriate prices.

(ii) **Calculation of waste treatment cost**

	ALF7	Red	Green
Quantity of waste by-product (m litres)	8.0	34.00	0.75
[m litres produced/no. of m litres to make 1 litre of waste]	[100/12.5]	[85/2.5]	[75/100]
Allocated total $300m according to quantity of waste as proportion of total 55m litres:			
Annual waste treatment allocated ($m):	43.6	185.5	4.1
	[8 × 300/55]	[34 × 300/55]	[0.75 × 300/55]

R&D cost

Allocated total $60m according to required hours of research as proportion of total 30,400 hours:

R&D treatment allocated ($m):	1.6	16.8	7.9
	[800 × 60/30,400]	[8,500 × 60/30,400]	[4,000 × 60/30,400]

(b)   Average unit cost of each product over total lifecycle

$m	ALF7	Red	Green
Revenue [given]	800.0	1,105.0	825.0
Direct material, labour and energy [given]	(524.0)	(724.0)	(565.0)
Factory overheads [given]	(80.0)	(122.0)	(74.0)
Waste treatment [from part (a) (ii)]	(43.6)	(185.5)	(4.1)
Total annual net profit	152.4	73.5	181.9
Lifecycle duration (years)	3	15	8
Total net profit over lifecycle (before other lifecycle costs)	457.2	1,102.5	1,455.2
Scientific study [$4m × 20 years]	–	(80.0)	–
Decommissioning cost	–	(45.0)	–
R&D cost [from part (a) (ii)]	(1.6)	(16.8)	(7.9)
Total net profit over lifecycle	455.6	960.7	1,447.3
No. of litres produced over the lifecycle (m)	300	1,275	600
Average profit per litre over lifecycle	$1.52	$0.75	$2.41

From the analyst's calculations in Appendix 1, Red has the highest profitability per litre of the three products at $2.26, but this only covers a single period. As such, it does not consider costs which occur before production commences or after it ceases. When the costs of the products over their entire life cycles are taken into account, Red has the lowest average unit profit, the highest being Green at $2.41. This change has occurred as the R&D costs, the cost of the study which will span 20 years and the decommissioning costs have now been recognised. Knowing the costs over the entire lifecycle of a product will help the agrochemicals division to better evaluate its investment decisions, determine appropriate prices and generate an acceptable margin.

(c)   EMA

Environmental management accounting (EMA) involves the production of non-financial and financial information to support internal environmental management processes. This could involve measuring the physical movements of inputs to a production process, such as materials and energy, and outputs such as waste.

The agrochemicals division could also record financial data on costs and savings related to the environment. It appears that, in common with most other businesses, these costs are not currently identified by Alflonnso's accounting system and they lie hidden within overheads.

Managers have no incentive to reduce these environment related costs as they are not even aware of them, or the costs of poor environmental practices. EMA allows an organisation to identify environment related costs and take steps to control them. Such costs are often categorised into conventional costs, contingent costs and reputation costs.

Conventional costs

These costs include the cost of energy and raw materials, and may remain hidden within overheads. The energy costs of the three new products in the analyst's income statement are simply combined with raw material and direct labour costs. This does not, for example, highlight the relatively high energy cost to produce Green. Being unaware of this cost, managers are unable to take steps to redesign the specification or production process for the product in order to reduce the cost.

Contingent costs

These are costs which are incurred in the future, for example, the decommissioning costs of plant used to manufacture Red. This cost is significant at an estimated $45m, but occurs 15 years in the future and so the estimation is unlikely to be accurate.

Identification of these contingent costs will at least allow the agrochemicals division to more accurately estimate the cost of each of the three new products. Also, by identifying these costs at an early stage, this may allow managers to redesign the specification or production process for the product in order to reduce the cost and help prevent managers from focusing only on short-term performance.

Reputation costs

Reputation costs are incurred where an organisation acts in a way which may cause harm to the environment, and include sales lost as a result of loss of reputation. These costs are hard to quantify. For example, the accumulation of the existing product, ALF6, in the soil is said to have a potential effect on crop yields which may lead to future claims from users of the product or to loss of sales due to its potential harm to the environment.

Similarly, Alflonnso's failure, by producing Green, to improve crop yields in countries where food production is already scarce is likely to arouse disapproval by public and governments in the 25 countries where it operates. This again may result in lost sales or refusal by governments to grant licences for Alflonnso to operate.

Making managers aware of these reputation costs should focus their attention on the need to manage the risks of them occurring.

Marking scheme			
			Marks
(a)	(i)	Generic explanation of purpose of ABC – 1 mark Application to scenario – 1 mark per point	
		Maximum	5
	(ii)	Waste treatment costs – 2 marks R&D costs – 1 mark	
		Maximum	3
(b)		Revenue, direct costs, overheads (given) – 1 mark Waste treatment costs – 1 mark Total net profit over LC (before other LC costs) – 1 mark Scientific study – 1 mark Decommissioning cost – 1 mark R&D cost – 1 mark Total litres – 1 mark Average profit per litre over LC – 1 mark Comments – up to 3 marks	
		Maximum	9
(c)		Description of EMA – up to 2 marks Each cost category – up to 3 marks	
		Maximum	8
Total			25

Examiner's comments

This 25-mark question was based on the consideration of environmental management accounting and the use of appropriate costing techniques. In general, this was the least popular question.

Part a) (i) was generally poorly done as candidates did not address the demands of the question. Most candidates gave a developed definition of the costing technique which, whilst technically correct on almost every occasion, did not address the specific question demands as to how it may help the entity determine the specifics of product profitability. This relates to the point made previously with regard to definitions and rote learning: a maximum of 25% of the marks can be gained in this way and candidates should also be aware that full marks could be obtained for this part of the question without any definitions being given and purely application being undertaken.

Part a) (ii) was a brief question on a specific calculation and was well done by those who undertook it.

Part b) was generally passed by those who undertook it but most candidates showed a fundamental lack of technical competence by being unable to distinguish between costs that occurred on an annual basis and those that related to the product's overall life. It is also worth highlighting to candidates that when a question asks for comment on the results that what is being sought is more than 'this figure is larger than another.' In the context of this type of question, the commentary being sought is with regard to the implications of the figures: would they change a decision, has the use of one technique as opposed to another fundamentally changed the product cost and what significance should be attached to that? Commentary on the figures here should add more than can be seen from the figures themselves.

Part c) asked for candidates to relate environmental management accounting to the entity. Several answers gave a brief response which only defined and/or explained EMA. The question is assuming that some technical competence in the area of EMA exists and asked for how the principles of it would potentially benefit the entity. Once more, and consistent with the demands of the paper and its level, it is the application of the technique to the entity's practices that is being assessed. Would practices change? How? What might be involved? These are useful trigger questions for a candidate to consider when faced with a question of this nature.

17 GODEL (JUN 14 – AMENDED)

Key answer tips

Part (a) requires a discussion of the implications for performance management of splitting variances into planning and operational elements. This area has been examined in the past and it demonstrates the importance of your brought forward knowledge from PM.

Part (b) asks for an evaluation of the budgeting system. Ensure that you include a full discussion of both the pros and the cons and relate your points back to Godel.

Part (c) on ZBB is core knowledge and should not cause too many problems. Try not to focus too much on the benefits – there are a number of reasons why ZBB is inappropriate for this business.

(a) Planning variances are those which arise due to inaccurate forecasts or standards in the original budget setting. Operational variances are then the remainder due to the decisions of operational managers. A planning variance is the difference between the original standard and a revised one set with the benefit of hindsight. An operational variance is the difference between this revised standard and actual performance.

The total variable cost variance considers all costs together and so it is unlikely that gains or problems can be attributed to one individual. It is of limited value and should be used to point to more detailed analysis to identify the specific source of the variance. Currently, at Godel, the standard costs have been set too high and it appears that the bulk of the cost improvements can be attributed to this. The operational managers have had limited impact in driving down costs overall in May 2014.

The sales price variance indicates how far sales prices were misestimated in the budget (planning) and how well the sales managers have done in negotiating high prices with customers (operational). It appears that the budget was overoptimistic in setting too high an initial price but the sales managers have done well in negotiations with customers. The best individual sales managers could be identified and their techniques communicated to the rest of the sales team. The initial price setting process should be examined as it may have been due to faulty market intelligence about the price setting of competitors or the commercial situation of the customers (supermarkets).

(b) **Purpose and benefits of budgeting**

Budgeting is a key control tool for management and of particular importance in controlling costs in businesses such as Godel which is seeking to be a cost leader. At Godel, it is succeeding in this as total costs show a favourable variance. Budgets help to communicate and coordinate all the management activities within the company towards a single plan. The budget helps to attribute responsibility for performance, for example, the favourable material usage variance indicates that fewer raw materials are required than was planned and this reflects the work of the production manager in cutting waste and, possibly, the purchasing manager in buying good quality raw materials. The participatory nature of the budget process will help to motivate managers to achieve budget figures which they themselves have helped to set. It is important for this purpose that the budget is achievable or else it is demotivating.

Budgets assist the evaluation of performance by identifying variances and then point to areas for corrective action or future learning. At Godel, sales are clearly under-performing the plan both in terms of the quantity and price achieved. On the positive side, the managers in charge of labour and the workforce are working efficiently and cheaply.

There are several problems with budgeting at Godel:

1 The time-consuming nature of the process which is unusual as the business is mature and stable and so budget-setting should not be a complex process. The exasperation of the managers probably results from the fact that they see little benefit coming from work involved in forecasting. The operating variances given are relatively small.

2 The planning variances explain the bulk of the variances at Godel and so the operational managers have good reason to be concerned as their performance affects the operational variances only.

3   The operational and planning variance analysis is limited in scope. Performing more detailed operating and planning variance could also assist in addressing the complaint that operational managers are being asked to explain variances which are not their fault, for example, by doing this analysis for all the different cost headings in the operating statement and not just the total cost variance.

4   The use of standard costs in budgeting could discourage a system of continuous improvements which would help a cost leader in making efficiency gains. However, Godel's senior management may view that it is unlikely that there will be a need to make such changes on a regular basis and that a review of the costs once a year is sufficient.

(c)   Zero based budgeting (ZBB) is a method of budgeting that requires each cost element to be specifically justified, as though the activities to which the budget relates were being undertaken for the first time. Without approval, the budget allowance is zero.

There are four distinct stages in the implementation of ZBB:

1   Managers should specify for their responsibility centres those activities that can be individually evaluated.

2   Each of the individual activities is then described in a decision package. The decision package should state the costs and revenues expected from the given activity. It should be drawn up in such a way that the package can be evaluated and ranked against other packages.

3   Each decision package is evaluated and ranked usually using cost/benefit analysis.

4   The resources are then allocated to the various packages

The approach of ZBB is considered appropriate in industries where there are rapid changes in the business environment, new product developments and/or where there are very higher levels of overheads, especially discretionary costs such as research and development.

This approach at Godel would appear to be inappropriate for a number of reasons:

1   There does not appear to be the need to have to justify every cost from scratch. There is little evidence of budget slack or excessive spending and the work generated in having to prepare decision packages may increase the complaints about time-consuming exercises from the operational managers.

2   The lower level managers would now need to prepare their own decision packages and would require training in this. They do not appear to have the appetite for such development.

3   There is no indication that there are rapid changes in Godel's business and little innovation, so the ZBB approach would not appear to yield many benefits.

Overall, then, there are insufficient benefits and many barriers to switching to ZBB at Godel and it is not recommended.

	Marking scheme		Marks
(a)	Definitions	up to	1
	Total variable cost variance	up to	3
	Sales price variance	up to	3
			___
		Maximum	**6**
			___
(b)	Benefits of budgeting for Godel including:		
	Planning and coordination – meeting overall strategy		
	Responsibility		
	Integration		
	Motivation		
	Evaluation		
	1 per point made up to 6 marks		6
	Problems with budgeting at Godel including:		
	Time-consuming and unnecessary		
	Lack of recognition of planning failures		
	Insufficient planning and operational analysis		
	Impedes continuous improvement		
	1 per point made up to 6 marks		6
			___
		Maximum	**11**
			___
(c)	Description	up to	3
	Appropriateness at Godel	up to	5
	Recommendation		1
			___
		Maximum	**8**
			___
Total			**25**
			___

Examiner's comments

This question was based on the current and possible future budgeting systems at a sweet manufacturer, Godel.

Part (a) called for a comprehension of planning and operating variances. Most candidates did not know the definitions of these and so talked about all the other variances in the appendix thus avoiding the question.

Part (b) was also inadequately attempted. As in the past, too many candidates only saw the negatives of the existing system and few identified the positives for a traditional company like Godel.

18   DIBBLE (MAR/JUN 16)

Key answer tips

A great revision question covering the core elements of ABC and ABM. Ensure that you are very comfortable with this before the exam.

(a) **(i)** **Implementation of ABC**

ABC is an alternative to absorption costing, which is the method currently used by Dibble. ABC is a detailed fact gathering and data analysis technique.

In order to implement ABC production, overheads need to be grouped into cost pools as in the analysis of production overheads for Dibble in the management accounts extracts.

Then cost drivers for each cost pool must be identified. Cost drivers are the activities which bring about the costs, for example, the setup of the CAM machinery in Steel Division will be driven by the number of batches of production.

Once the cost pools and their associated cost drivers have been established, the cost per unit of cost driver can be calculated for each individual activity. The overhead costs are absorbed into each unit based on how much of the activity the unit uses, therefore, for example, units which require more inspection and testing will be allocated more of those costs. The overhead costs are then added to the prime costs in order to calculate the full cost of production.

(ii) **Appropriateness of ABC**

ABC is especially useful where there is a wide range of complex products and where production overheads form a larger proportion of total production costs. In Steel Division, there is a large range of products, many of them bespoke or one-off designs. Production overheads form 28% (4,472/(20,605 – 4,533)) of total production costs, and the use of ABC will be appropriate in this division.

ABC enables a more accurate cost of production to be calculated, which is very --useful in setting product prices. This could be especially useful in Steel Division which has a wide range of products subject to a number of manufacturing processes. It will help to ensure that each product is priced high enough in order to produce an acceptable margin, but not so high so as to become uncompetitive. This is especially important as Steel Division's strategy is to produce bespoke products at prices comparable to competitors who produce simpler, more conventional products.

ABC enables managers to determine what activities drive the costs, and so focus on reducing those activities to control costs. Not all production overheads, for example, inspection costs of the coatings in Steel Division, are related to production volumes. It is equally possible to apply ABC techniques to overheads other than production overheads.

Problems with ABC

ABC is less useful in businesses such as Timber Division where there is a small range of relatively simple products and where production overheads only comprise around 1% of total production costs. Of the production overheads in Timber Division, storage is by far the biggest and is likely to be driven by production volumes.

It may be difficult to determine what the drivers of production costs are. Storage costs could also be related to the insolvency of a customer. It may be impossible to allocate all overheads to the specific activities which drive them and so management will have to apply judgement.

Calculation of ABC may be time consuming, complex and poorly understood by managers. As such, the time and expense of doing so may not be justified. This appears to be the case in Timber Division where there are only a few, relatively simple products and few production overheads. Whereas in Steel Division, where there is a wide range of more complex products and a high proportion of production overheads, ABC is more appropriate than the traditional absorption costing method currently used at Dibble.

(b) ABM is the use of ABC methods in order to improve organisational performance by meeting the needs of customers using the lowest possible amount of resources or costs. ABM can be applied at the operational level or to help develop strategy.

Product pricing

By accurately determining the cost of each product using ABC, Dibble would be able to ensure that prices are set so as to achieve an acceptable margin and also remain competitive with the prices currently charged in the rest of the market.

Steel Division charges customers a standard mark up of 10% on top of the $650k subcontractor's costs for the coating and painting of the steel. This means that customers are only being charged $65k whereas the costs of storage of goods awaiting subcontract work and of transporting the goods to the subcontractor total $695k.

By identifying the cost pools relating to the subcontract work, Steel Division can determine that it is making a loss on the subcontract work as a whole. It could therefore adjust the price of painted and coated products to ensure that an acceptable contribution margin is achieved. This is an example of operational ABM. At the strategic level, this type of information could help Dibble decide which product types to develop or discontinue.

The same principle may also apply where ABC can be used to identify which types of customers are the most profitable. In that way, resources can be focused on retaining and managing these customer groups. Action can be taken by additional advertising or product development in order to focus on these particular markets. By analysing customer profitability, it may be possible to reduce costs or increase revenue to make certain customer groups or product lines more profitable, both in the short and long term.

By identifying lines of business with poor profitability, Dibble could discontinue selling to particular customers, or selling particular products, if appropriate action could not be taken to improve profitability.

Analysis of activities

By analysing the activities which drive the costs, Steel Division could determine which activities may not be required or could be done in a more efficient way. It may be possible to introduce improvements in the short term, for example, changes in the production process which may improve efficiency. In the longer term, strategic changes could be made to the way in which activities are undertaken, such as by outsourcing other activities in addition to the painting and coating which is currently outsourced.

Identifying the costs of transporting painted finished goods back from the subcontractors to Steel Division could lead them to evaluate ways to reduce this cost, for example, by despatching goods to customers directly from the subcontractors' premises. This is a non-value added activity, i.e. one which consumes resources, such as time and cost to transport goods to and from the subcontractors, but which is of no additional value to the customer. In contrast, ABM may help identify value adding activities, such as the coating and painting, which customers are prepared to pay for.

Of the five categories of production overheads, only machining time is a value adding activity, sometimes categorised as a primary activity. Setting up the CAM machinery is a secondary activity, which does not itself add value, but is required in order to perform a value adding activity (machining).

The other overheads, storage, transfer and inspection, are all non-value adding activities which should be eliminated or reduced. By identifying the activities which drive these costs managers can attempt to do this.

However, given the nature of Dibble's products, it is likely that some inspection will still be required for safety or commercial reasons, as shown by the litigation case relating to the faulty product. The production manager's proposal to increase the costs of inspection is inappropriate, as having identified inspection as a non-value adding activity, it would be better to focus attention on getting the product right first time.

Design improvements

Steel Division has a wide range of relatively complex or even bespoke products. ABM can help managers take decisions at the product design stage, where many of the product's costs are already committed. These can include using fewer or more standardised components, such as a more limited range of paints and coatings.

Where strategic decisions are being taken, for example, about new product lines or lines of business, such as with Steel Division's strategy to develop novel innovative products, ABM can help assess whether such developments are likely to be profitable at an early stage. This would help avoid development costs for products which could turn out to be unprofitable. This could also help allocate resources, such as capital investment, to the most profitable lines of business.

Performance measurement

For ABM to be successful, it will require the commitment of senior management and effective communication and training of employees at all levels in the organisation as to the benefits and methods of ABM. This will incur management time and cost, and divert attention from existing management activities.

New performance measurement systems will need to be developed. Employee rewards will need to be aligned to key performance measures, such as the reduction of non-value adding processes like inspection. This will ensure that employees work towards the objectives of the organisation. Additional information gathering systems, or adaptations to existing information systems, will also be required, which will again incur additional cost and may disrupt existing activities.

Marking scheme			
			Marks
(a)	Implementation of ABC – 1 mark per point		
		Maximum	4
(b)	Appropriateness of ABC – up to 6 marks		
	Problems with ABC – up to 6 marks		
		Maximum	8
(c)	Improving performance using ABM – 1 mark per point		
		Maximum	13
			———
Total			25
			———

19   HERMAN SWAN & CO (DEC 12 – AMENDED)

Key answer tips

Burns and Scapens had not featured in the APM exam before this question, which should have presented few problems, provided you knew the content and applied it to the scenario.

(a)   Overview

Burns and Scapens have studied changes in management accounting and noted how it has changed focus from financial control to business support. So the management accountant has become more of a generalist within the business providing an internal consulting service for managers. They have named this new role a hybrid accountant. Traditionally, it was thought that accountants needed to be independent from operational managers in order to allow them to objectively judge and report their accounting information to senior management. Burns and Scapens also report that many accountants believe that there is an element of a current fashion in the need for change.

Burns and Scapens state that there are three main forces for change: technology, management structure and competition. Taking technology first, a significant change has occurred over the past 20 years in the quality and quantity of information technology. In the past, the accountant was one of the few people in the organisation who had access to the IT system and the information generated, as the outputs from the IT system were used to prepare highly sensitive financial reports to management. Data input was strictly controlled. Now, however, management information systems (MIS) allow users across the organisation to input data and run reports giving the type of analysis once only provided by the management accountant. So, the management accountant now just acts as another user of the system. This force is present at HS as it has seen the SBU managers gain more access to information via the new MIS.

Secondly, changes in management structure have forced change on the accountant. For example, responsibility for budgeting has often moved from the head office to operational management. This force is illustrated at HS where the increased autonomy of SBUs has driven the SBU managers to take more of the decisions that would have been reserved for the head office management accountant. These managers will be using financial and non-financial indicators and they will be producing forecasts.

The management accountant will be providing reports alongside the SBU reports, often trying to provide a link between the operational reports, the financial consequences and the strategic outcomes desired by the board.

Finally, the competitive environment also drives change in the role of the management accountant. Over the last 20 years, there has been a move in organisations to a more strategic focus with the need for competitive advantage being emphasised. As a result, the traditional accountant's focus on the final profit figure has been seen as short term and this has led organisations to focus on a range of measures to try to capture the longer-term trends in their performance.

This is evident at HS as it is a family firm focused on providing wealth and management opportunities to the family and not being driven by short-term outside shareholder demands. HS also faces global competition from expanding large brands that will try to enter and dominate its markets using their scale to competitive advantage. Therefore, HS will have to be flexible and innovative in response.

Benefits

All of the factors requiring the changes in the role of the management accountant are present at HS. It will be of particular benefit that the management accountant can take a supporting role to assist the SBU managers in getting the most from the new MIS. This will entail the accountant understanding the needs of the particular manager and then working with them to extract valuable reports from the MIS. It may also require the development of different performance measures beyond the traditional measure of profit.

From the organisation's perspective, the accountant will be a guide to the SBU manager to ensure that strategic goals are reflected in their performance management.

(b) Brand identity quickly conveys an image of quality and price that helps customers to identify the products and so helps to create customer loyalty to the brand. Loyalty results in repurchase and continued use of the products. Brand awareness is an indicator of the strength of a product's/organisation's place in the customers' minds.

From the customer perspective, at HS, the brand is part of the competitive advantage of the business. The history and quality of the products justify the high margins that are charged for such luxury goods. The customer will want to see the family story behind the company maintained and this will require a large annual marketing budget. The company will want to promote itself in places that match with that brand story, so sponsorship of public events may be large. Controlling such a budget will be difficult and the management accountant will want to regularly test the usefulness of the marketing spend against sales growth in order to identify the most effective marketing channels to use. HS will have to be sensitive to the needs and attitudes of the different markets in which it operates. The testing of the marketing will have to be appropriately segmented (geographically, by age, by gender, by income) as a result. This spending will be both regular, to maintain the general brand and its position, and irregular, to match specific product launches or marketing opportunities.

From the internal process perspective at HS, quality control is of great importance. This is true in both the production and retailing SBUs. In production SBUs, the spending on prevention of faults and the appraisal of products on the production line and their repair will all indicate the importance of quality at HS. In the retail SBU, service staff training will be high in order to give a high quality of experience to customers in the company's shops.

There will also be a need for high capital costs in order to fit out the retail premises to the standard expected of a premium brand such as HS.

(c)   Measuring brand awareness can be done crudely through the revenue and market share that HS enjoys. In more detail, consumers can be tested on the marketing of HS products in order to see if they recall the brand that is associated with HS' logos and products. Again, this will need to be done in each of the different markets that HS operates.

Measuring brand loyalty can be done through customer retention and repeat purchase rates. The elasticity of demand to price will also indicate customer loyalty. The ability of a brand to be able to push through price increases with little loss of demand is a key benefit of brand loyalty. It can also be measured by considering the profit margins that HS enjoys and comparing these to other companies that make similar products but without such a strong brand.

Marking scheme			
			Marks
(a)	Describe Burns and Scapens' view of the overall change	up to	2
	Identify the three factors driving change and illustrate at HS (up to 3 marks per factor)	up to	9
	Benefits of the change at HS	up to	3
		Maximum	**13**
(b)	Describe brand loyalty and awareness	up to	2
	Impact of brand loyalty and awareness	up to	6
	Customer perspective and internal process perspective		
			8
(c)	Evaluate measures of brand loyalty and awareness	up to	**4**
Total			**25**

Examiner's comments

In part (a) most candidates had a broad grasp of the issues being dealt with by Burns and Scapens and did well trying to weave these in to the specific circumstances at HS. However, few candidates could remember the detail of the report and so their analysis often missed out on one of the three factors mentioned (technology, management structure and competition).

With part (b) most candidates were able to discuss brand loyalty from the customer perspective and suggest suitable measures, fewer were able to clearly distinguish the internal process perspective although they had realised that quality was a key part of the product offering. The better candidates distinguished themselves by differentiating between loyalty and awareness with awareness preceding loyalty and being about beginning to attract new customers while loyalty was about retention of existing customers.

20 BOOXE (JUN 14)

Key answer tips

In part (a) a cost/benefit analysis is required. This should be reasonably straightforward but be careful to not spend too much time of the calculations here.

In part (b) do not just write everything you know about BPR. Take a few minutes to plan your answer ensuring that both areas of the requirement are addressed, that there are a sufficient number of points and that these points are prioritised.

Part (c) focuses on the HR aspects of performance management. Use your own experience to offer advice on the appraisal process at Booxe.

(a) **Annual costs of new system:**

	$
Hardware for warehouse and purchasing depts (depreciation)	27,500
Software total cost (depreciation)	34,375
On-going servicing cost	22,500
	———
	84,375

Benefit of new system (cost savings):

Staff costs		$	
	Warehouse	125,000	= 10 × $25,000 × 50%
	Purchasing	54,400	= $32,000 × 8.5/5
		———	
		179,400	

Net benefit $95,025

The BPR project will yield a net benefit of $95,025 p.a. and so the project is financially successful. However, there are other costs not included in this analysis such as redundancy/retraining of the staff whose workload has been reduced and the training costs for staff on the new system.

Tutorial note

An analysis using other methods such as payback or accounting rate of return would be equally acceptable.

(b) Business process re-engineering (BPR) is described as the fundamental rethinking and radical redesign of business processes to achieve dramatic improvements in critical contemporary measures of performance, such as cost, quality, service and speed.

It cuts across traditional departmental lines in order to achieve a more efficient delivery of the final product. At Booxe, this is evident in the effect which the BPR project has had on both warehousing and purchasing departments.

This change to a process view will require a change towards process teams rather than functional departments. Employees will need to retrain in order to gain additional skills. The organisational hierarchy will flatten with the employees being given more responsibility to make decisions. This is often aided by the introduction of a unified corporate database accessed through an ERP system. These will represent major changes at Booxe which appears to have become set in its ways. The change will require much communication and leadership from senior management as a result.

The implications for accounting at Booxe are that performance measures must be redesigned around processes rather than departments. The aim is to identify where value is being added and eliminate where resources are employed to no valuable outcome. An activity-based approach might be used to model the processes in the business as part of the BPR restructuring and this could be carried on in the accounting systems. The ABC system of costing is a more detailed method of allocating overheads in order to achieve a more accurate product cost and, therefore, a more accurate idea of the profit each product generates. It is more time-consuming and expensive to set up compared to traditional overhead absorption methods but in the context of the intended changes to processes at Booxe due to BPR, it will fit well. Financial reports will have to be redesigned around process teams and any variances to budget used may need to be reconsidered in the light of the activity-based approach.

Tutorial note

Other analysis models (for example from SBL) could be relevant to this answer and would be given appropriate credit within the mark limitations of the requirement.

(c) Appraisal is the process of collecting and reviewing data on an employee's work which will provide an assessment of their capabilities and potential in order to improve performance, for example, by training. It also presents an opportunity to deal with other HR issues, such as discipline, career management, motivation and determining rewards.

There is a general need for some kind of performance assessment; however, appraisal systems are often criticised as irrelevant to the work of the organisation. Indeed, the current system at Booxe has arguably become too informal, possibly as a result of neither side of the process taking it seriously. In order to make the process relevant, appraisal is seen as a means of control of staff and linking their activities to the overall organisational goals such as driving down costs. It will lead to improved development of appropriate skills and greater motivation on the part of the staff, especially if linked to a suitable reward system.

The balance between control and development within the appraisal process will link to the culture within the business. At Booxe, there is a culture of craft appreciation which implies the importance of development of skills and thus it may be that there has been a loss of the sense of control and this has led to the increased costs which the CEO is trying to drive down.

			Marks
Marking scheme			
(a)	Calculations		
	Costs:	Depreciation	1
		Total	1
	Savings:	Warehousing	1
		Purchasing	1
		Net benefit	1
	Comments:	1 mark for suitable comment on the calculations	1
			———
		Maximum	**6**
			———
(b)	Definition of BPR – 1 mark per point	up to	2
	Culture – 1 mark per point	up to	5
	Impact on accounting systems – 1 mark per point	up to	5
			———
		Maximum	**11**
			———
(c)	Definition of process – 1 mark per point	up to	2
	Purpose – 1 mark per point	up to	4
	Balance of control and development – 1 mark per point	up to	3
			———
		Maximum	**8**
			———
Total			**25**
			———

Examiner's comments

This question covered the impact of a BPR project and the performance management of staff at Booxe, a furniture manufacturer.

Part (a) was generally well done although many candidates muddled a per annum view of cost/benefit with a project lifetime view which left answers difficult to interpret.

Part (b) was again generally well done. Most candidates realised there were two areas to discuss and split their answers appropriately. A large number took the hints in the scenario to consider how this might link to activity-based approaches and the introduction of ERPS. The one weakness demonstrated was a simplistic grasp of what 'culture' might be.

Candidates who performed well in part (c) usually discussed the purpose of an appraisal system, considered the issues at Booxe and then suggested solutions to the problems identified. Those candidates that gave text-book answers did not score marks very efficiently.

21 GANYMEDE UNIVERSITY (JUN 12 – AMENDED)

Key answer tips

This question concerned a university (Ganymede) which was in the process of undertaking a benchmarking exercise with two other universities in its country. This was easily the most popular question in section B.

Overall, answers were disappointing to what ought to be a straightforward question in a APM examination. Make sure you understand the steps involved in a benchmarking exercise as well as how to interpret the results of such an exercise.

(a)   Benchmarking process

The benchmarking process is often described using seven steps. The following are the steps with the current state of the exercise:

1   Set objectives and decide the areas to benchmark

GU has set the objective of improving efficiency and is benchmarking all of its administration operations relating to teaching and research.

2   Identify key performance drivers and indicators

The performance drivers have been provided and the indicators are based on the activity per driver. The drivers might be improved by distinguishing between teaching staff and administrative staff.

3   Select organisations for benchmarking comparison

The government selected the three largest universities for benchmarking which excludes five other smaller universities. This can be justified if the large universities cover similar teaching and research areas while the smaller ones are narrower in focus (for example science and engineering subjects only). However, it may be that there are examples of good practice in university administration that will be missed as a result of restricting the exercise. It might be sensible to include foreign universities in the exercise. Differences in the mix of subjects researched and taught might also affect the results (e.g. managing teaching facilities in engineering and law will be different).

4   Measure performance of all organisations involved in benchmarking

The basic data has been gathered as required by government. This step would normally be more complex in a private sector situation as commercial secrecy would hinder the sharing of information.

5   Compare performances

This is the stage that has been reached. See answer to part (b) for results.

6   Specify improvement projects

The results of the comparison should lead to identification of areas for improvement. If GU is not demonstrating leading performance then it should send staff to the top performer to identify their best practice processes and devise projects to implement these at GU.

7   Implement and monitor improvements

Management should perform a post-project review in order to identify if the improvement has achieved or exceeded its goals and consider lessons that have been learned from the project.

(b) The benchmarking has been completed as follows:

	GU	AU	BU
	$	$	$
Research			
Contract management	78	87	97
Laboratory management	226	257	281
Teaching facilities management	951	1,197	920
Student support services	71	89	73
Teachers support services	506	532	544
Accounting	204	204	197
Human resources	156	156	191
IT management	817	803	737
General services	2,153	2,088	2,286

Research categories are considered per $000 of contract value supported.

Teaching facilities and student support are considered per student.

Other categories are considered per staff member.

From the results, it can be seen that GU is best at controlling costs associated with research contracts and it has the highest research funding ($185m). This may indicate that the government monitors such cost control and that GU should ensure its continued good practice in this area. AU spends most per student on its teaching facilities and student support although it has the smallest number of students. It might be expected that this would lead to higher student enrolment which may imply that student enrolment is not significantly dependent on these factors. However, lower dropout rates and higher student pass rates and future success in gaining employment may reflect the more expensive teaching environment at AU. These quality measures are not being reflected in the benchmarking exercise.

In accounting services, all the universities perform broadly in line. BU has achieved a small 3.5% advantage over the others.

In human resources management, BU is 22% more costly which is surprising given the larger staff numbers at BU over which to spread such a central cost.

In IT management, there is some variation of performance with BU costs being 10% lower than GU's. These variations may well be due to the subjects being taught (for example, universities that are more orientated to science and technology will probably demand larger computing resources).

In general services, all the universities perform broadly in line. AU has achieved a small 3% advantage over GU.

It is necessary to give a warning about the difficulty of comparing the performance of the universities due to differences in location and the mix of subjects taught and researched.

<table>
<tr><td colspan="2" align="center">Marking scheme</td><td></td></tr>
<tr><td></td><td></td><td>Marks</td></tr>
<tr><td>(a)</td><td>1 mark per point up to 8 marks. (Note only 2 marks are available for identifying the headings in the process.)</td><td></td></tr>
<tr><td></td><td align="right">Maximum</td><td>10</td></tr>
<tr><td>(b)</td><td>Up to 8 marks for calculations applying the appropriate drivers. Up to 8 marks for commenting on the results.</td><td></td></tr>
<tr><td></td><td align="right">Maximum</td><td>15</td></tr>
<tr><td>Total</td><td></td><td>25</td></tr>
</table>

Examiner's comments

Part (a) required candidates to assess the progress of the benchmarking exercise. This required knowledge of the steps involved in such an exercise and an ability to see what had and had not been completed in the scenario example. Answers were generally unstructured with those that laid out a set of steps in the benchmarking process scoring best. Nevertheless, a general understanding of the method was present but this had to be combined with suitable comments about Ganymede's current progress in order to gain a pass mark.

Part (b) required candidates to evaluate Ganymede's benchmarked position. This ought to have been a straightforward analysis of the data table given. However, as mentioned earlier, candidates displayed a disappointing lack of judgement over what constitutes useful advice in this scenario and failed to use the indicated drivers in order to calculate suitable relative measures. Also, as in Question 2 (a), the commentary was often restricted to the unnecessary writing out in a sentence the output of the table, e.g. 'GU has the highest research contract value', with no value-adding (and mark-scoring) comments attached.

22 MAXWELL (DEC 14 – AMENDED)

Key answer tips

Part (a) asked for an assessment of two given plans. You are expected to carry out some calculations here but note that the level of detail in the model answer goes beyond what is needed. Leave time to conclude on your calculations.

In part (b) it would be useful to explain the different categories of environmental cost. This will help to give your answer structure and depth.

Part (c) requires a discussion of lifecycle costing issues. Make sure that you adequately focus on the issues here.

(a) The environmental goal of Maxwell is to reach the CO_2 emission reduction target of 20% in five years while increasing capacity to cope with an expected rise of 10% in demand over that period.

The changes in mix of generating stations have the following effects:

Plan 1a

| | | Details for each type of station | | | | Totals for Maxwell | |
Power station type		Maximum generating power (MW)	Operating cost of electricity ($/MWh)	Capital cost ($m)	Number of stations	Total capital invested ($m)	Total CO_2 emissions (million tonnes)
Coal	(small)	300	25	1,320	3	5,280	3.15
	(large)	600	25	2,640	3	10,560	12.61
Gas	(small)	300	50	300	7	2,400	3.15
	(large)	900	50	900	2	1,800	7.10
Nuclear		1,200	20	6,000	3	12,000	0.50
						32,040	26.51

The new nuclear station will cost $6,000m. The total power output of Maxwell is maintained at 10,200 MW and the total CO_2 emissions falls by 15.4% to 22.43 million tonnes. The operating cost of electricity will fall on average as a nuclear station is the cheapest one to operate. Therefore, Maxwell will have maintained its capacity and reduced CO_2 emissions but it will not have covered the rise in demand nor met the government's target for CO_2 reduction. (Plan 1b will provide the same generating capacity as Plan 1a and it will be less expensive in capital terms but it will not reduce CO_2 emissions.)

Plan 2

The addition of a second new nuclear station would cost a further $6,000m and would increase power-generating capacity by 11.8% to 11,400 MW. This would cover the expected rise of 10% in demand for electricity due in the next five years. It would increase the total CO_2 emissions by only 1.1% (0.25/22.43, assuming it is done in combination with Plan 1a) and would, therefore, further reduce the average CO_2 emitted in the operation of the stations.

We do not have the detailed figures for actual power output for each station but if we use maximum power capacity, then currently, Maxwell produces 0.0026 tonnes of CO_2 per max MW (= 26.51/10,200).

If the company pursues plan 1a and plan 2 in combination, then it will produce 0.0020 tonnes of CO_2 per max MW (= 22.68/11,400). This is a 23% reduction and indicates the government's target may be achieved.

If the company pursues plan 1b and plan 2 in combination, then it will produce 0.0023 tonnes of CO_2 per max MW (= 26.76/11,400). This is a 12% reduction and indicates the government's target may not be achieved.

(b) Management accounts provide us with an analysis of the performance of the business. However, traditional accounting systems are unable to deal adequately with environmental costs. As a result, managers are unaware of these costs and have no information with which to manage or reduce them.

Specific areas include the following:

- Conventional costs, such as energy costs will not be prioritised by management since they often hidden within overheads.

- Contingent costs such as future compliance costs or remediation costs when a power station is decommissioned are often incurred towards the end of a project so are ignored by managers who focus on short- term performance. This aspect is addressed within environmental lifecycle costing below.

- Relationship costs such as the cost of producing environmental information for public reporting are often ignored by operational managers who are unaware of their existence. It is likely that a separate PR department within Maxwell will deal with communications to the local community to reassure them about safety, for example.

- Reputational costs such as costs associated with failing to address environmental issues may be ignored by managers who are unaware of the risk of incurring them.

(c)   Lifecycle costing records the costs of a product 'from cradle to grave', taking into account the environmental consequences across the whole life of the product. In order to appraise a project correctly, cost recording systems must capture all costs.

In particular for a nuclear power station, these must include:

- those costs incurred prior to production such as costs of handling regulatory difficulties and design choices, and also

- those costs incurred after production ceases such as the clean-up costs of decommissioning and decontaminating the site and safely storing all waste.

It is important that these costs are identified and included in the initial project appraisal. In the case of Maxwell building a new nuclear power station, there are the uncertain costs up front associated with the regulatory process which could include the financing costs associated with delays in the project while regulatory approval is sought. There is the normal uncertainty over the building cost when a project costs $6bn and takes five years to complete. Finally, there is the estimated $1bn in decommissioning costs which again carry uncertainty. If Maxwell is to be able to claim to be financially and environmentally responsible, then it must have plans in place to cover these costs.

Marking scheme		Marks
(a)	2 marks for identifying the detailed environmental goal 1 mark for choosing suitable ways to assess the goal (choice of indicators) Up to 4 marks for each plan	
	Maximum	10
(b)	Up to 2 marks for describing lifecycle costing Up to 6 marks for discussing issues associated with Plan 2	
	Maximum	8
(c)	1 mark for each well explained point or example	
	Maximum	7
Total		25

23   ENT ENTERTAINMENT CO (JUN 11 – AMENDED)

Key answer tips

This question uses the BCG matrix which is also covered in SBL. In APM you are more likely to have to calculate key inputs such as market growth and share and, more critically, evaluate its use for performance management.

(a)   The BCG matrix breaks a business into its component units and then considers their performance in terms of the growth of the unit (usually measured by revenue) and the relative market share of each unit.

The sector growth and market share for each of ENT's divisions is as follows:

	2010	2011	2012	2013	
Growth in sector					
Restaurants		1.0%	1.0%	0.0%	
Cafes		9.0%	11.0%	9.0%	
Bars		–2.0%	–3.0%	–3.0%	
Dance clubs		6.0%	6.0%	9.0%	
Market share					
Restaurants	0.5%	0.5%	0.5%	0.6%	
Cafes	1.0%	1.0%	1.1%	1.2%	
Bars	3.5%	3.5%	3.5%	3.6%	
Dance clubs	11.0%	11.0%	10.9%	11.0%	
Relative market share	2010	2011	2012	2013	*Mkt leader*
Restaurants	0.17	0.17	0.18	0.19	3.0%
Cafes	0.33	0.34	0.37	0.39	3.0%
Bars	1.17	1.17	1.18	1.22	3.0%
Dance clubs	0.73	0.73	0.73	0.73	15.0%

(Relative market share calculated as a ratio of division's market share to market leader's share. Figures calculated to nearest 0.1%.)

Additionally,

	Market growth (2011 – 2014) % pa	*ENT divisional growth (2011 – 2014) % pa*
Restaurant	0.67	4.67
Café	9.66	15.28
Bars (Shrunk)	–2.67	–1.34
Dance clubs	6.99	6.98

Tutorial note

There are more calculations given here than are needed for a good answer. They are intended to illustrate useful analysis of the data given.

(b) The restaurant and bar sectors are slow growth or in decline while the clubs and cafes appear to be growing at a pace well above the general economic expansion of 2% pa. ENT has a strong position in the bar and club sectors but is relatively small in the restaurant and cafe sectors.

Consequently, the restaurant division would be seen as a dog with low growth and poor market share which would make it a poor candidate for investment. A disposal could be considered unless there are other reasons to keep it (such as it acts as a feeder to dance clubs). The cafe division is a problem child where there is the possibility of good growth in the sector but the division lacks market share in such a fragmented market. The sector appears ripe for consolidation and so either the division should be financed to grow by acquisition or else sold on to another consolidator. The bar division is a cash cow as it has a strong share of a low growth sector. It will be managed for its cash generative capabilities and will be heavily cost controlled. Finally, the dance clubs represent another problem child with strong growth and a large market share (near the market leader). They would not be considered a star as they lack market leadership but would be considered an excellent candidate for investment to achieve that position.

This portfolio of divisions represents a good spread of businesses with the cash generative bar business supplying the financial resources for the development of the cafe and club businesses. It is unclear from this analysis how creative the company as a whole is at developing new businesses to replace the poorer performing entities.

(c) The BCG matrix can be beneficial as it allows the company to view the prospects of its different divisions. A different style of management should be applied to each division based on this analysis. Those businesses which are in faster growing sectors will require more capital to be invested and may not generate cash as efficiently from profits. However, those businesses in slower growing mature markets should have a focus on cost control and cash generation. Business units identified as cash cows and, particularly, dogs should not be dismissed since if they are properly managed they can provide a rich source of cash as they are run down.

The performance management systems and metrics used by the divisions should therefore be adjusted to reflect this analysis. The metrics for high growth prospects of cafes and clubs will be based on profit and return on investment, while those in lower growth, such as the bar division, will be focused on margins and cash generation.

However, the BCG matrix is a very simple method of analysis. For example, using relative market share measured against the largest competitor, where a value of 1·0 is used as cut off between large and small, means there is only one star or cow per market. It was designed as a tool for product portfolio analysis rather than performance measurement.

As a performance system, it seems to downgrade traditional measures of performance such as profit and shareholder wealth and therefore may not be well aligned with all of the key stakeholders' objectives. It should be seen as a starting point for considering the appropriate performance management for a business unit but not the final result.

Additionally, it may be that different products with each business unit may not fit the unit's classification. For example, the newly launched wine bar format seems to be in a higher growth sub-sector and so applying the performance systems and management style of a dog business would not be appropriate. It may also be difficult to distinguish the sectors from each other as, for example, it may be difficult to define the difference between a cafe and a restaurant. The model also fails to consider the links between the business units, for example, where the bars or cafes may serve as feeder businesses for late night dance clubs.

(d) The existing remuneration system is primarily based on the division's performance compared to budget. It is likely that the management style will be highly cost conscious and conservative as a result. This would be appropriate for the bar and restaurant divisions which foresee low growth. However, this could present particular problems for the divisions that are or could be grown (cafes and clubs). They will require a more entrepreneurial managerial approach and, therefore, should be using long-term profit measures of performance in order to align the manager's motivation with the business unit's needs.

The chairman is also correct to be concerned about the broad measure of divisional performance (EVA™) and whether this is coherent with the budgetary approach to management reward in the divisions. There is the possibility that if the budgets are not set in order to maximise EVA™ then the overall objectives are not reflected in the reward system at divisional level.

	Marking scheme		
			Marks
(a)	6 marks for appropriate calculations.		
		Maximum	6
(b)	Up to 5 marks for an appropriate classification with reasons.		
		Maximum	5
(c)	Up to 2 marks on general benefits of BCG analysis. Up to 2 marks on how BCG can be applied in performance systems. Up to 5 marks on limitations of the BCG approach. To score well the comments must be illustrated by application to the scenario.		
		Maximum	8
(d)	1 mark per point. Maximum of 6 marks.		
		Maximum	6
Total			25

Examiner's comments

With part (a) many candidates did not know that the growth element of the analysis referred to the growth of the market sector and either ignored this element or calculated the growth of the division instead. This lead to poor marks as half of the analysis was therefore missing and the conclusions compromised as a result. Also, some candidates chose to ignore most of the forecast numerical data and only calculate the current position of the company. This wasted an opportunity to score marks on the historical trends and also, the expected future position which is relevant if giving strategic advice.

Requirement (b) was also affected by this lack of knowledge of the method. However, there were a number of excellent answers in which, better candidates demonstrated good confidence in exposing the weaknesses of the BCG model and suggesting possible alternative solutions to performance management at ENT.

Requirement (c) requested an evaluation of the divisional managers' remuneration package. The candidates were asked to consider the link with the current divisional performance system and also the BCG analysis. The answers to this part often represented the candidate's best work on this question although few candidates displayed a clear grasp of the scenario. Better candidates noted the problem of applying a uniform package based on cost performance where they noted from the BCG analysis that some divisions showed growth or growth prospects that required a different style of management. They also commented on the lack of alignment of the divisional performance measure with the cost-based bonus element of the package.

24 PLX REFINERY CO (PILOT 10 – AMENDED)

Key answer tips

A useful question on the core areas of the environmental management accounting topic. This is a fantastic revision tool. Make sure you have the necessary knowledge in place and that you can apply it to the particulars of the scenario.

(a) Environmental cost categories

PLX will need to identify existing and new cost information that is relevant to understanding its environmental impact.

There are conventional costs such as raw material costs and energy costs which should be broadened to include the cost of waste through inefficiency. These and other conventional costs (such as regulatory fines) are often hidden within overheads and therefore will not be a high priority for management control unless they are separately reported.

There are contingent costs such as the cost of cleaning industrial sites when these are decommissioned. These are often large sums that can have significant impact on the shareholder value generated by a project. As these costs often occur at the end of the project life, they can be given low priority by a management that is driven by short-term financial measures (e.g. annual profit) and make large cash demands that must be planned at the outset of the project.

There are relational costs such as the production of environmental information for public reporting. This reporting will be used by environmental pressure groups and the regulator and it will demonstrate to the public at large the importance that PLX attaches to environmental issues.

Finally, there are reputational costs associated with failing to address environmental issues when consumer boycotts and adverse publicity lose sales revenue.

(b) **Explanation and evaluation of techniques**

A lifecycle view consists of considering the costs and revenues of a product over the whole life of the product rather that one accounting period. For an oil refinery, this might be taken to be the useful life of the refinery. A lifecycle view may take profit or discounted cash flow as the principal measure of performance. This is particularly relevant for PLX given the planned redevelopment programme at the refinery which will highlight the decommissioning costs of such plant. This will aid future long-term investment planning at PLX.

Activity-based Costing (ABC) is a method of detailed cost allocation that when applied to environmental costs distinguishes between environment-related costs and environment-driven costs. At PLX, related costs would include those specifically attributed to an environmental cost centre such as a waste filtration plant while driven costs are those that are generally hidden in overheads but relate to environmental drivers such as additional staff costs or the shorter working life of equipment (in order to avoid excess pollution in the later years of its working life). This will assist PLX in identifying and controlling environmental costs.

Input/output analysis (sometimes called mass balance) considers the physical quantities input into a business process and compares these with the output quantities with the difference being identified as either stored or wasted in the process. These physical quantities can be translated into monetary quantities at the end of the tracking process. Flow cost accounting is associated with this analysis as it reflects the movement of physical quantities through a process and will highlight priorities for efficiency improvements.

These techniques are not mutually exclusive and all can assist PLX in improving performance. However, cost/benefit analysis will need to be undertaken for each of the systems. This will be difficult, as benefit estimates will prove vague given the unknown nature of the possible improvements that may accrue from using the techniques. The non-financial benefits will include a better public image and reduced chance of protest by environmental groups and an improved relationship with the government who is likely to be a key supplier of crude oil to the business. Additionally, ABC and flow cost accounting will require significant increases in the information that the management accounting systems collect and so incur increased costs. As a result, the decision to use these techniques is likely to be based on the balance between known costs and estimated benefits of non-financial factors.

(c) **Lifecycle costing**

A traditional analysis of the costs of Kayplas might yield the product profit given in the original data. However, this ignores capital costs, environmental costs and the cost of decommissioning. A lifecycle analysis aims to capture the costs over the whole lifecycle of the product and it would show

Costs	
Production costs	82.3
Marketing costs	17
Development costs	8.6
	─────
	107.9
	─────

Environmental costs	
Waste filtration	8.1
Carbon dioxide exhaust extraction	5.3
	————
	13.4
	————
Other costs	
Decommissioning costs	18
	————
Total costs	139.3
	————

This should be compared to revenues of $149.4m and leaves only a small overall return on investment (surplus of $10.1m). It should be noted that the decommissioning costs are estimated at $18m in five years. It is likely that given the difficulty in dealing with specialised equipment and the fact that environmental legislation may get stricter, this could easily be a significant underestimate. This could destroy all of the added value of the product.

The value of lifecycle costing often lies in the visibility it gives to costs that are determined in the early stages of the design of the product and in this case, it emphasises the need to minimise the cost of decommissioning. This should be done in the design phase of the refinery extension.

The traditional product profit analysis shows a surplus of $41.5m over the life of the product failing as it does to capture the environmental and decommissioning costs.

Additionally, if volumes of production can be ascertained then a cost per unit of Kayplas could be calculated and this would assist in price setting.

Marking scheme		
		Marks
(a)	Up to 2 marks per cost area discussed. Points must include examples of relevance to the scenario to score full marks.	
	Maximum	8
(b)	Up to 2 marks per technique – an explanation and its link to environmental performance. 3 marks for an evaluation of the techniques.	
	Maximum	9
(c)	2 marks for calculation of lifecycle costs. Up to 2 marks for calculating the product profits of the two approaches. Up to 4 marks for discussion of improvements and issues identified by lifecycle costing.	
	Maximum	8
Total		25

25   FGH TELECOM (FGH) (DEC 10 – AMENDED)

Tutorial note

Requirement (a) could be answered using any sensible set of headings for example, PEST.

The working given in this solution is more detailed than would be required to produce a good answer to this question. It is here to give detailed explanation of the calculations.

(a)   Government regulations relevant to FGH's environmental strategy include requirements to recycle materials, limits on pollution and waste levels along with new taxes such as carbon levies to add additional costs. Performance indicators would be additional costs resulting from failure to recycle waste, fines paid for breaches and the level of environmental tax burdens.

The general economic climate is relevant to the strategy including factors such as interest, inflation and exchange rates. For FGH, the general economic environment is not good and cost savings from reductions in energy use would help to offset falling profits. Also, the difficulties indicated in raising capital could be monitored through the firm's cost of capital. This would be especially relevant if the environmental initiatives lead to significant capital expenditure for FGH.

Trends and fashions among the general public appear to be relevant for FGH as the public will be end-users of its services and environmental action could improve the brand image of FGH. Suitable performance indicator would be based around a score in a customer attitude survey.

Technological changes in the capabilities available to FGH and its competitors will affect its environmental strategy. New environmentally efficient technologies such as hybrid cars and solar recharging cells would be relevant to the cost and product sides of FGH. Performance indicators would involve measuring the impact of the use of new technology on existing emission data.

(b)   The company has a target of cutting emissions by 60% of their 2001 values by the year 2017. Overall, it has cut emissions by 38% in the first nine years of the 16-year programme. There was a reduction of 16% in the last year of measurement. If this rate of improvement is maintained then the company will reduce its emissions by 82% (62% × (84% ^ 7)) by 2017. However, it should be noted that it is unlikely that there will be a constant rate of reduction as it normally becomes more difficult to improve as the easy actions are taken in the early years of the programme.

The initial data are rather complex and so to summarise, three categories for the three types of transport were considered (Road, Rail and Air). The largest cut has been in rail related emissions (63%) while the contribution from road transport has only fallen by 38%. The road emissions are the dominant category overall and they are still falling within the programmed timetable to reach the target. However, it is clear that air travel is not falling at the same pace but this may be driven by factors such as increasing globalisation of the telecommunication industry which necessitates travel by managers abroad to visit multinational clients and suppliers.

One unusual feature noted is that the mix of transport methods appears to be changing. Rail travel appears to be declining. This is surprising as rail is widely believed to be the lowest emitting method from these forms of travel. However, caution must be exercised on this conclusion which may be due to a change in the emissions technology relating to each category of travel rather than the distance travelled using each method.

The major change that is apparent from the basic data is the move from petrol to diesel-powered motor vehicles which in the commercial fleet appears nearly complete. It will be more difficult to move company and private cars to diesel-power as there will be an element of choice on the part of the car user in the type of car driven.

Working:

	2001	2009	2010	Change on base year
Measured in millions of kgs	*Base year*			
Commercial Fleet Diesel	105.4	77.7	70.1	−33%
Commercial Fleet Petrol	11.6	0.4	0.0	−100%
Company Car Diesel	15.1	14.5	12.0	−21%
Company Car Petrol	10.3	3.8	2.2	−79%
Other road travel (Diesel)	0.5	1.6	1.1	120%
Other road travel (Petrol)	3.1	0.5	0.3	−90%
Rail travel	9.2	9.6	3.4	−63%
Air Travel (short haul)	5.0	4.4	3.1	−38%
Air Travel (long haul)	5.1	7.1	5.4	6%
Hire Cars (Diesel)	0.6	1.8	2.9	383%
Hire Cars (Petrol)	6.7	6.1	6.1	−9%
Total	172.6	127.5	106.6	
Index	100%	74%	62%	
	YoY change	−16%		

Simplifying categories

Road travel	*Base year*			
	153.3	106.4	94.7	−38%
Air travel	10.1	11.5	8.5	−16%
Rail travel	9.2	9.6	3.4	−63%
Total	172.6	127.5	106.6	−38%

Mix of travel method in each year

	Base year			
Road travel	89%	83%	89%	
Air travel	6%	9%	8%	
Rail travel	5%	8%	3%	

(c) The analysis could be improved by collecting data on the total distances travelled so that employee behaviour can be tracked. This would allow measurement of the effect of switching away from physical meetings and using teleconferencing facilities. This may be particularly effective in cutting air travel which has been noted as a problem area.

It would also allow assessment of the homeworking scheme which should reduce total distance travelled. Although, the full environmental benefit will not be apparent as much of the travel would have been a regular commute to work which an employee will not be able to claim and so is unlikely to record.

Finally, the collection of distance travelled data will allow a measure of the effect of changing modes of transport by calculating an average emission per km travelled.

	Marking scheme		
			Marks
(a)	1 mark per factor identified as relevant for each section of the broad sections of the analysis (PEST or PESTEL sections are appropriate and competition could be an additional area considered). Up to 1 mark for each performance indicator relevant to the factors identified. Maximum of 8.		
		Maximum	9
(b)	Up to 4 marks for analysis of basic data, commenting on overall picture and achievement of target		
	Up to 4 marks for simplifying data into broad categories and commenting		
	Up to 4 marks for analysis of mix of methods of travel and commenting (Another acceptable categorisation could be related to fuel type: petrol, diesel and aviation – rail is problematic as it is a mix of diesel and electricity but reasonable assumptions will be acceptable)		
		Maximum	12
(c)	1 mark per point reasonably	**made up to**	4
Total			25

Examiner's comments

Part (a) was generally well done although a number of good candidates ignored the request for illustrative performance indicators.

Part (b) was an analysis of a table of raw data which showed up basic weaknesses in some candidates' skill set. It was well-answered by only a minority of candidates.

Many candidates wasted their time by limiting their comments to only writing out lists of statements such as

'Commercial Fleet Diesel use has fallen from 105.4 to 70.1' or even 'Commercial Fleet Diesel use has gone down'. First, this is stating the obvious to anyone who read the table but also, this is far too detailed for most reporting purposes.

An appropriate plan of attack for this part might have been:

1   consider the 'big picture' – whether the overall target for emission reduction be met

2   break down the data into smaller but meaningful (and manageable) chunks – Road, Rail and Air transport; and

3   discuss the individual lines of the data table focussing on the data that explains the overall picture of emission changes, for example, the switch from petrol to diesel powered motor vehicles is complete in commercial vehicles and has led to large reductions in emissions but such a change may be more difficult in company cars as employees may resist such a change.

Good candidates analysed the numerical data given in the scenario. They created information from the data given and provided the reader of their answer with new insight into the key factors driving the reduction in emissions.

Part (c) was often poorly done as a result of the failure to address the requirement which asked for the data to be related to the reduction initiatives mentioned in the scenario. Many candidates got a mark for general suggestions of further useful data but few related this to the reduction initiatives.

26   GMB CO (DEC 07 – AMENDED) *Online question assistance*

Key answer tips

The whole question relates to activity based techniques. Firstly prepare an analysis of expense items, be careful not to ignore the information on batches and therefore arrive at an incorrect solution. Part (c) asks candidates to identify cost drivers and consider their appropriateness and part (d) asks for practical problems of implementing an activity-based system, not to describe what it is.

(a) **Activity-based management (ABM)** is a method of identifying and evaluating activities that a business performs using activity-based costing to carry out a value chain analysis or a re-engineering initiative to improve strategic and operational decisions in an organisation. Activity-based costing establishes relationships between overhead costs and activities so that overhead costs can be more precisely allocated to products, services, or customer segments. Activity-based management focuses on managing activities to reduce costs and improve customer value.

Operational ABM is about 'doing things right', using ABC information to improve efficiency. Those activities which add value to the product can be identified and improved. Activities that don't add value are the ones that need to be reduced to cut costs without reducing product value.

Strategic ABM is about 'doing the right things', using ABC information to decide which products to develop and which activities to use. This can also be used for customer profitability analysis, identifying which customers are the most profitable and focusing on them more.

A risk with ABM is that some activities have an implicit value, not necessarily reflected in a financial value added to any product. For instance a particularly pleasant workplace can help attract and retain the best staff, but may not be identified as adding value in operational ABM. A customer that represents a loss based on committed activities, but that opens up leads in a new market, may be identified as a low value customer by a strategic ABM process.

ABM can give middle managers an understanding of costs to other teams to help them make decisions that benefit the whole organisation, not just their activities' bottom line.

(b)   Order Number 377: Summary total cost statement

	$000	$000
Unit-based costs:		
Direct material cost ($180 × 5,000)	900	
Direct labour cost ($150 × 5,000)	750	
Power cost ($120 × 5,000)	600	
	———	2,250
Batch-related costs:		
Design work ($30,000 × 5)	150	
Machine set up ($34,000 × 5)	170	
Production scheduling ($60,000 × 5)	300	
Selling – batch expediting – ($60,000 × 5)	300	
Admin. – invoicing & accounting ($24,000 × 5))	120	
Distribution ($12,000 × 5)	60	
	———	1,100

Product sustaining costs:

Engineering design & support (per order)	350	
Production line maintenance (per order)	1,100	
Marketing (per order)	200	1,650
Total cost excluding business/facility sustaining costs		5,000
Total cost excluding business/facility sustaining costs		5,000
Business/Facility sustaining costs:		
Relating to production, administration, selling and distribution based on overall business/facility time used. 30% × $5,000,000		1,500
Total cost of order		6,500

Note: Number of batches = 5,000 units/1,000 = 5 batches

(c) A cost driver is the factor that determines the level of resource required for an activity. This may be illustrated by considering costs for each of the four levels in Order Number 377.

Unit based costs:

Direct material costs are driven by the quantity, range, quality and price of materials required per product unit according to the specification for the order.

Direct labour costs are driven by the number of hours required per product unit and the rate per hour that has been agreed for each labour grade.

Batch related costs:

The number of machine set-ups per batch is the cost driver for machines used.

The number of design hours per batch is the cost driver for design work.

Product sustaining costs:

The number of marketing visits to a client per order is the cost driver for marketing cost chargeable to the order.

The number of hours of production line maintenance per order is the cost driver for production line cost.

Business sustaining costs:

These costs are absorbed at a rate of 30% of total cost excluding business sustaining costs.

This is an arbitrary rate which indicates the difficulty in identifying a suitable cost driver/drivers for the range of residual costs in this category. Wherever possible efforts should be made to identify aspects of this residual cost that can be added to the unit, batch or product related analysis.

The cost drivers are useful in that they provide a basis for an accurate allocation of the cost of resources consumed by an order. In addition, investigation of the cause(s) of a cost driver occurring at its present level allows action to be considered that will lead to a reduction in the cost per unit of cost driver.

Examples of causes that might be identified are:

Material price may be higher than necessary due to inefficient sourcing of materials. This may be overcome through efforts to review sourcing policy and possibly provide additional training to staff responsible for the sourcing of materials.

The number of machine set-ups per batch may be due to lack of planning of batch sizes. It may be possible for batch sizes in this order to be increased to 1,250 units which would reduce the number of batches required to fulfil the order from five to four. This should reduce overall costs.

The amount of production line maintenance (and hence cost) required per order may be reduced by examining causes such as level of skill of maintenance carried out – by GMB's own staff or out-sourced provision. Action would involve re-training of own staff or recruitment of new staff or changing of out-source providers.

Tutorial note

Alternative relevant examples and discussion would be acceptable for all aspects of part (c).

(d) The benefits of an activity-based system as the basis for product cost/profit estimation may not be straightforward. A number of problems may be identified.

The selection of relevant activities and cost drivers may be complicated where there are many activities and cost drivers in complex business situations.

There may be difficulty in the collection of data to enable accurate cost driver rates to be calculated. This is also likely to require an extensive data collection and analysis system.

The problem of 'cost driver denominator level' may also prove difficult. This is similar to the problem in a traditional volume related system. This is linked to the problem of fixed/variable cost analysis. For example the cost per batch may be fixed. Its impact may be reduced, however, where the batch size can be increased without a proportionate increase in cost.

The achievement of the required level of management skill and commitment to change may also detract from the implementation of the new system. Management may feel that the activity based approach contains too many assumptions and estimates about activities and cost drivers. There may be doubt as to the degree of increased accuracy which it provides.

Tutorial note

Alternative relevant examples and discussion would be acceptable for all aspects of part (d).

Marking scheme		Marks
		Marks
(a)	Comments (on merit) – 1 mark per point	5
(b)	Unit level costs	1
	Batch related costs	2
	Product sustaining costs	1
	Business sustaining costs	1
		___
		5
		___
(c)	Identification and appropriateness of cost driver of levels 1 to 4 expenses	6
	Causes of the cost drivers 1–3	3
	Possible benefits	3
		___
		10
		___
(d)	Comments (on merit)	5
		___
Total		25
		___

Examiner's comments

In their answers to part (a) the vast majority of candidates discussed activity-based costing (ABC) as opposed to Activity-based management (ABM) and in doing so not only failed to achieve some relatively easy marks but also sacrificed precious examination time. Many candidates did not provide any answer whatsoever and in not doing so 'threw away' a potential six marks.

Many candidates provided a correct solution to part (b) and achieved maximum marks. Regrettably, many candidates ignored the information on batches and therefore arrived at incorrect solutions. Answers to part (c) were invariably of a satisfactory nature and many candidates provided very good answers to part (d).

27 FILM PRODUCTIONS CO (FP) (DEC 10 – AMENDED)

Key answer tips

This should be a reasonably straightforward question focussing on the core areas of CSFs, KPIs and their use. Unfortunately many students did not know the difference between CSFs and KPIs and/or were unable to apply their knowledge to the scenario.

(a) Information for establishing CSFs

The company can use information about the internal and external environment to set its CSFs. Relevant external information would include the structure of the industry and the strategy of FP's competitors. The geographical location of production and the main sales markets may also be relevant. Film is a hit driven industry where word of mouth can lead to success, therefore, recognition of the product and the brand ('Film Productions') by the public would lead to success. For example, the Walt Disney Company has achieved a high level of brand recognition that has enabled it to expand into other entertainment areas using characters from its films.

Relevant internal information would include measures of seasonality on sales which will dictate the timing of film releases and effectiveness of marketing campaigns. By forecasting the size of the market along with likely levels of competition, profit can be optimised.

However, these forecasts will be subject to uncertainty and so the information systems will need to be flexible and allow probabilistic analysis. A CSF based on the quality of these forecasts would therefore be appropriate. Other internal sources could include measures of the cost per film and the time taken to produce a film.

Other possible information could include contingent factors (those that depend on specific threats or opportunities facing FP).

(b) **Performance indicators linked to the CSFs**

Audience satisfaction – performance indicators are:

- Sales per film – currently the company releases an average of 6·4 films per year and makes about $31·25 million on each one. These figures should be compared to industry averages. Trends on sales per film should be monitored for indications of changes in consumer taste.

- Brand recognition – consumers should be surveyed to identify if the FP name is known and used as an indicator of quality when selecting films. If FP regularly uses certain artists (directors or film stars) then positive consumer recognition of these names will indicate satisfaction.

- Repeat viewings – with TV showings, it will be possible to measure viewers for each showing of the film and monitor the decline in viewing over repetitions. The level of DVD purchases following a cinema release will also indicate customer satisfaction with customers actively wanting to own their own copy of a favourite film.

- Awards won – number of awards won will indicate success. However, the level of recognition of any award must be brought into account as major ones such as those voted on by the public or those whose ceremonies are widely reported have the greatest impact.

- Response of the media – scores by film critics often appear in the media and these give a measure of satisfaction although this category must be treated carefully as critics often look for artistic merit while FP is seeking commercial success and broad audience acceptance.

Profitability in operations – performance indicators are:

- Industry average margin – collect data on competitor companies to set an appropriate benchmark. This will require care to ensure that appropriate comparator companies are chosen, for example, those with a production budget similar to FP's of $18 million per film.

- Time in production – the cost of a film will depend on the length of time it takes to produce. If the film is intended to meet a current customer demand it may require to be produced quickly, in order to meet revenue targets. Therefore, the time in production will affect both sales and cost levels so altering the gross margin. Again, it would be helpful to identify if films meet their production schedule and if these schedules compare favourably to those of other film companies.

- Costs – the costs should be broken down into categories such as those for artists, production technicians and marketing. The cost structure for each film should be compared internally, to others that FP produces and also externally, to available figures for the industry.

(c)   Impact on FP's information systems

The company website can collect audience survey results and comments posted on the site.

Consumers can be drawn to the site with clips and trailers from current films and those in production. The site can log the frequency with which films are viewed and if audience members create accounts then further detail on the age, gender and location of the audience can be collected. This will allow a more detailed profile of the customer base for FP to be created and will be used to help in decisions about what films to commission in the future. The account members can be given the opportunity to score each film providing further information about satisfaction.

The company could also consider scanning the websites of its competitors to identify their performance – especially their published results which will provide benchmark information on gross margin levels.

A management information system (MIS) will collate the information from individual transactions recorded in the accounting system to allow middle level management to control the business. This system will allow customer purchases to be summarised into reports to identify both products that sell well and the customers (such as cinema chains and TV networks) who provide the main sources of revenue (indicators of satisfaction). The level of repeat business on a customer account will give an indication of the satisfaction with FP's output. The system will also produce management accounts from which gross margins will be drawn and it should be capable of breaking this down by film and by customer to aid decision-making by targeting FP's output to the most profitable areas. This will aid decision-making about the performance of the production team on a film and can be used to set rewards for each team.

An executive information system (EIS) is one that will supply information to the senior management of the organisation allowing them to drill down into the more detailed transaction reports where necessary. The EIS will provide summarised information, focused on the key performance indicators in order to allow the directors to quickly judge whether the company is meeting its CSFs. It will draw on internal sources such as the MIS and also external sources such as market data on revenues that different films are earning at the box office.

Marking scheme		
		Marks
(a)	2 marks for the sources of information. 2 marks for each example including demonstration of why it is appropriate for FP.	
	Maximum	6
(b)	2.5 marks for each suggested performance indicator with 0.5 for identification and 2 for discussion of use and relevance to FP. Maximum of 10. (Students may also discuss different margin measures such as operating and gross profit but these must be related to actual operations in order to gain much credit.)	
	Maximum	10
(c)	3 marks for each relevant information system indicating how it links to the PIs.	
	Maximum	9
Total		25

Examiner's comments

Requirement (a) was poorly attempted. This part asked for the information used in setting CSFs and then, using their reading of the scenario and general business knowledge, suggestions of suitable CSFs. Many candidates were unable to address this part of the question due to lack of knowledge of the definition of a CSF and devoted their answer purely to KPIs, as a result scoring no marks. Those candidates that read the question requirement and responded to it were quickly rewarded.

Requirement (b) was generally well answered with many candidates getting 7 or 8 out of 10. The best answers were those that used the question requirement to give a methodical structure to their answer. Those candidates who did not score well tended to provide bullet point lists of many KPIs when the question asked for four.

Requirement (c) was generally adequately attempted. The better answers clearly linked the KPIs to changes that would be required in the design and use of the information systems mentioned. Thus, they could demonstrate knowledge of how such systems operate and the use to which the information produced is subsequently put.

B – IMPACT OF RISK AND UNCERTAINTY ON ORGANISATIONAL PERFORMANCE

28   SWEET CICELY (SEPT/DEC 17)

Key answer tips

If you are comfortable with PEST and risk then you should find this a manageable question.

(a) This is a good example of how PEST may be examined. Rather than simply listing the various PEST factors, you are expected to evaluate how the PEST factors may lead to risk and uncertainty and how they could be managed effectively by SC.

In (b) and (c), clear workings and relevant comments for minimax regret, maximax and expected values are required.

(a)   **Importance of incorporating risk and uncertainty in making long-term decisions**

Risk relates to the variability of outcomes, the probabilities of which are known, or can be estimated. Uncertainty occurs where the outcomes and their probabilities are unknown. The variability of demand for SC's chocolate bars is a risk, and the probabilities of different levels of demand can be estimated. The outbreak of conflict in a cocoa growing region affecting cocoa prices cannot be assigned a probability, and so is an uncertainty.

The market price of cocoa and the demand for chocolate bars are examples of exogenous variables which significantly affect the performance of SC. Exogenous variables arise from outside the business, but over which the business has no control. Climatic conditions, soil erosion, for example, all affect the price of cocoa, and therefore the performance of SC.

When investors evaluate businesses, they take into account prospective returns and the level of risk involved. Therefore, managers should consider risk and return when evaluating projects on their behalf. Long-term strategic planning requires forecasts to be made about future events, such as the price of cocoa. These future events are by definition unknown, and subject to risk and uncertainty. Risk and uncertainty must, therefore, be considered when making long-term plans, such as opening the new factory. The further into the future the plans project, the riskier, and more uncertain, events are likely to be, as it is harder to predict what conditions will be. This mean consideration of risk and uncertainty is even more important when making long-term decisions than for short-term decisions.

Use of PEST analysis

To incorporate risk and uncertainty into long-term strategic planning, SC must identify and monitor the most important exogenous variables, taking action to manage the risks they present. As a traded commodity, the risks of rising cocoa prices could be managed (hedged), for example, by using cocoa futures. The board member's comments suggest planning for the cake business was poor, and did not adequately consider the importance of exogenous variables. Risks in the macro environment could be identified using a PEST analysis.

Political factors

The market price of cocoa is affected by conflicts and political uncertainty, so consideration of these external factors is needed to incorporate risk and uncertainty into long-term planning. By identifying factors such as political instability or conflict, SC can improve its long-term performance by sourcing cocoa from more stable regions. The political situation in a region can change rapidly, which might make it difficult to incorporate these risks into long-term planning, as there is a high degree of uncertainty.

The introduction of increased taxes on products containing sugar is a political factor affecting the long-term demand for SC's products. Once introduced, this factor is likely to operate in the long term and be more predictable. Identifying this, SC could develop products containing less sugar and so reduce the amount of these additional taxes on its products.

Economic factors

Economic factors such as the variation in long-term interest rates can influence SC's performance by affecting exchange rates or overall consumer demand. By identifying these factors, SC could hedge against currency exchange rates. In the longer term, SC could locate its operations in a country where the risks from exchange rate fluctuations are lower, or diversify geographically to spread the risk.

Social factors

Overall demand for chocolate products will be influenced by social factors such as consumer tastes or increased awareness of healthy eating. SC can improve its long-term performance by not investing in a chocolate factory at all, if it believes demand for its products will fall sufficiently to make the venture unprofitable.

Technological factors

The increased cocoa yields from genetically modified crops may reduce long-term cocoa prices and SC could incorporate this into the net present value calculations for the factory. There may be unpredictable consequences which are harder to plan for, such as the acceptance by consumers of genetically modified foods.

Tutorial note

Ensure you add enough depth to your answer in (a) rather than focusing too heavily on the calculations in (b) and (c).

(b)   **Board**

The board wants to minimise the opportunity cost of making the wrong decision about the size of the new chocolate factory, which means to minimise the regret of making the wrong decision. The minimax regret rule would be the appropriate method to use so they would choose the project with the lowest maximum regret.

The regret table is as follows:

	Option 1	Option 2	Option 3
Annual demand			
50 million	0	(12.0)	(36.0)
60 million	(10.0)	0	(40.0)
70 million	(11.0)	(1.0)	0.0
Maximum regret	**(11.0)**	**(12.0)**	**(40.0)**

Option 1 is the option with the lowest maximum regret ($11m), and that would be the option preferred by the board according to their risk appetite. A drawback of using the minimax regret rule is that the probabilities of the outcomes are not considered.

New shareholders

The new shareholders are keen to increase the long-term performance of the business and are prepared to accept a high level of risk to achieve this. They will choose the option with the maximum possible outcome, which is option 3, with a maximum possible net present value of $17m. This is known as the maximax rule. This also takes no account of the probabilities of the outcomes, and also tends to be over-optimistic. It also ignores the fact that even risk seekers have a risk–return trade off.

(c)   **Expected values of each option**

Option 1 – (0.3 x 3.0) + (0.4 x 0.5) + (0.3 x –2.0)   = $0.5m

Option 2 – (0.3 x 5.0) + (0.4 x 2.0) + (0.3 x –1.0)   = $2.0m

Option 3 – (0.3 x .7.0) + (0.4 x 1.5) + (0.5 x –2.0)   = $2.1m

The risk neutral investor's choice, for year 1 only, would be option 3, with an expected value of $2.1m.

Problems of using an expected value approach

A risk neutral investor would use the expected value approach to choose between the three options. The expected value is a long run average, and is only appropriate where a decision is repeated many times. This does not appear to be the case at SC which has made only one attempt at strategic expansion in the last several years. For the same reason, the expected value will not equal the actual outcome.

Determining the probabilities, of the market price of cocoa for example, is subjective. Even analysis of historical market prices is not necessarily a guide to what will happen in the future. The expected value approach is suitable for a risk neutral investor. This does not apply to the key stakeholders at SC, and hence this approach is inappropriate for use in the decision on the three options. Determining the payoffs is also difficult when demand is subject to uncertainty. SC should not make a decision on the factory based only on the first year's operating profits, and should take a longer term view, for example, based on discounted cash flows.

	Marking scheme		Marks
(a)	Consideration of risk and uncertainty – 1 mark per point, up to 8 marks		
	Discussion of use of PEST analysis – 1 mark per point, up to 8 marks		
		Maximum	**14**
(b)	Calculations and comments on board's performance – 4 marks		
	Comments of new shareholders' preference – 2 marks		
		Maximum	**6**
(c)	Calculation of expected value – 1 mark		
	Conclusion and drawbacks of expected value approach – 1 mark per point		
		Maximum	**5**
Total			**25**

Examiner's comments

This question considered issues around risk and uncertainty at a manufacturer who is deciding on the size of a new factory. Candidates who chose this question often scored well.

Part (a) required a candidate to give reasons why consideration of risk and uncertainty are important in such decisions and then evaluate the use of PEST analysis in this project. This part was generally reasonably well done. Good answers illustrated the use of PEST analysis with reference to risks for this manufacturer.

Part (b) required an analysis of the preferred option for the factory size for two different stakeholders with different risk appetites. This part was usually well done although the calculation of a regret table caused some difficulties.

Part (c) required a recommendation for a risk neutral investor and an evaluation of the method used. This part was generally well done with expected values being correctly calculated and the limitation of this method in context of this business reasonably discussed.

29 TURING (JUN 14)

Key answer tips

This question is based on a joint venture arrangement showing the examiner's desire to focus on more complex business structures.

In part (a) a discussion of the different risk appetites of the two joint venture partners was required together with a recommendation of an appropriate method for decision making. This area has been examined a number of times and it is important to feel comfortable with the ideas discussed in the answer.

Part (b) requires the calculation of maximum and minimum payoff. A nice opportunity to do some calculations but don't get bogged down and lose track of time. In part (c) make sure that you have enough relevant points and that you relate your points back to the scenario – general book knowledge will score few marks.

(a) **Turing**

Risk appetite

The risk appetite of Turing will be dominated by the VCs who own 90% of the company. They are risk-seeking as they hold a portfolio of high-risk investments where they accept the failure of some investments provided others generate high returns. The other key stakeholders mentioned are management who has been given an equity stake in the business and so is likely to be comfortable with this high-risk approach.

Method of decision-making

Overall, therefore, Turing is likely to be risk-seeking and so a maximax approach to decision-making under uncertainty will be appropriate. In the maximax approach, the design selected will be the one which maximises (over the three designs) the highest profit for each design among the three demand scenarios.

Riemann

Risk appetite

The risk appetite of Riemann will be dominated by the financial investors, both the shareholders and any debt providers, as they have recently had to provide new funds to keep Riemann afloat. These investors will be concerned about the immediate survival of the business as will the management who could lose their jobs. The need for short-term cash flow gains from TandR emphasises this point.

Method of decision-making

Overall, therefore, Riemann is likely to be risk averse, focusing on the survival of the business and so a maximin approach to decision-making under uncertainty will be appropriate. In the maximin approach, the design selected will be the one which maximises (over the three designs) the lowest profit for each design among the three demand scenarios.

Tutorial note

Some credit will be given for a minimax regret solution as it is risk averse, although it is not as clearly focused on obtaining a minimum level of return needed to aid the survival of the business.

Other comments

The management at Turing will also be motivated to choose projects with an innovative edge such as the 8 MW unit proposed.

The high fixed costs of the 8 MW unit are unlikely to deter Turing's management as they represent a large investment in their education in potentially world-leading technology.

The wide range of demand forecasts (1,000 units to 2,000) will make Riemann nervous. The likely long timescale for development of the 8 MW unit, where $7.5bn will be invested, may not be attractive in meeting their short-term cash needs.

(b)

Type	Variable cost per unit $m	Fixed costs $m	Price per unit $m		
8 MW	10.4	7,500.0	20.8		
3 MW	4.8	820.0	9.6		
1 MW	1.15	360.0	4.6		
Demand	1,000	1,500	2,000		
Variable cost					
8 MW	10,400	15,600	20,800		
3 MW	4,800	7,200	9,600		
1 MW	1,150	1,725	2,300		
Total cost					
8 MW	17,900	23,100	28,300		
3 MW	5,620	8,020	10,420		
1 MW	1,510	2,085	2,660		
Revenue					
8 MW	20,800	31,200	41,600		
3 MW	9,600	14,400	19,200		
1 MW	4,600	6,900	9,200		
Profit				*Max payoff*	*Min payoff*
8 MW	2,900	8,100	13,300	13,300	2,900
3 MW	3,980	6,380	8,780	8,780	3,980
1 MW	3,090	4,815	6,540	6,540	3,090
Maximum of the maximums	8 MW	13,300			
Maximum of the minimums	3 MW	3,980			

Therefore, the risk-seeking decision makers at Turing will select the 8 MW design with the possibility of earning $13.3bn from the project. The risk-averse decision makers at Riemann will select the 3 MW design with the likelihood of earning at least $3.98bn from the project.

(c)   Considering first the problem of measuring performance in joint ventures, the primary difficulty is establishing the objectives of the joint venture (JV). The different JV partners may have different goals; in this case, Riemann wants fairly immediate cash flows while Turing wants the possibility of large returns (possibly over a longer time-frame). Performance metrics are likely to include a variety of financial indicators, such as profit, growth and cash flows. However, there may be different emphasis put on these metrics by each JV partner and there will be difficulties in attributing accountability for these different elements of performance where each partner in the JV is bringing different skills and knowledge to the venture.

The different timescales which Riemann (short term) and Turing (longer term) will emphasise will also lead to conflict in the choice of metrics: quarterly cash flows for Riemann to report to its shareholders and discounted cash flows over the project life for Turing.

At TandR, the different risk appetites of the key stakeholders will lead to conflict in the choice of key performance measures and these problems will be difficult to resolve as the ownership is split 50:50 between Turing and Riemann. The possibility of deadlock can only be avoided by having clearly laid out a path for resolution at the outset of the JV (possibly in the JV legal agreement).

This high level conflict can also appear in day-to-day co-ordinating and controlling the JV. The management of the JV must be given clear direction at the outset, otherwise this deadlock problem will appear whenever there is a disagreement between the managers selected by the JV partners. Therefore, the compatibility of the management styles and cultures of the JV partners will have an important impact on success.

Another potential issue in joint ventures and specifically at TandR is that, as well as sharing offices, assets and staff, the partners must also share information and intellectual property. It appears that Turing are bringing significant advantage for the JV with their blade design skill. However, it is often difficult to measure the contribution of such intangible assets to the performance of the JV and a suitable method of extracting these assets at the end of the life of the JV will need to be agreed at its outset.

It is likely that the venture partners will be reluctant to share too much information about their own businesses with their JV partner. It will be important for the success of the JV that a climate of trust exists which will again depend on issues such as management style and culture.

	Marking scheme		Marks
(a)	1 mark per point up to the following maxima:		
	Turing:		
	Risk appetite		3
	Method of decision-making		2
	1 for properly selected method		
	1 for description of method		
	Riemann:		
	Risk appetite		3
	Method of decision-making		2
	1 for properly selected method		
	1 for description of method		
		Maximum	**9**
(b)	Calculations:		
	Variable costs		2
	Total costs		1
	Revenue		2
	Profit		1
	Maximax result		1
	Maximin result		1
	Conclusion		1
		Maximum	**8**
(c)	1 per point made up to 8 marks		
	Points such as:		
	Different goals and performance metrics at JV partners		
	Handling different risk appetites		
	Deadlock in decision-making		
	Handling different time horizons for results		
	Different management styles and cultural differences		
	Information sharing		
	Intellectual property		
	– extra credit is available for relating point to TandR specifically.		
		Maximum	**8**
Total			**25**

Examiner's comments

Part (a) was generally well done with 8 or 9 marks often scored. It was especially cheering to note that most candidates understood that decision making 'under uncertainty' is different to 'under risk' or else, they realised that the lack of information on probabilities meant that expected values were not an optimal approach.

Part (b) was usually well done with many candidates scoring full marks. One point for future candidates to note is that the companies involved cannot choose to produce a certain number of units as this is the uncertain factor.

Part (c) was adequately answered with many candidates able to identify the problem areas but few could discuss the causes and impacts of these problems in anything other than vague terms.

30   FRANCHISING FOR YOU LTD (F4U) (JUN 09)

Key answer tips

A fairly straight forward NPV question. Candidates firstly need to calculate contribution as sales revenue less variable cost. Then calculate NPV, be careful about the timing of the cash flows especially the development costs. Remember the rule about inflation either inflate the cash flows and discount at the money rate or to make it easier and quicker remove the inflation from the money cost and ignore inflating the cash flows.

In part (b) you are required to understand 'intellectual capital', just think logically what the two words mean. Intellectual means analytical thinking in a professional capacity.

In part (c) imagine why focusing on financial measures is not enough when analysing performance. Then the final part (d) is based on the information given in the question and is very straight forward on maximax and maximin.

Tutorial note

The style of this question and the requirements are a little different to that used by the current examiner. However, this question does serve as useful revision of some important syllabus areas.

(a)   Contribution per franchise   = sales revenue – variable cost

= $20,000 – $6,000 = $14,000

Net operating cash flow each year before taxation = ($14,000 × 300) – $600,000 = $3,600,000 Net operating cash flow each year after taxation = $3,600,000 × 70% = $2,520,000

Net present value (NPV) at a discount rate of 11%

Net operating cash flow – initial investment – development costs

= (2,520,000 × 4.231) – (6,000,000) – (1,000,000 × 0.812) – (1,000,000 × 0.731) = $3,119,120

The positive NPV indicates that the proposal should be undertaken.

Tutorial note

A real discount rate of 11% has been used. It has been calculated as follows:
(1 + money cost of capital)/(1 + rate of inflation) – 1

= (1 + 0.1544)/ (1 + 0.04) – 1   = 0.11 or 11%

(b) There are barriers to the creation and revision of a performance measurement system. Key drivers are not easily measured. This applies specifically to the issue of intellectual capital.

Intellectual capital will include assets such as employee know-how, skills and creativity. Such assets cannot be measured using traditional financial measures. It is necessary to identify and value a number of alternative measures such as years of experience or service of key employees, or the proportion of employees generating new ideas for the development of the business.

The rise of intellectual capital statements has been driven by the decreasing information relevance of aspects of traditional financial statements.

There is a role for accountants (in particular management accountants) in classifying the intellectual (and intangible) assets in the organisation.

In F4U the development of new franchises will rely heavily on the intellectual capital input. This will require the ongoing development of existing employee knowledge and expertise and the recruitment of new expertise/knowledge as required by the trend in the franchise range.

There will be specific costs incurred in the retention and development of existing staff expertise and in the acquisition of new staff/expertise and its development within the ethos of F4U.

(c) A Performance Measurement system (PMS) must be comprehensive for the following reasons:

- Financial is only one dimension of value – as such it is inadequate in evaluating strategic performance of an organisation in its entirety.

- Financial measures are traditionally backward looking – in today's volatile markets, a poor predictor of future performance.

- Financial measures take no account of the intangible value drivers – especially important in knowledge intensive companies.

- Fixation with bottom line profit pushes for short-term decisions to boost earnings streams in short term.

- Alternative perspectives are needed to satisfy demands of providing a sustainable competitive environment.

The effectiveness of a PMS based solely on financial performance may be reduced due to key drivers not being easily measured such as, for example, the degree of innovation required for new franchises.

Also, there may be conflict between the PMS with the culture of an organisation. The culture will probably focus on innovation in franchise development. This will not be enhanced by a solely financial based PMS. It is important that a culture is developed which recognises and rewards the contribution of employees to achieving corporate goals and strategy fulfilment.

It is important to focus on sustaining competitive advantage through superior strategic management in all aspects of franchise development and implementation. There is a need for better business intelligence capability from both within the organisation and from external sources, in the assessment of likely demand for new franchise areas and how best to satisfy such demand. In this regard there is need for non-financial performance measures in order to enhance the effectiveness of the PMS.

(d) The maximax rule looks for the largest possible outcome. In this case F4U will choose a fee per franchise of $18,000 where there is a possibility of an NPV of $4,348,226. This may be seen as risk seeking since F4U has not been put off by the possibility of a lower NPV than if a $22,000 fee is charged and variable costs are $6,000 or $7,000.

The maximin rule looks for the fee per franchise which will maximise the minimum possible NPV. Hence maximin is a risk averse strategy. In this case F4U will choose a fee per franchise of $22,000 where the lowest NPV is $2,674,865. This is better than the lowest figures applying where franchise fees of $18,000 or $20,000 apply.

The minimax regret rule requires the choice of the fee per franchise which will minimise the regret from making the wrong decision.

Regret in this context is the opportunity lost through making the wrong decision. Using the calculation from the payoff matrix given in the question, a regret matrix may be created as follows:

Regret matrix

Fee per franchise ($000)

		$18	$20	$22
Variable cost	5	0	340,596	74,043
per franchise	6	177,702	355,404	0
($000)	7	429,446	444,255	0
Maximum regret		429,446	444,255	74,043

This shows that the minimax regret rule leads to the choice of a fee per franchise of $22,000. This minimises the regret to an amount of $74,043.

Marking scheme			
			Marks
(a)	Margin after tax		2
	Discount rate		2
	NPV		1
	Decision		1
		Maximum	**6**
(b)	Elements		4
	Issues		4
		Maximum	**6**
(c)	Comments (on merit)		6
(d)	Maximax		2
	Maximin		2
	Minimax regret criterion		3
		Maximum	**7**
Total			**25**

Examiner's comments

There were significant variations in the quality of candidates' answers to this question.

Answers to part (a) revealed that the majority of candidates were unable to calculate correctly the discount rate. A large number of candidates also included the development costs in the tax calculations of F4U.

In general, answers to part (b) were poor. A significant number of candidates appeared to attempt to 'guess' the answer and a sizeable number made no attempt to answer part (b).

There were a large number of very good answers to part (c) which achieved high marks. However, in answering part (c) many candidates offered a discussion of a variety of non-financial performance measures instead of discussing ways in which reliance solely on financial performance measures can detract from the effectiveness of the performance management system within an organisation, as required by the question.

There were many correct answers to part (d) with candidates achieving maximum marks. However, a significant number of candidates demonstrated a lack of knowledge of maximax, maximin and minimax regret decision rules. What is more, a significant number of candidates made no attempt to answer this subsection of the question which was potentially worth seven marks.

31 THE EQUINE MANAGEMENT ACADEMY (EMA) (JUN 10)

Key answer tips

The reference to expected values and probabilities in the question requirements should have told you that risk is a key focus within this question and should thus be incorporated in your discussion as well as the calculations. Risk is likely to be a key theme in the exam, so ensure you are confident incorporating it.

Tutorial note

This question is slightly different to the question style of the current examiner but it does serve as good question practise of some important syllabus areas.

(a) **Budgeted Income Statement for the year ended 31 May 2011**

		$	$
Equine College:			
Fee income – Working (1)	Student category:		
	Surgery	4,536,000	
	Dentistry	3,150,000	
	Business management	3,402,000	11,088,000
Operating costs			(6,760,000)
Budgeted profit of Equine College			4,328,000
Riding School:			
Fee income	Rider category:		
	Beginner	1,843,200	
	Competent	2,027,520	
	Advanced	3,379,200	7,249,920
Operating costs			(6,095,000)
Budgeted profit of Riding School			1,154,920
Budgeted profit of EMA			5,482,920

Workings:

(W1) Equine College fee income:

e.g. Surgery	
Number of students (30% × 1,200) =	360
Fee per student 12,000 × 1.05 ($)	12,600
Budgeted Fee income ($)	4,536,000

(W2) Riding School fee income

	Number of lessons	Charge per lesson $	Fee income $
240 horses × 4 per day × 320 days × 80% =	245,760		
Beginner (50%)	122,880	15	1,843,200
Competent (25%)	61,440	(30 × 1.1) = 33	2,027,520
Advanced (25%)	61,440	(50 × 1.1) = 55	3,379,200
			7,249,920

(b) **(i)**

% change in fee income	Probability	Lesson capacity	Probability	Combined probability	Equine College revenue $	Riding School revenue $	Total costs $	Net profit $	Expected value of net profit $
		90%	0.10	0.02	11,088,000	8,156,160	12,855,000	6,389,160	127,783
No change	0.20	80%	0.60	0.12	11,088,000	7,249,920	12,855,000	5,482,920	657,950
		70%	0.30	0.06	11,088,000	6,343,680	12,855,000	4,576,680	274,601
Decrease		90%	0.10	0.06	9,979,200	8,156,160	12,855,000	5,280,360	316,822
by 10%	0.60	80%	0.60	0.36	9,979,200	7,249,920	12,855,000	4,374,120	1,574,683
		70%	0.30	0.18	9,979,200	6,343,680	12,855,000	3,467,880	624,218
Decrease		90%	0.10	0.02	8,870,400	8,156,160	12,855,000	4,171,560	83,431
by 20%	0.20	80%	0.60	0.12	8,870,400	7,249,920	12,855,000	3,265,320	391,838
		70%	0.30	0.06	8,870,400	6,343,680	12,855,000	2,359,080	141,545
				————					————
				1.00			Expected value of profit =		4,192,872
				————					————

(ii) The use of expected values takes into account the relative likelihood of each of the possible outcomes occurring. The expected value of $4,192,872 is not one of the potential outcomes in the table, but is the weighted average of those outcomes. The use of expected values by the management of EMA implies that they have a risk-neutral attitude. A risk neutral decision-maker will ignore the variability in the range of potential outcomes and will be concerned only with the expected value of outcomes.

(iii) Possible reasons why the government of Hartland has decided to open an academy comprising an equine college and a riding school are as follows:

EMA operated the only Equine College in Hartland and operated at full capacity during the year ended 31 May 2010. This could well be an indication that the demand for equine specialists in Hartland exceeds the available supply.

Much transportation in Hartland is provided by horses and this might therefore account for the fact that the Equine College operated by EMA is currently operating at full capacity. It is reasonable to assume that the more that horses are used for transportation then the greater will be the need for specialists such as equine veterinary surgeons.

The government of Hartland 'actively promotes environmental initiatives' and therefore it might well be the case that it discourages the use of petrol and diesel propelled vehicles for both social and business purposes.

Hartland is a developing country which has a large agricultural sector and therefore it is probable that horses are used in day-to-day operations e.g. farming.

				Marks
(a)		**Equine College:**		
		number of students		1.0
		fee income	3 × 0.5	1.5
		operating costs		0.5
		Riding School:		
		number of lessons		1.5
		fee income	3 × 0.5	1.5
		operating costs		0.5
		EMA profit		0.5
			Maximum	**7**
(b)	(i)	Combined probability schedule		3
		Profit and loss schedule		3
		Expected value schedule		3
			Maximum	**9**
	(ii)	Likelihood of occurrence		1
		Risk neutrality		1
		Other relevant comments		1
			Maximum	**3**
	(iii)	Reasons	3 × 2	6
Total				**25**

Marking scheme

Examiner's comments

There were significant variations in the overall quality of candidates' answers to this question.

Most candidates offered excellent answers to part (a) on preparing a budgeted profit figure for the academy and many scored full marks.

However, when this basic understanding was tested in part (b) (i) (finding an expected value) candidates struggled. Stronger candidates scored full marks on this part but many others would have benefited from a structured approach. The issue of risk and its treatment are an important feature of business decision-making and are in the syllabus and have been mentioned in technical articles.

Additionally, much of (b) (i) is assumed knowledge from PM. This lack of knowledge was then reflected in answers to (b) (ii) where few candidates discussed the implication of the use of expected value in the risk appetite at EMA.

Requirement (b)(iii) for three reasons for the national government opening a competitor academy was generally well answered although some candidates did not read the question and offered six reasons briefly discussed rather than three reasons each more comprehensively discussed.

32   STOKENESS ENGINEERING (JUN 13)

Key answer tips

The key to success in this question is in reading the requirements carefully and answer the question asked. For example, in part (a) ensure you discuss the impact of Porter's five forces on performance management rather than performing a SBL style analysis.

The other danger with this question is to spend all of your time on part (a) to the expense of parts (b) and (c), so make sure you allocate your time accordingly.

(a)   **Porter's five forces analysis**

Threat of new entrants

The threat of new entrants will be dictated by barriers to entry into the fuel cell market. These appear to be high, given the long timescale and the high levels of technical expertise required to develop a viable product. Also, the developer will need to have cultivated a strong relationship with the major vehicle manufacturers who will be the customers for the product.

A suitable performance measure would be percentage of revenue derived from patented products to measure the legally protected revenues of the business and so indicate the barrier to entry. Stokeness will need to ensure that all technology developments are written up and assessed for their patent possibility.

[Other measures could include ratio of fixed cost to total cost (measures capital required) or customer loyalty (through long-term contracts to supply fuel cells to manufacturers).]

Threat of substitutes

The substitutes mentioned in the question are electrical batteries, compressed natural gas and improved existing diesel/petrol engines. However, it is clear that improved diesel/petrol engines would potentially have many lower barriers to cross as the technology is known to the car industry and the infrastructure exists to deliver the fuel to the end-users of the cars.

The threat of each of these substitutes would be measured by an analysis of the comparative cost of creating a viable alternative to the fuel cell. The performance in terms of power output of the engine and emissions reductions compared to price would be critical. Management of this aspect will entail monitoring fuel prices in the market, reviewing the appropriate technical journals and attending conferences in order to identify these threats and their progress. This will require the input of both finance and engineering staff at Stokeness.

Power of suppliers

The suppliers have considerable power. There are rare raw materials used in production and the price and availability of these will dictate possible output levels for fuel cell producers. This is especially important, given the possibility of increased production which could flow if fuel cells become the dominant way to power vehicles in the future. There is a danger that the market in these materials is controlled by a few suppliers who can then dictate price. The engineering subcontractors will also have power through their knowledge of the design elements of Stokeness' product. It will be important for Stokeness to protect this by legally enforceable non-disclosure agreements. There is a danger that this knowledge will lead the suppliers to consider pre-emptive forward integration by taking over Stokeness.

The power of suppliers could be measured by estimating the cost of shifting to an alternative supplier, which could be considerable, given the innovative nature of the technology. These costs would have to include the damage to value from the delay that such a shift would cause.

[Other measures could include cost of suppliers' product compared to total cost of the fuel cell, which indicates the importance of this component in production, and the number of suppliers as it indicates the level of competition in that market.]

Power of customers

The customers are the major bus and truck manufacturers. Again, the customers will have a large degree of influence, given their size and limited numbers if Stokeness wants to access the world market. There will need to be a partnership between the fuel cell maker and the vehicle manufacturer in order to ensure that the technologies are compatible. There is the threat that these powerful customers will seek to take over Stokeness if its products prove successful; however, this may be an attractive exit for the shareholders depending upon the price offered.

The power of customers can be measured by estimating their switching costs which are likely to be high, given the technological compatibility issue. However, these costs will only occur once the vehicle manufacturer has agreed to source from a particular supplier (e.g. Stokeness) and until an agreement is reached, the fuel cell supplier will be in the weaker position. The vehicle manufacturer will also have the commercial power to be able to become a new entrant to the market if it appears more profitable to do so.

Stokeness could seek to manage these problems in two ways:

(a) Quickly enter into an exclusive arrangement with one partner by emphasising the technological lead which they hold over the competition. This will be lower risk but will cut returns as the partner will then have pricing power; or

(b) Seek to develop a product which will be attractive to multiple vehicle manufacturers and then maximise price by playing them against each other. This appears less plausible in this scenario, given the limited number of large manufacturers.

[Other measures could be the number of alternative customers, the level of discounts customers demand and the number of alternative suppliers customers can chose from.]

Power of existing competition

The power of existing competition appears low as Stokeness has a two-year lead in development. It will be important to protect this legally by patenting innovations as soon as possible and, also, ensuring the strictest commercial confidentiality is maintained within Stokeness and their commercial partners.

The power of existing competitors can be measured by market share once the market forms. However, at this development stage of the industry, a measure such as time to market (the expected commercial launch date of a viable fuel cell) would be more appropriate. This will aid management focus on delivering the product as rapidly as possible, thus maintaining Stokeness' competitive advantage and avoiding time over-runs in development which will strain the cash flows of the company and may lead to unwelcome further calls for funding from the VCs.

[Other measures could be partnership agreements (with car manufacturers) signed or projected revenues/volumes under such agreements.]

Tutorial note

The use of ideas such as patent protection, time to market and partnering with a vehicle manufacturer are relevant under several of the headings and credit is given provided the point is suitably justified to the particular force being discussed at that point of the answer.

(b)   The CEO's concerns over the definition of market in market share are justified, as there are a variety of possibilities.

If Stokeness were to take an ambitious view, then they could measure the market as the total commercial vehicle market and measure the number of vehicles powered by Stokeness' fuel cell compared to the total number of vehicles. This would be a measure of competitive performance against all existing engine technologies including existing petrol/diesel. It would be more realistic to use the number of new vehicles sold rather than all vehicles in existence in this measure. A second possibility exists in this scenario for comparing the number of vehicles with Stokeness' fuel cell compared to the number using any of the **alternative** engine technologies (fuel cells, electrical, compressed natural gas).

However, Stokeness could take an even less ambitious view and consider just the market for fuel cells, therefore measuring Stokeness' performance against only other fuel cell makers.

The board must make a choice as to the market they are competing in or maybe decide the firms which they see as their main competitors, and then use this to define the market and so the performance measure.

(c)   The VCs are likely to be rational investors seeking maximum return for minimum risk. However, they will have invested in a number of companies and so are prepared for investments to fail, provided that some of their investments perform very well. Therefore, they will be risk seeking in technology start-ups such as Stokeness.

The VCs have placed employees within the management team and so have a high degree of influence on Stokeness. They will be looking at medium/long-term returns, given the nature of the project, through net present value based on projected revenues. Of more immediate concern will be the worry that Stokeness runs out of cash before it has a viable product to sell and so cost control measures (variances from budget) and cash outflow will be key measures at present. They will have stated a rough timescale to exit the investment on provision of the initial funds and they will monitor performance to plan on this basis. Progression towards an exit will require Stokeness to pass various milestones (e.g. to file patents, to sign contracts with customers); timely achievement of these would be useful performance indicators, as well as purely financial ones such as meeting the cash flow projections.

ACCA Marking scheme		
		Marks
(a)	Up to 4 marks for performance measure justified and performance management implications for each force	
	Maximum	16
(b)	1 mark per suitable point made	
	Maximum	4
(c)	Assess risk appetite up to 2 marks	
	Impact on performance measures up to 3 marks	
	Maximum	5
Total		25

Examiner's comments

Part (a) for 16 marks was generally well done with good use made of the information in the scenario to give useful performance management advice to Stokeness. However, many candidates chose to only partially read the second part of the requirement which asked for 'a justified recommendation of one new performance measure for each of the five force areas'. Instead, they produced only a list of performance measures for each area, often including market share – failing, in three ways, to answer the question.

Part (b) for 4 marks tested a common area of uncertainty in an important, strategic performance measure. This part was poorly done and often, the only point raised was that the market was new and involved new technology so defining it would be difficult. Again, many candidates chose instead to answer the question 'how do you measure market share?' and so missed the point. There were a few excellent efforts which realised that the definition of market (and so its size) depended on whether you were talking about hydrogen fuel cells, alternative energy power technologies more generally or any sort of power unit including existing petrol/ diesel engines.

Part (c) for 5 marks looked at risk appetites and their effect on performance measurement. Most candidates were able to justify a view on the risk appetite of the VCs although many wasted time with a rote-learned list of all the possibilities which in a 5-mark question was wasting time. However, few candidates could provide valuable comment on the impact on performance measurement and many chose to talk more generally about the impact on performance management at Stokeness when a focus on the choice of metrics was required.

C – PERFORMANCE MEASUREMENT SYSTEMS AND DESIGN

33 NELSON, JODY AND NIGEL (NJN) (MAR/JUN 17)

Key answer tips

Overall, this is quite a challenging question but if you have your knowledge and exam technique in place then you should be able to score a pass.

(a) Other than a broad knowledge of lean, little knowledge is required here. Instead you need to use the scenario information and should be able to identify the shortcomings of the existing system.

(b) There are only 6 marks available here so keep your answer brief. You should be able to identify the shortcomings of each proposal in terms of addressing the issues faced.

(a)   Manual input

At NJN, at least some of the inputs to the WIS are manual, and that means they are prone to error. This is time consuming and costly.

The packing lists which are received in the shipping containers are input manually. If incorrectly input, the quantities of items in the locations in the WIS will also be incorrect. Incorrect information in the WIS wastes time by needing teams to investigate the discrepancies, reconcile inventory records with those held by the manufacturer, and correct the information held on the WIS.

Furthermore, customers will not receive the items they have ordered, as in 8% of picking notes, items are not in the location they should be, or are in insufficient quantities. This is a high proportion of errors. Staff will waste time looking for items stored in the wrong locations. This will cause customer dissatisfaction and mean that larger quantities of inventory will need to be held, which is a wasteful use of storage space. Fewer complete orders can be fulfilled per unit of warehouse space, than would otherwise be the case. Both of these are sources of waste.

In the longer term, this means NJN staff must undertake a series of cyclical inventory counts in order to correct the information held in the WIS. This is wasteful activity which does not add value to customers, and should be eliminated.

The provision of accurate inventory information will also be of value to the retailers who can place orders only for items which are available, rather than only finding out about unavailable items by receiving an email from NJN. This would lead to increased customer satisfaction by avoiding having stock outs of particular items by ordering alternatives.

NJN should consider the use of barcodes or radio frequency identifiers (RFIDs) on products, to ensure that accurate data is input into the WIS. Using these devices, the product numbers and quantities of goods entering and leaving the warehouse could be automatically read into the WIS, without any intervention from warehouse staff. This would reduce the time taken to manually input the data and improve its accuracy.

An effective information system may interface directly with the manufacturer's and retail customers' information systems through electronic data interchange (EDI). This would increase service levels by ensuring that all parts of the value chain had access to accurate and timely information.

Time delays

The packing list batches are not available until up to 48 hours after receipt of the goods. The information held in the WIS will therefore be out of date. Items which are required for sales orders may be unavailable for picking. The use of automated input, where possible, will increase the timeliness of the information input into the WIS. This will reduce the labour cost of correcting the system and improve the number, accuracy, and completeness of orders despatched to customers.

Currently, all picking notes are printed in the warehouse office, which may be some distance from the area where items are picked. This also implies the existence of a bottleneck in the provision of information to the staff picking the items and wastes staff time moving to and from the warehouse office to pick up the reports. An improvement would be to ensure that information is available when and where it is needed, using terminals in the warehouse, or portable devices such as tablets. This would reduce time spent collecting picking information.

Similarly, in order to investigate discrepancies, staff have to obtain special reports which the warehouse manager extracts from the WIS. Again, this is a bottleneck which could delay staff getting the correct information, and may mean that the reports are inconsistent depending on the parameters set to run them. An effective system would eliminate these problems by providing standardised reports when requested, and in an optimal location.

Complex presentation of information

Effective systems add value to information when they organise and present the information in a clear way, without excessive detail. This allows the users to easily and quickly identify the information they need. It prevents wasting time obtaining the information in the first place, and correcting errors caused by interpreting it incorrectly.

The picking sheets show the 12-digit product codes which can easily be misread and increases the likelihood of errors. A better system would present the information in a more accessible way and prevent information overload, for example, showing product descriptions, or product codes, only for the items to be picked.

(b) There are two main types of waste at NJN which can be identified using lean principles: waste which does not add value to the customer and waste which occurs due to variations in demand and demands on staff.

Reorganising the warehouse to place high volume items near to the despatch area will help reduce the type of waste where the movement of staff to pick goods is more than should be required. Less movement, which means less staff time and cost, will be required by staff to pick these items and bring them to where they are to be despatched. It may be, however, that large and bulky items should be placed nearer to the despatch area instead, to save on the time spent transporting them to the despatch area. This may also address the increased seasonal demand for certain types of product as products which are popular for that specific period could be stored more closely to the despatch area.

The cost of absenteeism is a waste caused by demanding too much of staff at busy times to compensate for inefficient organisation in the warehouse and errors in the WIS. The cost of searching for items which have been put in the wrong physical location at busy times is a waste due to variation in activity levels.

Another type of waste which does not add value to the customer is holding excessive inventory, for example, the additional warehouse space which NJN has rented. By not making efficient use of the warehouse space it has, NJN is reducing its level of output, and revenue, relative to the resources available to it. In addition, the extra warehouse space means more time spent by staff moving through the warehouses trying to locate goods.

The cyclical inventory counts which the management consultant has suggested do not add value to the customer and are also more demanding for staff. This is a wasteful activity, correcting the errors which have occurred in the WIS. NJN should instead concentrate on ensuring that errors do not occur in the first place, which will cost less than correcting them.

(c) The 5Ss in the adoption of lean principles during the warehouse reorganisation are Structurise, Systemise, Sanitise, Standardise and Self-discipline.

Structurise

This involves introducing order where possible, for example, by ensuring that items in the warehouse are arranged so that they are easy to find. This would also include segregating damaged or obsolete inventory, or discarding it from the warehouse.

The management consultant has suggested the measure of the proportion of inventory not stored in order of its alphabetical description, with 'A' nearest the despatch area and 'Z' furthest away. This may measure how easy to find each product is, but would not necessarily make best use of all available space or make the picking process more efficient. It may also be subjective and prone to errors caused by the interpretation of the product description, for example, in deciding if cricket balls be measured under 'C' or 'B'.

Systemise

This principle involves organising items so that they are easy to use. At NJN, this means being able to accurately pick the correct items in the shortest possible time. It could also cover access to other resources, such as having computer terminals close to where they are needed.

The measure relating to the storing of goods alphabetically seems to conflict with the consultant's recommendation to place the high volume lines close to the despatch area. Whereas storing goods alphabetically may make items easy to find, it does not necessarily make them easy to use (pick). By storing the high volume items near to the despatch area, the average time taken to pick orders would be reduced.

Sanitise

This principle means to be tidy and avoid clutter. This helps make things easy to find, allows easy access of staff around the warehouse, and helps make a safe working environment. The warehouse manager's daily assessment of tidiness is a suitable measure of this principle, which is a subjective assessment.

There is the possibility that the assessment will be biased, especially if the warehouse manager who is undertaking the assessment is also having his performance evaluated on the tidiness of the warehouse. The characteristics of what constitutes a tidy warehouse, compared to an untidy one, will need to be defined. There is the possibility of inconsistent measurement if someone other the warehouse manager does the assessment, or the assessment is done at different times of the day.

Standardise

This principle involves finding the best way of undertaking a process or task, and applying it consistently. The suggestion of the number of accidents caused by goods which have not been stored or picked in the correct way would measure this. As NJN should aim to have no accidents, this should be a performance measure with a target level of zero.

Self-discipline

This principle relates to sustaining the other Ss by motivating employees. Motivation is subjective, and hard to measure. None of the performance measures the management consultant has suggested directly measure this principle. The consistency in which specific tasks or processes are performed could be a measure of how well they are being sustained.

Tutorial note

Ensure you have all of your APM knowledge in place. The examiner is willing to test any part of the syllabus.

A key concept in APM is 'what gets measured gets done'. Here you need to explain each 'S' in the context of NJN and then evaluate the metrics used in relation to that 'S'.

Marking scheme		
		Marks
(a)	1 mark for each valid point	
	Maximum	10
(b)	1 mark for each valid point	
	Maximum	6
(c)	Each S discussed - up to 3 marks	
	Maximum	9
		―――
Total		**25**
		―――

Examiner's comments

Question 3 examined the impact on performance management at a warehouse from improved information systems and workflow. Candidates who chose this question often scored well.

Part (a) required an assessment of the existing information system and was generally well done with candidates able to identify and discuss the problems from the scenario. The better candidates then tied these problems to the operation of the information system and often made good suggestions for improvements.

Part (b) asked for advice on whether three specific changes to the systems at the warehouse would reduce waste. The candidates were asked to view this as an application of lean principles. Few candidates structured their answers using lean ideas about waste but, by keeping their answers focused on the specifics on the scenario and the proposals, they nevertheless scored well.

Part (c) of the question required an evaluation of whether a set of new performance indicators adequately measured the application of lean ideas in the warehouse reorganization. This part offered a mixed performance by candidates as many candidates did not know the meaning of the lean principles given but could offer some useful evaluation of the indicators from first principles.

---

34 INTEGRATED REPORTING

Key answer tips

Integrated reporting is a relatively new syllabus area, so make sure you are aware of the different concepts and terms and keep an eye open for relevant articles for further guidance on how it may be examined.

This question is not exam standard. The Section B questions in the exam would contain a longer scenario. However, this question is useful for revision purpose and for consolidating knowledge on IR.

(a) In its simplest form, integrated reporting can be understood as the merging of the sustainability report and the financial report into a single 'narrative', as described by the Marketing Director.

However, the International Integrated Reporting Council (IIRC) does not use the word 'sustainability' in its definition of the concept.

According to the IIRC's 'International IR Framework,' an integrated report is 'a concise communication about how an organization's strategy, governance, performance and prospects, in the context of its external environment, lead to the creation of value over the short, medium and long term.'

The key emphasis of this definition is the idea of sustainable **value creation**, which makes the report and the processes underpinning it far more valuable than simply a compliance or reporting exercise.

Furthermore, this framework is intended as **guidance** for all businesses producing integrated reports, rather than compliance with a set of rules.

(b) The IR Framework recognizes the importance of looking at financial and sustainability performance in an integrated way – one that emphasizes the relationships between what it identifies as the 'six capitals':

Financial capital

This is what we traditionally think of as 'capital' – e.g. shares, bonds or banknotes. It enables the other types of Capital described below to be owned and traded.

Manufactured capital

This form of capital can be described as comprising of material goods, or fixed assets which contribute to the production process rather than being the output itself – e.g. tools, machines and buildings.

Intellectual capital

This form of capital can be described as the value of a company or organisation's employee knowledge, business training and any proprietary information that may provide the company with a competitive advantage.

Human capital

This can be described as consisting of people's health, knowledge, skills and motivation. All these things are needed for productive work.

Social capital

This can be described as being concerned with the institutions that help maintain and develop human capital in partnership with others; e.g. Families, communities, businesses, trade unions, schools, and voluntary organisations.

Natural capital

This can be described as any stock or flow of energy and material within the environment that produces goods and services. It includes resources of a renewable and non-renewable materials e.g. Land, water, energy and those factors that absorb, neutralise or recycle wastes and processes – e.g. climate regulation, climate change, CO_2 emissions.

The fundamental assumption of the IR Framework is that each of these types of capital—whether internal or external to the business, tangible or intangible—represents a potential source of value that must be managed for the long run in order to deliver sustainable value creation.

(c) The objectives for integrated reporting include:

- To improve the quality of information available to providers of financial capital to enable a more efficient and productive allocation of capital

- To provide a more cohesive and efficient approach to corporate reporting that draws on different reporting strands and communicates the full range of factors that materially affect the ability of an organisation to create value over time

- To enhance accountability and stewardship for the broad base of capitals (financial, manufactured, intellectual, human, social and relationship, and natural) and promote understanding of their interdependencies

- To support integrated thinking, decision making and actions that focus on the creation of value over the short, medium and long term.

(d) As well as external reporting to a range of stakeholders, the principles of IR can be extended to performance management systems. This is sometimes referred to as 'internal integrated reporting'.

An emphasis on these types of capital could result in more focussed performance management in the following ways:

- KPIs can be set up for each of the six capitals, ensuring that each of the drivers of sustainable value creation are monitored, controlled and developed.

- These can be developed further to show how the KPIs connect with different capitals, interact with, and impact each other.

- The interaction and inter-connectedness of these indicators should then be reflected in greater integration and cooperation between different functions and operations within the firm.

- This should result in greater transparency of internal communications allowing departments to appreciate better the wider implications of their activities.

- Together this should result in better decision making and value creation over the longer term.

35 BLUEFIN SCHOOL (DEC 11 – AMENDED)

Key answer tips

Make sure you answer the question set. In part (b) you were asked to evaluate the usefulness of the pack provided, rather than assess the performance of the school.

Also try to link your discussion to the organisation's mission and ethos to earn full marks.

(a) The controls necessary over management information would involve the use of standard templates and definitions for all information that has to be collated. This will be important at Bluefin where the information processing is decentralised to the departments. The department heads are preparing information in different formats using different methods of presentation. This could be potentially confusing to the governors if they were trying to compare departmental performance. Comparison will also be made more difficult if different performance measures are used by each department (such as average class marks and exam pass rates). These controls are important to ensure that time is not wasted in understanding the different formats or in devising different formats.

The reports should be examined periodically to ensure that they are actually being used. For example, the governors should be asked if the reports are read or the minutes of the board meeting should be reviewed for references to the reports.

The cost of producing the reports should be compared to the benefit that they supply. It will be difficult at Bluefin to quantify the benefits as it is not financially driven. The reporting will be to satisfy the major stakeholders such as the government who fund the school. Costs of the system would also be difficult to identify as this would require the measurement and costing of department heads' time.

In order to safeguard data, there should be a policy on regular backups. Bluefin has a decentralised information system where controls relating to the backup of records are more difficult to enforce.

The security concerns at the school will relate to the sensitive, personal nature of individuals' exam performance and the school's financial information. In a decentralised system, there are more locations from which sensitive data can be accessed. Security protocols are more difficult to enforce, for example, it is necessary to ensure that PCs are not in publicly accessible areas. It will also be important to ensure that password controls are observed (such as regular changes to passwords) and that they are not easy to guess or in a written form beside the relevant computer.

The current system of passing information by memory stick could easily lead to misplacement or loss of data. If memory sticks are to be used then data should be encrypted. It will also mean that there may be different versions of the data files on the department PCs and the administration system which will require to be controlled. It can also lead to virus infection being passed around the computers in the school. All files should be screened by anti-virus software that is installed across the school's computers.

(b) The positive aspects of the current governors' pack are that it addresses the financial and educational performance of the school; it provides the raw numerical data on which judgements about the quality of teaching and financial management can be made; and it utilises the skill of the department heads in giving them the choice of how to present data on pupil performance.

However, the current governors' pack for the annual review suffers from a number of basic flaws. Firstly, there is too much information being provided and that information is too detailed for a non-expert audience such as the governors. The financial information may well be too detailed and since this is a review rather than an executive control meeting it would be more helpful to provide a summary of the financial highlights.

The information on exam performance is also too detailed. The governors will not cope very easily with 11 department reports, each possibly listing about 20 sets of individual class average marks (if the mathematics department report is of average length).

Secondly, there appears to be a lack of narrative in the pack to explain the data given. For example, the class averages themselves are not explained in any commentary, although the previous year's comparative figure is provided.

Thirdly, the school's ethos provides a guide to the overall mission of the school. However, the governors' pack does not attempt to measure the performance of the school in areas such as citizenship and self-confidence. The current pack only provides information on the financial and examination performance of the pupils. Possible measures of citizenship could be number of pupil hours spent in community service. The additional information on self-confidence will be difficult to collect as it is qualitative and the measurement will be subjective.

Fourthly, no statement of financial position information is given which might allow an understanding of the school's investment in its buildings and equipment. This could be important in making a decision over the proposed IT improvements.

Finally, although not mentioned in the school's ethos, it would be expected that external comparisons of the school's performance would be appropriate, so this benchmark data should be provided along with the school's performance.

(c) The suggested improvements will bring the benefit of removing possible duplication of files and reducing storage requirements by unifying the data in one database. The network should facilitate the transfer of information between the departments and the school office making errors in transfer less likely. The centralising of the data in the school should make control over security tighter, it will be easier to enforce a policy on the backup of data and it should facilitate the standardisation of departmental report formats. By connecting the network on the internet, communication with key stakeholders such as the government will be improved. It may be possible to share data with other schools which could assist in a benchmarking exercise in order to identify best practice in the region.

However, the changes could lead to problems. The opening of the school network to the internet will provide additional opportunities for the spread of viruses and possibly open the network to hackers. The centralising of all data may make a loss more catastrophic although backup procedures will reduce this risk. The costs of such an upgrade may not be outweighed by the benefits as the benefits are all non-financial.

(d) Benchmarking could be used in several different ways at Bluefin. The most likely application is for the school to use internal benchmarking to compare the results of each department. The school could look at the particularly successful departments (measured in terms of exam results) and then investigate the teaching methods used here to determine best practice for the classroom.

Bluefin could also consider competitive benchmarking by comparing the performance of the school with other schools either in the local area or further afield. As the school is government funded and without a profit motive or competitive environment it may be relatively easy to access such information and support from other schools. Competitive benchmarking is much harder to implement in for-profit organisations.

Finally the school could consider process benchmarking to determine best practice in certain aspects of performance. One area where improvements could be made is in the performance reporting and this is something that other organisations could work with Bluefin on by sharing ideas on how to gather, collate and disseminate information.

Marking scheme			
			Marks
(a)	Controls and security	1 mark per point up to	**9**
(b)	Positive aspects	1 mark per point up to	2
	Information overload		2
	Information confusing and unexplained		2
	Failure to cover overall objectives		3
	Other – 1 mark per point made		
			___
		Maximum	**6**
			___
(c)	Benefits	1 mark per point up to	4
	Problems	1 mark per point up to	3
			___
		Maximum	**5**
			___
(d)	Up to 2 marks for each type of benchmarking described and properly applied to Bluefin up to a maximum of 5.		**5**
			___
Total			**25**
			___

36 QUARK HEALTHCARE (DEC 13)

Key answer tips

Make sure you answer the question set. In part (a) you were asked to assess the impact of the RFID system using the input from the CFO. This should have given you a clear set of points to structure your answer around.

In all parts of the question it was vital to relate your points to the specific context given, rather than relying on generic comments.

Tutorial note

Do not be frightened by this question. RFID may appear to be a small syllabus area and you may feel you have little knowledge to use here. However, there is a lot of information in the scenario that can be used to support your answer and to boost your mark.

(a) The new information will not be without cost to Quark. The costs of hardware and software to set up the system and then ongoing operation of the system in terms of maintenance, consumables and employee time are often considerable. However, these costs can be offset against the efficiency savings of lost employee time in searching for tagged items and quality improvements in patient care which will result from that quicker access.

The information now being collected is non-financial in the location and quantities of equipment and drugs. However, these are forms of information which exist in the current systems and so there need not be dramatic change. The significant difference from the old system will be the real-time nature of the information and also its accuracy as it is collected and updated automatically. The tags are attached to batches of high-value drugs and if one of these batches is opened, then the count of inventory will not be entirely accurate if only the RFID information is used. A physical count will still be required for accuracy but the locations of these items from RFIDs will speed this.

Performance reporting will change as weekly inventory check reports will no longer be filed for the high-value drugs and instead there will be real-time, screen-based information. The relevant staff will need to be trained to access and use the information in this new system. It would appear that many medical staff will need access and so terminals will need to be available throughout the hospital – if the speed gains in finding items are to be obtained.

Improved control will result from the knowledge of location of high-value drugs. It will be easier to ensure that they are all in secure locations which will reduce the opportunity for theft. Additionally, knowing the date of delivery it will easier to identify items which may become obsolete and so they can more easily be used first, thus reducing wastage. Regarding the items of equipment, identification of location will reduce staff time in searching and also allow the items to be placed in the stores where they are most often accessed, thus further reducing searching time. This will improve quality of patient care due to a faster response. It will also be simpler to check and ensure that these items are in secure locations and so reduce the risk of theft. Management will also be able to check if processes of tidying up and locking away are being observed by doing daily checks on this through the system.

(b) Lean systems are based on the Toyota production system whose overall goal was to get the right things to the right place at the right time, the first time. Additional aims were to minimise waste and be open to change. These objectives match closely with the RFID system at Quark.

The location information will allow assets to be in the right location or at least a more optimised location and so speed ('right time') delivery of the service. The reduction in obsolescence and staff time help to minimise waste while the introduction of such a different process will require a culture of change in the organisation.

The five Ss concept is often associated with lean principles and has the aim of creating a workplace which is in order. It should sit well with the high status of work in Quark as it engenders employees' pride in their work and results in higher quality performance.

The five Ss are:

- Structurise – Introduce order where possible. Thinking about optimal locations for storage of the tagged items will help to do this at Quark.

- Systemise – The new RFID system will help to arrange and identify items for ease of use.

- Sanitise – Be tidy. There is danger that the easy availability of the knowledge of the location of items may lead to a lack of care with them. However, by training staff that they will be judged on storing items in useful locations, this information can be used as a control tool by management.

- Standardise – Be consistent in the approach taken.

- Self-discipline – Maintain through motivation. The system should report by exception to management on a daily basis about any items misplaced and so corrective action can be taken.

In order to be successful, lean techniques must be more than just housekeeping and should be treated as signs of the importance of quality at Quark.

(c) The attitude of the medical staff to the system will be important. As they are high-status individuals, it will be necessary to persuade them to accept the new system rather than impose the change. There will be the danger that they see the system as spying on them and take this as an insult to their professionalism. They will need to see the benefits both in terms of reduced frustration in their own job and patient care. This will motivate them to change their current way of storing assets.

The new system will be screen-based but the use of information technology should not be shocking in Quark as it has the reputation of being advanced in this area. The reports will need to be carefully designed with input from the medical staff in order that they find the system easy to learn and use, as this is often a major barrier to the uptake of a new system. The design of the new method of recording drug administration by nurses may have been part of the problem with its implementation.

Promotion of responsibility and accountability will come through the management use of the new information. It may be possible to make specific staff (e.g. nursing staff) responsible for the storage of drugs and specific specialist doctors responsible for the storage of equipment related to their field of expertise. Regular checks on the position of assets will act as a control test of this staff activity. It may be necessary to break the hospital into departments or wards in order to identify the relevant responsible individuals. The managers must think carefully about how often to do their control reporting but daily exception reporting of any items not properly stored would appear appropriate, given the need to use the assets at short notice.

It will be important to select the correct individuals and groups to be responsible as there will be a demotivating effect if a staff member is being criticised for not securing an item when a higher status member of staff (e.g. medical specialist) has over-ridden their decision.

Marking scheme			
			Marks
(a)	Costs and benefits	up to	3
	Type of information supplied	up to	3
	Performance reporting	up to	3
	Improved control	up to	6
		Maximum	**12**
(b)	Definition of lean system	up to	2
	Analysis of impact of RFID system	up to	7
	Up to 2 for definition of five Ss		
		Maximum	**7**
(c)	Medical staff's behaviour will influence the design	up to	4
	Promotion of responsibility and accountability	up to	4
		Maximum	**6**
Total			**25**

Examiner's comments

Part (a) for 12 marks looked at the overall impact of the new system. The scenario listed a number of areas of concern for the CFO of Quark and those candidates that used this hint tended to provide more complete and better structured answers. Most candidates did well in identifying the control benefits of the system but in not addressing the CFO's concerns often found that they ran out of ideas for further comment to reach the 12 marks available. Very few chose to comment on the nature of the information supplied and the changes to performance reporting and as a result, there were many passing answers to this part but few that scored highly.

Part (b) for 7 marks required candidates to demonstrate their understanding of the 'lean' concept by applying it to the effect of the new information system. Few candidates had a clear idea of the definition of 'lean' in this context though most realised that it related to waste reduction/efficiency/accuracy. Most candidates scored some marks for their illustrations from the scenario of how the new system created these benefits. (Candidates should note that they were not required to mention the 5Ss in order to score full marks here, though it may have been useful in structuring an answer.)

Part (c) for 6 marks concerned the staff at the hospitals. The rigid hierarchy of the staff and previous information system problems were described in the scenario and those that made use of this as illustration of their general points scored well. The question asked for the influence that staff attitude would have on design and implementation and better candidates used these two phases (design and implementation) to discuss their answer. The final part of the requirement asked about the impact on responsibility and accountability and, as in previous diets, candidates only displayed a very vague grasp of what these terms might mean in the context of the RFID information system.

37 FORION ELECTRONICS (JUN 15)

Key answer tips

Make sure you answer the question set. In part (a) you were asked to assess the impact of the ERPS on performance management issues at Forion. This should have given you three clear points to structure your answer around. In part (c) make sure you evaluate reliability of information sources and don't simply list them.

(a) Enterprise Resource Planning Systems (ERPS) are software systems designed to support and automate the business processes of large enterprises. ERPS help in identifying and planning the use of resources across the organisation in all activities. As a unified database of corporate information, ERPS will aid the flow of information between all functions both within Forion and also with key outside stakeholders (e.g. suppliers such as BAS).

ERPS handle many aspects of operations including manufacturing, inventory, distribution, invoicing and accounting. They also cover support functions such as human resource management and marketing. These all seem appropriate for Forion.

ERPS can also contain SCM (supply chain management) and CRM (customer relationship management) software. Automated systems would seem appropriate at Forion given the number of customer and supplier relationships which Forion has to manage.

An ERPS also addresses the common issue of poor communication between departments. It will help across the three problems mentioned.

The inefficiencies arising from ordering the wrong volume of subcomponents would occur because purchasing and manufacturing are not using a common database so that purchasing may be using erroneous or out-of-date information. This will lead to extra costs in inventory handling and storing.

The stock-outs will result in poor customer service as goods are not available for immediate shipment. The obsolescence problems will result in direct financial losses as inventory is written off. Both of these problems will be the result of poor integration of the manufacturing schedule with the expected level of orders. ERPS will be welcomed as it will make use of the expertise of the marketing department in forecasting and making this available to manufacturing managers when setting their production plans.

The lack of vehicles available to meet delivery deadlines could be aided by the manufacturing schedule linking in to the delivery schedule so that optimal use can be made of the delivery fleet. This would also allow the delivery managers to plan for use of subcontractors to do delivery if there is not internal transport available and so avoid customer disappointment.

(b) Considering the points raised overall, it is surprising that they seem to be addressing the strengths of BAS. BAS will have been chosen as an ally because it is a good company. However, it may be worth considering if there are weaknesses and if measures should be put in place in the agreement to guard against these.

The points seem reasonable given the critical nature of the screen in the production process of a smartphone and the setting of penalties is wise. Taking each point in turn:

Manufacturing quality would be expected to be high given BAS' reputation; however, it will be a critical part of the assembly process and faults will lead to either delayed delivery (if spotted in internal inspection) or else lead to customer dissatisfaction and rework costs to repair faulty items.

The time of delivery will dictate the volume of screen inventory which Forion has to hold and so impact on any attempt to run a just-in-time system of manufacturing. It may be necessary to give BAS access to Forion's production scheduling system (via the new ERPS possibly) in order to achieve such a close working relationship.

Unlike the other two issues, the point on the provision of technical upgrades does not provide a metric for measuring this. It will be difficult to set a minimum performance level as such upgrades will be difficult to predict and it would be reasonable for BAS to reject (or ignore) a vaguely worded clause which would not be enforceable.

The size of the penalties would need to be commensurate with damage to the reputation of the product from BAS' failure. Mobile phone customers are notable for having rapidly dropped previous market leaders when their products fail to deliver (e.g. Nokia, Blackberry). Therefore, it would be reasonable for potentially large penalties to be payable. Forion should note that these will only be claimable if they hold to their side of the agreement and so must carefully attend to the information and resources which need to be provided to BAS.

(c) **Financial and non-financial data**

Financial data has the advantage of being heavily checked and policed as part of the annual audit regime operating in most organisations. Financial data also has the advantages of being quantitative and so objective, whereas it can be difficult to judge the relative value of, for example, two customer complaints.

For the accountant, the collection and interpretation of financial data is thus straightforward and an everyday activity. Qualitative, non-financial data will often require to be transformed into quantitative data by applying 1–5 scales but it will never escape from the problem of being judgemental and subjective. Not all non-financial data is qualitative; however, the planning and scheduling data will be quantitative.

Internal and external sources

Forion will have greater control over the accuracy of internal data within its own ERPS than the external data, such as might be supplied by suppliers for their deliveries. External sources of data such as for the SLA will obviously be highly contentious if there is the possibility of penalty payments resulting from breaches of the agreement. Therefore, Forion may want to put in place its own inspection regime in order to confirm such data. Unreconciled differences between information systems are often a source of dispute in alliances such as the one with BAS.

Marking scheme		Marks
(a) 1 mark per point up to 5 marks for description of ERPS and how it integrates information up to 6 marks for ERPS impact on problems at Forion		
	Total	10
(b) 1 mark per point In order to score highly, all three issues must be addressed		
	Total	8
(c) 1 mark per point In order to score highly, both issues financial/non-financial and internal/external must be addressed		
	Maximum	7
Total		25

Examiner's comments

Part (a) was worth 10 marks and involved discussing the integration of Forion's information systems within the new ERPS and its impact on performance management. This part was often fairly well done with many good answers relating to the three specific problem areas in information management at Forion.

Part (b) for 8 marks required the candidates to evaluate the usefulness of the three critical areas from the strategic alliance agreement described in the question for Forion to measure the performance of BAS. This part was generally fairly well done with candidates showing a good appreciation of how BAS's performance links to Forion's. The most common fault in answers was a failure to focus on the performance measurement aspects of the areas.

Part (c) for 7 marks required an evaluation of the reliability of financial and non-financial data from internal and external sources. This has been a common topic in past examinations and performance in this question was unexpectedly poor. Many candidates seem unaware of what constitutes internal and external sources and surprisingly many consider audited, financial data to be amongst the least reliable sources. Possibly as a result of these weaknesses, the markers saw numerous answers that discussed only the type of information that both parties to the alliance would need without discussing its reliability.

38 ALBACORE (PILOT 10)

Key answer tips

This is a really useful revision question on the evaluation of a performance report and management styles. The theory here is reasonably straightforward but this theory needs to be applied to the specifics of the scenario. Once you have attempted the question, have a thorough read through the answer and marking scheme. Would you be able to replicate something similar in the real exam?

(a) The branch information appears to be inadequate on a number of levels to appraise the shop manager's performance. The manager should only be held responsible for those areas of performance that they can control.

The branch manager should be appraised on a realistic sales budget. The overall market fall of 12% suggests that the original budget of no change on previous year was not realistic. It is possible to analyse this by calculating planning and operational variances as follows:

	$
Revised budgeted sales given market fall	234,080
Budgeted gross margin	60%
Revised budgeted gross margin	140,448
Original budgeted gross margin	159,600
Planning variance	19,152 A
Actual sales	237,100
Revised budgeted sales	234,080
	————
	3,020 F
Budgeted gross margin	60%
Operational variance	1,812 F

The operational variance reflects more accurately the manager's work and from this we can see the manager has done well by limiting the fall in gross profit by $1,812.

This analysis could be extended to other areas of the performance report. For example, if the breakdown of sales prices and volumes for individual product lines were given together with details of market volumes and price movements then the sales price variance could be broken down into operational and planning elements to reflect the manager's use of the limited discounting power that she has. Overall at the Tunny branch, the gross margin has remained constant (at 60%) which indicates that the manager may not have made use of the sales price discounting authority.

There are a number of other non-controllable costs in the branch information. It is unlikely that the branch manager can affect the price variance of heating and lighting costs as the prices are set through central purchasing although they will have some control over usage. The rental cost will reflect head office property management and is not controllable. The manager's own wages are not controllable although the staff costs will reflect the fact that the manager can choose to work longer hours and so save on part-time staff, therefore a labour efficiency variance would be appropriate.

A revised report would split the costs into two groups (controllable and on-controllable) so that a controllable profit would be shown as well as the overall shop profit. This would be the basic measure of performance of the store. A more detailed understanding of responsibility for the variances would be given by a breakdown of the operational (controllable) and planning (non-controllable) elements of each variance.

It might look like this:

Revised performance report

Albacore Chess Stores

Tunny branch – Year to Sept 2011

	Budget	Actual	Planning variance	Operational variance	Variance
	$	$	$	$	$
Sales	266,000	237,100	−28,900		
Cost of sales	106,400	94,840	11,560		
Gross profit	159,600	142,260	−17,340	−19,152	1,812
Controllable costs:					
Marketing	12,000	11,500	500		
Staff costs: Part-time staff	38,000	34,000	4,000		
Controllable profit	109,600	96,760	−12,840		
Non-controllable costs:					
Staff costs: manager	27,000	27,000	0		
Property costs	26,600	26,600	0		
Shop profit	56,000	43,160	−12,840		

Notes:

Property costs includes heating, lighting and rental.

Positive variances are favourable.

Summary

The manager's performance has been good in difficult general economic circumstances since if we exclude the gross margin planning variance ($19,152A) and allow that the part-time staff costs and marketing costs are controllable then we see that there is a favourable variance in controllable profit of $6,312 ($19,152-$12,840).

As indicated, additional variances that could be reported include operational and planning price variances for sales; part-time labour efficiency variances in operational variances; part-time labour rate variances in planning variances; and some price and usage variances for property costs. There is insufficient data to calculate examples of these variances here.

(b) The management style at Albacore is highly budget-constrained (Hopwood). It is driven by financial performance to meet the needs of the venture capitalist owners who have probably highly geared the business at the time of purchase. The cost control attitude is illustrated by the focus on achieving budget in the reward system and the enforcement of staff pay rates. This management style leads to stress for employees and difficult working relationships – as illustrated by the unhappiness of the shop managers. It also can motivate manipulation of performance reports although given the centralised nature of Albacore this appears unlikely at the shop level. It does however focus attention on achieving budget. This could be desirable in difficult economic circumstances.

Alternative styles are:

- profit-conscious where the performance is evaluated on longer-term effectiveness of the business unit in question (plausible here given Albacore's aim of profit maximisation)

- non-accounting where the budget is of low importance in performance evaluation

The performance appraisal system at Albacore reflects this cost-conscious, budget constrained approach. The shop managers are instructed as to their objectives and there appears to be no discussion of this target between the appraiser and the shop manager. For the branch given, it is striking that the failure to make budgeted profit (by $12,840) has led to no bonus being paid although the shop made an operating profit of $43,160 and the operating margin of the shop has held up at 18% compared to 21% per the budget.

The branch information needs to reflect the areas that the manager can control as mentioned in part (a) to this answer. Using the analysis of revised controllable profit, we have seen that the manager has returned a good performance $6,312 ahead of budget. The increased use of operational and planning variances should help to motivate the managers and reduce the friction with senior staff.

The current contract between the manager and Albacore could be described as coercive as it is imposed. The budget should be agreed between the manager and their appraiser using the detailed knowledge of both parties to improve the budget estimates. Although for Albacore, the likely budget will reflect the expectations of the senior management in order to achieve the business' overall financial objectives.

The reward system could move to a more calculative basis where the manager is paid a percentage of the profit above a certain level, usually this bonus is capped to a maximum as in the current system. The senior management will need to assess the trigger level based on head office costs (administrative support and financing costs). Therefore, the operational director's assessment would become more objective and this could remove lack of clarity in how performance is assessed.

Performance appraisal could also recognise longer-term and non-financial factors in the manager's performance such as innovative marketing ideas and customer feedback on their shopping experience. Additionally, as the branch manager handles the shop's staff development, recognition could be given for branch staff who progress from part-time to shop manager.

	Marking scheme		
			Marks
(a)	**Variances**		
	Calculations:		
	Flexed budget		1
	Operation and planning (1 mark per point up to 4)		4
	Controllable profit		1
	Revised performance report	up to	8
	Comments:		
	Structure		1
	Revenue budget unrealistic		1
	Controllable costs		3
	(general 1 specific justifications 2)		
	Controllable profit		1
	Other variances	up to	5
			———
		Maximum	**13**
			———
(b)	Management styles (1 mark per point up to 6)		6
	Performance appraisal system (1 mark per point up to 6)		6
	Improvements (1 mark per point up to 3)		3
			———
		Maximum	**12**
			———
Total			**25**
			———

D – STRATEGIC PERFORMANCE MEASUREMENT

39   CHICORY (SEPT/DEC 17)

Key answer tips

In part (a)(i) the calculation and evaluation of ROCE should be quite straightforward.

In (a)(ii) 10 marks are available for the calculation and evaluation of EBITDA. Do not view any syllabus area as 'fringe' or 'unexaminable'. This requirement demonstrates that the examiner is willing to test all syllabus areas.

In (b) a generic list of drawbacks will not be given much credit. Use of the scenario information to point out the large number of difficulties and differences in comparing the two companies is required.

(a)   (i)   **ROCE**

As can be seen in working 1, Chicory's ROCE is 13.6% and Fennel's ROCE is 14.9%. Fennel has apparently performed better than Chicory. One benefit of using ROCE as a performance measure in this benchmarking exercise is that it gives a percentage figure and can compare businesses of different sizes. ROCE does not, however, give the absolute level of return. In this case, Fennel has both a higher capital employed and a higher percentage return.

ROCE is easy to calculate and will be familiar to Chicory's management as it is currently one of Chicory's main financial performance indicators. The figures required to calculate ROCE are readily available from published data, which makes this a good financial performance measure for benchmarking.

ROCE shows a weak correlation with Chicory's objective to maximise shareholder wealth, which may limit ROCE's usefulness as a performance measure in this benchmarking exercise. ROCE may be distorted by accounting policies or where different businesses have different levels of intangible assets. This may lead to drawing incorrect conclusions from the exercise. A big disadvantage of using ROCE in this benchmarking exercise is that it may encourage managers not to invest in new non-current assets, which contradicts Chicory's strategy of investing in charging points.

Working 1

Chicory:

Opening capital employed (Total assets – Current liabilities)	$78.0m (138.0 – 60.0)
Closing capital employed	$59.0m (140.0 – 81.0)
Average capital employed	$68.5m ((78.0 + 59.0)/2)
ROCE (Operating profit/average capital employed)	13.6% (9.3/68.5)

Fennel:

Average capital employed $(170 \times 0.25) + (176 \times 0.75)$	$174.5m
ROCE	14.9% (26.0/174.5)

Tutorial note

In (a)(i), ideally the average capital employed figure should be used to calculate ROCE. However, do not get too distracted and waste time on this. A pass could still be achieved without using the average figure.

(ii)   EBITDA

Using Chicory's main financial performance indicators of ROCE, Fennel has performed better than Chicory. When depreciation of non-current assets and the write-off of goodwill in Chicory are added back to operating profit to calculate EBITDA, Chicory's performance, with an EBITDA of $52.0m, is slightly better than that of Fennel, which has an EBITDA of $51.0m.

EBITDA as a proxy for cash flow

EBITDA is easy to calculate from published data, and easy to understand. It is a measure of underlying performance, as it is a proxy for cash flow generated from operating profit. As Chicory is having cash flow difficulties following the unsuccessful acquisition, EBITDA would be a relevant measure for this benchmarking exercise. EBITDA does not, however, take into account the cash flow effect of working capital changes, for example, by Chicory negotiating longer payment terms with its suppliers.

Excludes items which are not relevant to underlying performance of the business

Tax and interest are distributions from profits, unrelated to the underlying performance of the business. Excluding them from measures of performance, therefore, gives a better understanding of the underlying performance of Chicory and Fennel. This is important for the benchmarking exercise since Fennel appears to suffer much lower rates of tax, probably due to the tax incentives given by the Veeland government. Loans underwritten by the Veeland government may be at artificially reduced rates of interest and should also be excluded when measuring performance.

Similarly, depreciation, amortisation and write-offs such as goodwill are not relevant to the current year's underlying performance and may relate to previous years. For example, adding back the write-off of goodwill in Chicory means the two businesses have identical EBITDAs, albeit that Fennel has much greater capital employed.

EBITDA affects comparability of benchmarking data

Using EBITDA as a performance measure in the benchmarking exercise makes the data for the two businesses more comparable and removes one element of subjectivity, such as in determining useful economic lives of non-current assets. EBITDA does, however, ignore the replacement costs of these assets. This might limit the usefulness of comparisons between Chicory and Fennel if one were to lease non-current assets and the other to purchase them. The introduction of a new accounting standard on the treatment of leases may, however, remove this limitation.

Unlike Chicory's existing measure of ROCE, which is a percentage measure, EBITDA is an absolute measure and so makes it difficult to compare businesses of different sizes. As a profit based measure, its usefulness is also limited by subjective assumptions made in the calculation of profit, or by inconsistent accounting policies. Development costs may be capitalised in Veeland, but not in Deeland, which may make a comparison against the benchmark difficult.

Working 2

$m	Chicory	Fennel
Operating profit	9.3	26.0
Add back:		
Depreciation on non-current assets	18.0	25.0
Write off of goodwill	24.7	–
	———	———
EBITDA	52.0	51.0

(b) Benchmarking the performance of Chicory against a similar business implies that there is a best way to operate. Though Fennel may be similar to Chicory, there is no indication that it is best in class and benchmarking against it may be inappropriate.

For example, Fennel has taken advantages of tax incentives and loan guarantees to finance new investments. These do not exist in Deeland, so Chicory may be unable to fund investment in this way. It may have to consider leasing assets instead, or accept a slower rate of growth if it wishes to set up charging points in Deeland.

Benchmarking is a catching up exercise. The financial data for Fennel is 18 months older than that for Chicory and may already be out of date. In 2015, Fennel improved operational performance by investment in IT. The effect of this is not reflected in the financial data given. Benchmarking performance against historical data may not be relevant for current or future performance. The electric car market in Veeland has grown rapidly in the last two years. This growth is not reflected in the financial performance data given for Fennel, nor is the falling price of components for the charging points.

Though Fennel has agreed to share data, this data may be inaccurate or misleading. Though initially the benchmarking exercise is only against Fennel, it may be difficult to find other comparable businesses to benchmark against in the future. The data required for calculation of the three financial performance indicators used in the benchmarking exercise is likely to be readily available and audited, however, which means it is reliable.

A large part of Fennel's business relates to providing charging points for charging electric cars. Though this is a business model Chicory intends to follow in the future, it is very different to its existing business, and so benchmarking against Fennel may be misleading unless more detailed data relating to the two activities can be obtained.

Similarly, Fennel operates in a different country, where the economy is much stronger. Performance targets set following the benchmarking exercise may be unachievable for Chicory. Fennel's financial data has been converted into $ from its home currency. Movements in exchange rates may make the benchmarking data less comparable, especially if the economies in Deeland and Veeland are growing at different rates.

Marking scheme		
		Marks
(a)(i)	Calculation of Chicory and Fennel's average capital employed	2
	Calculation of both companies' ROCE	1
	Comment of the results of the ROCE calculation	1
	Evaluation of ROCE as a performance measure	3
		———
	Maximum	**6**
		———
(a)(ii)	Adjustments to operating profit	2
	Calculation of both companies' EBITDA	1
	Comment of the results of the EBITDA calculation	1
	Evaluation of EBITDA as a performance measure	6
		———
	Maximum	**10**
		———
(b)	Problems of benchmarking exercise – up to 2 marks per point	
		———
	Maximum	**9**
		———
Total		**25**
		———

40 TOSEMARY AND RHYME HOSPITAL (TRH) (SEPT/DEC 17)

Key answer tips

Overall, this is a manageable question with clear requirements and adequate time.

In requirement (a), a good answer will focus on the need for NFPIs due to the multitude and diversity of objectives at TRH.

In requirement (b), ensure you outline the meaning of each 'E' (from the 3Es) before justifying a relevant performance measure for each of these.

In requirement (c), if you have your knowledge in place then it should be reasonably straightforward to identify that the organisation is largely budget constrained and that this would have potentially negative consequences for TRH.

(a) **Lack of profit-making objective**

Not-for-profit organisations do not, by definition, have profit as an overriding motive. Patients are not charged for receiving treatment, so TRH does not have a revenue stream. It may also be difficult to define a cost unit as this could be cost per patient arriving at hospital or cost per patient successfully treated.

Not-for-profit public sector organisations, such as TRH, have strict constraints on the amount of funding they receive, such as a fixed amount of funding received entirely from the government. They cannot obtain funding from elsewhere, so financial measures cannot be ignored completely. TRH must exist within its financial means, and the use of budgets to control costs is critical.

TRH provides an essential public service. Political, legal and social influences would prevent it from closing down a service just because it became more expensive or uneconomic to provide it. For all of these reasons, financial objectives are less relevant than for most commercial organisations, and its objectives are mainly non-financial in nature.

Not-for-profit organisations also undergo more public scrutiny and have multiple stakeholders, so non-financial indicators will be necessary to manage expectations. For example, patients are stakeholders who will have relatively little interest in how TRH exists within its financial constraints. They will have much more interest in non-financial performance, such as how quickly and successfully they are treated.

Multiple objectives

Not-for-profit organisations have multiple objectives, and it may be unclear which are the most important. Except for some aspects of giving value for money to the taxpayer, TRH's objectives are all non-financial.

The outputs or benefits of the services provided are non-financial in nature, for example, giving prompt and high-quality treatment to patients. Therefore NFPIs are required to measure performance.

(b) Value for money in public sector organisations can be measured using the 'three Es': economy, efficiency and effectiveness.

Economy

Economy means obtaining resources at the lowest cost. Doctors' salaries will be a significant expense for TRH, and salary per doctor is a suitable measure of economy. Doctors at TRH have an average salary of $150,000 ($3.75m/25), compared to the national average of $175,000 ($4.20m/24).

The relatively lower salaries of doctors may be due to differences in levels of experience or that they work unpaid overtime. It may also be one of the reasons why the staff satisfaction is so much lower at 9% compared to the national level of 89%.

Efficiency

Efficiency relates to obtaining the greatest possible outputs from the resources available. Treating patients is a key objective of TRH, and the number of doctors is an important resource. The number of patients treated per year by each doctor is a good measure of efficiency. In TRH, each doctor treats an average of 975 (24,375/25) patients per year, 17% more (975 v 833) than the national average 833 (20,000/24). This may be because they work longer hours than their colleagues in other hospitals.

Effectiveness

Effectiveness means how well TRH achieves its objectives. TRH has multiple objectives, one of which is to provide high quality medical treatment for patients. Where patients are re-admitted to TRH because their treatment had failed, this represents a failure to provide high-quality medical care, so the rate of re-admission of patients is a measure of effectiveness. The rate of re-admission at TRH is 7.5% (1,830/24,375), much higher than the national average of 1.5% (300/20,000). TRH seems to have performed relatively very poorly in this respect.

Summary

Overall, the results from the measurement of the 3Es are consistent with the doctor's comments that they are working without being paid overtime and treating more patients than their colleagues in other hospitals. TRH appears to deliver better economy and efficiency than the national average. This seems to be reducing performance, however, in respect of providing high-quality medical treatment for patients, where TRH is less effective than the national average.

(c) **Extent to which management style is budget constrained**

A budget-constrained management style emphasises the need to achieve short-term performance measures, for example, the annual financial budgets.

The doctor said that TRH has always achieved its total financial budgets, and this is supported by the fact that the doctors' salaries for the year to 31 August 2017 equalled the budget set for the period. Though it is unclear what NFPIs are measured at TRH as a whole, doctors receive only a limited set of financial and non-financial performance data. The discussion about this data, however, is mainly related to financial targets. This implies greater emphasis is given to performance against financial targets, rather than non-financial ones.

All of this suggests that TRH has a budget-constrained management style. An advantage of this is that it ensures TRH operates with the financial constraints of the fixed amount of funding received from the government.

Implications of a budget-constrained approach at TRH

This management style encourages short-termism, by encouraging doctors to work long hours without being paid overtime, or not making funding available to recruit new doctors to alleviate the situation. An implication of this is that TRH may reduce its performance against its objectives, and this is already seen by the relatively high rates of re-admission as an indicator of a reduced quality of medical treatment. Job-related tension is a consequence of a budget-constrained management style, and the low staff satisfaction score could have resulted from this.

This management style encourages manipulation of results, or the way they are measured, to show better performance. At busy times, more patients are referred to the nearby larger hospital. There is apparently no medical need for this, which is inconsistent with the objective to deliver high-quality treatment. It appears to be a way to distort waiting times to demonstrate improved performance in treating patients promptly. From patients' perspective, though, this will mean they are treated less promptly than if treated at TRH.

Being unable to recruit new doctors reduces TRH's flexibility in reducing waiting times at busy periods, as the steps already taken seem to have had minimal effect. This management style does not encourage innovation, probably because doctors have insufficient time for this. Though this may have long-term benefits, it seems to be taken as less important than the other key objectives, to provide prompt, high-quality treatment.

Marking scheme			
			Marks
(a)	Importance of NFPIs - 1 mark per point		
		Maximum	5
(b)	Definition of 3 Es – 1 mark		
	Each E – up to 4 marks		
		Maximum	10
(c)	Discussion of budget constrained style - 1 mark per point		
		Maximum	10
Total			25

Examiner's comments

Question 3 examined performance measurement and management at a not-for-profit hospital. This was the most popular question chosen in section B.

Part (a) required an explanation of the importance of non-financial performance indicators at the hospital. It was generally fairly well answered with better answers targeting issues specific to this hospital.

Part (b) asked for application of the value for money framework in justifying a performance measure for each of its three component parts and then an assessment of this performance. Although this has been a common topic in APM, some candidates seemed ill-prepared; with many unable to define the framework and so properly attribute an indicator to each of the three headings. Candidates who did not know the framework tended to only score tangentially as it was the application of this model that was being tested. Candidates who knew the model generally scored well.

Part (c) of the question required an evaluation of the management style at the hospital and its implications for performance. Strong candidates gave logical answers which firstly identified the style currently in use, evidencing this with proof from the scenario and then discussed the consequences in achieving the organisation's objectives. Weaker candidates offered short answers for a 10 mark part often ignoring the points on the implications for performance management and just giving lists of possible performance management improvements without reference to the management style.

This final point illustrates a key point for APM that remains poorly grasped in many diets and that is the importance in the assessment of an organisation (its performance/choice of measures) to relate this back to its mission/objectives/critical success factors.

41   PITLANE (MAR/JUN 17)

Key answer tips

This is a reasonably challenging question and highlights the importance of having you PM knowledge in place.

(a) You should be able to have a good attempt at this calculation if you know that the cost gap is the difference between the target cost and expected cost.

(b) To obtain a good mark you need to compare the current system with the use of target costing and then examine each stage of the target costing process in detail, with a specific focus on how Pitlane could take steps to reduce the cost gap.

As always in APM, in requirement (c) application to the scenario is required. For example, you are expected to give advice on empowerment of employees.

(a)

	2018	2019	2020
Basic selling price	180.0	170.0	160.0
10% uplift for features/packaging	18.0	17.0	16.0
Estimated selling price	198.0	187.0	176.0
Less: 15% net profit	(29.7)	(28.1)	(26.4)
Target total cost per unit	168.3	158.9	149.6
Current expected cost:			
Estimated total direct cost per unit	134.0	134.0	134.0
Estimated fixed cost per unit (W1)	44.1	44.1	44.1
Estimated total cost per unit	178.1	178.1	178.1
Cost gap	9.8	19.2	28.5

W1 – Fixed overhead cost per unit

= Total fixed overheads/Number of units sold

= $10,000,000/227,000 units = $44.05

(b)   Target costing

Pitlane currently operates a traditional cost plus pricing method, where customers pay a fixed mark up on Pitlane's standard cost. This has been appropriate because the components currently produced have been manufactured in the same way for some time and their cost structure is well understood. Actual costs of production are very close to the standard costs. There is little competition in the market for Pitlane's current products, as a long-term contract was recently renewed with its biggest customer.

In contrast, for the proposed Booster product, the market price is only estimated. To compete with similar products, the Booster will need to sell at a price reflecting that of competitors' products, taking into account the different benefits and quality which each product has.

Target costing begins with taking the price which the market will pay for the product for a given market share. From that, the required profit margin is deducted to arrive at a target cost. The difference between the estimated cost for the product and the target cost is the cost gap. Where the estimated costs exceed the target cost, steps are taken to reduce the cost gap. The product can then be sold at a price which the market will accept, and which generates an acceptable profit margin.

Determining the market price

Pitlane's marketing department has estimated the average market price of competitors' products and the likely market share over the three years of the scheme. The estimates are based on the success of a similar scheme in Veeland, and the assumptions used could be incorrect. Electricity prices may already be higher in Veeland than in Deeland, meaning consumers there would reduce their energy costs more by installing solar panels. Similarly, consumers in Veeland could save more on energy costs if there is more sunshine there than in Deeland, enabling solar panels to generate more energy. Both factors would, in this case, reduce the take up of subsidies by consumers in Deeland and the amount they would be willing to pay for solar panels.

The domestic solar energy market is new in Deeland, and Pitlane has no experience in estimating market share or price for this type of product. Pitlane's belief that consumers would be willing to pay a 10% premium for highest quality packaging, or for the Booster to communicate with consumers' mobile phones, may be incorrect.

Calculating the target cost using the required profit margin

Pitlane charges a 15% profit margin on its existing projects. The shareholders' financial objective indicates that they require the same profit margin to be earned on Booster.

For its existing products, Pitlane can set a selling price based on its own costs, whereas the Booster's price must reflect external market conditions more closely. Target costing will focus Pitlane on the external environment by considering prices and relative benefits of competitors' products.

Estimating total costs of Booster

The total direct costs of Booster have been estimated at $134.00. The fixed overhead per unit relating to Booster for the three years of the scheme is $44.05, making total estimated costs per unit of $178.05. The cost estimates may be incorrect, especially as Booster is new, and different from Pitlane's existing products. As Booster includes costs which are fixed, estimating sales volumes is also crucial in determining costs per unit.

Pitlane has no recent experience of developing new products or of estimating costs and sales volumes for them. This makes it more likely that the cost estimates for the Booster will be incorrect. Estimating the total costs is needed for the next stage in the target costing process, to identify the cost gap.

Reducing the cost gap

A big advantage for Pitlane of using target costing is that it is often easier to reduce costs of a product at the design stage rather than after it has entered production.

As Boosters are not sold directly to consumers, the buyers of the product, who are professional installers, may not see value in the highest quality packaging. This could be a significant yet unnecessary cost, to be eliminated at the design stage. In deciding what costs to eliminate, Pitlane will have to take into account the effect of these on the quality and perception of the final product.

The features where the Booster can communicate with consumers' smartphones, and the use of highest quality packaging, are believed to enable Pitlane to charge 10% more than competitors' products. The $3.8m (W1) of estimated additional total revenue from the packaging and smartphone features may not justify the $2.8m upfront development costs for the smartphone feature alone, especially if the time value of money were to be taken into account. Consumers may not value these two features or be prepared to pay more for them. Eliminating them would therefore have little effect on sales volumes and would enable Pitlane to charge a more competitive price, or obtain higher gross profit margins.

Due to damage of sub-components when assembling the prototype, the estimated assembly labour cost assumes highly skilled labour will be used. This is 30% more expensive than other labour. By providing additional training, lower paid labour could be used to produce the Booster, and hence reduce the cost gap.

Pitlane plans to purchase the four main sub-components in bulk from six different suppliers. Consolidating suppliers, or using suppliers in lower cost countries, could help reduce the cost gap by reducing purchase costs. Moving to a just-in-time production system, rather than buying supplies in bulk, would help reduce costs of holding inventory as suppliers would only deliver sub-components when needed. This may increase other costs such as by requiring investment in information technology. It would also take time to develop the close relationship required with suppliers.

Another source of waste is due to internal transport and handling, which forms over 5% of the total direct cost of the Booster. This will also increase production cycle times, and is an unnecessary process which does not add value. It could be eliminated by changing the layout of the factory, or reorganising production into teams and ensuring all production was done at a single factory, rather than in both of Pitlane's factories.

W1 – Additional revenue from smartphone feature and highest quality packaging

2018 – 60,000 units x $198 = $11.880m

2019 – 75,000 units x $187 = $14.025m

2020 – 92,000 units x $176 = $16.192m

Total revenue = $42.097m

= $42,097,000 x 10/110 = $3,827,000

Tutorial note

This is a detailed solution. You would not be expected to produce an answer of this length.

(c) Kaizen costing

Unlike target costing, which occurs at the beginning of a product's life, Kaizen costing is a process of long-term continuous improvement by cost reduction throughout the life of the product.

The Booster will be produced only for the three years during which the Deeland government offers subsidies and tax incentives. Generally, Kaizen costing is used over longer periods, and it is likely the full benefits of this approach will not be achieved in such a short timescale. The target cost is the starting point for Kaizen costing. After production begins, each period's target is based on the previous period's reduced costs.

Target costing can achieve large cost reductions at the design stage of the product, e.g. by choosing not to develop the smartphone feature. Kaizen costing, however, reduces costs in much smaller, incremental steps.

The need for continuous improvement

Even though Booster's share of the market rises over the three years of the project, the market price falls, as does the size of the market. Which means that in order to achieve the shareholders' financial targets, the direct costs of the Booster must fall over the three years. Continual incremental improvements using Kaizen costing, and measuring these improvements against targets from the previous period rather than the original estimated cost, could help to achieve this.

Ways to reduce waste using Kaizen costing

Traditional costing methods often see employees as the cause of high costs, whereas Kaizen costing sees the employees as a source of ideas on how to reduce costs. The manufacturing director's comments, that the damage caused by employees to delicate sub-components may mean it may not be possible to produce the Booster, indicates that Pitlane is currently following the traditional approach. Employees are seen as the source of the waste.

To benefit from Kaizen costing, Pitlane must undergo a culture change to encourage employees to suggest ideas, perhaps using quality circles, to reduce costs. That way, improvements could be made in the way sub-components are assembled during production, which would shorten the production cycle and lead to a reduced cost of scrapped items.

Marking scheme		
		Marks
(a) Estimated unit selling price – 1 mark Less: 15% net profit – 1 mark Target total cost per unit – 1 mark Less: Fixed costs per unit – 1 mark Target direct cost per unit – 1 mark Cost gap – 1 mark		
	Maximum	6
(b) General description of target costing – up to 2 marks Advice on target costing for Pitlane – 1 mark per point Additional revenue generated from features – 2 marks		
	Maximum	12
(c) General description of Kaizen costing – up to 2 marks Application of Kaizen costing to Pitlane – 1 mark per point		
	Maximum	7
Total		25

Examiner's comments

This question dealt with the use of target costing and Kaizen costing at a manufacturer.

Part (a) of the question required a basic calculation of the cost gap. Many candidates scored well on this part. However, a significant number chose to present their answers using absolute figures rather than per unit. This is both a failure to answer the question requirement and also, illustrates a lack of understanding about the application of the method, where per unit calculations are most helpful.

Part (b) of the question required candidates to apply the target cost method to the scenario to give advice about performance improvements. Candidates scored reasonably well on this part but often failed to score marks as they did not analyse all the problem areas mentioned in the scenario. The scenario will often provide hints of areas to consider in an answer and good candidates use these to efficiently compile high marks in the longer parts of questions.

Part (c) of the question was fairly well answered with candidates demonstrating a fair understanding of Kaizen costing and its application.

42   JENSON, LEWIS AND WEBB (JLW) (MAR/JUN 17)

Key answer tips

In part (a) the key concept being examined is 'controllability'. It is important to explain that the managers should only be appraised on performance they can control. In order to gain 7 marks, specific examples relating to controllability are required. However, it is also important to recognise that determining what is/ is not controllable can be difficult.

In part (b) you are expected to adjust the net profit and revenue figures for uncontrollable items and to draw a conclusion that the manager of the division should, in fact, be awarded a bonus.

In part (c) to gain a good mark you need to give relevant examples from the scenario and also need to recognise that only the Domestic division, as an investment centre, would be suited to using this measure.

(a)   A key characteristic of divisional performance measurement is that divisional managers, and the divisions themselves, should only be appraised on performance that they control. For example, costs which are not controlled by divisional managers, such as JLW's apportioned head office costs, should be added back to profit when appraising manager's performance.

Similarly, as Export division is a profit centre, divisional managers are not able to make capital investment decisions and so depreciation is out of their control and should be added back to profit for their appraisals. Domestic division is an investment centre, so managers there can make investment decisions, and depreciation is a cost which they can control.

On 30 June 2015, the $KL weakened by 15% against the £SL. This meant Export division benefited from an increase in revenue which was not under the control of the divisional manager. This amount must be deducted from revenue when calculating the controllable net profit for Export division.

The net profit arrived at after items which are not under managers' control are added back is known as the 'controllable profit'. This is what divisional managers should be appraised on. This is because it is unfair to appraise them on factors outside their control, and may mean they become demotivated or give up trying to improve performance, which is not in the interests of JLW as a whole.

Divisional performance should be evaluated on all the items which relate directly to the division which is its 'traceable profit'. Allocated head office costs do not directly reflect the activity of the division and should be excluded when calculating the traceable profit.

The traceable net profit for Export division, after adjusting for allocated head office costs, was $KL905,000 (W1), and the traceable net profit margin was 11%.

A difficulty with calculating controllable and traceable profits in this way may be that it is difficult to determine which items are controllable or not. For example, though the new machine purchased for Export division by head office did lead to improvements in productivity, the extent of this increase must be attributed to good management, or otherwise, by the divisional managers. This increase in productivity is therefore due partly to controllable factors, and partly to uncontrollable.

W1 – Traceable net profit

	$KL000
Reported net profit	545
Add back: Allocated head office costs	360
Traceable net profit	905
Traceable net profit margin: (905/8,000)	11%

(b) **Conclusion on payment of Export division manager's bonus**

The controllable net profit is arrived at after items which are not under the manager's control are added back. The net profit margin controllable by the manager of Export division is 10%. Given that it is difficult to assess the effect of the increased productivity on controllable net profit, the manager should be awarded her bonus for the year. This is because the controllable net profit margin of 10% exceeds the target of 8%.

W1 – Controllable net profit margin for Export division year ended 31 December 2016

Controllable net profit	$KL000
Reported net profit	545
Add back non controllable items: Depreciation	395
Allocated head office costs	360
Deduct currency gain (W2)	(522)
Controllable net profit	778

Controllable revenue	$KL000
Reported revenue	8,000
Deduct currency gain (W2)	(522)
Controllable revenue	7,478
Controllable net profit margin: (778/7,478)	10%

W2 – Currency gain

Six months revenue from 1 July 2016 was increased by 15% due to currency gain. Six months revenue before currency gain 4,000/1.15 = 3,478

Therefore non-controllable currency gain is 4,000 – 3,478 = 522

As the exact increase in productivity resulting for the new machinery on Export division is unclear, it is difficult to accurately adjust the controllable net profit margin to reflect this. It would seem the divisional manager is benefitting from productivity improvements which are not entirely under her control. To reduce the controllable net profit margin to 8%, the threshold at which the manager is awarded her bonus, the net profit would have to fall by approximately $KL179,760 (778,000 − (7,478,000 x 8%)). This is equivalent to 3.7% of cost of sales (179,760k/4,800,000). It is difficult to conclude, therefore, whether the 'significant' improvement in productivity would make the difference between the manager of Export division receiving her bonus or not.

(c) **EVA™ as a performance measure for Export and Domestic divisions**

EVA™ makes adjustments to the financial profit to calculate the economic value generated by each division, and then makes a deduction for the cost of the capital invested in the division. A positive EVA™ indicates a division is creating value above that required by those who finance the business. It is therefore consistent with JLW's objective to maximise shareholder wealth. Appraisal of divisional performance on this basis would therefore align the interests of managers with those of JLW's shareholders.

EVA™ involves making many adjustments to operating profit and capital employed. These may be time consuming, and be poorly understood by managers. The manager of Export division has already commented that she finds the bonus calculations difficult to understand. Failure of managers to understand the EVA™ calculations would make it difficult for them to work towards targets set for the division.

EVA™ avoids distortion from estimates and financial policies

EVA™ avoids the financial results from being distorted by accounting policies and estimates made by divisional managers, for example, the $KL75,000 bad debt provision made in Domestic division, as increases in provisions are added back to operating profit in the EVA™ calculation. Whilst this provides a consistent basis to evaluate performance of divisions within JLW, EVA™ is not suitable for comparing divisional performance as it is an absolute measure and does not make allowance for their relative sizes.

EVA™ encourages managers to take a long-term view

The advertising costs for the new range of paints would be capitalised as these generate future value. The use of EVA™ would encourage managers to incur costs, such as these, which will benefit the business in the long term.

However, the calculation of EVA™ is backwards looking, and based on historical financial information, whereas shareholders need information about future performance on which to base their decisions.

EVA™ takes into account the cost of capital

The current performance measure of net profit margin is a poor measure as it takes into account neither the absolute net profit achieved, the capital employed in the division, nor the cost of capital. By making a deduction for the cost of capital employed in the division, the EVA™ calculation makes managers consider both the capital employed and the cost of capital in their divisions.

Export division is a profit centre and managers do not have control of investment decisions and hence it is not a suitable measure for the evaluation of the performance on Export division because there is no controllable capital employed. Domestic division is able to control investment decisions, and does have controllable capital employed, so EVA™ would be a suitable measure for evaluating Domestic division's performance.

However, to use the weighted average cost of capital (WACC) in the EVA™ calculation requires a number of assumptions and estimates to be made, for example, in calculating the cost of equity or market value of debt. The WACC is normally based on historic data, which may not reflect circumstances in the future, and may not be accurate.

	Marking scheme		Marks
(a)	Evaluation of manager's comments – 1 mark per point Traceable net profit calculation – 2 marks		
		Maximum	7
(b)	Depreciation and allocated head office costs – 2 marks Currency gain – 2 marks Controllable revenue – 2 marks Controllable profit margin – 1 mark Conclusion – 1 mark		
		Maximum	8
(c)	Evaluation of EVA™ – 1 mark per point		
		Maximum	10
Total			25

Examiner's comments

This question dealt with the use of target costing and Kaizen costing at a manufacturer.

Part (a) of the question required a basic calculation of the cost gap. Many candidates scored well on this part. However, a significant number chose to present their answers using absolute figures rather than per unit. This is both a failure to answer the question requirement and also, illustrates a lack of understanding about the application of the method, where per unit calculations are most helpful.

Part (b) of the question required candidates to apply the target cost method to the scenario to give advice about performance improvements. Candidates scored reasonably well on this part but often failed to score marks as they did not analyse all the problem areas mentioned in the scenario. The scenario will often provide hints of areas to consider in an answer and good candidates use these to efficiently compile high marks in the longer parts of questions.

Part (c) of the question was fairly well answered with candidates demonstrating a fair understanding of Kaizen costing and its application.

43   THE BETTER ELECTRICALS GROUP (BEG) (JUN 10 – AMENDED)

Key answer tips

In part (a) make sure you address the question from an APM perspective, not a SBL one.

The rest of the question is on target costs rather than target costing so ensure you answer the question set.

Tutorial note

The style of this question and answer is slightly different to that used by the current examiner. However, there are some useful and relevant ideas discussed here.

(a)   The main way strategic analysis models can assist performance management is in the identification of critical success factors and corresponding key performance indicators.

For example, a PEST analysis might identify that the key driver of change in a market is technological development. The firm can then set this as a CSF and develop appropriate KPIs to ensure it can benefit from future market change.

In this case a Porter's five forces analysis has highlighted the importance of competitive rivalry as key to BEG's ability to make acceptable margins. This would then force the Directors to reassess their competitive strategy and identify CSFs that will enable a sustainable competitive advantage to be maintained and thus defend against the threats from the significant competitors mentioned.

(b)   At present, the variable manufacturing costs are targeted to be at a level of 35% of sales value. Fixed costs are expected to increase by $400,000 in 2012 which may be indicative of an increase in the level of activity.

The use of cost targeting would necessitate comparison of current estimated cost levels against the targets which must be achieved if the desired levels of profitability, and hence return on investment, are to be achieved. Thus where a difference exists between the current estimated cost levels and the cost target, it is essential that this gap be closed.

The gap between the cost targets and current expected cost levels regarding the application for 'platinum' status may be analysed into internal and external failure costs.

Internal failure costs arise when products or services fail to meet design quality standards and such failures are detected before the product or service is passed to the customer. For example, incorrect processing of customer orders prior to supplying goods or services to customers, excessive idle capacity of personnel would constitute internal failure costs.

External failure costs arise after products or services have been passed to the customer and would include costs incurred in order to address rectification claims from customers.

Internal failure costs are expected to fall from 21.92% of the cost target to 7.5% of the cost target in 2013. External failure costs are expected to fall from 27.2% of cost target to 6.13% of cost target in 2013.

Prevention and appraisal costs are discretionary costs incurred by management in an attempt to reduce the costs of internal and external failures. Prevention costs are incurred as a consequence of management actions with regard to achievement of the desired quality standards to enable the cost target to be achieved, such as for example the costs incurred in training sales administration staff. Prevention costs are expected to fall from $4.2m in 2011 to $1.32m in 2013.

Appraisal costs are costs incurred in order to ensure conformance with agreed quality standards. These would include costs incurred in ensuring quality negotiation procedures with customers. Appraisal costs are expected to decrease by $100,000 to $0.7m in 2012 and to remain at that level during 2013.

(c)   (i)   The application for 'platinum status' quality certification may be measured in both financial and marketing terms. The net profit/sales percentage is expected to increase each year. The figures are 8.33%, 31.67% and 43.89% for 2011, 2012 and 2013 respectively (e.g. 2011 = $2m/$24m). The profit increase is partly linked to the projected fall in quality costs, both costs of conformance (appraisal and prevention) and costs of non-conformance (internal and external failure) as shown in the appendix. It is also linked to the increase in volume of business as fixed costs have a reduced effect. Will BEG achieve market growth and an improved market position? The projected sales in the appendix shows growth of 25% in 2012 ($30m/$24m) and a further 20% in 2013 ($36/$30m). In addition, market position is anticipated to improve, with a market share of 8%, 9.38% and 10.59% in years 2011, 2012 and 2013 respectively (e.g. 2011 = $24m/$300m).

(ii) In order to achieve external efficiency BEG has to satisfy its customers. Customer satisfaction may be defined as meeting customer expectations. The quality of service provision and delivery are operational criteria that can be used to monitor levels of customer satisfaction. The success will require an efficient business operating system for all aspects of the cycle from product design to after sales service to customers. Improved quality and delivery should lead to improved customer satisfaction. Schedule 1 shows a number of quantitative measures of the expected measurement of these factors:

- Quality is expected to improve. The percentage of products achieving design quality standards is expected to rise from 92% to 99% between 2011 and 2013. In the same period, rectification claims from customers for faulty work should fall from $0.96m to $0.1m and the cost of after sales rectification service should fall from $1.8m to $0.8m.

- Delivery efficiency improvement may be measured in terms of the increase in the percentage of sales expected to meet planned delivery dates. This percentage is forecast to increase from 88.5% in 2011 to 99.5% in 2013.

(iii) Internal efficiency may be assessed by reference to flexibility and productivity. Flexibility relates to the business operating system as a whole whilst productivity relates to the management of resources such as staff time. This should be helped through reduced cycle time and decreased levels of waste. Once again the appendix shows a number of quantitative measures of these factors:

- The average total cycle time from customer enquiry to delivery is forecast to reduce from 49 days in 2011 to 40 days in 2013. This indicates both internal efficiency and external effectiveness.

- Waste in the form of idle capacity of service personnel is expected to fall from 12% to 1.5% between 2011 and 2013. Also, service enquiries not taken up by customers are expected to fall from 10.5% of enquiries in 2011 to 3% of enquiries in 2013. These are both examples of ways in which improved productivity may be measured. Both will be linked to the prevention and appraisal costs, which are intended to reduce the level of internal and external failure costs.

Whilst we do not know the precise standards that are required to be achieved in order to gain 'platinum' status quality certification one can conclude that BEG has forecast vast improvements in several aspects of its performance during the three-year period under review.

Marking scheme

				Marks
(a)	1 mark pre relevant point		Maximum	5
(b)	Comments (on merit):			
	Cost targets			4
	Costs of quality			4
			Maximum	8
(c)	(i)	Financial performance and marketing		4
	(ii)	External effectiveness		4
	(iii)	Internal efficiency		4
			Maximum	12
Total				25

Examiner's comments

In part (b) there was some evidence of misreading the question as being about target costing rather than the more basic use of target costs in achieving this quality standard. However, candidates who took this track made relevant points and were given some credit. Those candidates who scored well did so by appreciating that these were forecast numbers and so gave an indication of the company's plans not its history. Therefore, a good answer commented on how the increased quality costs of 2011 fed through to improved quality in the later years yielding lower costs. Many candidates would have benefited from considering the cost categories within each year rather than across each category.

There was frequently little evidence of understanding how spending in one category affects the others – especially, the effect of conformance activity on non-conformance activity.

In part (c) successful candidates made clear how their points linked to the specific headings demonstrating their appreciation of the meaning of that heading. They provided quantified analysis of the data in the appendix and linked it to business objectives under the heading. Again, the weaker candidates provided trend analysis but did not demonstrate an appreciation of how this then affected the business within the headings e.g. by satisfying customers and so being externally effective.

44 ESSLAND POLICE FORCE (DEC 13)

Key answer tips

This is a great question on league tables and should form a key part of your revision of this topic.

If you struggle with some APM concepts, then try to apply them to a range of scenarios that you are more familiar with, such as school or hospital league tables in this instance.

(a) Logically, the Force Score (FS) should reflect the aims and objectives of the department. The overall aim has two basic parts: (1) value-for-money service; (2) community safety. The score does use variables associated with community safety but does not measure value-for-money. Value-for-money would be reflected by measures which take account of the economy, efficiency and effectiveness of the police forces. For example, the other indicators given in Appendix 1 allow calculation of the following measures which could be useful in measuring performance of this objective:

Other indicators:	C	D	E	F
Number of police per 10,000 population	49.6	48.9	50.0	52.7
Cost per population member ($)	323.2	331.1	336.5	340.0

The more detailed goals of the police forces are:

- Tackle the underlying causes of crime and achieve long-term sustainable solutions – which is measured by Rank 1 for the number of reported crimes.

- Bring perpetrators to justice – which is measured by Rank 2 which measures the detection rate of crimes.

- Provide protection and support for individuals and communities at risk of harm – which is measured through the user satisfaction score (Rank 3).

- Respond to community needs by being accessible and engaging with their concerns – which is measured through the user satisfaction score (Rank 3) and the responsiveness is measured by call handling speed (Rank 4).

None of these ranks will perfectly measure all aspects of each of the goals but there is a broad coverage present. For example, an improvement might be to include a measure of community engagement through the number of public meetings between police and the community or a measure of community-based policing initiatives.

The choice of weightings used in the FS formula must be considered. Force F is top ranked and Force C is bottom ranked. However, among the four variables used to calculate the score, no one force dominates with three different forces being the best in each of the four variables. Therefore, the weightings are important in determining the final FS.

The formula used is simple as it recognises only four input variables and weights these equally. No explanation of the logic of the choice of variables or weightings has been offered. Different weightings would produce very different results. To illustrate this, if a simple weighting system were used where weighting was given only to Rank 3 (on user satisfaction), then Force D would rank top and Force F would be bottom. Also, relatively small variations can have big impacts on the final FS.

For example, the difference between each force in their call answering is not great with three percentage points separating best and worst but this generates a difference of 0.75 in the forces' final FS.

There is a danger of over-complicating the formula (with more variables and complex methods of allocating weightings) and thus losing one of its main advantages, which is its simplicity.

(b) The use of league tables effectively benchmarks performance and can have a positive effect on behaviour. The sharing of data on performance can indicate areas of best practice and so improve performance across all forces. Additionally, the use of league tables gives a single figure which gives a clear, immediate answer to questions of performance.

However, the use of league tables only measures relative performance. The best force in the table could still be producing an unacceptable performance in absolute terms. In order to avoid this problem, tables will often try to include comparable bodies from outside the area of control of the government (foreign police forces). However, to get comparable data in order to calculate an FS for a foreign police force will be difficult.

On introduction, if the police staff do not feel that they can affect the FS, then they will not be held accountable by it. They may ignore it or actively undermine it in public through their union. This will present the government with difficulty as the police are considered the experts on this area of public policy and their criticism will carry weight with the electorate.

Once the system is in use, the FS can be used as a target for the leaders of each force; however, it can lead to over-focusing by employees on the variables in the FS to the exclusion of other relevant issues, i.e. only doing what gets measured. This means that the FS must encompass the key variables which will drive desired performance.

The police staff may be demotivated by the league tables if they feel:

(i) that the FS does not reflect the valuable work which they do (as noted above, the current FS formula does not take account of the value-for-money aspects of the police force's efforts); or

(ii) that the FS is driven by factors outside their control. (For example, there may be a link between the number of crimes reported and the economic conditions in the forces area which they do not have power to affect.)

The use of league tables has stemmed from their introduction for schools. However, the comparison between police forces and schools may not be valid, as school league tables are helpful where parents have some choice in the school to which they send their children while with only four forces covering the country, residents will have to move a long distance to be under the protection of a different police force. The schools' league table only used the single output of pupils' performance while the FS is more complex as it tries to encompass a number of different outputs. This will lead to greater debate about the value of the measure for the reasons given above and possibly its reduced effectiveness.

Marking scheme		
		Marks
(a) Calculations:		
Other indicators	up to	2
Comments:		
Force score formula		
Choice of variables used for weighting		
– match to overall aim	up to	3
– match to detailed goals	up to	5
Allocation of weightings	up to	4
Other	up to	2
		———
Maximum		**14**
		———

(b)	General evaluation of league tables	up to	4
	Link of tables to targets and employee reaction		
	Introduction of tables	up to	2
	Behaviour under the system and sense of accountability	up to	5
	Comparison of use in schools and police sectors	up to	2
	1 mark each for other relevant points		
		Maximum	11
Total			25

Examiner's comments

Part (a) required candidates to understand the detailed method of calculation given in the scenario and then examine whether this would indeed measure the achievement of these objectives. Candidates did well when they structured their answer by taking firstly, the aims of value for money and community security then the four detailed goals and examined how the four variables in the force score would relate to these and then whether the formula weighted these appropriately. This again emphasises the helpfulness in taking a logical approach to question answering. Unfortunately, a minority of candidates discussed the use of league tables in this part although the requirement focusses on the force score. These candidates should have read the whole question requirement and they would have realised that this was subject of part (b).

Part (b) for 11 marks was split into two parts firstly, a general discussion of the merits of league tables which was well done followed by specific concerns on their use on these police forces. Again, it was worth noting that the scenario hinted at the specific areas to consider though many candidates chose only to address the staff issues while leaving unscored the marks on the comparable usefulness of tables in measuring schools and police forces.

45 TELECOMS AT WORK (TAW) (JUN 08 – AMENDED)

Key answer tips

This may appear a very complicated question in actual fact it is very straightforward. The key is to be able to analyse the costs into the different categories of quality costs. Then calculate the total for each type of quality cost and the overall total. The second part requires an assessment of which option gives the better savings. Presentation is important.

This question is not in the style or standard of the current exam but it does serve as a useful question for consolidating knowledge on how to categorise quality costs.

Tutorial note

The style of this question and answer is slightly different to that used by the current examiner but some useful ideas are covered here.

(a)

	Quantity	Rate $	Total costs $000	% of sales
Prevention costs:				
Design engineering	48,000	96	4,608	1.28
Process engineering	54,000	70	3,780	1.05
Training			180	0.05
Total prevention costs			8,568	2.38
Appraisal costs:				
Inspection (manufacturing)	288,000	50	14,400	4.00
Product testing			72	0.02
Total appraisal costs			14,472	4.02
Internal failure costs:				
Rework (Manufacturing)	2,100	4,800	10,080	2.80
Total internal failure costs			10,080	2.80
External failure costs:				
Customer support (Marketing)	2,700	240	648	0.18
Transportation costs (Distribution)	2,700	280	756	0.21
Warranty repair (Customer service)	2,700	4,600	12,420	3.45
Total external failure costs			13,824	3.84
Total costs (P, A, IF and EF)			46,944	13.04
Opportunity costs	1,800	7,200	12,960	3.60
Total quality costs			**59,904**	**16.64**

% of Total Quality:			
Prevention	2.38%	16.64%	14.30%
Appraisal	4.02%	16.64%	24.16%
Internal failure	2.80%	16.64%	16.83%
External failure	3.84%	16.64%	23.08%
Lost sales	3.60%	16.64%	21.63%
			100.00%

The total of prevention, appraisal, internal failure, and external failure costs should not be assumed to represent the total costs of quality for TAW or any other organisation. Quality cost statements frequently exclude opportunity costs such as foregone contribution margins and profit from lost sales, lost production or lower prices that are consequences of poor quality. This is because opportunity costs are difficult to estimate and are often not recorded by accounting systems. It should be recognised that opportunity costs can be substantial and provide much impetus to quality-improvement programmes.

(b)   Option:

Cost of quality items:	Rate $	Option 1 $	Option 2 $
Additional design engineering costs	2,000	96	192,000
Additional process engineering costs	5,000	70	350,000
Additional inspection/testing costs	10,000	50	500,000	
Savings in rework costs:			
Option 1	720	1,920	−1,382,400
Option 2	960	1,920		−1,843,200
Savings in customer support costs:			
Option 1	600	96	−57,600
Option 2	840	96		−80,640
Saving in transportation costs:			
Option 1	600	210	−126,000
Option 2	840	210		−176,400
Savings in warranty repair costs:			
Option 1	600	1,700	−1,020,000
Option 2	840	1,700		−1,428,000
Opportunity savings:			
Option 1	300	7,200	−2,160,000
Option 2	360	7,200		−2,592,000
Incremental savings/(costs)			−4,246,000	−5,578,240

Option 2, i.e. redesigning and strengthening the casings is preferable since it is projected to result in incremental savings amounting to $5,578,240 − $4,246,000 = $1,332,240.

(c)   Environmental costs

One approach to accounting for environmental costs is to take the view that environmental costs are incurred because of poor quality controls.

Therefore, an environmental cost report could be produced in the format of a cost of quality report, with each category of cost being expressed as a percentage of sales revenues or operating costs so that comparisons can be made between different periods and/or organisations.

The categories of costs would be as follows:

- Environmental prevention costs: the costs of activities undertaken to prevent the production of waste.

- Environmental detection costs: costs incurred to ensure that the organisation complies with regulations and voluntary standards.

- Environmental internal failure costs: costs incurred from performing activities that have produced contaminants and waste that have not been discharged into the environment.

- Environmental external failure costs: costs incurred on activities performed after discharging waste into the environment.

Marking scheme		
		Marks
(a) Prevention costs		2
Appraisal costs		1
Internal failure costs		1
External failure costs		2
Opportunity costs		1
Correct percentages		1
Opportunity costs – comment		2
Presentation		1
		___
		11
		___
(b) Additional design engineering costs		0.5
Additional process engineering costs		0.5
Additional inspection and testing costs		0.5
Savings in rework costs:	2 × 0.5	1
Savings in customer support costs:	2 × 0.5	1
Saving in transportation costs:	2 × 0.5	1
Savings in warranty repair costs:	2 × 0.5	1
Opportunity savings:	2 × 1	2
Advice/reason		1.5
		___
		9
		___
(c) **1 mark per relevant point**		**5**
		___
Total		**25**
		___

Examiners comments

This was the least popular choice from among the option questions. However, when attempted, the question produced some excellent answers which earned very high marks. In general answers to part (a) were satisfactory. Poorer answers demonstrated confusion regarding the different categories of quality costs. There was a significant variation in the quality of answers to part (b) with a number of candidates achieving maximum marks for a correct solution. However, there was also a number of unsatisfactory answers which invariably comprised poorly laid out, incorrect calculations.

46 WESTAMBER (PILOT 07 – AMENDED)

Key answer tips

When considering the style of the current examiner it is questionable as to the extent by which you will be asked to answer a question in this way. However, it is still a good question and considers some important areas.

(a) (i) The hospitals have differing objectives. Eastgreen is a profit-seeking organisation whereas Westamber is, in part, a not-for-profit organisation.

(ii) The hospitals have different fee structures. Westamber undertakes the treatment of government-funded patients and receives a lower fee in respect of such operations.

(iii) The level of operating costs differs as evidenced by the fact that annual depreciation in Eastgreen is 100% greater than Westamber.

(iv) Eastgreen is partially funded by loan finance as evidenced by the $500,000 of loan interest charged to its profit and loss account during the year whereas Westamber hasn't any loan finance in its capital structure.

N.B: Other reasonable explanations would be acceptable.

(b) Adjustments:

	Westamber 20X6 Budget $000	Westamber 20X6 Actual $000	Eastgreen 20X6 Actual $000
Original Profit/(Loss)	(9,572)	(15,838)	2,000
Income shortfall due to subsidised operations (see note)	5,840	8,760	
Cost of emergency operations	1,000	800	
Loan interest adjustment			500
Operating profit/(loss) after adjustments	(2,732)	(6,278)	2,500

Note:

Income shortfall (budget) = 11,680 operations × 50% government-funded × $1,000 average shortfall per operation = $5,840,000.

Income shortfall (actual) = 11,680 operations × 75% government-funded × $1,000 average shortfall per operation= $8,760,000.

Where the average shortfall per operation of $1,000 = (Total operation fee from private patients of $3k + $4k + $5k) – (Total operation fee from government-funded patients of $2k + $3k + $4k) ÷ 3 types of operation.

(c) The statement of the recently qualified accountant is correct insofar as the fees received from private paying patients are higher than those received in respect of government funded patients.

However, there is an ethical issue in that government funded patients require medical treatment and that fact should always be considered especially since Westamber is a government-funded hospital. The mission statement of the hospital states that it 'is committed to providing high quality healthcare to all patients' and therefore it should not give priority treatment to private fee-paying patients.

(d) The following performance measures could be used to assess the quality of service provided by the management of either hospital:

(i) The time spent waiting for non-emergency operations which could be measured by reference to the time elapsed from the date when an operation was deemed necessary until it was actually performed

(ii) The number of successful operations as a percentage of total operations performed which could be measured by the number of remedial operations undertaken

(iii) The percentage of total operations performed in accordance with agreed schedules which could be measured by reference to agreed operation schedules

(iv) The standards of cleanliness and hygiene maintained which could be measured by observation

(v) The staff: patient ratio which could be measured by reference to personnel and patient records; and

(vi) The responsiveness of staff to requests of patients which could be measured via a patient survey.

NB: Alternative appropriate performance measures would be acceptable.

47 ALPHA DIVISION (DEC 07)

Key answer tips

Candidates are required to calculate residual income and comment on their findings and the relevance of three particular performance measures given in the question. Be clear and not too superficial in your answer. Finally candidates are required to calculate EVA, stating any assumptions made and three disadvantages of EVA as a measure. The final part of the question requires thought and application to the scenario and does not ask for advantages.

(a) (i)

	Year 1 $m	Year 2 $m	Year 3 $m
Net cash inflow	12.5	18.5	27.0
Less: Depreciation	15.0	15.0	15.0
Profit/(loss)	(2.5)	3.5	12.0
Less: cost of capital (at 10% of wdv)	(4.5)	(3.0)	(1.5)
RI	(7.0)	0.5	10.5

A positive NPV of $1.937m indicates that the performance is acceptable over the three-year life of the proposal.

The RI shows a negative value of $7m in year 1. This is likely to lead to its rejection by the management of Alpha Division because they participate in a bonus scheme that is based on short-term performance evaluation.

The short-term focus on performance evaluation might lead to the rejection of investment opportunities such as the one under consideration which would be detrimental to the Delta Group.

Management of the Delta Group should give immediate consideration to changing the focus of the bonus scheme.

(ii) Measures of divisional profitability may be viewed as evaluating managerial performance and/or economic performance of the division. Management are likely to take the view that any contribution value used as a measure of their performance should only contain revenue or cost elements over which they have control. If each of the measures 1 to 3 shown in the question are considered the following analysis may be made:

1 Variable short run contribution margin:

This measure may be viewed as unacceptable to divisional management where it contains inter-divisional transfers.

In this case this should not be a problem since the use of adjusted market price is in effect equivalent to external selling price after the deduction of cost elements (e.g. special packaging) that are not appropriate to inter-divisional transfers.

2 Controllable profit:

This measure will be calculated by deducting controllable fixed costs from the variable short-run contribution. These costs may include labour costs and/or equipment rental costs that are fixed in the short term but are subject to some influence by divisional management. For example, divisional management action may enable efficiency gains to be achieved in order to reduce the level of fixed labour or equipment rental costs that are incurred. In addition, it will be relevant to determine whether divisional management is free to source such items as they wish or if there is some direction for them to use, for example, a Delta Group Service Division for equipment rental requirements.

The inclusion of depreciation of fixed assets as a charge in evaluating controllable contribution may be debated depending on the extent to which divisional management has control over investment decisions.

3 Divisional profit:

Depending on the extent to which investment decisions relating to Alpha Division are ultimately authorised at Delta Group level, depreciation may be viewed as a non-controllable cost, chargeable in arriving at the divisional profit and hence as part of divisional economic performance measurement.

Other non-controllable costs attributed to the division may be a share of Group finance and legal staff costs for services provided to the division. Such costs are non-controllable by divisional management and may be viewed as avoidable only if the division was closed.

The divisional profit figure is useful in evaluating the economic performance of the division in that it represents the contribution made by Alpha Division towards the overall profitability of the Delta Group.

(b) **(i)** In order to compute EVA, adjustments must be made to the conventional after tax profit measures of $67m and $82m shown in the summary income statements.

Since we know that financial accounting depreciation is equal to economic depreciation then no adjustment is required to take into account the fact that economic depreciation differs from financial accounting depreciation. In calculating EVA the calculation of adjusted profit represents an attempt to approximate cash flow after taking into account a charge in respect of economic depreciation. Hence non-cash expenses are added back to the profit reported in the income statement. Net interest is also added back to the reported profit because the returns required by the providers of funds are reflected in the cost of capital adjustment. It is the net interest i.e. interest after tax that is added back to reported profit because interest will already have been allowed as an expense in the computation of the taxation liability.

In computing EVA, the calculation of capital employed should be based on adjustments which seek to approximate economic value at the commencement of each period.

Due to the lack of sufficient information the book value of shareholders' funds plus long-term capital loans at the end of 2005 is used as a basis for the determination of economic capital employed at the commencement of 2006.

Goodwill is a measure of the price paid for a business in excess of the current cost of the net separable assets of the business. Payments in respect of goodwill may be viewed as adding value to the company.

Therefore any amounts in respect of goodwill amortisation appearing in the income statement are added back to reported profit since they represent part of the intangible asset value of the business.

By the same token, the cumulative write off of $45 million is added back to capital employed in order to show a more realistic value of the capital base realistic value of the capital employed. This is because goodwill represents an element of the total value of a business. The value placed on goodwill should be regularly reviewed and any diminution in its value should be recognised immediately in the income statement.

The calculation of EVA in respect of the two years under consideration is as follows:

	2006 $m	2007 $m
Adjusted profit:		
Profit after tax	67	82
Amortisation of goodwill	5	5
Other non-cash expenses	12	12
Interest expense	4.2	4.2
Adjusted profit	88.2	103.2
Adjusted capital employed:		
Year beginning	279	340
Non-capitalised leases	16	16
Goodwill	45	50
Adjusted capital employed	340	406

The weighted average cost of capital should be based on the target capital structure of 50% Debt: 50% Equity.

The calculations are as follows:

WACC 2006: $(16\% \times 50\%) + (10\% \times 0.7 \times 50\%) = 11.5\%$

WACC 2007: $(18\% \times 50\%) + (10\% \times 0.7 \times 50\%) = 12.5\%$

Therefore EVA in respect of both years can be calculated as follows:

EVA 2006 = $88.2 - (340 \times 11.5\%) = \$49.1$ million

EVA 2007 = $103.2 - (406 \times 12.5\%) = \$52.45$ million

The EVA measures indicate that the Gamma Group has added significant value during each year under consideration and thereby achieved a satisfactory level of performance.

(ii) Disadvantages of an EVA approach to the measurement of financial performance include:

- The calculation of EVA may be complicated due to the number of adjustments required.

- It is difficult to use EVA for inter-firm and inter-divisional comparisons because it is not a ratio measure.

- Economic depreciation is difficult to estimate and conflicts with generally accepted accounting principles.

Marking scheme			
			Marks
(a)	(i)	Calculation of RI	3
		Comments (on merit)	3
	(ii)	For each of measures 1 to 3 including reference to managerial/ economic performance and to illustrative items given in the question	
		3×3	8
			14
(b)	(i)	Adjusted profit after tax	3
		Adjusted capital employed	3
		WACC	1
		EVA	1
		Comment	1
	(ii)	Disadvantages of EVA 3×1	3
			11
Total			25

Examiner's comments

It was noticeable that a large number of candidates did not attempt all parts of this question. Also frustrating was the significant number of candidates who provided 'advantages' of using EVA[TM] in the measurement of financial performance when Part (b) (ii) required a brief discussion of 'disadvantages'.

48   BEESHIRE LOCAL AUTHORITY (BLA) (DEC 14)

Key answer tips

This question is based on a local authority. The scenario is reasonably long and contains some numerical information to absorb.

Requirement (a) asks for an explanation of why NFPIs are useful for public sector organisations, giving relevant examples. This is a test of core knowledge and as long as you make a decent attempt to relate your points to the scenario you should be able to score a pass/good pass here.

Requirement (b) tests performance indicators once again (a very popular area) but now in the context of value for money. The link between value for money and performance indicators should be anticipated.

Requirement (c) asks for difficulties in measuring qualitative factors. In addition to the difficulties outlined make sure that you offer relevant solutions.

(a)   Public sector organisations have a number of problems which can be at least partially addressed with the use of non-financial performance indicators.

- **Lack of profit measure**

    BLA's waste management is not expected to make a profit. This is obvious from the fact that there is no specific charge for the service and so no clear revenue stream associated with it. The danger is that the only financial measure is cost and, in the current state of Seeland, this would mean that positive progress would only be seen in its reduction. This would be to the detriment of service and the three goals for the department (safe, clean, environmentally friendly).

- **Multiple objectives**

    It is difficult to say which is the single, overriding objective unlike in a profit-making organisation. This requires an approach which takes account of all the perspectives. BLA shows this in its three goals, none of which are financial.

- **Difficulty in defining a suitable financial measure**

    Many non-profit seeking organisations provide services for which it is difficult to define a cost unit. At BLA, should the cost unit be cost per tonne of waste collected or cost per household or cost per tonne of waste landfilled? Also, the benefits of the service are mainly non-financial such as clean streets.

    The three goals of BLA's waste management department could be addressed by looking at health statistics, tourist/resident surveys and tonnage of recycled waste. These are all non-financial in nature.

(b)   The standard criteria for analysis of the value-for-money of a service are:

- Economy – the optimisation of the resources which the organisation has; ensuring the appropriate quality of input resources are obtained at the lowest cost

- Efficiency – the optimisation of the process by which inputs are turned into outputs

- Effectiveness – how the outputs of the organisation meet its goals.

At BLA:

Economy could be measured by looking at the cost of buying equipment such as the lorries or fuel or the major cost of staff (44% of the total). The current average staff pay is $31,429. This is above the national average pay of $29,825. However, paying more for each member of staff could result in greater efficiency as staff members have improved skills.

Efficiency could be measured by the number of tonnes of waste moved per staff member (629 tonnes/staff member) or the cost of collection of waste per tonne ($114) or the staff cost per tonne collected ($50). Benchmarking these against national averages, the cost of collection of waste per tonne and staff cost per tonne collected are below the national averages of $123 and $51 respectively while the tonnes of waste moved per staff member (583 tonnes/staff member) is higher than the national average. This implies that BLA is showing good efficiency in its use of resources. The balance of capital and staff costs would also indicate how labour intensive the department's work was, for example, the value of the lorry fleet per tonne collected compared to the staff cost per tonne collected. No figures are given for lorry fleet value, so no quantification of this can be done.

Effectiveness has to be measured against the departmental goals:

1   Public health concerns – this is a vague objective and could be measured against many indicators such as level of vermin or levels of diseases related to waste. The lower frequency of collections (17% below national average) may present a public health problem.

2   Clean and attractive streets – this is a subjective goal as discussed above. The level of tourism and return visits may give a rough measure of this goal. The trend in complaints by residents will be a more reliable measure.

3   Increased recycling – the trend in tonnes recycled would be one measure but an imprecise one. If waste collected is generally going up, then this will rise too. A better measure of the effort to increase use of recycling would be the percentage of waste which is recycled compared to the government's target. (BLA is recycling 43% of its waste which is already ahead of the target of 40% by 2015. It is also ahead of the national average of 41%.)

(c)   The major problem in interpreting qualitative data is that it is subjective since it is based on people's opinions. For example, in assessing quality of service people have different expectations and priorities and so are unlikely to be consistent in their judgements. At BLA, customer complaints will be driven by such opinions. Some customers may wish to see effort focused on recycling, while others may be more concerned about unsightly waste in the streets and others will focus on the frequency of waste collections. Some customers may not understand that improved waste collection is only possible with spending implications which may not be acceptable due to the current recession in Seeland.

One way to reduce the effect of subjectivity is to look at trends in performance since the biases in opinion will be present in each individual time period but the trend will show relative changes in quality.

The recording and processing of qualitative data can be difficult. Opinions are expressed in language and it can be difficult to tell if a complaint which describes service as 'awful' is more or less serious than one which describes service as 'unacceptable'. The current data for BLA does not contain any such information and this is often the result of these difficulties in collection.

The most common way to try to overcome this problem is to turn the data into quantitative data. For example, surveys often use scoring systems to capture data on service. A scoring system will often ask the customer to rank their satisfaction at the service provided on a scale of 1 to 5 with '1' representing 'completely satisfied' and '5' representing 'totally dissatisfied'.

However, the problem remains that such scoring systems are still subjective, and it has often been found that there is a tendency to score toward the middle as people tend to feel uncomfortable using the extreme scores of 5 or 1.

BLA waste management will suffer from these problems particularly in their goal of keeping the streets attractive as this will clearly require subjective judgement in its assessment.

Marking scheme		Marks
(a) Up to 4 marks for general discussion Up to 4 marks for examples relevant to BLA		
	Maximum	6
(b) Up to 3 marks for a description of a general approach to VFM 1 mark per point – discussing each heading at BLA		
	Maximum	12
(c) 1 mark per point made		
	Maximum	7
Total		25

49 SSA GROUP (DEC 09 – AMENDED)

Key answer tips

This is a tough question on transfer pricing, so it is vital that you focus on the key aspects – in particular how transfer prices affect managers' decisions from a divisional perspective and whether those decisions are best for the company as a whole. More recent questions on transfer pricing have been less challenging. However, this is an extremely useful question for consolidating knowledge on how to evaluate transfer pricing.

(a)   The objectives of a transfer pricing system are as follows:

Performance measurement

The buying and selling divisions will be treated as profit or investment centres. The transfer price is a cost to the receiving division and revenue to the supplying division and should allow the performance of each division to be assessed fairly.

Divisional managers will be demotivated if this is not achieved.

Goal congruence

The decisions made by each profit centre manager should be consistent with the objectives of the organisation as a whole, i.e. the transfer price should assist in maximising overall company profits.

A common problem is that a transfer price is set that results in suboptimal behaviour, where the best decision for a division is not necessarily the best for the company or group as a whole.

Autonomy

The system used to set transfer prices should seek to maintain the autonomy of profit centre managers. If autonomy is maintained, managers tend to be more highly motivated but suboptimal decisions may be made.

Recording the movement of goods and services

In practice, an extremely important function of the transfer pricing system is simply to assist in recording the movement of goods and services.

Tax management

In global companies or groups the transfer price can effectively move profits from one tax jurisdiction to another. Such companies can thus set transfer prices to minimise global tax liabilities, although there is extensive anti-avoidance legislation in this area.

(b) **(i)** As regards Quotation 1 in respect of the year ending 31 December 2010, the management of Division B would purchase ankle supports from a local supplier in order to increase the profitability of Division B. An internal transfer price from Division A of $10.50 ($15 less 30%) would appear unattractive in comparison with a locally available price of $9. The management of Division B is encouraged to seek the maximisation of reported profit as its key objective.

Division A has spare production capacity of 10,000 units (Maximum available = 160,000 units and the 2010 budget total demand is 150,000 units). Division A could, therefore, supply 10,000 units of ankle supports at its marginal cost of $7 per unit ($350,000/50,000) i.e. at a total cost of $70,000.

However the external supplier would charge $9 per unit, giving a total price of $90,000 for the 10,000 units.

In order to have decisions leading to the maximisation of SSA group profit, Division A should, therefore, quote its marginal cost of $7 per unit for each of the 10,000 units required by Division B.

SSA Group profit will then increase by ($9 – $7) × 10,000 = $20,000.

As regards Quotation 2 in respect of the year ending 31 December 2010, the management of Division B would again purchase from a local supplier in order to increase the reported profitability of the division if Division A quotes a transfer price of $10.50 ($15 less 30%).

Division A could potentially have supplied 18,000 ankle supports by using (i) spare capacity for 10,000 units and (ii) switching 8,000 units of production from sales of the type of support that earns the lowest contribution per unit.

The 10,000 units of spare capacity can be supplied at marginal cost of $7 per unit as in Quotation 1.

The additional 8,000 units would have to be diverted from the type of existing support that earns the lowest contribution per unit. The situation is as follows:

Product	Knee Support	Ankle Support	Elbow Support	Wrist Support
Selling price per unit ($)	24	15	18	9
Variable cost per unit ($)	10	7	8	4
	——	——	——	——
Contribution per unit ($)	14	8	10	5

Division A should offer to transfer the additional 8,000 ankle supports by diverting production from the least profitable type of support. The wrist support earns the lowest contribution per unit ($5).

Hence Division A should offer to transfer the additional 8,000 ankle supports at marginal cost + contribution foregone = $7 + $5 = $12.

In this case, Division B would reject the offer and would buy externally at $9 per unit. This would ensure that SSA Group profit is not adversely affected by any transfer decision.

(ii) The management of the SSA Group needs to ensure that the management of all divisions takes into consideration all internal and external information relevant to divisional and, much more importantly, group circumstances.

As a starting point, the basic principle which underpins transfer pricing is that transfer prices should be set at a level which covers the marginal costs plus any opportunity cost to the SSA Group. If the basic principle is applied correctly then any subsequent decision made regarding whether to make internal transfers or external sales of products or internal purchases as opposed to external sourcing of products should lead to the most profitable outcome from the standpoint of the group as a whole.

What is best for the SSA Group as a whole is dependent upon the capacity utilisation of its divisions. In this example everything depends on the capacity utilisation of Division A.

What is of vital importance is that the marginal revenues and marginal costs of the SSA Group are known, understood and applied by management.

(c) If Division B buys from a local supplier the financial implications for the SSA group are as follows:

	$
Division A sales:	
60,000 wrist supports at a contribution of $5 per unit	300,000
Taxation at 40%	120,000
	———
After tax benefit of sales	180,000
Division B purchases:	
18,000 ankle supports at a cost of $9 per unit	162,000
Taxation benefit at 20%	32,400
	———
After tax cost of purchases	129,600
Net benefit to SSA Group = $180,000 – $129,600	$50,400

If Division B buys internally from Division A the financial implications for SSA group are shown below. **The SSA group will be $50,400 – $42,600 = $7,800 worse off if Division B purchases** the ankle supports from Division A, as opposed to purchasing an equivalent product from a local supplier.

Division A sales: $ External:

52,000 wrist supports at a contribution of $5 per unit	260,000
18,000 ankle supports to Division B at a contribution of	
($15 × 70%) – $7 = $3.5 per unit	63,000
	————
	323,000
Taxation at 40%	129,200
	————
After tax benefit of sales	193,800
Division B purchases:	
18,000 ankle supports at cost of $10.50 per unit	189,000
Taxation benefit at 20%	37,800
	————
After tax cost of purchases	151,200
Net benefit to SSA Group	$42,600

Marking scheme			
			Marks
(a)	1 mark per explained point		5
(b)	Quotation 1	Up to 4	4
	Quotation 2	Up to 4	4
			———
			8
			———
	Comments (on merit)	Up to 2 each	4
(c)	Calculations (on merit)		
	Purchase from local supplier		3
	Purchase from Division A		4
	Conclusion		1
			———
			8
			———
Total			25
			———

Examiner's comments

There were some very good answers to parts (b)(i) and (b)(ii) which achieved very high marks. In their answers to part (b)(i) a significant number of candidates did not recognise that Division A had spare production and consequently were unable to provide a correct solution. It was disappointing to observe a number of candidates being unable to correctly identify which of the products yielded the lowest contribution. In general, answers to part a (ii) were satisfactory with a significant number of candidates achieving all four available marks. There were a significant number of poor answers to part (c). Some candidates confused themselves by applying the 30% discount to the market price of the buying division (B), not that of the selling division (A).

50   LOCAL GOVERNMENT HOUSING DEPARTMENT (JUN 10 – AMENDED)

Key answer tips

This question requested analysis of concepts surrounding the upgrading of housing stock by a local authority. To improve your answer, ensure you use the scenario of a local authority working for the benefit of the community as a base for your explanations.

(a)   The stated mission can be criticised on the following grounds:

Identifying stakeholders – 'The community'

The mission identifies key stakeholders as the 'community' and presumably includes groups such as local residents, local voters, local businesses, tourists to the area and so on.

While such a vague term may encourage staff to think beyond simply serving residents, it fails to give any clear direction as to which stakeholders are more important or their extent. As such it will not ensure that the council does focus on meeting all stakeholder needs.

Setting objectives – 'Caring'

The term 'caring' could be taken to mean very different things to different stakeholders and makes it difficult for the council to formulate objectives and identify critical success factors.

For example, caring could incorporate any or all of the following:

- quality of life for residents, reducing Nosie and pollution

- job creation

- keeping council taxes low

Decision making

The stated mission gives no way of resolving conflicting objectives when making decisions.

For example, suppose the council is considering replacing a Memorial Park in the city centre with a much needed car park for shoppers. On the one hand this would create jobs and bring wealth to the city but on the other hand it might result in more pollution and road congestion. The mission is of little help in making this decision.

(b)   (i)   Value for money audits may be seen as being of particular relevance in not-for-profit organisations where they are an important performance assessment tool. The VFM audit focuses on the achievement of objectives of the organisation in a way that ensures the most economic, efficient and effective manner. This may be complicated by the inter-relationship of objectives.

In the scenario the principal objective is the provision of the upgrade of the air-conditioning systems, ensuring that the quality of the system is satisfactory to LGHD. A subsidiary objective is to ensure satisfaction of the occupants of the premises with the quality and ease of use of the upgraded system.

An extension of the objectives is to ensure that the upgrade is seen to satisfy cost-benefit criteria, both in terms of the upgrade and the subsequent maintenance and operational advice to be provided by the contractors.

The principals are LCGD as the provider of funds and the house occupiers as recipients of the improved service.

The agents are the contractors who are tasked with the installation and maintenance of the upgrade plus the advice to users (occupants) during the initial two year period.

(ii) The focus on the achievement of the objectives of the proposed improvements will benefit from consideration of the relevance of each of Economy, Efficiency and Effectiveness. The three Es are likely to be seen as possibly being in conflict with each other in terms of the achievement of objectives.

Economy will be seen as being achieved by aiming at minimising the average cost per house for the upgrade and subsequent maintenance and advice. This may be aimed at choosing the lowest quote per house for the proposed upgrades. A possible problem with this approach is that the quality of the work done may be compromised resulting in dissatisfaction of occupants.

Efficiency may be seen as the maximisation of the input:output ratio. In this exercise, this may be measured through maximising the number of houses that can have the air-conditioning upgrade with the funds available.

Effectiveness requires the achievement of the objectives (both principal and subsidiary) of the proposal. This may be measured by focusing on factors such as:

- The quality of upgrade obtained

- The level of improvement in air-conditioning achieved

- The extent to which external noise is eliminated

- Residents' feedback indicates that the benefits will outweigh any inconvenience caused by the upgrading work

- LCGD considers that 'value for money' has been achieved.

(iii) Intangibility in the context of the LGHD proposal relates to the likelihood that it is less likely that there will be a single measurable output. The upgrading of the air-conditioning systems is likely to require different amounts of input effort from one property to another. In addition, the provision of maintenance and advice to occupiers over the first two years after the upgrade is unlikely to be able to be valued with certainty. Intangible factors such as the professionalism of the contractors may be difficult to value. Also the level of advice likely to be sought by occupiers may vary considerably.

Heterogeneity refers to a possible variability in the standard of performance in the provision of the service. The quality of advice given to house occupiers may vary according to the expertise and/or level of commitment of the engineer giving the advice. Alternatively, the engineer may be underperforming because of some work stress factor.

Simultaneity refers to the provision and consumption of the service coinciding and hence making it difficult to apply all relevant checks and tests before its use. In the LGHD exercise, it should be possible to test the quality of an upgrade before it is accepted by LGHD. However, the provision of maintenance and operational advice will take place throughout the two-year period after installation. This means that there should be some safeguard provisions in the contract to ensure that deficiencies from the agreed maintenance and advice aspects can be addressed as required.

Perishability refers to the inability to 'store' the service in advance. A particular problem may be where extreme weather conditions (hot or cold) lead to an overload of the air-conditioning units. Will there be any provision in the contract to ensure that the contractors will provide additional help – especially during the initial two year period?

Marking scheme			
			Marks
(a)		1 mark per explained point	5
(b)	(i)	Value for money	3
		Principal and agent	3
	(ii)	Economy, efficiency, effectiveness Up to 2 each	6
	(iii)	Explanation of terms, the extent of their influence and problems arising for each heading Up to 2 each	8
Total			**25**

Examiner's comments

Requirement (b)(i) regarding a value for money audit was reasonably answered although many candidates did not appreciate there are multiple principal/agent relationships in the scenario (home occupants/LGHD; LGHD/contractors). A number of candidates did not read the requirement and offered general comment about VFM in the scenario when the relevance of a VFM audit was requested.

Requirement (b)(ii) was typically well done with most candidates displaying knowledge of the meaning of the 3Es and their application to the scenario.

Requirement (b)(iii) was generally poorly done with few candidates indicating clearly that the four terms relate more to services than tangible products. Some candidates understood the meaning of the four terms but did not clearly relate them to the situation at LGHD. Candidates would score high marks by giving examples of how each term affects LGHD's situation and then providing any problems to which this would give rise.

51   TENCH CARS (DEC 11 – AMENDED)

Key answer tips

The keys to scoring well on this question are (1) knowing the content and (2) being able to apply your knowledge to the scenario given. The latter skill was the main discriminator between good and weak scripts.

(a)   The costs of quality will probably be hidden in overheads in the standard costing system at Tench. They relate to design, inspection and repair and reworking. The existing system will need to be modified to separate these costs.

The quality costs that will need to be collected will include the following:

- Costs of conformance: ensuring that cars produced are at the acceptable quality standard. This includes prevention costs such as training for staff, building quality into the design of the cars and the design of the business processes in order to avoid quality rejections. It also includes appraisal costs which include the inspection of components from suppliers before they are used and inspection of work-in-progress and finished cars.

- Costs of non-conformance: cost of dealing with cars that do not meet the prescribed quality standards. These costs include internal failure costs when a quality fault is noticed before the car leaves the factory and is rectified. External failure costs also arise when a customer finds a fault with the car which must be handled through customer complaints.

There are quality costs that an accounting system will tend to omit such as the opportunity cost of lost future sales resulting from customer dissatisfaction and the knock-on effects of faulty component purchases in lost time in the rest of the manufacturing process.

The identification and collection of these costs will probably lead to greater management focus on the quality issue as 'what gets measured, gets done'. This will help Tench to raise the quality of its products in order to compete more effectively with the new imports.

The issues discussed above represent the traditional view of quality costs where there is an optimal effort that minimises but does not eliminate quality faults. There is a trade-off occurring since the reduction of non-conformance costs requires an increase in conformance costs in order to prevent product failures and there comes a point where the cost of reducing the error rate further is greater than the benefit from preventing that additional fault. For a national manufacturer faced with multinational competitors, this may seem an appropriate approach as Tench will not have the resources to be able to drive out all quality faults.

(b) The Kaizen costing process focuses on producing constant, small, incremental cost reductions throughout the production process during the product's life. Kaizen can be translated as continuous improvement. Kaizen costing applies functional analysis in the design phase to create a target cost for each production function. These are totalled to give a product target cost which, after the first year of production, is used as the baseline for further on-going reductions. These reductions in turn reduce the baseline cost and so on as the production process improves. The cost reduction rate is set as a target and managed by exception throughout an accounting period often on a monthly basis compared to the annual setting of standard costs.

The effect of this on the standard costing system at Tench is significant since, in a process that is continually improving, standard costs have much less value as they are fixed over the relevant period. Therefore, Kaizen costing can respond more easily to a dynamic business environment. Standard costing is used to control costs while Kaizen costing focuses on cost reduction.

The management attitude to employees is different in the two systems, as in continuous improvement systems they are the source of the improvement solutions while in standard costing systems with its analysis of variances of labour rates and efficiencies, the employees are often seen as the source of problems. In the Kaizen system, the employees often work in teams and are empowered to make changes to production that would have to be cleared through a management hierarchy in a more static standard costing system. Changing the costing system would be likely to represent a major cultural change at Tench with its history of bureaucratic control.

The benefit of continuous improvement, which has been successfully followed at many multi-national car manufacturers such as Toyota, is that it will allow the company to address quickly the changing nature of Tench's competitive environment. It will increase staff motivation through empowerment. However, there may be significant management difficulties initially in getting workers who are used to a command and control structure to change their behaviour and speak out about possible improvements.

(c) Just-in-time (JIT) is a demand-pull system of ordering from suppliers which aims to reduce inventory levels to zero. It can be broken into two parts: purchasing and production. Each part has a similar goal to produce the components for the next stage of the production process only when they are needed (hence demand-pull). The system is often used in conjunction with the continuous improvement methods discussed earlier.

For Tench, this will bring benefits and problems. The benefits will be measured in lower working capital requirements, factory floor space savings and increased flexibility in meeting the customer's individual needs (faster response times to product specification changes).

There are a number of problems to be overcome. There will be an increased reliance on suppliers as any component quality failures are not necessarily rectifiable by going to inventory to pick a replacement. This can lead to costly stoppages to production. For Tench there could be difficulty in finding local suppliers who are capable of meeting the required component and delivery standards needed in order to run such a system. Quality systems are therefore a driver of the feasibility of JIT and the metrics associated with quality costs (mentioned above) will become important as a result.

Output must be matched to demand and each stage of the production process must match its output speed to the demand level. Teams must be formed to work by component or product rather than by the type of work performed. Staff will require training in order to work in these teams as they will have to be multi-skilled (able to operate and maintain the machinery in use by their team). This means that traditional functional divisions of costs become less appropriate, again requiring cultural change at Tench. Measures of spare capacity and bottlenecks in production will be critical to achieving these aims. Also, the amount and effectiveness of staff training will need to be measured during the implementation of these changes.

(d) Tench's existing performance reporting system uses standard costing and variance analysis for monitoring and control purposes. This is likely to have been adequate under the old regime when the focus was on production but will not necessarily drive the business forward. As the surrounding markets begin to see the effects of deregulation there is likely to be a greater rate of change in prices and availability of goods and labour and Tench may find it difficult to keep the standard costs up to date and appropriate. This could lead to significant variances being reported and time wasted on analysis and investigation. Tench may find it useful to analyse and report on a wider range of performance measures going forward and will need to consider performance relative to the competition as well as simply comparing against budget. The variance analysis system may also constrain managers as there may be insufficient focus on growing the business and taking advantage of the greater wealth enjoyed by the population. Tench could consider a system which incorporates a range of different measures and takes into account both internal and external factors. A system such as Fitzgerald and Moon's building blocks would achieve this and could also help the business consider the impact of quality management on performance.

Marking scheme		
		Marks
(a)	Describe quality costs	2
	Impact of quality costs 1 mark per point up to 4 marks	4
	Use of quality costs	
	And traditional view of quality costs 1 mark per point up to 5 marks	5
		___
	Maximum	**6**
		___
(b)	Describe Kaizen costing	4
	Comparison of standard and Kaizen costing 1 mark per point up to 3 marks	3
	Effect on management of employees 1 mark per point up to 3 marks	3
		___
	Maximum	**8**
		___
(c)	JIT	
	Description	2
	Benefits 1 mark per point up to 2 marks	2
	Problems 1 mark per point up to 3 marks	3
		___
	Maximum	**6**
		___
(d)	Issues with standard costing and variance analysis –	
	1 mark per point up to a maximum of 5	5
		___
Total		**25**
		___

Examiner's comments

Requirement (a) asked about the impact of collection and use of quality costs on the current costing systems. The better candidates began by realising and describing what is meant by the current standard costing method at Tench. Their subsequent comments then showed how it would be difficult to implement the collection and use of quality costing given this system.

Requirement (b) concerned the impact of Kaizen costing on two aspects of Tench [its costing systems and its employee management]. Again, good candidates addressed the detailed requirement by considering the difficulties and opportunities of taking Tench from its old command and control style systems and culture into performance management style that is common in the current car industry.

Requirement (c) provided an opportunity to consider the use of just-in-time (JIT) manufacturing at Tench. Many answers wisely used the requirement to breakdown their comments into sections on JIT in purchasing and JIT in production. However, most answers were poorly connected to suitable performance measures.

52 THEBE TELECOM (JUN 12 – AMENDED)

Key answer tips

While the use of templates and checklists can help structure an answer, they can also become a problem. For example, DMAIC is perfect for part (b) but if you tried to use it in part (a), then you may have struggled. If a checklist isn't working, then try something else.

(a) There are a number of broad ways in which the implementation of Six Sigma improves quality in an organisation. These include:

- an increased focus on customers illustrated at Thebe by the strategic need to improve customer service and the project objective of improving customers' bills

- management decision-making being driven by data and facts not intuitions such as the use of customer satisfaction scores or numbers of complaints as key performance measures

- the identification of business processes' improvement as key to success which is exemplified by the mapping of the processes and then their redesign

- the proactive involvement of management such as the CEO championing the billing improvement project. Six Sigma depends on leadership which is provided by various experts who interact with the various Six Sigma projects which will be improving processes in the organisation

- the increased profile of quality issues and the increased knowledge of quality management that comes from the use of different layers of trained experts in the project. There are green belts who will often be line managers, who in additional to their normal work will lead Six Sigma projects. There are black belts who will exclusively specialise on Six Sigma and lead specific projects and there are master black belts who are Six Sigma experts in statistical methods who consult across several Six Sigma projects; and

- Six Sigma implementation requires collaboration across functional and divisional boundaries so bringing the focus of the whole organisation to quality issues as illustrated at Thebe by the involvement of all the business units in the billing project.

(b) The DMAIC process is as follows:

1 Define customer requirements/problem

Here the problem is the complaints on bills that result in customer dissatisfaction and delayed revenue receipt or potential loss of business. Customer requirements can be divided into those that are the minimum that is acceptable (e.g. billing errors are corrected), those that improve the customer's service experience (e.g. billing corrections completed swiftly) and those that go beyond the customer's expectations (e.g. offering additional services as compensation). The customers could be surveyed in order to identify if different customers have different needs (e.g. based on the three business units).

2 Measure existing performance

The number of customer complaints or scores below a threshold level on customer surveys will have to be measured and targets set (e.g. number of complaints per million bills issued or average time to resolve complaints). Measurement should focus on areas where the customer will value improvement. A key issue at this point is ensuring that the measurement system is reliable and this may require redesign of the existing customer survey forms/procedures.

3 Analyse the existing process

This step involves data collection in order to identify the root causes of problems and then techniques such as Pareto analysis will improve the focus of action on the issues that give raise to the majority of complaints based on the idea that 20% of the categories of causes will give rise to 80% of the complaints. For example, the analysis at Thebe could look at causes of delays in complaint resolution such as staff motivation or processing time for rebilling.

4 Improve the process

This is the implementation stage for any changes that are suggested and it is important at this stage to check on the cost and resource consequences of any suggested improvement.

5   Control the process

The improvement project will be monitored after implementation to ensure that the benefits of reduced complaints are maintained. This can be done through exception reporting if complaint numbers begin to exceed the tolerance set or continued monitoring of the time taken to resolve complaints. The general performance measure of the success of the project will be the retention of customers which is commonly measured through the churn rate of customers (percentage of existing customers lost per year).

(c)   One quality practice which Thebes could consider is Total Quality Management. TQM is a philosophy of quality management that is applied to the whole organization and aims for continuous improvement and prevention of all errors. In this sense it is consistent with the introduction of Six Sigma. TQM is more frequently used in manufacturing organisations where the impact of quality failures in the production process may be that goods are scrapped. However it is possible to apply the concepts to an organization such as Thebes and a focus on improvement to process and minimizing errors in all aspects of the business could enhance the customer experience which is a key aim of Thebes. A TQM approach would also provide support to the Six Sigma programme and ensure quality is maintained and improved in all aspects of the business.

Kaizen costing is another quality practice which Thebes could introduce. This practice focuses on small, incremental cost reductions throughout the production process. Again it is more commonly found in manufacturing but elements of the concept may be applied to service industries. One key aspect of Kaizen costing is the involvement and empowerment of staff. As Thebes is aiming to differentiate with respect to customer service, involving staff could be beneficial. However Kaizen costing does have the overall aim to make cost reductions which is not considered by the CEO to be the main focus for Thebes.

Target costing is something which also may be applied. This concept focuses on the customer and their requirements in terms of quality, service and price and takes into account all costs occurring in the product life-cycle. This is appropriate for Thebes in the sense that it starts with external factors and customer needs. However identifying and therefore analysing the appropriate costs may be difficult for Thebes due to the nature of the business.

It is recommended that Thebes consider a Total Quality Management approach which will support the Six Sigma programme. Kaizen costing and Target costing are not recommended for the reasons given above.

Marking scheme		
		Marks
(a) Up to 3 marks per theme for each of three themes.		
	Maximum	8
(b) Up to 3 marks per stage of the process with 1 mark for a general description and 2 marks for application to the scenario.		
	Maximum	9

(c) Up to 4 marks per quality practice including:
           TQM
           Kaizen costing
           Target costing		

	Maximum	8
Total		25

Examiner's comments

Part (a) was poorly answered with much evidence of candidates trying to use DMAIC as a template for an answer when the question was asking about the six sigma method (in general) and not a specific implementation method. Nevertheless, it was possible to score some marks with this approach although the themes of Pande and Holpp were more relevant and those who used these scored close to full marks in this part.

Part (b) required candidates to illustrate how a specific method of implementing six sigma (DMAIC) could be applied at Thebe. This part was usually done very well by the candidates who attempted it. Many candidates scored full marks by describing each of the steps and then illustrating the step with a relevant comment for Thebe.

53 LINCOLN & LINCOLN ADVERTISING (DEC 12 – AMENDED)

Key answer tips

In parts (a) and (b) ensure you address your advice to the individual circumstances of the three offices instead only offering generic comments for the whole company. The scenario gives much detail on the three offices and each faces their own challenges requiring a tailored response – indeed, the CEO in the scenario specifically advises you to avoid 'a one-size fits all policy'.

(a)   **Regional office performance**

Fundamentally, all three offices are doing well.

	North	East	West
	$m	$m	$m
Net income	20	65	80
Net cash flow in year	24	86	46

They have all delivered profits at its most basic level (net income) and positive cash flows. In addition, there have only been positive residual incomes and returns on capital employed of over 50%. However, these are not effective performance measures for a service company such as LLA. The intangible nature of many of the assets and services provided will make traditional measures based on capital employed less reliable. A more thorough analysis of performance would require data on customer satisfaction and retention.

However, the offices do show differences in their growth and liquidity prospects.

1   The North office has seen a decline in revenues over the three periods (by 1.9% in the most recent year). As a result, net income has fallen by 4.8% in the last year. The office has the lowest operating margins.

2   The East office has stable revenues growing slightly (although it would help to gain a clearer perspective on this figure by benchmarking against the wider market for advertising). The East office has managed to hold down cost of sales and this has driven a strong increase in net income (by 12.1% over 2011).

3   The West office has seen the highest growth in revenues (by 8.9% over 2011). But this has led to strains in working capital as receivable days has risen to 93 days (well above the 54–59 day range for the North and East offices). This, and a higher level of capital expenditure, helps to explain why West is seeing a fall in cash flows generated while driving its profits higher. It should be noted that West is obtaining significantly higher operating margins than North or East as well. This may be as a result of the large capital expenditure that seems to be going into that office.

(b)   Suitable performance measures at LLA

Net income is not wholly the responsibility of the regional management as head office costs are allocated outside of their control. Therefore, measures based on operating profit are more appropriate for the regional managers at LLA. However, even using operating profit, residual income and return on capital employed are less meaningful for a service-based business, since the business will not use a great deal of tangible assets compared to a manufacturing business. More meaningful measures would be revenue growth and, in cost terms, the ratio of staff costs to revenue. If residual income were to be used, it may be more appropriate to use different notional interest rates for the different offices. This is justified as it seems that West may be in a different environment and with its higher capital spend, it may be taking more risks, for example, by investing in technology to aid the creative design process.

Specifically, at present, the following performance metrics match to the issues at each office:

1   At North, the need is to turn around the decline in revenue and so revenue growth would be set as a target. However, this must not encourage the 'buying' of revenue by slashing prices and so an operating margin measure would be an appropriate additional control.

2   At East, the business appears stable and therefore efficiencies should be sought. East should focus on staff costs as it is paying 37% of revenue to its staff compared to as little as 31% at West. There may be economic reasons for this – the East office may be in the richest and most expensive part of Veeland and so it costs more to attract good employees to work there. The East office could pass on to the other offices how it has driven such high gross margins (72% as opposed to 66% at West).

3   At West, the business needs to continue its growth at the best operating margins but it must maintain control of working capital and so turn profit into cash. Therefore, debtor days or current assets should be targeted.

It would assist decision-making if suitable benchmarks internal (office to office) and external (competitors) to LLA were also found and included in performance reporting. A further suitable external measure may be the market share that each office holds in its region.

Therefore, it is recommended that operating profit is a more appropriate general measure for the offices at LLA with revenue growth and staff costs ratio as subsidiary indicators of performance. There are additional detailed indicators noted above to address each office's specific problems.

(c)   Remuneration packages

Generally, using industry norms as a basic benchmark will help to ensure that staff are kept broadly happy, although it will not motivate them to outperform their peers.

Taking each of the staff levels in turn:

Senior management

Their basic salary reflects historic norms and the bonus should motivate performance. It is notable that no account is taken of the different economic conditions that each office may find itself in and so there may be resentment from those in offices where the general economy is doing poorly to those who are in a region with good performance and so profits are growing easily.

It may be worthwhile trying to benchmark the performance of each office against its regional competitors, although it can be hard to obtain such detailed information.

Creative staff

The creatives' packages are set when recruited. This could lead to a loss of motivation, especially for those who get only a fixed salary. If a bonus is paid, then it is currently based on revenue and not profits and so there is no mechanism to control costs on projects with these employees. There will be tension between the need for imaginative ideas and cost efficient ones. Overall, it is likely that each staff member should have a personalised package with a performance element that would be based on the assessment of a superior manager. In order to maintain some sense of objectivity, the criteria that the manager might use to judge performance should be agreed across the firm and could include, primarily, winning new business in tender competitions and, secondarily, winning industry awards.

Buying staff

The packages for the buying staff appear to be based on appropriate performance, although the setting of such targets depends heavily on the expertise of the finance team and, as they are based in the East office, they may lack the local knowledge to set the budget accurately. It may be wise to maintain the bulk of the buyers' remuneration as a fixed salary element as a result.

Account management staff

It is surprising that this group of client-facing staff are not paid on performance. It would seem that their performance could be directly measured by client retention and new business won, so it would be common for such staff to have a high percentage of their remuneration based on performance and not be wholly fixed. Measures such as numbers of clients and total client revenues would be appropriate for these posts.

Administration staff

This is a common method of remuneration for these types of jobs and in line with the general market. A small bonus based on the overall performance of the firm may help to create a culture of loyalty throughout the business. It is unlikely to be efficient to set individual targets for such employees, given that there will probably be a large number of them.

	Marking scheme		
			Marks
(a)	Discuss overall performance	up to	1
	Evaluate measures calculated and offer suggested improvements	up to	3
	Discuss performance of each office	up to	7
		Maximum	**10**
(b)	1 mark per point	**up to a maximum of**	**8**
	(To obtain a good mark a candidate must address the issue of controllability and responsibility)		
(c)	1 mark per point	**up to a max of**	**7**
Total			**25**

Examiner's comments

In part (a) most candidates understood that there were differences between the offices but failed to bring them out in their answers. The marks in this question were for analysis of the data not its repetition. Therefore, those candidates who explained the implications of the data or succeeded in connecting trends in one indicator with another scored well (e.g. falling revenue plus fixed costs leads to larger falls in profit). The best answers offered a general overview of the three offices performance and then took each office in turn to bring out the commercial issues present there e.g. West's rapid growth but dangerous increase in receivables. Future candidates should consider the reader in writing their responses. In this situation, the board would have found an answer divided into sections by office much more helpful than split into sections based on the standard headings of an accountant's ratio analysis.

Similarly in part (b) candidates scored well if they appreciated the need to address the regional offices' specific requirements. Many candidates offered a reasonable set of generic suggestions for the company as a whole but missed out on the regional differences. The first part of the requirement sought an evaluation of the existing performance measure (net income) and a recognition of two key facts – this measure contained uncontrollable costs and it was too general to cover the issues across the company. Other criticisms of the measure were credited as well, however, these were the main areas.

The second part required justified recommendations of alternative metrics. Most candidates realised that nonfinancial indicators would be useful and those that made suggestions appropriate to LLA scored well. Those that offered lists of metrics that could apply to any company scored significantly less well. There were many answers that provided lengthy (possibly rote-learned) proposals of ROCE, EVA™ and RI although these were of limited use in this scenario, as they did not address the issues in the different offices nor did they address the fact that LLA would be likely to have a large intangible asset base.

The better solutions made sure that their comments on these alternatives were consistent with their criticism of the existing measure.

Part (c) was typically well done. Most candidates addressed their comments to the five different grades of staff given in the scenario. However, many candidates assumed that all of the existing policies must be wrong and so only made negative comments – future candidates need to be aware that evaluate means to give a balanced assessment (including both the positive and negative aspects of an issue). On the suggested improvements, most candidates provided practical suggestions addressing the weaknesses previously discussed.

For example, the best candidates suggested that the account management staff should have part of their remuneration based on measures of client satisfaction such as retention. However, many candidates seem to be under the misapprehension that share schemes solve all remuneration policy issues. These schemes can address alignment of interests of staff with shareholders but do not necessarily address the short-sighted nature of many bonus schemes.

54   LANDUAL LAMPS (JUN 13)

Key answer tips

The question required an assessment of the current transfer pricing system and then the consideration of two changes: one to the transfer pricing policy and one to the divisional structure of the company. To answer this question well it is vital that you consider the implications of any changes, recalculating the figures in part (a), if necessary.

(a)   **Current transfer pricing policy**

A good transfer pricing system will ensure goal congruence and fair performance measurement between the divisions and maintain a suitable level of managerial autonomy within each division. Generally, the use of variable costs is helpful as it leads to optimal decisions for the company as a whole. The use of fixed production costs obscures these marginal costs and can lead to sub-optimal decisions by the divisions.

Electrical components

The use of a market price basis for electrical components makes sense, as these are generic products for which there is a ready external market. Therefore, the performance of the components division in their production can be readily compared to this market and the assembly division will accept such a price, as this is its alternative to sourcing internally. This activity does return a small contribution to head office costs, currently $383k (1,557 – 804 – 370). This small contribution reflects the generic nature of the products.

However, the assembly division could reasonably argue that the market price is too high, since an internal transfer of components does not require a number of costs (transport, marketing and bad debts). These should be deducted from the market price in order to get an adjusted market price. If this is done, then the contribution to head office costs from electrical components within the components division falls to $114k (1,288 – 804 – 370 or 383 – 269), as shown below.

Housing components

The housing components are currently priced using actual production costs. This makes sense, as these components are uniquely produced for the assembly division and there is no external market since this would give away Landual's competitive advantage. It could be argued that the unique work in housing components should be rewarded with greater divisional profit. The components division only covers its actual production costs and gets no contribution towards the allocated head office costs from these components. Thus, since housing represents the bulk of the division's revenue (84% = 8,204/9,761), it will be difficult for the components division to ever earn a significant profit. A mark-up on actual total production costs of 30% (say) would not seem unusual for such unique products and would lead to additional divisional profit of $2,461 (30% of $8,204k). This would significantly shift the location of the divisional profit from assembly to housing.

However, by using actual rather than budget costs, this means that there is no incentive to reduce on costs by the components division, as it will always receive these back from the assembly division. This lack of incentive could explain the failure to meet budget by $575,000 caused in the production of the housing components.

Applying all of these changes, divisional reports would be:

Data for the year ended 31 March 2013 Notes:

	Components Division $000	Assembly Division $000
Sales Electrical	1,288	
Housing	9,918	
sub-total	11,206	15,794
Cost of sales		
Electrical	804	1,288
Housing	6,902	9,918
Fixed production costs		
Electrical	370	
Housing	1,302	
sub-total	1,672	1,268
Allocated HO costs	461	2,046
Profit	1,367	1,274

Notes:

1   Transfer price for electrical components is reduced by additional costs of external sales.

	$000
Previous market price for electrical	1,557
Less: additional costs for external sales	(269)
Adjusted market price	1,288

2   The transfer price for housing is now budgeted total production cost (7,629 = 6,902 + 1,302 – 575), marked up by 30%.

(b)   The change in transfer policy has the effect of reducing the revenue/cost of sales of the components/assembly divisions by the fixed production costs of the housing components ($1,302k). It shifts this amount of divisional profit from the components to the assembly division. This change seems unusual since the competitive advantage of the business lies in the housing designs, and yet this change is further emphasising the importance of the assembly division which does not seem to be the value-adding element of the business.

There is a danger, here, that the company focuses on the work of the division with higher profits and so downgrades the unique work done by the components division. However, the clarity of using variable costs only in transfer pricing may assist the company overall in achieving optimal pricing and profit.

There is no change to the company's profit from such a change.

Working:

Data for the year ended 31 March 2013

		Components $000	Assembly $000	Landual Lamps $000
Sales	Electrical	1,557		
	Housing	6,902		
	sub-total	8,459	15,794	15,794
Cost of sales				
	Electrical	804	1,557	
	Housing	6,902	6,902	
	sub-total	7,706	8,459	7,706
Fixed production costs				
	Electrical	370		
	Housing	1,302		
	sub-total	1,672	1,268	2,940
Allocated HO costs		461	2,046	2,507
Profit		(1,380)	4,021	2,641

Note: Only change is that housing is now charged to assembly on variable cost only.

Tutorial note

This calculation is much more than required as the change is simple – it is presented here for clarity only.

(c)   Housing division

The housing division is now a cost centre and so it will be easier for it to focus on cost control (avoiding adverse budget variances) and quality of its output (as it makes the key components for the company's products). However, there may be an adverse effect on the motivation of divisional managers through losing profit centre status and this must be countered by altering their reward packages to focus them on costs.

Electrical division

The electrical division can be seen to be making a small divisional profit ($335k). Its treatment as a profit centre makes sense, as it can be compared to similar companies for benchmarking purposes and also so that Landual can consider easily the 'make or buy' decision for such generic components. Obviously, at present, electrical is making a contribution to HO costs, which means that it should continue to obtain the business from the assembly division.

Assembly division

The assembly division is unaffected by the changes, although the greater clarity of results in the electrical division will allow the managers of the division to ensure that the electrical division remains competitive.

Landual Lamps

The change has no effect on the company profit reported but it would be hoped that the change would bring the benefits noted above (cost savings in housing and greater motivation to compete in electrical) and so improve profits in the future.

Working:

	$000	$000	$000	$000
Sales			15,794	15,794
Electrical		1,557		
Housing				
Cost of sales				7,706
Electrical		804	1,557	
Housing	6,902		8,204	
Fixed production costs			1,268	2,940
Electrical		370		
Housing	1,302			
Allocated HO costs	413	48	2,046	2,507
	(8,617)	335	2,719	2,641

Note: Head office costs have been reallocated *pro rata* with cost of sales.

Marking scheme		
		Marks
(a) Electrical components Basic policy – up to 2 marks Use adjusted market price – 1 mark Housing components Basic policy – up to 2 marks Need for mark-up – up to 2 marks Use of budgeted costs – up to 2 marks Workings: New divisional profit – electrical policy 1 mark housing policy 2 marks		
	Maximum	10
(b) New component revenue figure – 1 mark New profit figures, 1 for each entity – up to 3 marks Comments – 1 mark per point up to 4 marks		
	Maximum	6
(c) New profit figures, 1 for each entity – up to 4 marks Comments – 1 mark per point up to 7 marks		
	Maximum	9
Total		25

Examiner's comments

This question was generally poorly done with weak (often no) efforts at handling the quantification issues – recalculating the current transfer price, calculating the impact of the two proposed changes on the various entities in the scenario. Again, this meant that candidates often had very little to say in evaluating or giving advice in the commentary parts of their answers. Also, candidates did not focus their answers on the stated area of competitive advantage for Landual in making the housing components. This ought to have been a priority.

Part (a) for 10 marks required an evaluation of the current system of transfer pricing at Landual – the requirement emphasised the need for calculations. There were a number of faults in the existing system which needed to be pointed out with the impact that correcting these would have on the divisions in the company.

In part (b) 6 marks were available for advice for the finance director on the impact of changing the transfer pricing policy for housing components to using variable costs. A useful answer here would provide firstly, what this change would do to profit in the two divisions and for the company as a whole and then, from this, consider the likely reactions of the key stakeholders (the three sets of management). Unfortunately, if the (simple) quantification work was not done then very few candidates could see that this change lead to lower profits in the division that was the key competitive advantage of the company (the difficult process of design and manufacture of the housing components).

Finally, in part (c) an evaluation of the impact of the change in proposed divisional structure on the profits for the various entities was required for 9 marks. The question provided an illustration of the impact of changing the emphasis of a division from profit centre to cost centre as well as increasing the number of divisions. Again as in part (b), the calculations were straightforward but where they were done at all, they were often done poorly.

A common basic mistake was imputing a revenue stream to the new housing division when it was stated that it was to become a cost centre. As a result, much ink was spilled discussing the impact that the reduction in profit for the housing area would have on the morale of its management, rather than focussing on the change to a cost control emphasis that this change would affect.

Future candidates would be advised to consider, during their revision, the impacts that strategic changes such as designation of cost, profit and investment centres would have on the performance management of divisions or departments within a company.

55 BEACH FOODS (JUN 15)

Key answer tips

Make sure you apply the models mentioned to the specific scenario in the question as much as possible.

(a) **Economic value added (EVA™) as a divisional performance measure**

The main benefit to EVA™ is its link to the overall corporate objective of adding shareholder value. It is an appropriate measure to use if the company is applying value-based management. Therefore, by using it as a divisional performance measure, divisional managers should also be motivated to work in the best interest of the company as a whole and this ought to be one of the main objectives of a divisional performance measure.

The other advantages of EVA™ are that:

- It gives an absolute measure so showing the overall contribution to the company.

- The basic test of performance is simple since if EVA™ is positive, then the division is generating a return above that required by the providers of finance. (ROI requires a target level to be set usually based on benchmarking to the industry sector.)

- The adjustments within the calculation of EVA™ mean that the measure is closer to cash flows than accounting profits and so is less subject to choices in accounting policies.

- EVA™ encourages investment for the future (for example, in advertising and development) by removing such costs from the performance period and treating them like capital expenditure. This will reduce the dysfunctional temptation for management to engage in some short-term decision-making, which can be a problem with the capital employed figure from the financial statements which is used in ROI and RI. This is likely to be particularly appropriate at Beach, where R&D is significant.

However, EVA™ does have disadvantages, some of which are common to the two suggested alternative measures and some which are specific.

All three measures are dependent on historical data and so are only of limited use in forecasting future performance.

The specific criticism of EVA™ that it is complicated is reasonable as the full version requires more than 100 adjustments to the information in the normal financial statements. RI and ROI are derived from headline information in the financial statements which would be more familiar to the board.

EVA™ (like RI) uses a charge for the capital employed in the division. EVA™ uses the weighted-average cost of capital for the company as a whole and may not reflect the risks of the division. However, RI uses a notional cost of capital based on the risk of the division, which will be subject to an element of judgement and estimate. Also, as an unlisted business, the estimation of WACC is difficult.

Unlike ROI, EVA™ would not help to judge relative divisional managerial performance at Beach if the divisions are not of similar size.

It is sensible to avoid consideration of the R&D division in this discussion as it is not a revenue-generating division.

(b) **Workings:**

Baby division

	2015 $m
Revenue	220
Divisional operating costs	121
	——
Controllable profit	99
R&D costs recharged	11
	——
Profit after R&D costs	88
Apportioned head office management fees	28
	——
Divisional profit before tax	60
	——

	ROI	RI $m
Based on controllable profit	23%	52.4
Based on profit after R&D	21%	41.4
Based on divisional profit	14%	13.4

The key assumption in the calculation of both metrics is which profit figure to use. Controllable profit relates to those revenues and costs under direct control of the divisional manager but this does not reflect the R&D costs, although it takes account of the revenues which new products are generating. It would be more appropriate to include these costs in an assessment of the divisional managers' performance, especially if the product development was at the request of the divisional management and the transfer price was widely agreed. The assessment of the division itself should include all relevant operating costs and so the divisional profit would be the appropriate figure to use.

The RI and EVA™ give the same assessment that the division is performing well (both figures are positive). It is not possible to do a simple comparison between RI and EVA™ as there are different tax and R&D cost treatments to take into account. The ROI figure should be compared to the comparator; however, this is not possible as the profit used in calculation of the comparator is not specified.

(c) **Baby division**

As the star of the Beach portfolio and with new products launching, it would appear sensible that Baby was an investment division with the autonomy to continue to develop its business successfully. However, it is unclear where the decision to commit to a new product rests as the R&D division actually does the development work. In that case, it may be appropriate to make Baby a profit centre and manage it according to its profit generating ability.

The business is rapidly growing and so a budget-constrained style would be inappropriate as it would stifle the creativity necessary for such a division. Alternatively, a non-accounting style where criteria other than profit such as revenue growth and new product development may be appropriate. Once the market sector has matured further then given a strong market share, the focus of the division will move to optimising profit.

Chocolate division

As the cash cow of the Beach portfolio, Chocolate should be run for the profit which it generates. It could be classified as a profit centre since its sector is mature and there are unlikely to be plans to make new investment. Alternatively, it could be classified as an investment centre so it does not have to wait for approval of limited capital expenditure such as happened with the production line upgrade. The management style should be budget-constrained with special emphasis placed on the ability of the division to generate cash not just profit.

R&D division

The R&D division has no source of revenue other than internal recharge of its services and so it should be a cost centre. However, the value of the division will only be appreciated if the overall profit generated from these new products can be demonstrated. This may be the cause of the problem with the Baby division managers. They only see the recharge cost appearing in their performance reports without the revenue which these new products are generating being specifically disclosed. It may be helpful to have a profit calculated for each product over its lifecycle to demonstrate the value of the division which is seen by Beach as vital.

A budget-constrained style of management would be appropriate where the budget is set separately for each new product development project. However, it would be important not to constrain the division within a fixed overall budget if there is a number of good product development ideas. The generation of ideas may be helped by using a non-accounting style, giving priority to more than just budget numbers (e.g. number of new product ideas/favourable press comments on new product launches).

A specific approach will therefore need to take account of all these factors in order to arrive at a style of management which meets the needs of the company as a whole.

	Marking scheme		Marks
(a)	1 mark per point		
		Maximum	8
(b)	Calculations:		
	RI – method 1 mark		
	ROI – method 1 mark		
	Correct calculation of both RI and ROI for more than one profit figure – 1 mark per profit figure used		
	Max 4 marks		
	Comments:		
	1 mark per point up to a max of 4 marks		
		Maximum	7
(c)	Up to 4 marks for any one division		
	— all recommendations must be justified within the answer to gain credit		
	— high marks within the answer for any one division can only be scored by discussing both the type of centre and management style		
		Maximum	10
Total			25

Examiner's comments

Part (a) for 8 marks required an assessment of the use of EVA^{TM} as a divisional performance measure at Beach. Generally, this was done reasonably well. Those candidates who attempted to show how EVA^{TM} could be affected by conditions in the two relevant divisions scored well. However, the question did not require any lengthy description of how EVA^{TM} is calculated. This should have been obvious as the company is already using this measure for its overall performance.

Part (b) for 7 marks required a calculation of two alternative divisional performance measures (return on investment and residual income) and an assessment of the assumptions made in these calculations on divisional and managerial performance. Those candidates who realised the nature of the assumptions in their calculations, specifically the difference between divisional and managerial performance, scored highly. They considered the choice of profit to use in their calculations as central and calculated the profit from multiple perspectives. Many candidates realised that there were different profits to use but did not do the numerical work and so their answers lacked the evidential support that was clearly within their ability to produce.

Part (c) was worth 10 marks and required justified recommendations on divisional control and management style at Beach. This part was poorly answered as many candidates clearly did not know the criteria for the choice of responsibility centre (the centre headings to choose from were given in the scenario). This lack of knowledge has been noted in previous diets and continues to surprise the examining team. Lengthy descriptions of the three management styles were not helpful here as the candidate was expected to demonstrate that understanding through the application of the ideas to the scenario.

The general lesson for future candidates from this question is to learn not just the models or jargon but how to apply them in a specific scenario. This is typically only possible through question practice and not merely learning generic answers that can be ported from one question to another. Candidates should also make sure that they understand issues around responsibility accounting and the choice of responsibility centre for controlling a business unit.

56   POSIE FURNITURE (SEPT/DEC 15)

Key answer tips

Make sure you learn the DMAIC model and how to apply it, particularly focussing on the implications of each stage on the business.

(a)   The DMAIC process is a technique used to implement six sigma to improve existing processes and is split into five phases as described below.

Define the process

The CEO is concerned that the increase in returns from customers is increasing costs and threatens to affect the Posie brand. Six sigma focuses closely on the requirements of the customer and it is important to be clear exactly what customers' requirements are and in this case specifically why products are returned.

The objective of the project needs to be clear, in this case to reduce the number of customer returns.

Customers will expect certain minimum requirements from the manufacturing and packaging process, for example, that the furniture is able to be properly assembled and all the necessary components are included in the box. They will also expect the goods to be delivered undamaged within a reasonable time and at the time and date promised when the order was placed. Customers' perceptions of quality should correspond to the price paid, though different customers will have different expectations of this.

Beyond this basic requirement, there may be aspects of the manufacturing product which further enhance the customers' experience of the product and presumably of the Posie brand. Customers may be particularly pleased with furniture which is delivered early or at a time especially convenient to them, or which is robust, durable and 'well-made'. These perceptions are subjective and may equally relate to design or the quality of raw materials as to the manufacturing process. By identifying where the products exceed customers' expectations, it may be possible to focus more on these aspects in the future. While products which significantly exceed customers' expectations will enhance the Posie brand, it may also indicate a quality of manufacture which is too high and allow Posie to reduce manufacturing costs in accordance with its cost leadership strategy whilst still having mainly satisfied customers.

Measure the existing process

The current returns figures do give some data to as to why products are returned, but its usefulness is limited as it is unclear which of the categories relates to defective manufacture, and which relate to activities of other divisions. The ambiguity of the data and category definitions will need addressing to enable the process to be measured effectively.

Returns in Category 1 could be because the goods were not manufactured or packed properly in the manufacturing division, but could also be due to poor design, customers losing components or simply being unable to assemble furniture.

Damaged goods in Category 2 probably do not arise because of defective manufacturing either, though customers may wrongly categorise defective goods as damaged. For the other categories it is less clear. Though goods may become damaged by the distribution company, it seems that only a small number of returns relate directly to them.

Returns in Categories 3 and 4 could be due to defective manufacture or if the customer had simply changed their minds and no longer wanted the product. In Category 3, the identification of 'defective' items is too broad.

Returns in Category 5 which arrived late are clearly not due to manufacturing defects and as this causes only 2% of returns, is relatively insignificant.

Currently 10% of Posie's sales are of products from other manufacturers. There is no indication from the data given how many of the returns relate to these products, nor of the total number of returns relative to the number of items sold.

Therefore the existing data are insufficient to reliably measure existing performance and take no account of inputs such as raw materials. Only items which customers value should be measured. The CEO has suggested more detailed data are required, for example, on overall customer satisfaction with the manufacturing, but this is at 93% which already seems high and there is little point in incurring costs to measure what customers are already satisfied with. In the context of the six sigma project at Posie, there is little that can be done to improve this particular area and such items should not be measured.

Analyse the process

This stage is where the root causes of the problems are identified. Additional information may be needed, for example, to analyse customer returns by type of product, by country of sale or with a clearer definition of what is meant by 'defective'. By doing so, Posie may identify areas of the business where customer returns are particularly high and so be able to focus on these.

Improve the process

At this stage the proposals for improving the process are implemented and availability of resources and likely costs of making the improvements need to be carefully considered. Posie may need to consider which aspects of the production or packaging process could be improved, for example, by better maintenance or calibration of machinery. Additional training of staff may also be required.

Control

This is the on-going monitoring that the reduction in customer returns due to defective manufacturing is being maintained. Reporting on the number of returns may be done by exception if they reach a particular level. In Posie, it seems likely that the data on customer returns used to manage this process will need to be redesigned to make it clearer in which responsibility centre the problems arise. The ongoing monitoring may indicate that some of the earlier stages in the DMAIC process need to be revisited.

(b)   (i)   The CEO wants to identify which responsibility centres are the root causes of the problem of customer returns. A responsibility centre is a part of the business where a manager has specific authority and accountability for its performance and so Posie will need information relating to aspects of performance specific to the centre. For example, performance data relating to the reasons for customer returns need to be clearly segregated between responsibility centres. Currently, the information compiled on customer returns does not do this and some categories of return may result from manufacturing defects but some will be from problems outside the manufacturing division, or even outside Posie itself, for example, from poor quality raw materials purchased externally, or because of late deliveries or damaged goods caused by the distribution company.

Once information has been analysed and responsibility has been identified, then the managers of those areas will need the information drilled down into even further, as in order to improve they need to know which specific areas they can control.

It would be unfair to make managers responsible for aspects of performance which they are unable to control, and the board member responsible for manufacturing quality has recently resigned because of this.

Posie needs to ensure it produces performance data to an appropriate level of detail so as not to overload the users with too much data. For board level reporting, the information in the current board reporting pack may be too detailed and it would be sufficient just to produce summary data on the overall level of returns relative to sales. Responsibility centres would need much more detailed information, perhaps even down to product or production line level.

However, Posie should also consider the costs and resources required to provide more detailed performance data. Given Posie's cost leadership strategy, the costs of data collection may outweigh the benefits of doing so.

Performance data should be provided at an appropriate frequency. For the Posie main board, monthly reporting may be sufficient to alert them to any problems. Responsibility centres will need much more frequent, even daily or weekly details of the levels of customer returns so that they can react quickly to any problems identified. At the moment, the returns data are compiled every six months, possibly due to the difficulties in obtaining data from the IT systems in the overseas businesses. Even for a board level report, this seems much too infrequent.

(ii) At the moment, the overseas subsidiaries are being designated as profit centres and managers will be held accountable for both revenues and costs. As they do not manufacture, it seems reasonable to designate them as revenue centres. As such, managers would be held accountable for just revenues as they have little or no control over costs as most goods for resale are purchased from the manufacturing division.

The performance data produced by Posie's subsidiaries' IT systems will therefore switch to focus more on revenues rather than costs. As revenue centres they may well have some freedom to change selling prices. Posie will need to ensure the subsidiaries have information to monitor the impact of different pricing strategies and will need to provide the management of these subsidiaries with information gleaned from the external environment. It will be important to evaluate competitors' pricing strategies when making pricing decisions.

A potential problem with providing only performance data relating to revenue is that managers could focus too much on achieving revenue targets rather than maintaining or improving profitability. As they are autonomous subsidiaries, there will be aspects of their own costs, such as staffing costs and other overheads, which they will be able to have some control over. It is important that Posie ensures the management still has sight of this information to ensure that such costs are still controlled effectively.

Furthermore, if the overseas managers are only held responsible for sales, this may mean they do not focus sufficiently on addressing reasons why goods are returned, and so levels of returns may increase. This means that once Posie undertakes the exercise to identify the root causes of the returns from customers, this information is shared and monitored.

Posie needs to be aware of these issues when determining information requirements if the reclassification of the subsidiaries goes ahead. It will not be as simple as assuming that they will now only need information on revenues.

		Marking scheme		*Marks*
(a)		Use of DMAIC		
		Define		
		1 mark per point	up to	4
		Measure		
		1 mark per point	up to	6
		Analyse		3
		Improve		3
		Control		3
				___
			Maximum	**15**
				___
(b)	(i)	Definition		1
		Impact on information requirements		
		1 mark per point	up to	6
				___
			Maximum	**6**
				___
	(ii)	Impact on information requirements		
		1 mark per point	up to	4
				___
			Maximum	**4**
				___
Total				**25**
				___

Examiner's comments

Part (a) asked for specific advice about how a six sigma project could be implemented using DMAIC methodology. A key focus to the question was the use of DMAIC methodology and it was clear that a few candidates had little knowledge about how this methodology worked. Given that the use of the methodology was being tested, knowledge of it was essential and candidates who could not demonstrate this scored very few, if any, marks.

An explanation of the DMAIC methodology scored a few marks though the majority of credit in this question was to be gained from applying the methodology to the scenario. One of the main shortcomings in many responses to this question was a failure to recognise properly how to use the data given with each part of the methodology – Define, Measure, Analyse, Improve, Control and actually how all this connected to customer requirements and expectations. Answers were not provided in sufficient depth.

Part (b) (i) asked for an evaluation of the impact on the organisation's information requirements of the need to identify and improve on the level of customer returns. This part was badly done overall as many candidates did not read the requirement of the question and offered responses which considered the effect on the organisation's performance. Such responses scored few marks. The need to recognise the effect upon information requirements is fundamental with the introduction of a six sigma project and a DMAIC methodology. The data that has to be captured is significant and it is important for a candidate sitting APM to recognise the effects of the introduction of a major development such as this. This is part of the overall process of analysis and evaluation of the adoption of any technique and should be part of a revision mind-set, perhaps in a self-prompt sense to consider questions such as – if this is introduced, what are the overall effects on information, personnel, etc.

Part (b) (ii) asked for an evaluation of the information requirements that would arise from the proposed re- designation of parts of the organisation from profit centres to revenue centres. Few candidates attempted this question in a meaningful way and a number failed to differentiate between the two types of responsibility centre.

It is clear that a valuable lesson which candidates can take forward is that they should always read the question and come prepared to consider the effects on a company's systems of the introduction of something new.

57 UNIVERSITIES IN TEELAND (MAR/JUN 16)

Key answer tips

Part (a) – Value for money (VFM) is a key tool for assessing performance in a not-for-profit organisation (NFPO). It is important to be able to explain VFM in terms of the 3Es, i.e. economy, efficiency and effectiveness.

Part (b) should be relatively straightforward if you have your core knowledge of the advantages and disadvantages of league tables in place. Make sure you reference your points back to the scenario.

Tutorial note

The solution given is very detailed and candidates would not have to provide an answer of this length to score maximum marks. It is provided to give an idea of the scope of the relevant points which could have been made.

(a)   Public sector organisations such as the Teeland universities receive all their funding from central government and do not have the generation of profit as an objective. Furthermore, their objectives such as 'improving the standard of education of the citizens of Teeland' cannot be measured in financial terms. The value for money of the universities can be assessed using the '3Es' framework of economy, efficiency and effectiveness.

Economy

This involves obtaining the inputs to the service at the lowest possible cost, while still maintaining the quality of the inputs. In practice, this may be difficult to do, and a reduction in cost may lead to a reduction in quality.

From the performance data given, the average annual payroll cost per member of academic staff is highest in Northcity University at $62,286 ($109m/1,750). This is 51% higher than Eastcity University, which has the lowest cost at $41,237 of the four universities given. The high costs in Northcity University may reflect the fact that staff there may be more highly qualified or that highly skilled, trained staff are attracted to work there because of the high standards of teaching and academic research.

A higher payroll cost per member of academic staff may not necessarily mean a particular university is not giving good value for money. The relatively high salary costs in Southcity University of $62,083 may simply reflect the higher costs of living in the capital city and so comparison between the regions may be inappropriate.

As such, there may be a conflict between this performance measure and the ability of the universities to achieve their objectives, such as to improve educational standards in Teeland. The politician's proposal to reduce salary levels for new recruits may reduce the number of appropriately qualified and skilled staff who wish to work there. This may reduce the standard of teaching and academic research, and as a result, the universities' performance against their stated objectives. This means that focusing solely on economy would not ensure the universities achieve value for money.

Efficiency

Efficiency measures the amount of outputs relative to the amount of inputs. The number of academic staff per student may be a suitable measurement but there may be differences between universities which would make it hard to compare results.

For example, there are 10.1 (17,600/1,750) students per member of academic staff in Northcity University, which is ranked number one in the Teeland government's provisional league table. There are 17.9 in Westcity University which is ranked much lower at 21. It would seem therefore, that increasing the number of students relative to the number of academic staff as per the politician's proposal may reduce the performance of the universities against their stated objectives and as such will not increase value for money.

The politician's comparison with the number of students per academic staff in neighbouring Veeland may not be appropriate. Whilst the politician's assertion that educational standards are higher in Veeland may be correct, the undertaking of high quality academic research may not be a key objective of the universities there, or the quality of research may be lower than in Teeland.

Effectiveness

Effectiveness measures whether the objectives of the organisation are being met. The stated objectives of the Teeland universities are to improve the overall standard of education of citizens in Teeland, to engage in high quality academic research and to provide well-qualified university graduates to meet the needs of the graduate jobs market in Teeland.

Objective to improve the overall standard of education in Teeland

Currently, there is no direct measure of the performance of the universities' stated objectives to increase the level of education of the citizens of Teeland. The number of graduates entering graduate jobs and the results of the TSOR survey may indirectly measure the effectiveness of the universities in achieving this aim. More direct measures such as the number of students completing their studies, or obtaining good results in university exams may be more appropriate.

The effectiveness of the universities in improving the standard of education should really be related to the entry requirements of each university. Westcity University is the lowest ranking of the four universities in the provisional league table and has the lowest proportion of graduates entering graduate jobs at 50% (1,750/(11,200/3.2)). It also receives the lowest amount of research funding per student at around $1,250 ($14m/11,200), but it has the lowest entry requirements, which have been relaxed to encourage students from a more diverse range of backgrounds to study there. Therefore, the improvement in educational standards relative to students' attainment on entry may be higher than the position in the league table may suggest.

Objective to engage in high quality academic research

The stated aim of the universities to engage in high quality academic research is also not currently measured. The amount of research funding received from government and other organisations by each university may indirectly reflect the quality of the research there as providers of funds for research would probably look to fund high quality research.

This measure may, however, equally reflect that some types of research are more expensive than others. Southcity University, which is successful in science and technology subjects, receives $15,592 per student compared to $5,000 in Eastcity, which specialises in arts and humanities subjects. The funding received may be more indicative of the past quality of academic research rather than future quality, or may not even reflect the quality of the research and may be high due to wastage or inefficiency. The definition of 'quality' of research is unclear.

Objective to meet the needs of the graduate jobs market

The number of graduates from each university obtaining graduate jobs each year is an indirect measure how well each university is achieving this objective. However, the number of graduate jobs filled may simply reflect the number of students at each university and demand for graduate jobs in the economy.

Many graduates, including the most talented of them, may take graduate jobs overseas. In which case, the measure of graduate jobs filled may not be a clear measure of the objective to meet the needs of the graduate jobs market in Teeland. A more precise measure of graduates entering graduate jobs in Teeland may be more appropriate. Even this may be misleading, if graduates later return from overseas to enter graduate jobs in Teeland.

The definition of what is a 'graduate' job is subjective and likely to change over time, for example, as a result of changes in the economy. This again limits the usefulness of this measure in determining whether universities have met this objective.

The TSOR survey is a measure of effectiveness reflecting a basket of measures, one of which is students' own perceptions of their future job prospects. The measures in the TSOR survey are, however, highly subjective according to individuals' personal perceptions, for example, about students' job prospects and the quality of teaching at the university. Furthermore, the survey also covers a wider range of factors such as their overall satisfaction with university life. As such, this may not reflect the stated aims of the universities in Teeland. The TSOR score for Westcity University is considerably higher than for all the other universities, despite it having the lowest overall ranking.

(b) **Effect of league tables on the quality of the Teeland universities**

League tables encourage competition between universities

The publishing of league tables of the performance of the universities in Teeland should stimulate competition for high ranking between them. This should encourage them to find better ways to improve the quality of the service, achieve their performance objectives, and deliver greater value for money.

Sharing of resources may be discouraged

However, this may discourage knowledge or even resource sharing between the universities if they see themselves in competition for the best students and limited research funding. This could particularly be a problem if the university leaders were given performance targets and rewards based on their university's position in the league table. They may be encouraged to undertake 'gaming' and focus solely on their position within the league table to the detriment of other aspects of performance. This may mean the objectives for the universities overall in Teeland may not be achieved.

University leaders may focus on a narrow range of objectives

Students' overall experience of university life may be influenced by access to social, pastoral and sporting facilities. Management time and resources may be diverted away from these important areas by focusing on a narrow range of performance objectives such as improving educational standards and high quality research in order to boost the position in the league table.

Use of league table to ensure accountability of the universities

If the performance league tables are made publicly available, for example, on the internet as they are in Veeland, this should ensure the performance of the universities is transparent. This will mean that they are held accountable by the public for the quality of service and value for money which they provide.

League tables give choices to students and staff

To be really effective, league tables should provide users of the performance data, such as the public, with the ability to make choices based on the data given. Prospective students and staff will be able to make choices about which university to study or work at according to their position in the league tables. In addition, providers of funding such as the government will be able to identify where corrective action or additional funding may be required.

This could also be a disadvantage of using league tables, as the best students are likely to be attracted to the best universities, which are in turn likely to attract the most funding for academic research. This may cause a reduction in the overall performance of lower ranking universities, and therefore a failure of the universities as a whole to achieve the stated aim of improving educational standards in Teeland.

League tables may not reflect variation of standards at each university

There may also be considerable variation of the standards within one university, which a ranking in a league table will not address. For example, Southcity University offers courses in a variety of subjects and is particularly successful at science and technology subjects. This may mean that it achieves a high overall ranking in a league table, whereas its performance in other subjects may be weaker. For all of these reasons, the provision of league tables or performance data at a lower level, such as by subject area, may therefore be a better way to make the universities accountable to the public.

Regions may not be directly comparable

There may be inherent differences between universities which make comparison using league tables misleading or of limited value. For example, Eastcity University specialises in teaching arts and humanities. It may be inappropriate to compare it to universities offering a wide range of courses or specialising in science and technology subjects. Similarly, it may be misleading to compare universities of different sizes or in locations in different parts of Teeland. Universities which also attract students from outside Teeland, for example, those in capital or major cities, are likely to have more access to the most able students.

Due to its capital city location, Southcity University may incur additional costs of providing facilities and have to pay staff more to reflect the higher cost of living there. It may be more appropriate to produce league tables at a lower level, like within individual cities, to make the comparisons more meaningful and eliminate the effect of regional variations such as this.

There may be differences in the way different universities collect and report performance data. These problems can be reduced by the use of consistent and enforced policies for compiling performance data.

Resources required to produce league tables

Other problems relate to the targets chosen, external influences on results and cost of collating and measuring performance for the league table.

In Veeland, there is a sizeable government department dedicated to measuring performance. The cost of collecting performance data and compiling the league tables may therefore outweigh the benefits to be gained from doing so. It will use up resources which could be used, for example, in providing additional funding to the universities themselves.

Performance measures used to create league tables may be confusing and conflicting

By having a large number of targets such as in Veeland, this may cause confusion to managers, who may not know which to focus on. Similarly, it may be difficult to decide which performance measures are the most important.

Many performance measures chosen are likely to conflict. Reducing the salaries paid to academic staff may make it harder to recruit and retain experienced and well-qualified staff, which may lead to failing to meet the universities' key objectives. Similarly, increasing the number of students per member of academic staff is unlikely to help achieve any of the universities' objectives as staff will have less time available for teaching and for engaging in high quality research.

The use of league tables may demotivate staff and students

The Teeland politician's proposed target of a 5% annual increase in the number of students entering graduate jobs sounds very challenging and may be unrealistic. This will be especially so if accompanied by a reduction in the number of academic staff and a reduction of the salaries of new recruits. If the targets are felt to be unachievable by the university leaders, they may become demotivated, and give up on trying to achieve them altogether. This will especially be the case if this is an 'all or nothing' target. A more realistic target may at least ensure that some progress is made.

Students may also become demotivated if their university ranks poorly in league tables, even if the students themselves are satisfied with the standard of education they are receiving.

Similarly some performance measures, such as the number of students entering graduate jobs, which may be highly dependent on the economic conditions in Teeland, are not entirely under the control of the university leaders. The economic conditions in Teeland will be a key factor in determining the number of graduate jobs available there. University leaders may become demotivated by this measure as well and stop trying to improve.

The relative importance of different performance measures is subjective

The weighting of the different performance measures used by the Teeland government in arriving at the provisional ranking of the universities is subjective. It is difficult to determine which measures are the most important, and hence how each should be weighted. The opinions of different stakeholders on which are the most important measures will also vary. Academic staff and students may view different measures as important compared to the providers of finance (the Teeland government) and organisations who recruit university graduates.

Determining the relative importance of different performance measures in order to publish a league table is therefore difficult. Furthermore, the measures chosen, and their relative weightings, could differ from those in other countries. This would make it difficult to benchmark performance against universities in other countries, such as Veeland.

Marking scheme		
		Marks
(a)	Description of 3Es in public sector organisations – up to 3 marks Application of 3Es – 1 mark per relevant point	
	Maximum	12
(b)	Potential benefits – up to 6 marks Problems – up to 10 marks	
	Maximum	13
Total		25

Examiner's comments

This 25-mark question was about performance measurement in the public sector (universities).

Part (a) called for advice on how to assess value for money at the universities. Many candidates made good use of the 3Es to structure their answer. A good answer also utilised the data in the scenario to illustrate their points.

Part (b) required an assessment of the benefits of league tables in improving performance of the universities and problems of their use. This part was generally fairly well done with candidates breaking their answers into two parts (benefits and problems) and illustrating their answers with specific issues between the universities in the scenario.

58   LAUDAN ADVERTISING AGENCY (LLA) (SEPT/DEC 16)

Key answer tips

Part (a) – CSFs and KPIs are commonly tested. Make sure you practise a number of questions on this area.

Parts (b) and (c) cover transfer pricing and are entirely discursive. Make sure that you are comfortable with the discussion around transfer pricing and not only the calculations. The challenge here was to ensure the answer had enough relevant points and that there was some depth to these points. An answer plan should help with this.

(a)   (i)   CSF of high quality design

The directors of LAA have identified the importance of producing high quality creative designs as a CSF to ensure successful advertising campaigns, and therefore client satisfaction. It is likely that having this as a CSF will help LAA achieve its objective to 'delight clients with the quality of work', as creative design is an important part of the service which LAA provides.

It is not clear, however, whether this CSF will help achieve the second of LAA's objectives to provide excellent value for money. It may be that other agencies produce a similar quality of work, but charge a lower price. Alternatively, the quality of LAA's design work may exceed that required by the client, who will be unlikely, therefore, to perceive it as good value for money.

Identifying this CSF will not directly help achieve the stated objective of providing clients with access to local and specialist knowledge. External suppliers may have more specialist knowledge than LAA can realistically replicate in its own design department.

The relationship between the quality of the creative design and the clients' perception of its value for money will determine whether the fourth objective, to have returning clients, will be achieved or not. All other things being equal, high quality design work will probably make clients more likely to return. Other aspects of LAA's service though, such as designing effective advertising campaigns and negotiating competitive rates for media buying, may be at least as important to the client.

(ii)   KPI to buy 90% internally

Setting a KPI should lead managers to try and achieve this target, as they are appraised (and presumably rewarded) according to their performance against the target.

Having this target will only help achieve the objective of delighting clients if the quality of the design done internally exceeds that done by third party external designers. Though LAA has set up the 'centre for design excellence', this does not automatically mean the quality of work is any better than external agencies.

Encouraging managers to buy creative services internally does not necessarily help achieve the objective of giving value for money for clients. Managers at both B and C have indicated that the prices charged by the in-house design department are significantly higher than other agencies in the market. The use of the internal design department may not be best value for the client.

Encouraging the use of internal services may not help achieve LAA's third objective to offer specialist and local knowledge to clients. The design department is based entirely in Geeland and may not meet the needs of clients in other countries. The manager of B has already commented that the department did not understand the requirements of consumers in Veeland. This is also inconsistent with the objectives to delight clients and to have them return to LAA.

Similarly, managers in A have also commented that the internal department did not have specialist knowledge to meet the needs of a new client. Again, encouraging managers to use the internal department seems contrary to the objectives of providing clients with specialist knowledge in order to delight them and to have them as return customers.

(b) Transfer pricing policy

Autonomy of the subsidiaries

The purposes of a transfer pricing policy are to encourage subsidiaries' autonomy, facilitate performance evaluation and to promote overall goal congruence with the aim of LAA to maximise shareholder wealth.

As the three subsidiaries are profit centres, they will tend to make decisions which maximise their own profit. This may be at the expense of the other subsidiaries. By charging a higher transfer price to B and C for design services, A will increase its own revenue and also the costs for B and C. This may also be at the expense of LAA as a whole, for example, as C's client was unhappy by the high charges levied by A.

A transfer pricing policy helps to prevent subsidiaries from acting in an entirely self-interested way where this may not be in the best interests of LAA as a whole. Though a transfer pricing policy should promote autonomy of the subsidiaries, LAA's head office should have the power to impose a transfer price to maintain goal congruence across the organisation. This is not currently happening, and the high transfer prices charged for design services are causing dissatisfaction.

Both B and C have commented that they have spent large amounts of time trying to negotiate transfer prices with A. This is a waste of managers' time. The ability of head office to impose a transfer price, or the existence of a clear transfer pricing policy, would allow managers more time to deal with other key aspects of the business, such as ensuring client satisfaction.

Performance measurement in the three subsidiaries

A transfer pricing policy will enable the performance of the individual subsidiaries to be fairly measured. If the policy is unfair, for example, the gross margin at subsidiary C was reduced by the seemingly excessive transfer prices charged by A, managers' motivation will be reduced, especially if this reduces the subsidiaries' managers' rewards.

Setting clear, transparent and understandable transfer prices

Managers at B have complained that the basis for setting the transfer price from A is unclear. A transfer pricing policy should ensure that the basis for setting the prices is transparent, straightforward and well understood by managers so that they do not see prices as being set unfairly and thus become demotivated.

The basis for the prices set between subsidiaries in different countries should also be clear about how exchange rate movements are reflected in the transfer price, so that managers' performance is not appraised on factors which are outside their control.

Also, the transfer pricing policy for transfers between different countries should ensure that the prices are likely to be acceptable to the local tax authorities. The tax authorities in Veeland, where B is located, are already investigating the transfer prices charged by A. This is presumably because the authorities suspect that the transfer price may be set at an artificially high level in order to reduce tax paid on profits earned in Veeland. Having a clear transfer pricing policy may help to demonstrate that B is operating within relevant taxation laws and is acting ethically in setting a fair transfer price. As the internal design department has no external customers, then it may be preferable to operate it as a separate cost centre and make all transfers at marginal cost.

Tutorial note

An approach which addressed the question based on the aims of a transfer pricing system, i.e. encourage autonomy, facilitate performance evaluation and promote goal congruence, would have been acceptable.

(c) **Advantages of setting transfer prices on the basis of market value**

Transfer prices on the basis of market value reflect the prices of purchasing creative design services on the open market. Both buying and selling subsidiaries will know what the market price is and be able to compare this to the price they are paying or charging internally.

Where subsidiaries have autonomy to negotiate their own transfer prices, in order to maximise the performance of the individual subsidiaries, the transfer price agreed is likely to reflect market price. The buyer will be unwilling to pay more than the price it can pay on the open market. The seller will be unwilling to charge less to sell internally than can be obtained on the open market. This encourages efficiency in A, which has to compete with external suppliers of creative design services.

Where a market value transfer price is used, it will usually be beneficial for buyer and seller, as well as for LAA as a whole, to transfer internally. This is because selling and administration costs overall for both parties are reduced, and the buyer should get better customer service and reliability of supply by buying internally.

The transfer price charged by A currently includes an allowance for marketing costs and bad debts. These are unlikely to be incurred where internal transfers are made. The costs savings may be shared by both parties and the transfer price reduced to a level below the market value. This lower transfer price is known as the adjusted market price.

If the transfer price charged by A is calculated on a different basis from market value, which appears to be the case as A's prices are higher than the market rates, the subsidiaries will waste time arguing over the transfer price. This current approach may improve the subsidiaries' own performance, but this is not in the best interests of LAA overall.

Disadvantages of using market price

The use of external market price will only be the optimal transfer price when a perfectly competitive external market exists. For example, though creative services can be purchased on the open market, those services may not be identical with those provided internally. Subsidiary A had to use a third party design agency for its new client as it did not have the industry knowledge to do the work itself. In this case, there may not be an equivalent service available internally to those available externally, and vice versa. There may therefore be no realistic option to buy on the open market in this situation and the use of an external market price as a transfer price would be inappropriate.

The market price may be temporary, changing according to capacity of the service providers, changes in economic circumstances, or in the case of LAA, short-term variations in the exchange rate. In which case, the transfer price would need to be frequently changed if it were to continue to reflect market conditions. This would be time consuming and probably confusing to the subsidiaries' managers.

Where allowance is made in the transfer price for the reduced costs, for example, of marketing and bad debts, it may be difficult to agree an adjusted market price which is acceptable to both A and the subsidiary purchasing design services from A.

	Marking scheme		
			Marks
(a)	Discussion of CSF with objectives – up to 6 marks		
	Discussion of KPI with objectives – up to 6 marks		
		Maximum	8
(b)	Each relevant point – 1 mark		
		Maximum	9
(c)	Benefits of a market value approach – up to 6 marks		
	Problems with a market value approach – up to 6 marks		
		Maximum	8
Total			25

Examiner's comments

This 25-mark question asked about how stated CSFs and KPIs might help the entity achieve its stated objectives followed by a consideration of the need for a transfer pricing system then a recommendation as to whether market value transfer pricing was appropriate.

Part a) was done quite badly with many candidates focusing on the areas they felt the entity should specialise in or on actions that the company would need to undertake in order to be successful. This is an analysis of business performance, not on whether the CSFs and KPIs are appropriate measures that help the entity in their overall management of performance.

Part b) tended to see candidates scoring better: the scenario was rich with data as to how the transfer of goods between different divisions was causing many problems in terms of performance management, autonomy and the achievement of overall entity objectives and most candidates were adept at highlighting where those areas specifically were and relating it to the theory of transfer pricing.

Part c) asked for a specific focus on one area of transfer pricing and in this area it was clear that candidates were lacking in technical knowledge. Many could explain the basic technique but did not advise as to whether it should be used or not: such a suggestion involves an in-depth analysis of the advantages and disadvantages of this technique relative to the scenario and very few candidates engaged in this level of analysis. Also common was an explanation/definition of all types of transfer pricing. This is irrelevant to the question in two ways: a) what was presented were mere definitions that contained neither discussion nor recommendation and b) it did not address what the question was looking for, which was a specific analysis of the relevance of one technique to the scenario depicted. Future candidates are advised again to focus on the specific requirement of the question.

59   THE HEALTH AND FITNESS GROUP (HFG) (JUN 08 – AMENDED)

Key answer tips

In answering this question you must be able to calculate and a comment on ROI/RI and economic value added (EVA).

Candidates are required to calculate the sensitivity analysis, and give key arguments of writers such as Fitzgerald and Moon's (building block model) and application of these to the scenario.

(a)   To: **The Directors**

From: **Management Accountant**

Subject: **The performance of our three health centres**

Date: **6 June 20X8**

Further to your recent request please find below my detailed responses to the questions you have raised.

A summary of the financial performance of the three centres is shown in the following table:

Heath centre	Return on investment (%)	Residual income ($000)	Economic value added ($000)
Ayetown	23.02	180.00	42.08
Beetown	13.96	33.00	−123.27
Ceetown	18.40	187.00	−30.09

Which of the three centres is the most successful?

This very much depends on the method used to assess the performance of the three health centres. As requested, I have undertaken calculations based on three performance measures namely, return on investment (ROI), residual income (RI) and economic value added (EVA). I have included the workings for each respective calculation in an appendix to this report.

Using ROI as a measure of financial performance indicates that Ayetown is the most successful of the three centres since its ROI was 23.02% compared with the 18.40% achieved by Ceetown and the 13.96% achieved by Beetown. However, you should bear in mind that the use of ROI can be grossly misleading since it is a relative measure and ignores absolute returns. In this respect I wish to draw your attention to the fact that Beetown earned $45,000 (11.4%) more operating profit than Ayetown and Ceetown earned $397,000 (77.5%) more profit than Ayetown.

The use of RI as a measure of financial performance indicates that Ceetown is the best performing centre, generating $187,000 of residual income. It is worth observing that Ayetown was not far behind Ceetown in terms of generating residual income of $180,000. However, Beetown only managed to generate $33,000 of residual income.

EVA™ is a specific type of residual income calculation which has attracted a considerable amount of attention during recent years. Economic Value Added equals after-tax operating profit minus the (after-tax) weighted average cost of capital multiplied by total assets minus current liabilities. EVA™ substitutes the following numbers in residual income calculations:

(a)   Income is equal to after-tax profits

(b)   A required rate of return is equal to the after-tax weighted average cost of capital; and

(c)   Investment is equal to total assets minus current liabilities.

Ayetown has the highest EVA. Indeed, it is the only centre which has a positive EVA. In common with RI, EVA charges managers for the cost of making investments in long-term assets and working capital. Value will only be created in circumstances where post-tax operating profit exceeds the cost of investing the required capital.

In order to improve EVA, managers need to earn more operating profit using the same amount of capital, or invest capital in higher-earning projects. The use of EVA is often preferred to RI because it takes into account tax effects of investment decisions whereas pre-tax residual income measures do not.

(b)   The ROI of Beetown is currently 13.96%. In order to obtain an ROI of 20%, operating profit would need to increase to (20% × $3,160,000) = $632,000, based on the current level of net assets. Three alternative ways in which a target ROI of 20% could be achieved for the Beetown centre are as follows:

1   Attempts could be made to increase revenue by attracting more clients while keeping invested capital and operating profit per $ of revenue constant. Revenue would have to increase to $2,361,644, assuming that the current level of profitability is maintained and fixed costs remain unchanged. The current rate of contribution to revenue is $2,100,000 – $567,000 = $1,533,000/ $2,100,000 = 73%. Operating profit needs to increase by $191,000 in order to achieve an ROI of 20%. Therefore, revenue needs to increase by $191,000/0.73 = $261,644 = 12.46%.

Or alternatively 632,000 less current level of 441,000 = a 191,000 increase.

Contribution is uncertain therefore 191,000/1,533,000 *100 = 12.46%

2   Attempts could be made to decrease the level of operating costs by, for example, increasing the efficiency of maintenance operations. This would have the effect of increasing operating profit per $ of revenue. This would require that revenue and invested capital were kept constant. Total operating costs would need to fall by $191,000 in order to obtain an ROI of 20%. This represents a percentage decrease of 191,000/1,659,000 = 11.5%. If fixed costs were truly fixed, then variable costs would need to fall to a level of $376,000, which represents a decrease of 33.7%.

Or alternatively variable costs are uncertain therefore 191,000/567,000 *100 = 33.7%

3   Attempts could be made to decrease the net asset base of HFG by, for example, reducing debtor balances and/or increasing creditor balances, while keeping turnover and operating profit per $ of revenue constant. Net assets would need to fall to a level of ($441,000/0.2) = $2,205,000, which represents a percentage decrease amounting to $3,160,000 − $2,205,000 = 955,000/ 3,160,000 = 30.2%.

Or alternatively as net assets would need to fall to 2,205,000 this is a decrease of 955,000. Net assets are uncertain therefore 955,000/3,160,000* 100 = 30.2%.

(c)   The marketing director is certainly correct in recognising that success is dependent on levels of service quality provided by HFG to its clients. However, whilst the number of complaints is an important performance measure, it needs to be used with caution. The nature of a complaint is, very often, far more indicative of the absence, or a lack, of service quality. For example, the fact that 50 clients complained about having to wait for a longer time than they expected to access gymnasium equipment is insignificant when compared to an accident arising from failure to maintain properly a piece of gymnasium equipment. Moreover, the marketing director ought to be aware that the absolute number of complaints may be misleading as much depends on the number of clients serviced during any given period.

Thus, in comparing the number of complaints received by the three centres then a relative measure of complaints received per 1,000 client days would be far more useful than the absolute number of complaints received.

The marketing director should also be advised that the number of complaints can give a misleading picture of the quality of service provision since individuals have different levels of willingness to complain in similar situations.

The marketing director seems to accept the current level of complaints but is unwilling to accept any increase above this level. This is not indicative of a quality-oriented organisation which would seek to reduce the number of complaints over time via a programme of 'continuous improvement'.

From the foregoing comments one can conclude that it would be myopic to focus on the number of client complaints as being the only performance measure necessary to measure the quality of service provision. Other performance measures which may indicate the level of service quality provided to clients by HFG are as follows:

- Staff responsiveness assumes critical significance in service industries. Hence the time taken to resolve client queries by health centre staff is an important indicator of the level of service quality provided to clients.

- Staff appearance may be viewed as reflecting the image of the centres.

- The comfort of bedrooms and public rooms including facilities such as air-conditioning, tea/coffee-making and cold drinks facilities, and office facilities such as e-mail, facsimile and photocopying.

- The availability of services such as the time taken to gain an appointment with a dietician or fitness consultant.

- The cleanliness of all areas within the centres will enhance the reputation of HFG. Conversely, unclean areas will potentially deter clients from making repeat visits and/or recommendations to friends, colleagues etc.

- The presence of safety measures and the frequency of inspections made regarding gymnasium equipment within the centres and compliance with legislation are of paramount importance in businesses like that of HFG.

- The achievement of target reductions in weight that have been agreed between centre consultants and clients.

APPENDIX

Calculations of ROI:

ROI:	(A) Operating profit	(B) Total assets less current liabilities	(A) ÷ (C) Return on investment (%)
Ayetown	396	1,720	23.02
Beetown	441	3,160	13.96
Ceetown	703	3,820	18.40

Calculations of RI

RI:	(A) Operating profit ($000)	(B) Required rate return	(C) Total assets ($000)	(D) = (B) × (C) Required return on investment ($000)	(E) = (A) – (D) Residual income ($000)
Ayetown	396	12%	1,800	216	180
Beetown	441	12%	3,400	408	33
Ceetown	703	12%	4,300	516	187

Calculations of EVA

EVA	(A) Pre-tax operating profit ($000)	(B) = (A) × 70% Post-tax operating profit ($000)	(C) WACC	(D) Total assets less current liabilities ($000)	(E) = (C) × (D) WACC × (ta – cl) ($000)	(F) = (B) – (E) EVA ($000)
Ayetown	396	277.2	13.67%	1,720	235.12	42.08
Beetown	441	308.7	13.67%	3,160	431.97	–123.27
Ceetown	703	492.1	13.67%	3,820	522.19	–30.09

Calculation of weighted average cost of capital (WACC) for use in calculation of EVA is as follows:

	Market value ($000)			
equity	9,000	Ke	0.15	1,350
debt	1,800	Kd	0.07	126
	———			———
	10,800			1,476
WACC = 1,476/10,800				13.67%

Note that the cost of equity is 15% and the after-tax cost of debt is

$$\frac{(100 - 30)}{100} \times 10\% = 7\%$$

	Marking scheme		
			Marks
(a)	Calculations:		
	ROI		1.5
	RI		1.5
	EVA		4
	Comments (on merit) re ROCE/RI/EVA		9
			—
		Maximum	**14**
			—
(b)	Comments (on merit):		
	% changes in Turnover, Total costs, Net assets	3 × 2	**6**
(c)	Comments (on merit):		
	Success/quality relationship		1
	Number of complaints as performance measure		2
	Reduce existing level of complaints		1
	Other measures		2
			—
		Maximum	**5**
			—
Total			**25**
			—

Examiner's comments

The requirement of part (a) revealed a very large number of candidates who could not provide a commentary on, and/or a detailed calculation of economic value added (EVA). Moreover, few candidates were able to calculate correctly the sensitivity analysis calculations required by part (b) of the question. In dealing with requirement (c) many candidates simply summarised the key arguments of writers such as Fitzgerald and Moon but failed to apply these to the scenario thereby producing answers that would be of little value to readers of this part of the report.

E – PERFORMANCE EVALUATION AND CORPORATE FAILURE

60   ROYAL BOTANICAL GARDENS

Key answer tips

This question tests your knowledge of the balance scorecard, how to apply the model and the process employed to develop the scorecard for the botanical gardens. It is not a past exam question but serves as useful revision.

The scenario has a lot of very important information which can be applied to your answer. Ensure you go through each perspective and relate them to the botanical gardens.

(a)   **Board briefing**

The concept of the Balanced Scorecard was introduced by Kaplan & Norton in the early Nineties to recognise what they considered to be two primary deficiencies in the implementation phase of many corporate plans.

First, they recognised that, although many organisations measure performance ratios these are primarily focused on historical figures and may have little to do with future success. Although such ratios are important they do not address important aspects of future strategy, particularly those concerned with the satisfaction of customers and their loyalty, organisational learning and the commitment of employees.

Additionally, they believed that, although strategic initiatives were formulated, these often had little impact on organisational behaviour or performance since they were not translated into measures which management and staff could understand and use.

Moving away from purely financial measures they claimed that what really mattered was the strategy implementation process and described **three processes**:

1   Management – how the leader runs the organisation, how decisions are made and implemented

2   Business – how products are designed, orders fulfilled, customer satisfaction achieved, for example

3   Work – how work is operationalised, purchased, stored, and manufactured.

The Balanced Scorecard was developed to address any deficiencies in these areas and encompasses **four key principles**:

1   Translating the vision through clarifying and gaining consensus

2   Communicating and linking by setting goals and establishing rewards for success

3   Business planning to align objectives, allocate resources and establish milestones

4   Feedback and learning to review the subsequent performance against the plan.

They recognised that there should be, on every scorecard, **four perspectives**:

1   Financial perspective – 'To succeed financially, how should we appear to our shareholders?'

2   Customer perspective – 'To achieve our vision, how should we appear to our customers?'

3   Internal perspective – 'To satisfy our shareholders and customers, what business processes must we excel at?'

4   Future – the innovation and learning perspective. 'To achieve our vision, how will we sustain our ability to change and improve?'

For each perspective, a number of objectives, appropriate measures and target levels of performance together with initiatives for their achievement, would be defined. Thus the measures chosen under each perspective would reflect the strategic imperatives under which the organisation operates at the time.

Although the Balanced Scorecard was originally developed for commercial organisations, over the last few years it has found increasing use in the not-for-profit sector, where the same perspectives are equally important, but measured in a different way.

The Royal Botanical Gardens would benefit from the introduction of a Balanced Scorecard by:

•   Placing the whole organisation in a learning process, aligning everyone to strategy in a single framework. The Balanced Scorecard has potential to improve itself over time by testing cause – effect hypotheses, refinement of the metrics selected, the measurement processes employed, resource allocation and identification of suitable initiatives.

•   Encouraging more rational budgeting in a world of rapid change where resource allocations are based on performance and systematic, fact-based management replaces intuition.

•   Encouraging and facilitating the anticipation of future outcomes and their impact on the organisation.

•   Raising the visibility of what is happening, prioritising what most needs to be changed and helping to identify best practices.

In addition to the internal, managerial, benefits that the balanced scorecard can bring to the organisation it has the potential to demonstrate to external stakeholders that their mandates and objectives are being met. In this particular case, where the Government will need to be convinced to maintain, or even increase, the grant in aid, the measures incorporated can demonstrate that objectives over and above value for money are being achieved. It would make it easier for the Garden's negotiators to demonstrate the achievements in terms of assistance to education, industry, tourism and national prestige.

However, it must be recognised that it requires sustained effort to implement fully and requires a high level of organisational commitment.

Its introduction may create fear and uncertainty since it raises both visibility and accountability. As with all other performance measurement techniques it will not solve problems – only strategy and initiatives and their successful implementation can do that.

(b)   It is important that the Balanced Scorecard is developed by a team of individuals and the commitment of the senior management is obtained. The team should be cross organisational and contain representatives of all functional groups within the Gardens.

The main tasks of the teams are as follows:

- Identify strategic themes

- Define perspectives and desired outcomes

- Create a strategy map

- Define performance measures and targets

- Develop strategic initiatives to achieve targets.

Once the team has been established the mission statement should be analysed to identify the strategic themes that are encompassed by the statement. This will provide a more specific focus for planning.

For instance the following themes, among others, might be distilled from the mission statement:

- Knowledge and understanding through research

- Knowledge and understanding through display

- Conservation by living and preserved collections

- Belonging to the Nation.

The next task will be to define the perspectives – the diverse ways of looking at the organisation from the perspective of different stakeholders. Also to define the meaning of mission success for each perspective and strategic theme.

The different stakeholders for The Royal Botanical Gardens are many and would include, for example:

1   Financial perspective – government and research foundations that fund some of the work

2   Customer perspective – universities who use the facilities

3   Internal perspective – botanists using the facilities for research

4   Future – the innovation and learning perspective – educationalists attached to the Gardens.

Within the strategic theme of knowledge and understanding through research, these perspectives might lead to the following desired outcomes:

1   Financial perspective – government funders would look for value for money in the collection of novel plants and materials and the production of research papers.

2   Customer perspective – universities who deal with the Gardens would look for seamless access to any plants and materials they required in a cost-effective way.

3   Internal perspective – the botanists who work within the Gardens would look for support in their research so that they can work productively and advance the boundaries of science.

4 Future – the innovation and learning perspective – the educationalists might wish to raise the profile of the facilities and attract people to this area of study and would look to find innovative ways to bring people in.

For each strategic theme, the team would need to develop a chain of causes and effects that would be expected to lead to the desired outcomes. Each of these chains would be mapped onto a strategy map. Systems dynamics techniques would help in this area.

For instance considering the provision of samples to Universities from a future perspective would mean enhancing information management, improving the employee climate and changing the skills gap. The botanists who work in the Gardens might see themselves in competition with the Universities. A co-operative approach would improve relationships, while seeking citation or acknowledgement in any research published. From the internal perspective looking for process efficiencies in picking and despatch would lead to more cost effective operations satisfying the financial perspective, while the enhanced service levels would, from the customer perspective, make them more likely to acknowledge assistance in research publications.

The definition of performance measures and targets would be achieved by answering the question 'how will we know if this theme/desired outcome is being achieved?' and deciding how each goal should be measured for example surveys or other means of data collection. If available, baseline data should be examined to set schedules and targets for improvement.

For instance, measures for the theme/outcome of provision of samples to Universities might include:

- Financial – cost per sample provided, revenue generated from advice and consultancy

- Customer – satisfaction surveys, amount of repeat business

- Internal – citations in published research, published research

- Future – new universities seeking samples; reduction in number of unsatisfied requests.

61 BLA (DEC 03 – AMENDED)

Key answer tips

Part (a) is standard bookwork. Part (b) requires you to comment on the performance of BLA using the information supplied and the dimensions from Fitzgerald & Moon's building block model.

Part (c) asks for three factors in determining standards i.e. ownership, achievability and fairness. This is core book knowledge.

Tutorial note

The question was set by a previous examiner but serves as good revision of the building block model.

(a) **Fitzgerald and Moon's building block approach**

The building block model is an analysis that aims to improve the performance measurement systems of service businesses such as BLA. It suggests that the performance system should be based on three concepts of dimensions, standards and rewards.

Dimensions fall into two categories: downstream results (competitive and financial performance) and upstream determinants (quality of service, flexibility, resource utilisation and innovation) of those results. These are the areas that yield specific performance metrics for a company.

Standards are the targets set for the metrics chosen from the dimensions measured. These must be such that those being measured take ownership of them, possibly by participating in the process of setting the standard. The standard must be achievable in order to motivate the employee or partner. The standards must be fairly set, based on the environment for each business unit so that those in the lower growth areas of, say, audit do not feel prejudiced when compared to the growing work in business advisory.

Rewards are the motivators for the employees to work towards the standards set. The reward system should be clearly understood by the staff and ensure their motivation. The rewards should be related to areas of responsibility that the staff member controls in order to achieve that motivation.

(b) **Downstream results**

(i) **Financial performance**

Summary Income statement for the year ended 31 October 20X3

	Budget $000	Actual $000
Fee income (W1)	6,075	6,300
Costs:		
Consultants' salaries (W2)	2,025	2,025
Bonus (W3)		90
		2,115
Other operating costs	2,550	2,805
Subcontract payments (W4)	0	18
	4,575	4,938
Net profit	1,500	1,362

Workings:

(W1) Fee income

    Budget   40,500 chargeable consultations × $150

    Actual   42,000 chargeable consultations × $150

(W2) Consultants' salaries

    45 consultants × $45,000

(W3) Bonus

    40% of $(6,300,000 − 6,075,000)

(W4) Subcontract payments

    120 consultations × $150

It is clear that BLA has not performed as well as expected during the year to 31 October 20X3. Whilst client income is above budget, other operating expenses reached a level which is more than 10% higher than the budget for the year, and thus it would be extremely useful to have a more detailed breakdown of other operating expenses for the year. Consultants have earned an aggregate bonus of $90,000 (42,000 − 40,500) × $150 × 40% in respect of activity above budgeted levels. Payments to subcontractors amounted to $18,000. Actual profit amounts to $1,362,000 against a budget of $1,500,000. It would be extremely useful to see the results of the previous two years in order to assess whether there are any discernible trends in revenues and costs. The budget for the following year should be reviewed in the light of the actual performance of this year with particular reference to checking the footing of the assumptions upon which it has been prepared.

(ii) **Competitiveness**

Competitiveness may be measured in terms of market share or sales growth and the relative success in obtaining business from enquiries made by customers. The turnover of BLA for the year to 31 October 20X3 is above budget. Again it is desirable to see the results of recent years since it might well be the case that BLA has achieved steady growth which is indicative of a high level of competitiveness in future years.

BLA provided 1,200 consultations on a no-fee basis with a view to gaining new business. Also, during the year BLA consultants provided 405 non-chargeable 'remedial' consultations. Both of these non-chargeable activities might be viewed as initiatives to increase future levels of competitiveness.

It is useful to look at the extent to which BLA were successful in converting the enquiries received from both existing and new client enquiries into new business.

The percentages are as follows:

	Budget		Actual	
Conversion rate from enquiries				
New clients	(24,300/67,500)	36.0%	(22,400/84,000)	26.7%
Repeat clients	(16,200/32,400)	50.0%	(19,600/28,000)	70.0%

70% of enquiries from the existing client base resulted in additional consultancy work for BLA. This is indicative of strong customer loyalty, suggesting that existing clients are satisfied with the service provided. However, the company was unable to reform as well with regard to enquiries from potential 'first time' customers, only achieving a conversion ratio of 26.7%, which is approximately 74% of the intended number of 'first time' clients that were budgeted for. This indicates that there is probably room for improvement in the ways in which BLA deals with enquiries from prospective clients.

The company should review its marketing strategies with a view to improving its conversion ratio.

In absolute terms new business was approximately 7.8% below budget whereas repeat business was 21.0% above budget.

As regards the nature of the chargeable activities undertaken by the consultants, it can be seen that Exterior Design is 14.6% below budget, whereas Interior Design and Garden Design are 6.4% and 35.1% above budget.

Upstream results

(iii) Service quality

Quality of service is the totality of features and characteristics of the service package that bear upon its ability to satisfy client needs. Flexibility and innovation in service provision may be key determinants of service quality. To some extent the increase in the number of complaints and non-chargeable consultations associated with the remedying of those complaints is indicative of a quality problem that must be addressed. This problem needs to be investigated. BLA only provides advice to clients and only recommends contractors when asked to do so by clients. It would be interesting to see how many of the complaints related to recommendations made by BLA. Assuming consultants could have otherwise undertaken chargeable work, the revenue forgone as a consequence of the remedial consultations was $60,750. Client complaints received during the year were nearly double the budgeted level. Also the number of remedial consultations was 405 against a budgeted level of only 45, which is exactly nine times higher than budget!

Perhaps BLA should review and, if necessary, limit the amount of remedial consultancy provided to any one particular client. The business development consultations can be viewed as an innovative measure with a view to gaining additional business.

(iv) Flexibility

Flexibility may relate to the company being able to cope with flexibility of volume, delivery speed or job specification.

Hence, flexibility might be substantiated by looking at the mix of work undertaken by the consultants during the year. The following table gives a comparison of actual and budgeted consultations by category of consultant.

Consultations by category of consultancy service

	Budget %	Actual %	Increase/(decrease)
Exterior Design	40.0	32.9%	(7.1%)
Interior Design	40.0	41.0%	1.0%
Garden Design	40.0	26.1%	6.1%

It is a deliberate policy of BLA to retain 45 consultants thereby maintaining flexibility to meet increasing demand. The delivery speed will be increased as a consequence of the retention of consultants. It would appear that a change has occurred in the mix of consultants which may well be a response to changing market requirements. Again, it would be useful to see recent years' statistics in order to consider trends but notably garden design looks to be a growth area hence the three new consultants recruited during the year. The mix of consultants should be such that BLA can cope with a range of job specifications. The fact that links have been retained with retired consultants will give an added dimension of flexibility in times of very heavy demand upon its consultants.

(v)   Resource utilisation

Resource utilisation measures the ratio of output achieved from those resources input. In this scenario the mean number of consultations per consultant may be used as a guide.

Average consultations per consultant

	Budget	Actual	Increase/(decrease)
Exterior Design	900	922	2.4%
Interior Design	900	957	6.3%
Garden Design	900	912	1.3%

It is interesting to note that all categories of consultant are being utilised above budgeted levels. Consequently an aggregate bonus amounting to $90,000 was paid in respect of the year ended 31 October 20X3. There are potential problems if the quality of the service provision is falling. In this regard it would be useful to have more detailed analysis of the client complaints in order to ascertain whether a large proportion relate to any one category of consultancy and/or contractor. BLA has adopted an innovative approach that requires consultants to undertake non-chargeable business development consultations which have at their heart the intention of generating new business. Hence in the immediate sense there is a trade-off between resource utilisation and innovation.

(vi)   Innovation

Innovation should be viewed in terms of its impact on financial performance, competitiveness, service-quality, flexibility and resource utilisation in the short, medium and long term. Certainly the non-chargeable activity in terms of 'business development' is an innovative feature within the business of BLA, as is the non-chargeable remedial consultancy provided to clients who experience problems at the commencement of building works. The acquisition of 'state of the art' business software is by its very nature innovative.

The result of its use is reflected in the significant increase of 35.1% above budget achieved in garden design consultations. This has probably enabled BLA to differentiate its services from those of its competitors and enhance its reputation. Certainly the management of BLA will be hoping for a similar increase in business as a consequence of the use of the software by its external and interior design consultants. The management should ensure the introduction of the software has not caused the increase in the number of complaints received.

(c)   Ownership:

In establishing targets, the importance of individuals taking ownership of the standards has long been established: this is often facilitated by the adoption of a budgetary system based on employee participation.

This is also considered to be beneficial to the organisation since it alleviates, or at the very least reduces, many of the dysfunctional consequences associated with particular control models. In particular, managers who participate in the standard-setting process are more likely to accept the standards set, feel less job-related tension and have better relationships with their superiors and colleagues.

Participation does, however, provide opportunities for the introduction of budgetary slack in order that any subsequent monitoring of activities presents a favourable outcome.

Achievability:

Budgets need to be realistic enough to encourage employees to perform, but not set at levels so high that they are demotivated.

The challenge to management lies in finding the balance between what the company views as achievable and what the employee views as achievable as this often proves to be a source of organisational conflict.

Fairness:

It is important that the standards of performance measurement chosen by management facilitate a fair comparison across all similar business units and that equity is seen to prevail in measuring the performance of those units.

There may be circumstances where some business units have an inherent advantage unconnected with their own deliberate initiatives. For example, some business units will be subject to higher levels of environmental uncertainty than others. In situations where higher levels of uncertainty exist, there will be a need for greater reliance to be placed on subjective judgement in appraising performance, with consequently less reliance being placed on objective, financial data.

It would be inappropriate and inequitable to measure the performance of two completely different business contexts in an identical manner.

62   CULAM (DEC 14) (SPECIMEN 18)

Key answer tips

This question is typical of the examiner in that it does not expect you to carry out long calculations or remember complex formulae but instead focuses on the useful interpretation of calculations that have already been done.

In part (a) do not solely focus on the calculations – remember to also discuss the pros and cons of the two models.

In part (b) you should be able to come up with a handful of relevant points but be sure to relate these points to the scenario.

Part (c) is a nice requirement and you should be able to come up with some good, relevant suggestions here.

(a) The results from both models indicate that Culam is not likely to become insolvent in the next two years. However, there are good reasons to question the applicability of these models to Culam's business and so it would be dangerous to place too much reliance on these results.

A quantitative model such as those presented here identifies financial ratios which significantly differ in value between surviving and failing companies. Statistical analysis is then used to choose the weightings for these ratios in a formula for a score which can be used to identify companies which exhibit the features of previously failing companies. Obviously, the company being analysed must be similar to those being used to build the model for the results to be relevant.

The Altman Z-score was originally developed in the late 1960s and was based on data from US companies, primarily in the manufacturing sector. Therefore, there are three reasons to question the applicability of such data to Culam.

1   The world economy has changed significantly since Altman's original work. The data for this model is now nearly 50 years old.

2   The economy of the USA may not reflect the market in which Culam works.

3   The mining sector is not like general manufacturing, for example, it is highly capital intensive with long periods of no revenue generation.

The Q-score model was based on recent data from Teeland businesses. As for the Z-score, Culam is not likely to be appropriately modelled by such data. The problems are:

1   The Q-score is based on data for Teeland listed companies and Culam is a mining company with an unusual pattern of revenue and costs supplying a global market. It is therefore unlikely to be similar to the companies on the small Teeland exchange, both in its markets and its business model.

2   If Teeland's exchange is small, there may not be much data from failing companies on which to base the model.

Neither of the models addresses factors which may have a large impact on Culam's survival such as world commodity prices and foreign exchange rates.

(b) The lifecycle issues for Culam relate to the long timescale (23 years) for development and use of a mine and the uneven cash flows over this lifecycle.

The initial development phase of two years will require large capital investments with no revenue being generated. There is then a 20-year revenue-generating phase followed by a final year of decommissioning costs with no revenue.

This will impact on the Z-score by making the score very volatile as the mines go through the three phases of their lives.

- During the development phase, total assets are growing while revenue is zero. This will mean that the X5 variable will be zero and the X1 and X3 variables will be falling, thus lowering the score.

- During the working phase of the mine, the total assets will be static or falling (depending on the accounting for reserves) while the revenue is high.

- Finally, during the decommissioning phase, the assets will be falling and again there will be no revenue, so a low Z-score could be expected.

The fact that Culam has only four mines will mean that the phase of any one mine will have a significant impact on the score. If two mines are in development at the same time, then there is likely to be a large effect in lowering the Z-score. It will be the scale of the financial resources which Culam can call on over the life of the mines which will dictate its survival.

(c) The type of action which Culam's board can take to reduce the risk of collapse of the business is to grow the business by buying or developing many more mines, so that the failure of any one project does not bring down the business. Staggering the development of the mines would also help to address this issue.

The board could also seek to alter the proportion of revenues generated from long-term contracts rather than the more volatile spot market. By signing over more of the production to contracts of fixed revenues, the business's cash flows will be more reliable.

The board could learn from the mistakes of their competitors by avoiding over-priced acquisitions or other large project failures by performing suitable due diligence and risk analysis in advance of the investment.

The board could be proactive in managing other major risks by using hedging techniques in order to reduce volatile revenues due to:

- foreign exchange rate changes when the costs of the mines will all be denominated in local currency; and
- commodity prices on the spot market.

Although the use of such techniques will be limited by the availability of long-term hedging contracts.

Tutorial note

This solution may look short (of ink) but it is an illustration of how a good compact answer can look. More work in description and justification would have to be done to gain credit for more obvious advice such as increase revenue' or 'reduce costs'.

Marking scheme		
		Marks
(a)	1 mark for general interpretation of calculation	
	4 marks for general description of how a quantitative model works	
	Up to 9 for problems with the models	
	Maximum	10
(b)	2 marks for general issues	
	1 mark for description of lifecycle	
	6 marks for impact of lifecycle on Z-score	
	Maximum	7
(c)	Up to 2 marks on each improvement – 1 mark for the description of an improvement and 1 mark for the justification	
	For example:	
	Increase size of business – portfolio effect	
	Use of fixed price contracts to avoid volatile commodity prices	
	Use of FX hedging to avoid revenue volatility	
	Learn from the mistakes of others – avoid big project failures	
	Maximum	8
Total		25

63 PERFORMANCE PYRAMID (JUN 06 – AMENDED)

Key answer tips

The question draws on a variety of topics relating to concepts of performance management in a service environment. The key point to appreciate is the distinction between effectiveness (the achievement of required outcomes at minimum cost) and efficiency (achieving maximum output from given inputs). A good answer to this question demonstrates an appreciation of the range of financial and non-financial performance metrics that can be used to measure both efficiency and effectiveness, and the need to take account of qualitative issues as well.

(a) (i) EAJ

Financial performance and competitiveness

Summary Income Statement for the year ended 31 May 20X6

	Budget $000s	Actual $000s
Fee income:		
New	2,940	3,150
Existing	6,930	8,085
	9,870	11,235
Costs:		
Consultants salaries	5,000	5,000
Bonus		294
Other operating costs	3,600	4,500
Total costs	8,600	9,794
Net profit	1,270	1,441

It is clear that EAJ performed well during the year ended 31 May 20X6. Fee income was 13.8% above budget, in spite of the fact that other operating costs were 25% higher than budget.

The management of EAJ should investigate what caused this significant overspend and therefore it would be extremely useful to have a more detailed breakdown of other operating costs.

Consultants earned an aggregate bonus of (($11,235,000 – $9,870,000) – (450 × 2 × $700)) × 40% = $294,000 in respect of activity above budgeted levels. Actual net profit was $1,441,000 against a budgeted net profit of $1,270,000. In spite of the overspend on other operating costs, EAJ is achieving rapid growth in levels of net profit. In 20X5 (its second year of trading) net profit was 50% higher than in its first year. In 20X6 net profit has increased by 60.1% over 20X5 net profit.

EAJ could measure its competitiveness in terms of sales growth and the relative success in obtaining business from enquiries made by customers.

In assessing sales growth it needs to be borne in mind that this is the 'start-up' phase of EAJ. However, EAJ increased sales revenue from $4,000,000 in its first year to $11,235,000 in its third year of operation, which is very impressive. EAJ's success in obtaining business from enquiries made by customers for the year ended 31 May 20X6 is shown in the following table.

Conversion rate from enquiries:	Budget	Actual
New clients	35.0%	30.0%
Repeat clients	50.0%	60.0%

60% of enquiries from existing clients resulted in additional chargeable consultancy days for EAJ. This may well indicate that EAJ is starting to build customer loyalty despite the fact that the organisation has only been in existence for three years. With regard to enquiries from potential 'first time' clients, EAJ achieved a conversion ratio of 30.0%, against a budgeted conversion ratio of 35% that was budgeted. However, in absolute terms new business was approximately 7.1% above budget whilst existing business was 16.7% business above budget.

As regards the nature of the chargeable activities undertaken by the consultants it can be seen that Distribution software implementation was 20.6% below budget, whereas Accounting and Manufacturing implementations were 26.2% and 33.3% respectively above budget.

EAJ provided 300 consultations on a no-fee basis with a view to gaining new business. Also, during the year EAJ consultants provided non-chargeable 'remedial' consultations. Both of these non-chargeable activities might be viewed as initiatives aimed at increasing future levels of competitiveness. However, each remedial consultation could be viewed as inefficiency.

(ii)   External effectiveness

In order to achieve 'external effectiveness' EAJ has to satisfy its customers. Customer satisfaction may be defined as meeting customer expectations. The quality of service provision and delivery are operational criteria that can be used to monitor levels of customer satisfaction. To some extent, the increase in the number of complaints and non-chargeable consultations associated with the remedying of those complaints is indicative of a quality problem that must be investigated and addressed. In particular the number of chargeable days for implementation of distribution applications is significantly below budget and it might well be the case that poor service 'delivery' is giving rise to the need for remedial consultations.

Assuming consultants could otherwise have undertaken chargeable work at a rate of $700, revenue amounting to $630,000 was lost as a consequence of having to undertake remedial consultations. It would appear that EAJ does not budget for complaints.

A summary of client complaints received by EAJ is shown in the following table:

Year ended 31 May	20X4	20X5	20X6
Number of complaints	160	225	280
Number of clients	320	500	700
Complaint: client ratio (%)	50%	45%	40%

Whilst it can be seen that the complaint: client ratio is improving, it should be recognised that this may be due to the fact that the size of the client base is increasing very rapidly. Such a trend might be expected during the first few years of operation, especially in a business such as EAJ.

The harsh fact is that the number of complaints is increasing in absolute terms. In order to be able to better assess customer satisfaction, complaints need to be analysed since the nature of complaints may well be of far more relevance than the number of complaints!

The number of customer support desk queries resolved is improving; i.e. 20X4 (85%); 20X5 (95%) and 20X6 (99%). This will further enhance the level of customer satisfaction. The fact that the number of accounts in dispute is falling whilst the number of clients is increasing significantly on a year-on-year basis may also be an indication of improved customer satisfaction. The increase in the number of new customers and the increased revenues generated per customer are probably indicators of increasing levels of customer satisfaction.

(iii)   **Internal efficiency**

Internal efficiency may be assessed by reference to flexibility and productivity. Flexibility relates to the business operating system as a whole whilst productivity relates to the management of resources such as, in the case of EAJ, consultants time.

Flexibility might be substantiated by looking at the mix of work undertaken by the consultants during the year. The following table gives a comparison of actual and budgeted consultations by category of consultant.

Consultations by category of consultant:

	Budget %	Actual %	Increase/(decrease)
Accounting	40.0	44.2	4.2%
Distribution	30.0	20.8	(9.2%)
Manufacturing	30.0	35.0	16.7%

It is a deliberate policy of EAJ to retain 100 Consultants thereby maintaining flexibility to meet increasing demand. The delivery speed will be increased as a consequence of the retention of consultants. It would appear that a change has occurred in the mix of consultants which may well be a response to changing market requirements. Again, it would be useful to see recent year's statistics in order to consider trends.

Productivity can be measured by the ratio of output achieved from those resources input. In this scenario the average number of chargeable days per consultant may be used as a guide.

	Average number of chargeable days per consultant		
	Budget	Actual	Increase/(decrease)
Accounting	168	212	26.2%
Distribution	168	160	(4.8%)
Manufacturing	168	192	14.3%

The implementation of distribution application software was more than 20% below budget. Chargeable distribution consultancy days based on the original budget of 168 days per consultant would produce a total of 4,200 chargeable days which is 200 more than the actual levels. Again this might be indicative of a quality problem.

'Cycle time' would appear to be improving as evidenced by the increasing number of on-time implementations as well as the reduction in the implementation time of each application. In this respect EAJ needs to be certain that the reduction in implementation time has not caused a diminution in the quality of service delivery. Consequently an aggregate bonus amounting to $294,000 was paid in respect of the year ended 31 May 2006. EAJ needs to ensure that the incentive provided by the bonus is not causing a loss of 'internal efficiency'.

With regard to the bonus paid to consultants then it is questionable whether the bonus should be shared equally by consultants since chargeable activity levels clearly vary between categories of consultant.

Tutorial note

Such a detailed analysis of performance is not representative of the current examiner's style. However, this requirement does serve as useful practise of such analysis and this may form a smaller part of an exam question.

(b) Particularly at higher levels of management, non-financial information is often not in numerical terms, but qualitative, or soft, rather than quantitative. Qualitative information often represents opinions of individuals and user groups. Decisions often appear to have been made on the basis of quantitative information; however qualitative considerations often influence the final choice, even if this is not explicit. In both decision making and control, managers should be aware that an information system may provide a limited or distorted picture of what is actually happening. In many situations, sensitivity has to be used in interpreting the output of an information system.

Conventional information systems are usually designed to carry quantitative information and are sometimes less able to convey qualitative issues. However the impact of a decreased output requirement on staff morale is something that may be critical but it is not something that an information system would automatically report.

The following difficulties in measurement and interpretation mean that qualitative factors are often ignored:

- Information in the form of opinions is difficult to measure and interpret. It also requires more analysis.
- Qualitative information may be incomplete.
- Qualitative aspects are often interdependent and it can be difficult to separate the impact of different factors.
- Evaluating qualitative information is subjective, as it is not in terms of numbers – there are no objective formulae as there are with financial measures.
- The cost of collecting and improving qualitative information may be very high.

Despite the challenges it presents, there may be ways of improving the use of qualitative information. Where it is important to make use of qualitative information, it is essential to ensure that users are aware of any assumptions made in analysis and of the difficulties involved in measuring and counting it. It is sometimes possible to quantify issues which are initially qualitative, by looking at its impact. For example when looking at service quality it is possible to consider the cost of obtaining the same quality of service elsewhere. Even if it is not possible to quantify issues precisely, attempting to do so is likely to improve decision making as the issues are likely to have been thought through more thoroughly.

64 BPC (DEC 07 – AMENDED)

Key answer tips

Part (a) requires candidates to not only describe Porter's five forces model but more importantly apply it to the scenario contained within the question.

With part (b) the requirement is to discuss performance indicators which might indicate that JOL Co might fail as a corporate entity, not the use of performance indicators in a more general sense.

(a) In order to assess the attractiveness of the option to enter the market for spirally-wound paper tubes, the directors of BPC could make use of Michael Porter's 'five forces model'.

In applying this model to the given scenario one might conclude that the relatively low cost of the machine together with the fact that an unskilled person would only require one day's training in order to be able to operate a machine, constitute relatively low costs of entry to the market. Therefore one might reasonably conclude that the threat of new entrants might be high. This is especially the case where the market is highly fragmented.

The fact that products are usually purchased in very large quantities by customers together with the fact that there is little real difference between the products of alternative suppliers suggests that customer (buyer) power might well be very high. The fact that the paper tubes on average only comprise between 1% and 2% of the total cost of the purchaser's finished product also suggests that buyer power may well be very high.

The threat from suppliers could be high due to the fact that the specially formulated paper from which the tubes are made is sometimes in short supply. Hence suppliers might increase their prices with consequential diminution in gross margin of the firms in the marketplace.

The threat from competitive rivals will be strong as the four major players in the market are of similar size and that the market is a slow growing market. The market leader currently has 26% of the market and the three nearest competitors hold approximately 18% of the market.

The fact that Plastic Tubes Co (PTC) produces a narrow range of plastic tubes constitutes a threat from a substitute product. This threat will increase if the product range of PTC is extended and the price of plastic tubes is reduced.

The fact that a foreign-based multinational company is considering entering this market represents a significant threat from a potential new entrant as it would appear that the multinational company might well be able to derive economies of scale from large scale automated machinery and has manufacturing flexibility.

Low capital barriers to entry might appeal to BPC but they would also appeal to other potential entrants. The low growth market, the ease of entry, the existence of established competitors, a credible threat of backward vertical integration by suppliers, the imminent entry by a multi-national, a struggling established competitor and the difficulty of differentiating an industrial commodity should call into question the potential of BPC to achieve any sort of competitive advantage. If BPC can achieve the position of lowest cost producer within the industry then entry into the market might be a good move. In order to assess whether this is possible BPC must consider any potential synergies that would exist between its cardboard business and that of the tubes operation.

From the information available, the option to enter the market for cardboard tubes appears to be unattractive. The directors of BPC should seek alternative performance improvement strategies.

(b)   It would appear that JOL's market share has declined from 30% to $(80 – 26)/3 = 18\%$ during the last three years. A 12% fall in market share is probably very significant with a knock-on effect on profits and resultant cash flows. Obviously such a declining trend needs to be arrested immediately and this will require a detailed investigation to be undertaken by the directors of JOL. Consequently loss of market share can be seen to be an indicator of potential corporate failure. Other indicators of corporate failure are as follows:

Six performance indicators that an organisation might fail are as follows:

Poor cash flow

Poor cash flow might render an organisation unable to pay its debts as and when they fall due for payment. This might mean, for example, that providers of finance might be able to invoke the terms of a loan covenant and commence legal action against an organisation which might eventually lead to its winding-up.

Lack of new production/service introduction

Innovation can often be seen to be the difference between 'life and death' as new products and services provide continuity of income streams in an ever-changing business environment. A lack of new product/service introduction may arise from a shortage of funds available for re-investment. This can lead to organisations attempting to compete with their competitors with an out of date range of products and services, the consequences of which will invariably turn out to be disastrous.

General economic conditions

Falling demand and increasing interest rates can precipitate the demise of organisations. Highly geared organisations will suffer as demand falls and the weight of the interest burden increases. Organisations can find themselves in a vicious circle as increasing amounts of interest payable are paid from diminishing gross margins leading to falling profits/increasing losses and negative cash flows. This leads to the need for further loan finance and even higher interest burden, further diminution in margins and so on.

Lack of financial controls

The absence of sound financial controls has proven costly to many organisations. In extreme circumstances it can lead to outright fraud (e.g. Enron and WorldCom).

Internal rivalry

The extent of internal rivalry that exists within an organisation can prove to be of critical significance to an organisation as managerial effort is effectively channelled into increasing the amount of internal conflict that exists to the detriment of the organisation as a whole. Unfortunately the adverse consequences of internal rivalry remain latent until it is too late to redress them.

Loss of key personnel

In certain types of organisation the loss of key personnel can 'spell the beginning of the end' for an organisation. This is particularly the case when individuals possess knowledge which can be exploited by direct competitors, e.g. sales contacts, product specifications, product recipes, etc.

(c) If a company starts exhibiting signs of financial distress and even potential corporate failure, then its performance management systems may need to change in the following ways:

Choice of CSFs

When facing potential failure, a company will need to focus on a different set of CSFs. For example, under normal trading conditions a company may not see cash flow as a critical success factor but it is perhaps the most important issue when facing failure.

Choice of KPIs

Liquidation or receivership are often triggered by a company exceeding its overdraft limit or other limits set in place under loan covenants. In times of distress a firm would wish to monitor these more carefully – for example a loan covenant may place limits on various ratios.

The need for up to date information

Some companies may only produce some reports on a monthly basis. In times of financial distress information will be needed that is as up to date as possible to make better informed decisions.

Timescales

With a healthy company the directors may be happy to review cash flow on a rolling monthly basis. If a company is in distress, then this may need to be a weekly or even daily event to ensure that overdraft or loan covenant limits are not breached.

Basis of reporting

Management and financial accounts are normally prepared on the assumption of the business being a going concern. Should this assumption no longer be valid then some figures will have to be restated, particularly for external reporting – for example, the valuation of inventory and WIP.

	Marking scheme		
			Marks
(a)	Comments (on merit):		
	Each of the five forces 5 × 2		10
	Conclusion		1
			___
		Maximum	10
			___
(b)	Comments (on merit)		
	Fall in market share significant		1
	(with percentage 18%)		1
	Indicators 6 × 1.5		9
			___
		Maximum	10
			___
(c)	1 mark per explained comment		5
			___
Total			25
			___

Examiner's comments

Part (a) was generally well answered with a significant number of candidates achieving maximum marks. However, many candidates who could describe Porter's five forces model were unable to apply it to the scenario contained within the question. Answers to part (b) were generally not as good as those to part (a).

A significant number of candidates did not observe the requirement to discuss performance indicators which might indicate that JOL Co might fail as a corporate entity, but discussed the use of performance indicators in a more general sense.

65 THE SENTINEL COMPANY (TSC) (DEC 08 – AMENDED)

Key answer tips

Read the requirements of this question carefully. Remember when a target is for delays a business would like to achieve less than the target!

In (b) the question is clearly referring to the building blocks model so you need to know what the measures refer to within the model. Use as many examples from the scenario as possible.

(a) **Summary analysis of points gained (1) or forfeited (0) for quarter ended 31 October 2008**

	Donatello-town	Leonardo-town	Michaelangelo-town	Raphael-town
Revenue and profit statistics:				
Revenue	0	1	1	1
Profit	1	0	1	0
Customer care and service delivery statistics:				
Late collection of consignments	1	0	1	0
Misdirected consignments	0	1	1	0
Delayed response to complaints	1	1	1	0
Vehicle breakdown delays	0	0	1	0
Lost items	1	1	1	0
Damaged items	1	0	1	1
Credit control and administrative efficiency statistics:				
Average debtor weeks	0	1	1	0
Debtors in excess of 60 days	1	1	1	1
Invoice queries (% of total)	1	1	1	1
Credit notes (% of revenue)	1	1	1	0
Total points gained	8	8	12	4

(b) The summary analysis in (a) shows that using overall points gained, Michaelangelotown has achieved the best performance with 12 points. Donatellotown and Leonardotown have achieved a reasonable level of performance with eight points each. Raphaeltown has underperformed, however, gaining only four out of the available 12 points.

Michaelangelotown is the only depot to have achieved both an increase in revenue over budget and an increased profit:revenue percentage.

In the customer care and service delivery statistics, Michaelangelotown has achieved all six of the target standards, Donatellotown four; Leonardotown three. The Raphaeltown statistic of achieving only one out of six targets indicates the need for investigation.

With regard to the credit control and administrative efficiency statistics, Leonardotown and Michaelangelotown achieved all four standards and Donatellotown achieved three of the four standards. Once again, Raphaeltown is the 'poor performer' achieving only two of the four standards.

(c) The terms listed may be seen as representative of the dimensions of performance. The dimensions may be analysed into results and determinants.

The results may be measured by focusing on financial performance and competitiveness. **Financial performance** may be measured in terms of revenue and profit as shown in the data in the appendix of the question in respect of TSC. The points system in part (a) of the answer shows which depots have achieved or exceeded the target set. In addition, liquidity is another aspect of the measurement of financial performance. The points total in part (a) showed that Leonardotown and Michaelangelotown depots appear to have the best current record in aspects of credit control.

Competitiveness may be measured in terms of sales growth but also in terms of market share, number of new customers, etc. In the TSC statistics available in (a) we only have data for the current quarter. This shows that three of the four depots listed have achieved increased revenue compared to target.

The **determinants** are the factors which may be seen to contribute to the achievement of the results. Quality, resource utilisation, flexibility and innovation are cited by Fitzgerald and Moon as examples of factors that should contribute to the achievement of the results in terms of financial performance and competitiveness. In TSC a main **quality** issue appears to be customer care and service delivery. The statistics in the points table in part (a) of the answer show that the Raphaeltown depot appears to have a major problem in this area. It has only achieved one point out of the six available in this particular segment of the statistics.

Resource utilisation for TSC may be measured by the level of effective use of drivers and vehicles. To some extent, this is highlighted by the statistics relating to customer care and service delivery. For example, late collection of consignments from customers may be caused by a shortage of vehicles and/or drivers. Such shortages could be due to staff turnover, sickness, etc or problems with vehicle maintenance.

Flexibility may be an issue. There may, for example, be a problem with vehicle availability. Possibly an increased focus on sources for short-term sub-contracting of vehicles/collections/deliveries might help overcome delay problems.

The 'target v actual points system' may be seen as an example of **innovation** by the company.

This gives a detailed set of measures that should provide an incentive for improvement at all depots. The points system may illustrate the extent of achievement/non-achievement of company strategies for success. For example TSC may have a customer care commitment policy which identifies factors that should be achieved on a continuing basis. For example, timely collection of consignments, misdirected consignments re-delivered at no extra charge, prompt responses to customer claims and compensation for customers.

(d) The performance measurement system used by TSC appears simplistic. However, it may be considered to be measuring the right things since the specific measures used cover a range of dimensions designed to focus the organisation on factors thought to be central to corporate success, and not confined to traditional financial measures.

Internal benchmarking is used at TSC in order to provide sets of absolute standards that all depots are expected to attain. This should help to ensure that there is a continual focus upon the adoption of 'best practice' at all depots. Benchmarks on delivery performance place an emphasis upon quality of service whereas benchmarks on profitability are focused solely upon profitability!

Incentive schemes are used throughout the business, linking the achievement of company targets with financial rewards. It might well be the case that the profit incentive would act as a powerful motivator to each depot management team. However, what is required for the prosperity of TSC is a focus of management on the determinants of success as opposed to the results of success.

	Marking scheme		
			Marks
(a)	Revenue		½
	Profit		½
	Customer care and service delivery		2
	Credit control and administration efficiency		3
			___
		Maximum	6
			___
(b)	Overall comment on ranking		1
	Analysis of each of the three sections in table		5
			___
		Maximum	5
			___
(c)	Inter-relationship of dimensions/results/determinants		2
	Definition/examples of financial performance and		
	competitiveness as aspects of results	2 × 1½	3
	Definition/examples of determinants of quality,		
	resource utilisation, flexibility and innovation	4 × 1½	6
			___
		Maximum	9
			___
(d)	Comments (on merit)		
		Maximum	5
			___
Total			25
			___

Examiners comments

In part (a) a minority of candidates reversed the 1/0 notation but nevertheless demonstrated an understanding of the need to rank the depots of TSC according to the 12 measures provided in the Appendix to the question and were rewarded favourably. It was also pleasing to observe that the majority of answers to part (b) were satisfactory as most candidates provided acceptable comments on the relative performance of each depot. That said, many candidates limited their evaluation of the performance of the four depots to ranking them 'first', 'second', 'third' and 'fourth' (or last)' and thereby ignoring which depots had in fact achieved (or had not achieved) the 'target values' which were at the heart of the performance measurement system of TSC.

In general, answers to part (c) were satisfactory, and indeed, some were excellent. Poorer answers were offered by candidates who did not relate answers sufficiently to the examples contained in the scenario and/or chose to state that there was insufficient information contained within the question to enable them to provide a relevant assessment of TSC using the required criteria.

The quality of answers to part (d) varied significantly. Many candidates achieved maximum marks whilst poorer answers referred solely to the need for more financial performance measures within TSC. In general, candidates provided satisfactory comments relating to the simplistic nature of the performance measurement system within TSC but few answers indicated the need to focus on the determinants of success rather than the results.

66   THE SPARE FOR SHIPS COMPANY (SFS) (JUN 10 – AMENDED)

Key answer tips

This is a fairly tough question that looks at ABC and ABM. Ensure that you have learnt the key knowledge aspects of both of these and appreciate the difference.

In particular, make sure you are comfortable considering how different models and methodologies can work together.

(a)   (i)   The differences in the reported cost estimates calculated under each of the two costing systems are significant. This is especially the case with regard to Job order 973. The management accountant's calculations for the cost estimates produce the following increase/(decrease) in reported costs:

	Job order 973	Job order 974
	$	$
Unit cost per job under existing system	1,172.00	620.00
Unit cost per job under activity based costing	1,612.00	588.89
Increase/(decrease) in reported cost	37.54%	(5.02)%

Job order 973 shows an increase in reported cost of 37.54% [(1,612 – 1,172)/1,172] whereas Job order 974 shows a decrease in reported cost of 5.02% [(88.89 – 620)/620].

A common occurrence when activity-based costing is implemented is that low-volume products show an increase in their reported costs while high-volume products show decreases in their reported costs. This is very much the case with regard to the products which are the subjects of Job orders 973 and 974.

The reported costs also differ due to the following:

- Job orders 973 and 974 differ in the way they consume activities in each of the five activity areas within SFS's premises

- The activity areas differ in their indirect cost allocation bases. In particular no activity area uses direct labour hours as the basis of allocating indirect costs.

Two areas where the differences in reported product costs might be important to SFS are as follows:

Product design – since it is more probable that those involved in the design of products will find the results produced by the activity-based approach to be much more credible. This is especially the case in a machine oriented environment where direct labour hours are unlikely to be the major cost-driver. Activity-based costing can be of more assistance to product designers and may signal areas where cost reductions can be achieved, for example using fewer cuts on the lathe and/or reducing the number of machine hours required in the milling area.

Product pricing – The application of activity-based costing shows that the cost of Job order 973 is being understated while the cost of Job order 974 is being overstated. The management of SFS should be aware of the danger of failing to recover the costs incurred on Job order 973. Conversely, they may well be overpricing Job order 974 which might well entail losing business to its competitors.

(ii) Two problems SFS would have had to deal with in the successful implementation of an activity-based costing system are as follows:

   (i) initially it would be very time consuming to collect a large amount of data concerning the activities relating to each job undertaken by SFS. Hence the cost of buying, implementing and maintaining a system of activity-based costing is likely to be significant

   (ii) it would be vital to identify the real 'cost-drivers' within the activity-based costing system of SFS otherwise results given by the ABC system would be inaccurate leading to incorrect decisions by management.

Tutorial note

Additional credit was available for staff/culture issues which would be resolved by adequate training and motivation to change.

(b) Operational ABM is about 'doing things right'. Those activities which add value to products can be identified and improved. Activities that do not add value should be reduced in order to cut costs without reducing product value. Where for example a product or service has been estimated to require a longer activity time than other products or services then every effort should be made to find ways of reducing the number of hours required.

Strategic ABM is about 'doing the right things' using the ABC information to decide which products to develop and which activities to use. It can focus on profitability analysis, identifying which products/customers are the most profitable and for which sales volume should be developed.

An activity may have implicit value not necessarily reflected in the financial value added to any service or product. SFS might decide to cut back on the level of expenditure involved in servicing customers. This may lead to a poorer perceived value by customers of the service provided by SFS with a consequent fall in demand.

There are risks attaching to the use of ABM insofar as ABM can give the wrong signals. For example a particularly pleasant work environment can help attract and retain the best staff, but may not be identified as adding value in operational ABM. By the same token, a customer that represents a loss based on committed activities, but that opens up leads in a new market, may be identified as a low value customer by a strategic ABM process.

Tutorial note

Other risks or potential problems were also accepted such as pricing errors arising or the cost/benefit of such an expensive system.

(c) ABM can be used alongside performance management improvement strategies, such as Total Quality Management, Six Sigma and Business Process Reengineering, where the information provided can support the projects.

TQM

In TQM, costs are analysed into costs of conformance (appraisal and prevention costs) and costs of non-conformance (internal and external failure costs). The aim of TQM is to reduce the costs of non-conformance.

ABM enables organisations to more accurately calculate these quality related costs by identifying the appropriate cost drivers and then monitoring improvements.

Six Sigma and Business Process Reengineering

Six Sigma and BPR typically involve projects to achieve large one-off improvements in particular business processes relating to efficiency and better customer satisfaction.

ABM can support these approaches in several ways:

- Identifying processes that need improvement and establishing priorities

- Providing cost justification for proceeding with the project, for example by enabling more useful cost-benefit analysis

- Monitoring the benefits of the projects.

Marking scheme				
				Marks
(a)	(i)	Comments (on merit):		
		Cost per unit comparisons		2
		Reasons for differences		2
		Potential consequences	Up to 2 each	4
			Maximum	**8**
	(ii)	Problems	Up to 2 each	4
(b)		Comments (on merit):		
		Operational ABM		2
		Strategic ABM		2
		The implicit value of an activity		2
		Risks		2
			Maximum	**8**
(c)		1 mark per relevant point		**5**
Total				**25**

Examiner's comments

Overall, answers to this question were mixed. The comparison of different methods of costing and performance measurement is a basic element of this exam and surprisingly, many candidates seem unprepared for part (a) (i). Better answers to this part focussed on how the two methods can produce different answers by comparing their underlying approaches. Again, candidates scored more heavily if their answer used the information in the scenario as illustrative example of the general points made about the different costing methods. Most candidates realised that there were price implications arising from the two costs but few realised the internal process implications for example in designing products.

Requirement (a) (ii) requested two problems associated with implementation of an activity-based costing system using 'state of the art' IT systems. Candidates who focussed on the implementation stage and considered how it might be affected by such an IT system scored well. A few candidates cleverly took two subheadings and then discussed issues within these in order to ensure that they scored the two marks available for each problem.

Requirement (b) related the ABC system used earlier in the question to the broader use of activity analysis in management of the company. There were effectively four parts to this question the three topics itemised plus the risks of using ABM.

There was a wide spread of marks to this part with a few knowledgeable candidates scoring close to full marks but a number of weaker answers which failed to relate the general definitions of operational and strategic ABM to SFS. Many candidates did not realise that implicit value was the value which does not immediately appear in traditional performance measurement systems but nevertheless, is important in a long-term management of a successful business.

67 THE SUPERIOR BUSINESS CONSULTANCY (SBC) (JUN 10 – AMENDED)

Key answer tips

To score well in this question you have to make your answer relate to the specific circumstances in the question. So in part (a) have you written generic KPIs or are they relevant to SBC. Similarly in part (c) have you explained the trends using typical issues or ones specific to SBC's circumstances?

(a) The use of non-financial performance indicators (NFPIs) has become more widespread during recent years to assess performance in organisations.

This is largely attributable to the fact that many important aspects of organisational performance cannot be measured in purely financial terms. It follows that if performance measures are restricted to financial measures alone then many important non-financial aspects of organisational performance may be ignored.

Furthermore there is a widely held view that 'what gets measured gets done' and if performance measures are restricted to financial measures alone then the focus of managers will be myopic and consequently they may be motivated by the wrong stimuli.

In the past the important measure of performance have been financial in nature, with little or in extreme cases no focus whatsoever, being given to other important aspects of performance. Many commentators have argued that financial measures encourage short-termism to the detriment of the longer-term prospects of organisations.

Many NFPIs are 'lead indicators' insofar as they give an indication of likely future financial performance and therefore their measurement might reveal problems which might be addressed by management in time to take remedial action.

Skill and care must be exercised by management in the selection of NFPIs given the vast number of potential NFPIs in order to avoid an 'information overload' which could be damaging to an organisation.

The increasing attention given to NFPIs was a key factor in the development of Kaplan and Norton's 'balanced scorecard' which proposed that business performance is reviewed from four perspectives, these are:

- The financial perspective – How does an organisation appear to the shareholders?

- The customer perspective – How does an organisation appear to the customers?

- The internal business perspective – What must an organisation excel at?

- The innovation and learning perspective – Can an organisation continue to improve and create value?

For each of the four perspectives goals and measures will need to be defined – typically five measures for each perspective. The goals and measures are designed to focus attention on important factors and precipitate improved organisational performance.

The internal logic of the balanced scorecard is that goal-setting originates with customers. Then an organisation must determine what it must excel at in order to satisfy customer expectations. The innovation and learning perspective contains goals which relate to how an organisation will maintain progress and develop its processes, products and services. The results from these three perspectives will be mirrored in the financial perspective.

The directors will need to agree the 'vision' of the organisational strategy with middle management and to ensure that the vision is also shared by all employees within the organisation thereby creating an 'understood environment'. The creation of such an environment should ensure that sufficient attention is focused on all important factors within the organisation's environment which will lead to higher levels of profitability.

The following are possible measures that might feature within a balanced scorecard for SBC:

Customer perspective:

- % of sales from new clients

- % of clients from whom repeat business is gained

- Ratings from client satisfaction surveys

Internal business perspective:

- % of client projects completed on time and within budget

- % of bids for new clients which are successful

- % of employee time billed to clients

Innovation and learning perspective:

- % of time used for staff development

- % of revenues earned from new products or services

Financial perspective:

- Growth in operating cash flow

- Gross margin earned from clients

- Percentage increase in operating costs

- Expected value added (EVA ^{TM}) generated in relation to the budget.

(b) Calculation of the cost per consultation is as follows:

		Advertising	Recruitment	IT Support
Number of consultants		20	30	50
Salary ($)		40,000	35,000	30,000
Total salaries		800,000	1,050,000	1,500,000
Number of consultations per annum	(200 per consultant)	4,000	6,000	10,000
Business Development Activity		(280)	(1,320)	(1,200)
Chargeable days		3,720	4,680	8,800
Demand for chargeable consultations		4,200	6,250	10,250
Subcontractor days		480	1,570	1,450
Cost per subcontractor day ($)		300	220	200
Cost of subcontractors ($)		144,000	345,400	290,000

Cost per chargeable consultation ($)		Advertising	Recruitment	IT Support
Full-time consultants	Total salaries plus operating costs/chargeable days	277.55	286.86	232.95
Subcontractors	= Cost of subcontractors/ number of subcontractors	335.71	255.71	235.71

Tutorial note

Any reasonable method for allocating operating costs was given credit. Here, chargeable days have been used but allocating by the number of consultants in each area or the number of consultations (inc BDA) were also accepted.

(c) The figures contained in the appendix reveal a forecast reduction in level of total demand of 8% over the next two years.

Specifically hard hit is the recruitment business with a fall of 20% over this period with the number of recruitment consultants dropping by 33%. The figures also show that salary levels will remain constant from 2011 to 2012. This may be due to reasons such as increased competition or an economic downturn.

The forecast increase 'across all activities' in days spent on Business Development Activity, notwithstanding the projected fall in activity levels in 2011 and 2012, represent an attempt by SBC to broaden and/or retain its existing customer base.

(Additional points such as the increased use of subcontractors (based on answer to part (ii)) were also given credit.)

Marking scheme			
			Marks
(a)	Importance of NFPIs	Up to	4
	Balanced scorecard – discussion	Up to	2
	Balanced scorecard – SBC	Up to	7
			———
		Maximum	**13**
			———
(b)	Chargeable days		3
	Subcontractor days		2
	Costs per consultation		2
			———
		Maximum	**7**
			———
(c)	Comments (on merit)	Up to 2 each	6
			———
		Maximum	**5**
Total			**25**
			———

Examiner's comments

In general, answers to requirement (a) were good with a number of candidates gaining maximum marks by ensuring that their example metrics were relevant to SBC. Weaker responses often lacked focus on the importance of non-financial performance indicators and a surprisingly large minority of candidates lacked basic knowledge of the balanced scorecard, which should be considered a core topic in APM.

Requirement (b) received answers of variable quality with many candidates not appreciating the importance of calculating the chargeable days which would exclude the business development work. A surprising number of candidates did not appreciate that the main purpose of business development was as a marketing activity.

Requirement (c) was reasonably answered but the answers could have been improved by candidates offering more in terms of commercial reasoning, for example, the key trend in the appendix was the drop in forecast activity and this was the likely driver of the changes in the company – it was less commercially realistic to be suggesting that the drop in numbers of consultants in a previously growing business was driving the drop in demand.

68   LOL CO (DEC 10 – AMENDED)

Key answer tips

This was a reasonably straightforward question provided you understood the main ideas surrounding VBM and EVA. Unfortunately many students were uncertain on these key concepts.

(a)   The value-based approach takes the primary objective of the business to be maximising shareholder wealth and seeks to align performance with this objective. The principle measure used at the strategic level will be economic value added (EVA™). EVA™ is equivalent in the long term to discounted cash flow which is widely used as the valuation method for shares by equity analysts. (Other relevant value measures might be market value added and shareholder value added.)

By using this as the sole measure of performance, management is focused and they will be able to avoid conflicts which occur when there are multiple objectives and measures. The measure can be applied to decisions at all levels within the organisation (strategic, tactical and operational) so that the company is unified in its goal. As only a single measure is used, the variables which drive performance are clear within the calculation of EVA™. These value drivers can be used by managers to achieve their value-based targets which are set from the strategic value-based goal.

(b)   The performance of LOL has declined with earnings per share falling by 23% (W2) from last year. Normally, this would imply that the company would be heavily out of favour with investors.

However, the share price seems to have held up with a decline of only 12% compared to a fall in the sector of 26% and the market as a whole of 35% (W3). The sector comparison is more relevant to the performance of LOL's management as the main market index will contain data from manufacturing, financial and other industries. Shareholders will be encouraged by the implication that the market views LOL as one of the better prospects within an outperforming sector.

This view is consistent with the calculated positive EVA™ for 2010 ($22·6m, (W1)) which LOL generated. EVA™ has fallen from 2009 but it has remained positive and so the company continues to create value for its shareholders even in the poor economic environment. It therefore remains a worthwhile investment even in a falling market.

Workings:

(W1) EVA calculations for the periods given are

	2009 $m	2010 $m
Profit after interest and tax	35.0	26.8
Interest (net of tax at 25%)	3.0	5.9
Net operating profit after tax (NOPAT)	38.0	32.6
Capital employed (at year start)	99.2	104.1

Assumptions:

Economic and accounting depreciation are equivalent.

There are no non-cash expenses to adjust in the profit figure.

There are no operating leases to be capitalised.

There are no additional adjustments to make regarding goodwill.

Cost of capital

WACC = (%e × Ke) + (%d × Kd)

2009 (50% × 12.7%) + (50% × 4.2%) = 8.45%

2010 (50% × 15.3%) + (50% × 3.9%) = 9.60%

EVA = NOPAT – (Capital employed × WACC)

2009 38.0 – (99.2 × 8.45%) = 29.6

2010 32.6 – (104.1 × 9.6%) = 22.6

(W2)

	2009	2010	Change
EPS (profit after interest and tax/ av no of shares) cents	21.88	16.75	−23.4%

(W3)

Stock market information	2009	2010	Change
Main market index	2,225.4	1,448.9	−34.9%
Retailing sector index	1,225.6	907.1	−26.0%
LOL share price ($'s)	12.2	10.7	−12.3%

(c) VBM provides focus on shareholder wealth but it can be argued that a single profit measure can do the same. Value measures are considered to be superior to profit measures because they take into consideration the capital employed and cost of capital. These variables are less clear in a profit measure. Also, although value measures are calculated from profit figures they are adjusted in order to bring them closer to a cash flow measure of performance which is less affected by the various accounting adjustments such as depreciation. (Here we have assumed in calculating EVA™ that accounting and economic depreciation are the same but with greater information on the company we may be able to make a better estimate to the cash performance of the company.)

A disadvantage of value-based measures like EVA™ compared to profit is the unfamiliarity and complexity of the calculation. The calculation of the cost of capital is encumbered by the assumptions of CAPM and it is based on historic data which may not be repeated in the future (share values are based on expected dividend flows). These difficulties can be overcome by a process of education and training for the staff and shareholders. Additionally, the use of EVA™ as the sole value-measure as suggested by Stern Stewart may be too simple and overlook other value drivers.

As a tool for decision-making, EVA™ can be subject to manipulation by choosing projects with low initial costs to provide a short-term boost to the value measure in the same way as profit measures. It may not address the weaknesses in project appraisal that drive many companies to use net present value, which recognises the increase in shareholder wealth over the life of the whole project in question.

(d) The principal objective of financial management is to maximise shareholder wealth. This raises two key questions – how can we measure whether shareholder value is being created or destroyed, and which performance appraisal targets ensure that managers act in such a way as to generate shareholder value?

We therefore require a wealth metric for measuring shareholder value, and a performance metric to use for target setting.

NPV is mainly used as a wealth or investment metric for project appraisal. The main advantage of this approach is the high correlation between NPV and shareholder value, so the technique should result in projects being selected that will increase shareholder wealth.

What is lacking, however, is an operating performance measure for managers that will help them to maximise NPV. Some firms attempt to use cash flow targets but with mixed success. Many more firms set targets based on traditional measures, such as profit and ROI, without resolving the inconsistency of using NPV for project appraisal and then ignoring it when appraising managers.

The EVA™ approach is primarily a performance metric rather than a wealth metric and has the advantage that it is consistent with the use of NPV.

Marking scheme		Marks
(a)	Up to 2 marks on the explanation of VBM and then up to 2 marks on how it aids focus in the management process	
	Maximum	**4**
(b)	**Workings:**	
	NOPAT	1
	Capital employed	1
	Cost of capital	1
	EVA™	1
	Assumptions 0.5 each up to a maximum of	1.5
	EPS	1
	Share price 3 × 0.5	1.5
	Comments: 1 mark per reasonable point up to 2 on EPS and share price and 2 on EVATM.	——
	Maximum	**12**
		——
(c)	1 mark for each point made up to a maximum of	**4**
(d)	1 mark for each point made up to a maximum of	**5**
Total		——
		25
		——

Examiner's comments

Requirement (a) requested an explanation of value-based management (VBM) and how it aids management focus. Candidates often scored a pass but not full marks on this part. There were often lengthy and irrelevant discussions about non-financial factors which suggest incomplete knowledge of VBM.

Requirement (b) asked for an evaluation of LOL's performance using EVA, EPS growth and the share price. It was also typically passed but few candidates scored 9 or more out of 12. The assessment of the numerical work was often lacking. Candidates infrequently compared the change in share price of LOL to the market and sector performance – which demonstrated that the company was doing well in a falling market. Some candidates could not perform the EVA computation which was surprising as this is a key performance measure and the scenario offered few of the possible technical adjustments. Having performed the calculation of EVA, a significant minority then failed to note that it was positive choosing to focus on the fact that it had fallen from the previous year. This again showed weak understanding of such a key concept.

Requirement (c) was the most difficult part of the question and was generally poorly done, probably as a result of the failure to explain VBM which was illustrated in part (a).

69 RM BATTERIES CO (DEC 10)

Key answer tips

This was a reasonably straightforward question on corporate failure provided you answered the question set. Many students failed to add value to their comments in part (b) and often misread or ignored the requirement in parts (c) and (d).

(a) Quantitative models such as the Altman Z-score use publicly available financial information about a firm in order to predict whether it is likely to fail within the two-year period. The method uses a model equation into which the financial data is input and a score obtained. The advantages of such methods are that they are simple to calculate and provide an objective measure of failure. However, they only give guidance below the danger level of 1.8 and there is potential for a large grey area in which no clear prediction can be made. Additionally, the prediction of failure of those companies below 1.8 is only a probabilistic one, not a guarantee. The model is based on a statistical analysis of historic patterns of trading by a group of companies and may not be relevant unless the company under examination falls within the same economic circumstances and industry sector as those used to set the coefficients in the model. These models are open to manipulation through creative accounting which can be a feature of companies in trouble.

Qualitative methods are based on the realisation that financial measures are limited in describing the circumstances of a company. Models such as Argenti's rely on subjective scores to certain questions given by the investigator. A score above a certain level indicates potential disaster. The advantage of the method is the ability to use non-financial as well as financial measures and the judgement of the investigator but this is also a weakness as there is a danger that the investigator will give scores to ensure the conclusion agrees with first impressions.

(b) Analysis requested:

	2008	2009	2010
Share price ($)	1.56	1.67	1.34
No of shares (millions)	450	450	450
Market value of Equity ($M)	702	752	603
X1 WC/TA	−0.163	−0.103	−0.087
X2 RE/TA	0.151	0.167	0.167
X3 PBIT/TA	0.227	0.136	0.078
X4 Mve/Total long-term debt	1.510	0.758	0.478
X5 Revenue/TA	1.077	0.756	0.780
Z	2.746	1.770	1.452
Gearing [debt/equity]	107%	173%	197%

(c) The Z score of RMB in 2010 is 1.45 which is below the danger level of 1.8 and so indicates that RMB is in danger of becoming insolvent within the next two years. The Z score has been falling for the last two years through the grey area between the safe level of 3 and the danger level of 1.8.

During this period, the variables in the model have been roughly static or have shown significant declines. About half of the decline of the Z-score from 2.7 to 1.4 can be explained by the deterioration of variable x4 which measures the market value of the company's shares to its debt.

Debt has been building due to the investment programme and the share price (and so the market value) has fallen by 14% over the last year. It would be helpful to identify the relative performance of the share price against RMB's competitors to see if this is related to the company's specific problems or is due to general market conditions. The other significant reduction is in variable x3 which shows a failure to derive profit from the assets available. However, this could be a timing effect as the profits from the new product will occur over many subsequent accounting periods but the asset value will increase immediately in line with the investment programme.

(d) The qualitative problems can be broken down according to the Argenti model into three broad areas: defects, mistakes made and symptoms of failure. RMB exhibits the following defects – a domineering CEO, a failure to split CEO/Chairman roles and a passive senior management. These are structural problems within the company that will obstruct any effort to change direction if that direction is leading the company downwards.

It appears that RMB may also be making mistakes (in fact, the company illustrates all three of the classic errors noted by Argenti). It is overtrading as revenue rises and this is mainly funded by debt. As a result, gearing has risen from 107% to 197% and interest cover has fallen from 8.8 to 2.0. Additionally, the future of the company seems to depend on one big project. The higher gearing increases the financial risk that the company will fail to make its loan repayments. The dependence on the single new product demonstrates a lack of diversification which also signals greater risk.

Finally, symptoms of failure are not yet apparent from the information to hand. This may imply that there is still time to correct matters as these are often the final signals of failure e.g. creative accounting being employed to massage the financial statements.

(e) The outlook for RMB appears bleak when only looking for the bad points, however, the company is still making profits ($65m in 2010) and its revenues are growing (by 23% over the last year). This suggests that customers are taking up the new product. It is not surprising that in the early stages of this project that the capital expenditure is high and returns have yet to materialise.

Overall, the company is clearly showing signs of financial strain from the project but more work is required before coming to a final conclusion. Further data required would include a cash flow projection to ensure that as the product matures there will be funds to pay the new borrowings. The decline in operating margin from 21% to 10% requires explanation and action as this indicates problems in control of the business. Detailed cost information would assist in identifying the source of margin problems. The share price movement should be compared to the change in the market as a whole to identify if the fall in price is due to problems unique to RMB or if this is due to general economic conditions.

Marking scheme		
		Marks
(a)	1 mark for each point made. Up to 3 for each type of model. Discussed.	6
(b)	1 mark for the Z score for each year	3
	1 mark for market capitalisation and 1 mark for gearing	2
	Maximum	5
(c)	1 mark for each point made. Maximum of 5 marks.	5
(d)	0.5 mark for identifying problem and up to 1 mark for explaining how this relates to corporate failure. Maximum of 5 marks.	
	Maximum	5
(e)	1 mark for each point explained. To score full marks some appreciation of the information not captured by parts (b) and (c) must be demonstrated. Maximum of 4 marks.	
	Maximum	4
Total		25

Examiner's comments

Part (a) required a general discussion of the strengths and weaknesses of both qualitative and quantitative models. This was generally done well although some candidates tried to structure their answer as the strengths and weaknesses of models in general which would not be a helpful method in real life, where a comparison of the models is likely to be more useful.

Answers to part (c) were generally good although many candidates restricted their comment on the Z-score to repeating the comment given in the question (RMB is 'at risk of failure within two years') when the data given was requiring a more analytical answer about which factors within the model were driving the score down and so leading to this prediction. A minority of candidates restricted their comments to the company's statements of income and financial position when the question required comment about the spreadsheet data and consequently their answers lacked relevance.

Part (d) asked for the application of qualitative-type models to failure prediction at RMB. This was generally well done with many candidates making good use of the Argenti model and the factors mentioned in the scenario. Unfortunately, some candidates ignored the word 'qualitative' in the requirement and wasted time writing about quantitative factors.

Part (e) was poorly answered with many candidates ignoring the requirement to assess the results of previous answers and only picking up marks for suggesting additional data to gather.

70   APX ACCOUNTANCY (JUN 11 – AMENDED)

Key answer tips

Make sure you learn the details of different models fully – for example, the building block model is more than simply a list of 6 dimensions – there is the distinction between results and determinants as well as dimensions v standards v rewards.

This is also a good example of a question where it is essential that you answer the question set! In the exam requirement (b) asked 'Evaluate the existing performance management system at APX by applying the building block model' but was often wrongly interpreted to mean 'Evaluate the existing performance of APX' – responses to this imagined question were often quite good but sadly, irrelevant and so scored poorly.

(a)   Fitzgerald and Moon's building block approach

The building block model is an analysis that aims to improve the performance measurement systems of service businesses such as APX. It suggests that the performance system should be based on three concepts of dimensions, standards and rewards.

Dimensions fall into two categories: downstream results (competitive and financial performance) and upstream determinants (quality of service, flexibility, resource utilisation and innovation) of those results. These are the areas that yield specific performance metrics for a company.

Standards are the targets set for the metrics chosen from the dimensions measured. These must be such that those being measured take ownership of them, possibly by participating in the process of setting the standard. The standard must be achievable in order to motivate the employee or partner. The standards must be fairly set, based on the environment for each business unit so that those in the lower growth areas of, say, audit do not feel prejudiced when compared to the growing work in business advisory.

Rewards are the motivators for the employees to work towards the standards set. The reward system should be clearly understood by the staff and ensure their motivation. The rewards should be related to areas of responsibility that the staff member controls in order to achieve that motivation.

(b)   The current system

APX's performance management system does not cover all the areas that the building block model would suggest are necessary. The downstream dimensions appear to be covered as the competitive performance (market share) and financial performance (revenue growth and profit margin) can be measured. However, the determinants of this performance appear less well covered with only the quality of service aspect handled by the customer satisfaction rating.

The standards are unclear from the information provided. It appears that the industry averages can be used to compare competitive performance but there are no figures for the industry on profitability. The measure must therefore be internal, comparing practice areas to each other. This may breach the fairness criterion as it is likely that business advisory can negotiate better fees than audit or tax due to market conditions being favourable from that area. No standard is mentioned on the document for quality of service.

The non-partner reward system at APX is related to performance as assessed by the line manager but this will be compromised by the limited measurement of the dimensions of performance. The partner reward system appears to be based on the level of responsibility of the partner and the performance of the whole firm rather than that individual's contribution to performance. Therefore, there is a strong probability that the reward level is not controllable by the partner and this may affect their motivation.

For example, a tax partner may view the growth in recovery work as sufficient to merit reward to all partners and so not optimise the performance of their own area of the practice.

(c)   Main building block improvements

The first improvement obtained by using this model will be to ensure that all the key determinants of success in performance are being measured. The next benefit will be that the targets set for each measure are set in such a way as to engage the staff. Finally, the reward system will operate in a way to optimally motivate the individual staff members.

Improvements to existing performance measurement system

The existing performance measurement system requires measures for flexibility which address the speed of delivery of the service (e.g. a punctuality measure of percentage of jobs delivered on time), the customer's attitude (e.g. the existing customer service survey could be broken down to include the customer's perception of whether objectives were achieved) and the degree to which the practice handles busy periods (e.g. amount of overtime worked).

It is surprising that APX does not seem to measure resource utilisation, for example, by considering the percentage of billable hours worked to the total working hours of the firm. This is a commonly used measure of the productivity of staff in accounting practices. Finally, the dimension of innovation is not measured. Innovation is an important source of competitive advantage. The efficiency of the innovation process can be measured by the time it takes to launch a new service once the initial customer need is identified. The outputs of innovation process within APX could be measured by the number of new customer initiatives launched or by the revenue that they generate.

Marking scheme		Marks
(a)	Taking each building block, up to 1.5 marks for a description. Maximum 4 marks.	
	Maximum	4
(b)	Taking each building block, up to 3 marks for evaluating the existing system at APX. Maximum 8 marks.	
	Maximum	9
(c)	Main improvements from use of model 1 mark per point up to 4 marks. Specific suggestions for APX 1 mark per point which must relate to the scenario by way of examples up to 8 marks.	
	Maximum	12
Total		25

Examiner's comments

Requirement (a) asked for a brief description of the model and often only the dimensions aspect was correctly identified. Within each of the building blocks, weak knowledge of the aspects emphasised by the model were demonstrated. For example, very few candidates appreciated the distinction between the upstream determinants of performance and the downstream results of performance within the dimensions block.

Requirement (b) requested an evaluation of APX's performance management system using the model. Many candidates offered an irrelevant assessment of APX's performance. To illustrate why this is irrelevant consider the analogous question 'evaluate the accounting system at company X' and then consider the response, ' Company X is performing well with profit increasing by 10% to $100m in the last year.' The response does not address the question which is about the system and not the performance. Many candidates only evaluated the performance measures with little comment given to the standards applied to these or the reward system at APX.

Requirement (c) sought suggestions for improvements for APX from the analysis in the previous parts. Better candidates had read the full requirement and so held back from offering improvements to the faults recognised in part (b) until the answer to this part. Again, answers were limited due to the poor quality of responses to the earlier parts although some candidates offered valuable practical ideas to the management at APX.

71   COD ELECTRICAL MOTORS (DEC 11 – AMENDED)

Key answer tips

Try to ensure you understand the rationale behind performance management models such as the performance pyramid. A key element here is the hierarchy where measures near the bottom of the pyramid are more relevant to people doing day to day operational tasks, whereas those at the top are more strategic and intended for Board use. Many students failed to develop this split in their answers.

(a) The key features of performance measures are that:

- they should measure the effectiveness of the business and its processes in meeting the organisation's objectives in order to link to the overall strategy

- they should measure the efficiency of resource utilisation within the organisation

- they should contain internal and external measures of performance

- they should comprise a mix of financial and non-financial (quantitative and qualitative) methods

- they will require to make clear the different dimensions of performance so that judgements on trade-offs between them are explicit (e.g. quality and cost)

- they will link to the targets set for employee motivation

- they should cover both the short-term and long-term performance of the organisation; and

- they should be flexible in order to respond to changes in the business environment.

The key performance indicators (KPIs) at Cod fail to have many of these key features. The KPIs at present are purely focused on financial performance and do not address issues of quality, customer service and product innovation which are all mentioned in the mission statement. The KPIs have no strong external features such as customer satisfaction or share price performance. It is unclear how they will link to employee motivation and indeed, the board recognise this fact and intend to use the performance pyramid in order to address it. The overall picture of the performance measurement system is a traditional one which will lack the flexibility to address the concerns of the key stakeholders of Cod.

(b)

The pyramid diagram is:

The pyramid firstly focuses on the development of a coherent set of objectives from the overall corporate vision. The pyramid views a range of objectives from the strategic to the operational, linking these through the themes of external effectiveness and internal efficiency.

The strategic level concerns relate to market and financial factors and these are fed by the tactical level drivers of customer satisfaction, flexibility and productivity. These objectives will reflect that business systems at this level will cross functional boundaries and so cannot be drawn into the specifics of the operational details. The operational objectives are then derived from the tactical drivers.

The performance measurement system is then built up to reflect the objectives and so ensure that each of the performance measures at the operational level feed the tactical level requirements and measures at this level drive the strategic objectives of the organisation. For example, cycle time reductions will improve productivity which will enhance the profitability of Cod.

This will help Cod to achieve the coherence that the board desires in the performance measurement systems.

(c)   The driving forces, according to Lynch and Cross, that are appropriate to meeting an organisation's objectives are customer satisfaction, flexibility and productivity. At present Cod's KPIs do not address these as they lack any mention of areas of customer satisfaction (quality and service standards), flexibility (innovation and the ability to adapt to change in the external business environment) and productivity (efficiency and waste). It could be argued that some of these are more appropriate at the tactical and operational levels of the management hierarchy but the existing measures have only a tenuous link to them and hence the board is right to be concerned by the current KPI system.

The additional performance information provided would allow the calculation of various indicators appropriate to these driving forces. For example:

Customer satisfaction

- Percentage of orders generating a complaint (5.4% in 2011 compared to 5.0% in 2010) measures customer satisfaction.

- Preferred supplier status (58% of market in 2011 and 50% in 2010 [if we assume that there are only 24 possible customers that offer this status]).

Flexibility

- New products launched in the year (one each of 2011 and 2010) measures innovation.

Productivity

- Quality costs ($4.35m in 2011 and $3.46m in 2010) measures inefficient production.

These should be added to the current KPIs used by the board.

The operational performance measures suggested by the pyramid will involve the four areas of quality, delivery, cycle time and waste.

Quality

The existing measures of failure costs supply a measure of quality, although variances to budget may be a more helpful presentation. The customer complaint numbers also address this issue, although they are a weak measure as no indication of the strength or ease of resolution of the complaint is given. It should be noted that the complaint category of 'other' is unacceptably large compared to the other categories and it should be broken down into further subcategories. The level of training days and long-term unfilled posts indicates the employee environment that will also impact on quality and delivery. It would be helpful to have industry benchmarks for these figures in order to understand them better.

Delivery

The preferred customer status indicates customer satisfaction and is fed by the complaint numbers on delivery and service. As before, it is worth noting that the severity of the complaint is not being measured, for example, by discounts offered or orders lost as a result.

Cycle time

There is no useful information currently collected to allow measurement of the cycle times of processes.

Possibly the indicative numbers on products being developed may give an idea of time to market, however, an average measure of this in months would be more useful.

Waste

No figures are collected that indicate waste in production. Variance analysis of idle time for employees and materials usage would be helpful in measuring this area.

	Marking scheme		
			Marks
(a)	Key features		
	Describe – 0.5 mark per point		4
	Assess – 1 mark per point	up to	6
			—
		Maximum	**7**
			—
(b)	Diagram – 1 mark per point	up to	2
	Explanation – 1 mark per point	up to	4
			—
		Maximum	**6**
			—
(c)	Strategic level		
	Describe drivers – 0.5 mark per point		1.5
	Assess current system – 1 mark per point	up to	2
	Suggest new KPIs – 1 mark per point	up to	3
	Operational level – 1 mark per point made	up to	8
	(in order to score full marks all four areas of the operational level of the pyramid must be addressed)		—
		Maximum	**12**
			—
Total			**25**
			—

72   CALLISTO (JUN 12 – AMENDED)

Key answer tips

This question, concerning an e-tailer with a complex business structure, is tricky as it does not lend itself some pre-ordained template or method. However, provided you use the information in the scenario to good effect, you should be able to gather the marks to pass.

(a)   **Performance measurement problems at Callisto**

In a virtual organisation such as Callisto, performance measurement can be difficult due to the fact that key players in the business processes and in the supply chain are not 'on site'. Callisto has the problem of collecting and monitoring data about its employees working from home and the outsourcing partners.

At Callisto, there is a reliance placed on information technology for handling these remote contacts. Collecting and monitoring performance should therefore be done automatically as far as possible. A large database would be required that can be automatically updated from the activities of the remote staff and suppliers. This will require the staff and supplier systems to be compatible.

The employees can be required to use software supplied by Callisto and in fact, at Callisto, they use the internet to log in remotely to Callisto's common systems. Although this solution requires expenditure on hardware and software, it is within the control of Callisto's management. Even with reviews of system logs to identify the hours that staff spend logged in to the systems, there are still the difficulty of measuring staff outputs in order to ensure their productivity. These outputs must be clearly defined by Callisto's managers, otherwise there will be disputes between staff and management.

One further outstanding issue is the need to ensure that such communication is over properly secured communication channels, especially if it contains customer or financial data.

The strategic partners, such as RLR, will have their own systems. A problem for Callisto is that there is disagreement over the measurement of the key SLAs. In order to resolve such disputes, lengthy reconciliations between Callisto's and RLR's systems will have to be undertaken otherwise there are no grounds for enforcement of the SLAs and the SLAs represent Callisto's key control over the relationship. The solution would be for the partners to agree a standard reporting format for all data that relates to the SLAs which would remove the need for such reconciliations.

Finally, there is the problem that Callisto and the partner organisation may have differing objectives – the obvious conflict over price between supplier and customer being one. However, at Callisto, this is being addressed by the use of detailed SLAs which both organisations can use to develop performance measures such as inventory levels and delivery times.

Performance management problems at Callisto

The performance management of employees is complicated due to the inability of management to 'look over their shoulder' since they are not present in the same building. However, employees will enjoy the advantages of home-working, such as lower commuting times, more contact with family and greater flexibility in working hours.

The disadvantages are the difficulties in measuring outputs mentioned above and ensuring motivation and commitment. The motivation and commitment can be addressed through suitable reward schemes which would have to be tied to agreed outputs and targets for each employee. Work could be divided into projects where the outputs are more easily identified and pay and bonuses related to these.

The performance management issues of handling the strategic partners include:

- confidentiality where the partners will have access to commercially sensitive information about customers' locations and suppliers' names and lead times

- reliability where the partner is supplying a business critical role (as for RLR with Callisto) such that it would take considerable time to replace such a relationship and affect customer service while this happened

- relationship management where the interface between the organisations can create wasteful activity if there is not an atmosphere of trust. At Callisto, this is illustrated by the problem of reconciliation of performance data

- profit sharing where given the collaborative nature of the relationship and the difficulty of breaking it combine to imply that it will be in the interest of both parties to negotiate a contract that is motivating and profitable for both sides. For Callisto, the business aim is to increase volume and this will require customer loyalty so the quality of service is important.

(b)   **Performance measures**

It is important that performance measures used for Callisto are in line with the overall business objectives.

Employees

There are likely to be a wide range of roles performed by employees across the functions of production, finance and supplier relationship management and the chosen measures need to reflect these differences.

Volume based measures could be used to assess those working in video clip production, for example the number of minutes of video produced. However the videos produced are not part of the physical product being sold by Callisto and so an increase in volume will not have any positive impact on the level of complaints which are received, a key concern for the company. Measures applied to these employees should concentrate more on the quality of the video produced and its ability to attract customers to the site. Web based measures relating to the number of 'hits' each video has and the number of purchases that then result would be more appropriate. This information should be readily available through the company's website.

Finance employees should be measured according to the quality and timeliness of the information they provide such as the number of deadlines met within a period of time. This should prove relatively easy to monitor through a review of the reports produced each period.

In order to accurately measure the performance of those employees involved in supplier relationship management, Callisto should consider the quality of communication between employees and strategic partners. From the employees perspective this can be measured by looking at the number of breaches in an SLA although this may be difficult due to the way the information is currently gathered. Regular reviews of the SLAs should allow this information to be collated.

Strategic partners

Performance of the strategic partners working with Callisto should be measured through delivery of the SLAs. Each of these agreements will have different terms depending on the nature of the supplier. So for example, a suitable measure for RLR may be that 90% of orders are despatched within 3 working days of receipt. Customer receipt documentation will ensure this can be tracked and regular reviews of the SLA should identify any areas of concern.

	Marking scheme		Marks

(a)	Performance measurement
	Up to 2 marks per point made.
	For example on:
	    geographical distance
	    reliance on IT
	    difference between employees and strategic partners
	    technology solutions
	    use of SLAs
		Maximum	9

	Performance management
	1 mark per valid point made
	    Employees up to 4 marks
	    Strategic partners up to 6 marks
		Maximum	8

(b)	Performance measures:
	    Employees – up to 4 marks
	    Strategic partners – up to 2 marks
	Methods of data collection – 1 mark per point
		Maximum	8

Total			25

Examiner's comments

Requirement (a) focused on the difficulties of performance management and measurement in such a complex business as Callisto. Candidates were correct to split this into areas such as the general impact of such a complex structure on the business as a whole and then the impact on employee management and strategic partner management.

The key to scoring well was making relevant points for Callisto – the difficulties of measuring and managing home-working employees and strategic outsourcing partners.

73 COAL CREEK NURSING HOMES (DEC 12 – AMENDED)

Key answer tips

Here, as in all APM questions, it is vital to answer the question set. In part (a) for example, the key verb was 'discuss', meaning the examiner wanted a discussion as to whether or why liquidity and gearing were more useful than profitability.

Also in part (a) make sure you do not limit your understanding of 'gearing' to simply financial gearing. In APM 'gearing' is much more likely to refer to operating gearing, requiring you to understand and comment upon the cost structure of the business concerned.

(a)   The current measures of performance at CCNH are based on profits. These are often insufficient to grasp issues to do with the survival of the business, both in the long and the short term. In the short term, liquidity covers the degree to which there are readily available funds in order to meet immediately payable liabilities, for example, the cash to pay suppliers. In the long term, gearing measures risk. This could be financial risk or it could be operational risk. Gearing indicates the size of the fixed regular liabilities of the company compared to the cash generators that will cover them. So, financial gearing is measured by the ratio of debt to equity – debt being the fixed liability and equity the capital equivalent that generates funds to cover this liability. If the ratio is high, then there are large fixed liabilities to cover with only a small equity investment and so the business is at financial risk. (The ability to cover the annual payments needed on the loans is often measured by the interest cover which is the ratio of profit before interest to interest payable.) Operational gearing compares the ratio of fixed costs to variable costs (or sometimes the ratio of contribution to the operating profits). If it is high, then the business is more risky as the fixed costs are a large part of the overall costs of the business and so if revenue falls the variable costs fall but the fixed ones do not.

Liquidity at CCNH is difficult to measure in detail as we are only given the current assets figure. However, we can compare the current assets and liabilities in the current ratio and we get 0.62. Therefore, CCNH does not have readily available assets to pay its creditors.

There is no breakdown into receivables, inventory and cash which might aid a detailed understanding of the maturities of the different items. However, we do know that there is no cash on deposit and since CCNH is a service company, it is unlikely that there is much value in inventory.

Therefore, the bulk of current assets must be receivables. So we can deduce that SC has difficulty collecting its receivables compared to GC, as it has much higher receivables on lower revenues. It may be helpful to use receivables days which measures the time taken to collect receivables as a key performance indicator for SC and also for SC to compare its collection procedures with those at GC in order to identify possible improvements. (Currently, SC has 68 receivables days compared to 9 at GC, assuming all current assets are receivables.)

Financial gearing at CCNH is fairly low with a debt to equity ratio of 54%. There is, however, a financial risk as the interest payments are barely covered by profits in the most recent year and this could jeopardise the relationship with the bank which has recently proved so valuable in getting the overdraft extension.

Operational gearing at CCNH is probably what the director was referring to when speaking to the CEO. From the income statement, it can be clearly seen that rents, which are a fixed payment, are a large percentage of revenues (27%). Given that central costs and home payroll costs will probably also be fairly fixed this means that CCNH has a high operational gearing of 7.5 ((536 + 257 + 30) ÷ 110) which means that any fall in revenues is not matched by a fall in costs and so the company moves quickly into loss as seems to be the case in the most recent period.

There are few simple ways to change the nature of the costs in the business. However, using more temporary staff would mean that home staff costs would become more variable, although this may compromise the quality of the service provided. Also, it may be possible to renegotiate the terms of the leases on the homes so that the landlord accepts part of the risk by taking a lower rent combined with a percentage of revenue that the home generates. However, landlords are notoriously risk averse and it will have to be an attractive deal to obtain such a renegotiation.

(b) Qualitative models of business failure such as Argenti use a variety of qualitative and some non-accounting factors to predict corporate failure. The types of factors included are management experience, dependence on one or a few customers or suppliers, a history of qualified audit opinions and the business environment including the industry sector and the general economic situation.

The Argenti model is a qualitative model used to predict corporate failure which is based on non-accounting or qualitative variables. The model suggests that there are three connected areas that indicate likely failure: defects, mistakes made and symptoms of failure. Each of these areas is divided further and an assessor gives scores under each of these headings. A score of more than 25 is considered to indicate that the company is at risk of failing. The scores in the three areas themselves are also of interest as high scores in mistakes made indicate poor management. Failing companies often score highly, around 60.

The Argenti score has, therefore, attempted to quantify the causes and symptoms associated with failure. Its predictive value has not been adequately tested, but a misclassification rate of 5% has been suggested.

Defects are divided into management defects and accounting defects. Management defects are to do with the characters and strengths of senior management. Facts that would cause concern are a dominant CEO, the failure to separate role of chairman and CEO, a passive board of directors, poor skills and experience in the management team and a poor record of responding to change in the business environment. Here, the recent loss of senior management at CCNH would be a black mark. Examples of accounting defects are lack of budgetary control, lacks of cash flow planning and costing systems. The one defect that we have evidence of at CCNH is the lack of cash flow planning which has resulted in the near failure to pay the landlords.

If a company's management and accounting systems are weak, then it is suggested that this will lead to mistakes being made. The mistakes are scored too under three headings: high gearing; overtrading and the failure of a large project. There may be evidence of some overtrading at the Special Care division, where rapid growth has led to a failure of credit control and so high receivables which are straining the working capital of the business.

Finally, the model suggests that the weaknesses noted above will lead to specific symptoms of failure where the prospect of corporate collapse becomes more publicly clear.

The symptoms are financial such as poor ratios in the financial statements; the use of creative accounting to window dress the financial statements; and non-financial signs such as frozen salaries, delayed investment projects, falling market share, high staff turnover. A glance at the financial statements of CCNH indicates problems with no profits generated, high operational gearing of 7.5 and low interest cover (5/5 = 1). The difficulty in paying creditors such as the landlords is often an indication that failure is close at hand. The other public signs of weakness at CCNH are the need to extend the overdraft, the directors' resignations and the police investigation of theft.

Overall, the picture at CCNH is bleak and will require immediate and possibly drastic action in order to avoid insolvency.

Tutorial note

The model solution has included some comments about the actual scores although these were not necessary for a good answer. They are included here for teaching purposes. The Argenti model has been used as the basis for the answer but suitable credit will be given for any reasoned approach. Further detail on failure prediction models can be found in the technical article 'Business Failure'.

Marking scheme			Marks
(a)	Explain liquidity, financial and operational gearing	up to	4
	Illustrate each at CCNH		
	Liquidity	up to	4
	Financial gearing	up to	2
	Operational gearing	up to	4
		Maximum	**14**
(b)	Describe qualitative models (possibly use Argenti as an example) (includes examples of possible failure indications)		
		Maximum	**5**
	Identify weaknesses at CCNH		
	Culture of fraud in previous management		1
	Lack of senior management		1
	Poor cash flow planning		1
	Overtrading at SC		1
	Weak financial ratios noted		1
	Inability to pay landlords/Seeking emergency funding from the bank		1
		Maximum	**6**
Total			**25**

Examiner's comments

Scores on part (a) were mixed with only the better candidates addressing the question requirement. Most candidates scored the incidental marks available for illustrative calculations from CCNH – although it was disappointing to see how many could not accurately calculate simple ratios. However, having done this work they allowed it to lead them into believing that the question asked for a general assessment of the financial situation of CCNH when in answering the question, this should be used as an illustration of why indicators of liquidity and gearing are needed alongside those of profitability. It was also notable that although many candidates successfully dealt with issues around financial gearing, only a few candidates addressed the operational gearing at the business. There appeared to be lack of identification of the cost structures (variable/fixed) within CCNH that ought to be a basic point in the financial assessment of a business by a management accountant.

In part (b) few candidates demonstrated a clear understanding of the issues in using a qualitative model and in particular, in the Argenti model only a minority could explain defects, mistakes made and symptoms of failure. Many could quote the headings but few could explain what they referred to – the wiser candidates tried to cover this by illustrating each heading with an example from CCNH. However, given the above comments, it was pleasing to see that many candidates scored reasonably well by identifying the specific issues at CCNH.

74   GRAVITON CLOTHING (DEC 13)

Key answer tips

As with many APM questions you need not only to know the content – here the performance pyramid – but also to be able to apply the model to the specific circumstances given. The examiner is interested in application of knowledge and so simply providing book-learned definitions of terms scored only a few marks.

(a)   The performance pyramid is based on the belief that each level of an organisation has different concerns but they must support each other in order to achieve the overall objective of the organisation. The aim is to produce a set of performance measures which cover the outputs and drivers of the outputs of the organisation. The pyramid shape is to emphasise that the measures from the operational up to the strategic levels should support the corporate vision.

A general criticism of the system at Graviton could be that it is suffering from tunnel vision which is over-focusing on those areas which are actually measured. This can be managed by ensuring that the set of performance measures are comprehensive in examining the results and the determinants of those results for the organisation. The performance pyramid is a systematic method which tries to achieve this goal. Tunnel vision may explain why, although revenue is rising rapidly, the operating profit is fairly static. There is a danger that the company is focusing on making more sales to the exclusion of making higher profits. This may result from the measuring of revenue growth but not of cost related metrics or profit margins. It is notable that there are no variances from budget given in the performance report.

The pyramid diagram is:

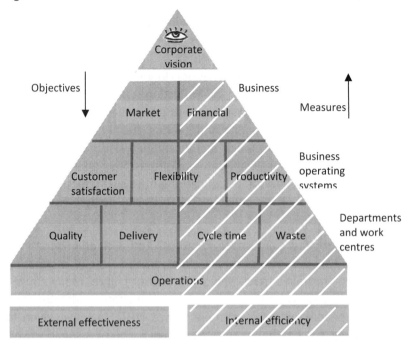

The pyramid begins with the corporate vision. At Graviton, the company objective is to maximise shareholder wealth by being flexible in response to market demand and controlling the production chain closely. The current performance measures as illustrated in the example report do measure all of these factors in some way but may not be comprehensive.

- Return on capital employed (ROCE) is reported but this is not directly measuring shareholder wealth and it is surprising that there is no mention of measures such as total shareholder return which will cover dividends and share price growth. The failure to provide a dividend measure may be a reason why the dividend growth has been allowed to slip.

- Flexibility in manufacturing is measured through the time to market for new designs. The design awards won indicate the innovative abilities of the employees at Graviton. The ability of the manufacturing chain to replenish successful lines and so take advantage of a fast-selling product is not measured.

- Close control of production is not evident as the problems with quality of clothes (durability complaints by customers) demonstrate. There may be a lack of cost control which explains the disconnection between growing revenue and the operating profits performance.

The next level of the pyramid is the driving of the vision by satisfying the market and performing well financially. As noted above, the financial measures are lacking a focus on costs through profit margins (such as gross margin) or key cost headings such as labour costs which would highlight the higher costs of designers. Therefore, the danger exists at Graviton that profitability is being sacrificed for revenue growth. Productivity measures of waste are likely to be important as designs become obsolete in this market quickly and the manufacturing process for clothes can lead to waste of materials in production. The problem of obsolescence can be significant in a fashion-driven industry since it is important to get the right garments in the right place at the right time. Inventory write-offs would measure such waste.

Market satisfaction is driven by customer satisfaction and flexibility. Graviton measures flexibility through time to market and delivery and these are obviously given a high priority in order to meet this objective in the corporate vision. Customer satisfaction can be considered to be measured through the revenue growth and indirectly through the winning of design awards but the failure to address quality may detract from this in the long term. (There is also evidence of short-term thinking at factory site 2 where the reason for the excess equipment repairs could be the failure to invest in new equipment which may be driven by the desire to keep the capital employed figure low to enhance ROCE.) An exercise should be undertaken to identify how strongly customers value the durability of Graviton's products and if this is significant, then measures of quality such as level of complaints should be made. It is possible that in a fast-changing, trend-driven industry such as Graviton's, there is little interest from customers in the durability of their garments, as they will be purchasing new ones on a regular basis to keep up with fashion.

(b) Myopia is prioritising short-term issues over long-term ones and is evident here in factory site 2. The variance in repairs expenditure could be due to a failure to invest in new machinery and so having excess repair work to do on old machinery. This could be exacerbated by using ROCE as a performance measure, since continuing to use old machinery (possibly written off) will require little or no capital employed. The use of longer term measures rather than those over just one accounting period might help to capture the effect of such behaviour.

Gaming is dysfunctional behaviour (from the organisation's perspective) where an individual manager is trying to meet their individual targets while ignoring the good of the whole organisation. There is evidence at factory site 1 of this behaviour where a manager is manipulating revenue and profit across the accounting cut-off. This behaviour can be dealt with by emphasising a culture of honesty in the organisation and by ensuring that the manager is rewarded for average gains over long periods rather than block payments for hitting simple profit-triggers in a single period.

Ossification is the unwillingness to change from an existing performance system, especially when it shows adequate or good results are being achieved. The board is clearly exhibiting this problem in resisting change at Graviton. The CEO will need to persuade them that there are issues in the omissions from the current set of performance measures which will lead to long-term difficulties in achieving their overall goal of enhancing shareholder wealth. The targets and remuneration of the board should be set so that the board is rewarded if current good performance is sustainable in the future.

	Marking scheme	
		Marks
(a)	General description of model – up to 3 marks (including diagram)	
	Remaining marks must have relevance to Graviton –	
	Tunnel vision – up to 5 marks	
	Up to 4 on the link of the metrics to the vision	
	Then 1 mark per point up to 6 marks on	
	Market satisfaction	
	Financial performance including:	
	Customer satisfaction	
	Flexibility	
	Productivity	
	Quality Delivery	
	Cycle time	
	Waste	
	1 mark per point for other relevant points	
	Maximum	**15**
(b)	1 mark for clear definition of the term then 1 mark per point made of relevance to Graviton and possible management solutions up to 3 on any one topic.	
	Myopia	
	Gaming	
	Ossification	
	Maximum	**10**
Total		**25**

Examiner's comments

Although many candidates showed a clear understanding of the terms of the pyramid in part (a), many were unable to apply these to the dashboard at Graviton. As with Question 1 of this exam, too many candidates simply listed new indicators without justification to the circumstances at Graviton. Those that scored well took each heading within the pyramid and discussed a) how it linked to the aim of the business (maximising shareholder wealth by focussing production on changing trends through maintained flexibility and close control of the supply chain) and; b) evaluated how the existing dashboard addressed these issues. For example, a valuable (but often ignored) connection could be made between flexibility in a fashion business and the time to market indicator.

With part (b) many candidates could not describe the terms (especially ossification) which indicates a lack of knowledge of the subject. However, most candidates did score some marks for suggesting suitable, justified solutions to the problems discussed even if they had not been able to state clearly which of the buzzwords was being addressed. (One detailed point of note on the suggested solutions is that these need to be justified, for example, a minority of candidates simply threw in a suggestion to use EVA^{TM} with no explanation at this point.) A successful structure for an answer to this part was to define the buzzword then show how it related to a particular issue at Graviton and finally, suggest a solution to the issue.

Future candidates should note that explanation and appropriate application of jargon (rather than merely bandying those terms) will often feature in APM as the valuable accountant is one who can demystify the subject.

75   VICTORIA-YEELAND LOGISTICS (JUN 15)

Key answer tips

As with many APM questions you need not only to know the content – here the balanced scorecard – but also to be able to apply the model to the specific circumstances given and give commercially valuable advice. The examiner is interested in application of knowledge and so simply providing book-learned definitions of terms scored only a few marks.

(a)   The success factors in the customer perspective will drive improved customer satisfaction. This should improve the customer perception of our service and so drive revenue growth. The increase in revenue could come through two routes:

1   winning customers from the competition and thus increasing volume or

2   increased selling prices as we may be perceived to offer a premium service.

Increased selling prices will immediately improve the profit margin of the service.

Increased volumes may indirectly improve our margins as we can spread the increased activity over our existing fixed cost base, for example, by increasing capacity utilisation (having more packages on each lorry).

As these improvements to operating profit occur without additional capital expenditure, they may feed through to an increased return on capital employed.

(b)   **Ability to meet customers' transport needs**

This is a measure of the flexibility of the business and would be measured by the percentage of customer requests which Victoria can actually undertake:

$$\frac{\text{Total number of packages transported}}{\text{Total number of customer transport requests}} = \frac{548,000}{610,000} = 89.8\%$$

Ability to deliver packages quickly

The difficulty of this measure is that different packages may travel different distances and so take longer. Therefore, a measure based on time taken per kilometre which a package travels is appropriate:

$$\frac{\text{Total minutes spent in transit by each package}}{\text{Total package kilometres travelled}} = \frac{131,520,000}{65,760,000} = 2.0$$

Ability to deliver packages on time

This is measured by the number of packages delivered within the time window given to the customer:

$$\frac{\text{Deliveries within window}}{\text{Total number of packages transported}} = \frac{(548,000 - 21,920}{548,000} = 96\%$$

Ability to deliver packages safely

This is measured by the number of undamaged packages delivered within the time window given to the customer:

$$\frac{\text{Deliveries of undamaged packages}}{\text{Total number of packages transported}} = \frac{(549,000 - 8,220)}{548,000} = 98.5\%$$

Problems with measurement using customer complaints

There are two dangers with measuring performance through customer complaints. The first is under-reporting where the customer does not bother to report a problem although it negatively impacts on their perception of Victoria. The customer simply walks away from Victoria's service. This could be alleviated by automatically discounting the invoice of any late delivery as Victoria should be recording its own delivery performance and not only relying on customers to provide data nor delay the process by waiting for their complaint.

The second is reporting of unjustified complaints to obtain compensation payments/credits. As the measures stand, they record all customer complaints whether reasonable or not. This could be addressed by using the number of customer credits issued for the fault rather than the number of complaints.

(c)   The senior management rewards system appears open to manipulation as the board is effectively setting their own rewards. There is the danger that targets are set to be easily achieved and so the profits of the business are siphoned off to the managers rather than the shareholders. The introduction of the BSC should assist in creating coherence between the objectives of the senior management and those of the shareholders. However, it appears that the major, financial measures suggested in the BSC do not directly address shareholder wealth although return on capital will be related. Finally, in a market where competition is fierce, the ability of management to grow revenue will be heavily constrained and there appear to be important factors in profit which are outside of the control of senior managers (fuel costs).

The operational managers should have their measures of performance set through a cascade down from the strategic measures in the BSC. These measures will often come from the customer and process perspectives. In this way, the reward system should be consistent with the overall objectives of the business. The suggestion that operational managers should be involved in setting their own targets should be treated carefully as it may present problems. This suggestion often arises from a confusion of the idea of explaining the target setting process to the manager with the idea of actually setting the target. The setting of the target should be done by a higher level of management so that the target is achievable with above normal effort. The target should not be set to be unreachable as this can cause demotivation. The target set should then be explained to the employee involved so that they understand what they have to do in order to earn this additional reward. It would be advisable for operational management, where most improvements are incremental, that the target is one where the bonus increases as the performance improves rather than a simple one of obtaining a given level of performance.

Tutorial note

The building block model headings of fair, achievable, owned standards and clear, motivational and controllable rewards are relevant to this answer but the answer needs to distinguish between the standards used and the targets set.

Marking scheme			
			Marks
(a)	1 mark per point		
	To score 5, must discuss all three financial metrics		
		Maximum	5
(b)	For each success factor, 1 mark for justification and 1 mark for calculation of suitable metric		
	Up to 4 marks for problems identified		
		Maximum	11
(c)	Up to 5 marks on senior management rewards		
	Up to 5 marks on operational management		
		Maximum	9
Total			25

Examiner's comments

Part (a), for 5 marks, asked for a discussion of the links between the customer perspective (and four success factors were given in an appendix for this) and the three financial metrics also given in the appendix. Those candidates that showed how success under each factor linked to changes in each of the three metrics scored all the marks. However, many candidates chose not to answer the question and instead discussed how the customer perspective factors aided achievement of the business strategy or else had a broadly positive effect on the financial position of the business. These were inadequate answers from APM candidates who are expected to be able to talk in detail about factors affecting ROCE, profit margin and revenue growth.

Worryingly, many candidates assume that revenue growth automatically means profit margin improvement and so improvement in ROCE, without any further consideration of cost or capital implications.

Part (b) for 11 marks required a justified recommendation of a suitable metric for each of the four customer perspective success factors, followed by comments on the problems of using customer supplied data. This part was well done by most candidates with many scoring 10 or 11 out of 11.

Part (c) for 9 marks required advice on reward management issues at Victoria. The CFO had supplied specific issues around senior and operational management rewards. This part was surprisingly poorly answered. Many candidates used the building block model as a template for their answer but failed to go further than a generic response and did not address the specific issues for Victoria. Successful candidates briefly outlined the model and then showed how each aspect could be applied to the situation at hand.

Candidates seemed unwilling to say that the employees (senior management/operational managers) may be unhappy but that need not be an issue for Victoria as there will usually be a conflict of interest between the employees and the company/shareholders. Good answers identified and discussed how to address this issue fairly. Baldly stating that employees should set their own targets is not a practical solution.

Future candidates should address the specific issues in a scenario in order to give commercially valuable advice to those involved.

76   SOUP RAIL SERVICES (SEPT/DEC 15)

Key answer tips

As with many APM questions you need not only to know the content – here the balanced scorecard – but also to be able to apply the model to the specific circumstances given and give commercially valuable advice. In part (a) you had to justify how the balanced scorecard would improve the performance management system. The examiner is interested in application of knowledge and so simply providing book-learned definitions of terms scored only a few marks.

(a)   The balanced scorecard consists of four perspectives: customer, internal, innovation and learning and financial. It requires an organisation to have a number of goals supported by performance measures in each perspective. The customer perspective measures what it is that customers value from the business; internal looks at what processes does the organisation need to be successful; innovation and learning considers how future value can be created and financial measures whether performance is acceptable to investors.

It is useful because it uses both internal and external information to assess performance and measures financial and non-financial aspects of a business to ensure long-term future success, rather than just focusing on historic results. It can also be used as a mechanism to link KPIs into the CSFs which are vital to deliver strategy.

Soup currently uses return on capital employed (ROCE) as its key financial performance measure, but this does not correlate directly with the objective to maximise shareholder wealth and could encourage short-term decisions to be taken at the expense of long-term success. This is the case at Soup which purchased old trains and subsequently failed to reinvest, meaning that Soup's ROCE is probably higher than its rivals. However, the trains are becoming unreliable and their condition is deteriorating. In the long term this will reduce customer satisfaction and financial performance.

Using the scorecard, Soup should have a broader range of financial measures which encourage managers to take decisions, such as investment decisions, consistent with the objective to maximise shareholder wealth in the long term. EVA^{TM} would be a suitable measure to help achieve this, and would be preferable to the current focus on ROCE.

Soup does measure growth in passenger numbers which could be a measure of customer satisfaction. However, it is a limited, quantitative measure. Though Soup does have rivals and is likely to be required to operate a specified level of service under the terms of the licence from the government, some passengers may be forced to travel on Soup trains, rather than those of another operator because of where they live or the times they need to travel. The number of operators (competitors) is limited by the capacity of the railway infrastructure as well as by passenger demand. This means that the level of repeat customers may not be appropriate for Soup.

Passenger numbers are also externally focused but again this fails to fully consider the environment in which Soup operates.

Within the customer perspective Soup could use a range of performance measures. This will be beneficial as where passengers are able, they are likely to choose to use Soup if they provide a good service. This can be easily measured by surveying or asking passengers' opinions. This will give Soup more qualitative information about their customers and their expectations, which will vary, for example, passengers will have different perceptions of overcrowding, or what is an acceptable delay. Certain groups may be more affected by overcrowding like frequent travellers and the elderly. Passengers who are unable to find a seat will probably be the most dissatisfied, though this will depend on how long their journey is. Other aspects of Soup's service may be less valued than reliability and occupancy, like wireless access and the on-board cafe, but will be important to certain groups.

Another key element of customer satisfaction will relate to the amount of fare paid. Fares are regulated in Deeland so the interaction between fares and other aspects of the service is unknown. Many customers while valuing a particular aspect of the service may be unwilling to pay more for it; some may accept a reduction in the level of service if fares were reduced.

This detailed information about customers will allow Soup to focus performance improvements on key areas using more external data to make decisions.

Measures of the internal processes are likely to be closely linked to customer satisfaction. Soup apparently neglects this area in its performance management system. The scorecard could be used to help to address reliability, overcrowding and environmental factors.

Reliability will be highly valued by customers especially those who travel frequently and who rely on rail travel to get to work. The number of trains arriving late would be a suitable measure of reliability, as would the number of train services cancelled, though the length of the delay is also critical and should be carefully defined. The scorecard would allow more detailed measures as some of the factors affecting reliability will be within Soup's direct control but others such as failures in the railway infrastructure are controlled by the government. This is useful information for Soup to effectively assess their controllable performance and feedback as necessary to external parties.

Seat occupancy, the number of passengers on a train compared to the number of available seats on different routes and at different times, is a suitable measure of train overcrowding and is important for passenger safety. To fully utilise its trains and achieve its objective of maximising shareholder wealth, Soup must try and maximise both the seat occupancy and the amount of time its trains are actually running. These internal measures would then help to support financial targets.

Soup's licence to operate rail services in Regions A and B expires in three years' time, and as with the operator from whom Soup purchased the trains, it may not be renewed. Soup must balance the needs of shareholders for short-term increases in dividends and share price with the long-term need to renew to its operator's licence.

The creation of long-term future value can be addressed by the innovation and learning perspective. The immediate scope to innovate the service experienced by the passenger is limited, but there are some quick wins available in the choice in the on-board cafe and improving the reliability of the internet access. Also time spent training staff may improve customer satisfaction and reduce maintenance time. Fundamental innovation like the use of faster or environmentally less harmful trains requires long-term planning and large capital investment. The scorecard will encourage Soup to be forward looking, unlike the present system which is limited to historic performance.

(b)   To measure the extent of overcrowding, some measure of occupancy is needed. The number of passengers per available seat can be used as a measure of occupancy.

Seats available per train is 490 (7 coaches × 70 seats) in Region A and 420 (7 coaches × 60 seats) in Region B.

Seats available per day	Region A	Region B
Peak times	1,960 (490 × 4)	1,680
Other times	2,940	3,360

Seat occupancy	Region A	Region B
Peak times	128%	83%
Other times	83%	55%

Total seat occupancy = 82.5% (8,200/9,940)

Overall occupancy is below 100% which means on average there are more seats available than passengers, which is not consistent with the government's claims that the trains are overcrowded. However, these averages may be misleading as trains running on certain days or at certain times may be relatively overcrowded. This may generate customer dissatisfaction even on services which are on average not fully occupied. The total number of passengers without seats would be a better measure.

There are significant variations between regions and times travelled with only the trains in Region A travelling at peak times being over occupied. This affects only 18% (4/22) of all services.

Most affected by this will be the 28% of the passengers travelling at peak times in Region A who are unable to obtain a seat. This represents only 9% (28% × 2,500/8,200) of total passengers per day. There is some overcrowding but the claim that Soup's trains are overcrowded seems exaggerated given the data provided. However, certain routes or specific times or sections of the trains may be more affected and more analysis is needed.

The impact of overcrowding on passengers also depends on journey times, with passengers being less satisfied by not obtaining a seat on longer journeys rather than on short ones. Assuming trains are available for 14 hours per day and there are 22 services, each service is on average almost 1.5 hours which may be a significant length of time for passengers to stand on a train.

(c)   When applying the balanced scorecard in Soup, the measures need to be chosen carefully. A balance needs to be struck and only measures which help Soup to achieve its objectives should be chosen. Currently Soup focuses on short-term financial measures such as return on capital employed, whereas the balanced scorecard considers more long-term measures.

Some measures are more important than others, so prioritising measures will be difficult. Customers may value some aspects of the service more than others, for example, the choice available in the on-board cafe is probably unimportant to most passengers provided they can obtain some food and drink. The punctuality of Soup's trains or whether they even run at all is fundamental to achieving customer satisfaction and needs careful measurement. Soup must have measures for regulatory or safety reasons too.

Some aspects of the business may be harder to measure than others. For example, it may be relatively easy to measure seat occupancy as a measure of overcrowding, but passengers' perceptions of overcrowding may differ. Non-financial aspects such as customer satisfaction may be subjective and any surveys done may not reflect the experience of the majority of passengers. Performing and analysing surveys would also be time consuming and resource intensive.

Measures chosen may conflict. Overcrowding may be unwelcome by passengers but making them less crowded conflicts with Soup's presumed objective of fully occupied trains. Time spent maintaining trains to reduce their impact on the environment or ensure reliability will mean they are not operational for periods of time, though safety will be a key factor here.

Care must be taken to avoid overloading with too many performance measures. The current objective to maximise shareholder wealth is very broad. Having a clearer strategy would enable Soup to determine suitable performance measures so it is not overloaded with KPIs which do not contribute towards achieving this strategy.

	Marking scheme		
			Marks
(a)	1 mark per relevant point		
	No marks for a list of new measures without justifying why they would benefit Soup		
	1 mark only for a generic description of the balanced scorecard without clear references to the scenario		
		Maximum	**10**
(b)	Calculation		
	1 mark each for:		
	Seats available per train		1
	Seats available per day by region/time		1
	Seat occupancy by region/time		1
	Total seat occupancy		1
	Comment on whether consistent with governments claims about overcrowding		1
	Other comments		
	Up to 2 additional marks for identifying journey time is an important factor and for attempting to quantify journey times from the data given		2
		Maximum	**7**
	Maximum of 3 marks if general points not applied to Soup		
	Selection of appropriate measures – up to 2 marks		
	Prioritisation of measures – up to 2 marks		
	Difficulties of making measurements – up to 2 marks		
	Conflicting measures – up to 2 marks		
	Overload of measures – up to 2 marks		
		Maximum	**8**
Total			**25**

Examiner's comments

Part (a) required advice on how the balanced scorecard could improve performance management systems. The majority of candidates clearly knew the structure of the theory, although some merely listed the four perspectives as opposed to explaining what they were. Candidates should be aware that few marks are awarded at this level for providing superficial lists.

The emphasis of the question was how the balanced scorecard can improve the system. Therefore it is essential that candidates recognise that they need to identify specific aspects of the model and how they would benefit the system. Simply listing potential metrics scored few marks unless the candidate could clearly demonstrate the benefit. For example, explaining that the company could use EVA as a measure under the financial perspective provides little evidence that a candidate understands how using the balance scorecard is beneficial. However, to score well, a candidate could explain that the approach aims to ensure the long-term success of the company and using EVA would be an improvement on using, say, ROCE.

Part (b) required candidates to evaluate claims that the services were overcrowded. The calculations for this part of the question were generally performed well. Credit was given to various approaches to show whether or not overcrowding was evident given the data presented. It is therefore worthwhile mentioning that candidates do not have to follow prescribed methods to demonstrate a point as long as there is a logical approach and the answer is well explained.

However, few candidates attempted to discuss the claim of overcrowding in any detail other than to say whether or not capacity was exceeded. Candidates should be aware that the scenarios on APM are written to reflect real world examples and as such, in this scenario, discussing practical considerations would be beneficial.

Part (c) required candidates to assess the problems that may be encountered when selecting and interpreting performance measures when applying the balanced scorecard. This part of the question was well attempted by many candidates. This is a clear example of where understanding the advantages and disadvantages of a model, and then demonstrating how they relate to the given scenario, will allow candidates to score well. One of the main shortcomings in many responses to this question was a failure to specifically answer the question, which focused on selecting and interpreting, for example, there can be conflicting metrics. Several candidates simply discussed the difficulties in adopting a balanced scorecard approach, such as commitment from management, and a general discussion of target setting, such as measure fixation. Again, re-iterating earlier comments, candidates should ensure that they specifically answer the question that has been set.

77   PHARMACEUTICAL TECHNOLOGIES CO (PILOT 10)

Key answer tips

Stakeholders are rarely examined as a standalone requirement but it is a syllabus area. This question is a good opportunity to practise a question on stakeholder influence.

(a)   Evaluation of proposed performance measures

The financial perspective has not been altered from the existing measures of strategic performance. These are appropriate to address the objectives of enhancing shareholder wealth although it has been argued that measures such as economic value added or shareholder value added are better long long-term measures of this topic. Also, it is more common to use share price and dividend per share to reflect total shareholder return. Additionally, measures of survival (cash flows) and growth (in eps) could also be considered.

The customer perspective mainly seems to address the patient (end user) viewpoint. However, it should also reflect the concerns of those paying for the products (the government and insurers). Therefore, measures of cost in comparison to competitors would be appropriate.

The internal process perspective reflects appropriate measures of manufacturing excellence and efficiency in the testing process. This directly addresses the second of the board's objectives.

The learning and growth perspective would appear to be an obvious area to address the third objective on innovation. Again, the ranking of the measures is unclear and it would be surprising if training days were considered the principal measure. From the learning perspective of learning, it would be the improvement in the time to market from product to product that would better indicate learning and the improvement in percentage of drugs finally approved that would indicate learning. It may be appropriate to benchmark these measures against industry competitors as well as internally.

It is not clear if the points in the proposed scorecard are already prioritised and it may be appropriate to reconsider the order of measures, for example, in the internal perspective, the measure of time to gain approval seems to be more directly relevant to the objective of efficiency of the development process.

The suggested scorecard does not consider the difficulty of collecting data on some of the non-financial measures. For example, the measurement of above-industry standard design and testing is likely to be subjective unless the company undergoes a regular quality audit which can be scored.

(b)   Stakeholders and their influence

The key stakeholders of BDR are the government, the drug companies being tested, the healthcare providers and their funders, and the patients.

A measure of influence of different stakeholders could be obtained by considering the degree to which they have power to affect decisions in the company and the likelihood that they would exercise their power (their degree of interest in the decisions). (Mendelow's matrix would be a suitable technique to perform this analysis.)

The government is an influential stakeholder on this basis as they have power over senior appointments and the funding of BDR. They are unlikely to use this power having delegated authority to the trustees, unless they are provoked by some financial or medical scandal.

The drug companies will be highly interested in the day-to-day workings of BDR as it sets the testing environment without which the drug companies will not have products. However, they will have little influence in the decisions within BDR as BDR must be seen to be independent of them. Nevertheless, it is in BDR's interest to have a successful drug development industry in order to achieve its goal of encouraging new drug development.

The healthcare providers will have interest principally in the quality of the approval process so they can have confidence about the cures that they dispense. They will have limited influence mainly through the pressure that they can bring to bear through the government.

The patients will be concerned that there is innovation as new cures are quickly and safely brought to market. They have limited secondary influence on decisions decision-making in BDR, as for the healthcare providers. Their influence will mainly be felt by affecting the actions of the government.

(c) Differences in the application of the balanced scorecard

The objectives at BDR are less obviously financial than at PT. The use of the balanced scorecard approach will be of great use to BDR as it emphasises non-financial performance which fits with BDR's objectives relating to quality of drugs and the relationship with key stakeholders. This can lead to difficulty in setting quantifiable measures due to the soft issues involved, e.g. measuring the level of user understanding of the risk/benefit profile of products. There is also the danger of setting quantifiable measures which are then obsessively pursued without regard to the softer aim of the organisation. An example could be the need to encourage drug innovation at the expense of making sure that each new product was a material improvement on existing drug products.

BDR will have a more complex balanced scorecard than PT due to the diverse nature of important stakeholders. As a public service organisation, the customer perspective may be more significant. The principal stakeholder is the government and so there will be a complex, political dimension to measuring performance.

The primary objective at PT is financial while at BDR there are several key objectives among which there is no clear ranking. Stakeholders may have conflicting objectives, for example, patients want effective drugs but the same individuals as taxpayers/ insurance premium payers may not be willing to foot the bill if the price is too high. This will lead to difficulties in setting priorities among the various measures identified on the balanced scorecard.

	Marking scheme	
		Marks
(a)	1 mark per point. There is a wide range of good answer points to be made. Points should be made about the measures suggested (whether they cover the perspective intended) and also, if there are other suitable measures. Other marks are for linking the measures to the stated company objectives, commenting on the difficulty of collecting appropriate data and ranking the measures.	
	Maximum	**10**
(b)	Up to 2 marks on method of analysis. Up to 2 marks on each stakeholder. Answers must display a consideration of both the power and the likelihood of exercising it in order to score full marks.	
	Maximum	**8**
(c)	1 mark per point. In order to score highly, a candidate must give examples that are relevant to the scenario. Maximum of 7 marks.	
	Maximum	**7**
Total		**25**

78 BETTASERVE (PILOT 07)

Key answer tips

When considering the style of the current examiner it is questionable as to the extent by which you will be asked to evaluate a proposal in this way. However, it is still a good question to consider the implications of decisions.

(a) (i) Corporate vision may be seen as looking forward through the defining of markets and the basis on which the company will compete. Bettaserve plc has defined the 'gold standard' proposal for one of its product ranges as a specific market opportunity. It envisages competing through the identification of key competitors and by close co-operation with its customers in providing services to meet their specific design and quality standards.

The corporate vision is seen as being achieved through a focus on internal efficiency and external effectiveness.

The 'gold standard' proposal may be seen as illustrating a specific sub-set of the corporate mission since it:

- has its own distinct business concept and mission – the 'gold standard' focus

- has identified the key competitors; and

- is a suitable area for the management of its own strategies – close co-operation with customers and the provision of services to meet their design requirements.

(ii) The 'gold standard' proposal may be measured in both marketing and financial terms. Will it achieve market growth and an improved market position? The projected sales ($m) in schedule 1 shows growth of 20% in 2008 ($36m/$30m) and a further 11.1 % in 2009 ($40m/$36m). In addition, market position is anticipated to improve, with a market share of 12.5%, 14.4% and 15.4% in years 2007, 2008 and 2009 respectively (e.g. 2007 = $30m/$240m).

The net profit/sales percentage is also expected to increase each year. The figures are 6%, 29.3% and 37.25% for 2007, 2008 and 2009 respectively (e.g. 2007 = $1.8m/$30m).

The profit increase is partly linked to the projected fall in quality costs, both costs of conformance (appraisal and prevention) and costs of non-conformance (internal and external failure) as shown in Schedule 1. It is also linked to the increase in volume of business as fixed costs have a reduced effect.

(iii) The marketing success of the proposal is linked to the achievement of customer satisfaction. The success will require an efficient business operating system for all aspects of the cycle from service design to after sales service to customers. Improved quality and delivery should lead to improved customer satisfaction. Schedule 1 shows a number of quantitative measures of the expected measurement of these factors:

- Quality is expected to improve. The percentage of services achieving design quality standards is expected to rise from 95% to 98% between 2007 and 2009. In the same period, rectification claims from customers for faulty work should fall from $0.9m to $0.2m and the cost of after sales rectification service should fall from $3m to $2m.

- Delivery efficiency improvement may be measured in terms of the increase in the percentage of sales expected to meet planned delivery dates. This percentage rises from 90% in 2007 to 99% in 2009.

(iv) The financial success of the proposal is linked to the achievement of high productivity. This should be helped through reduced cycle time and decreased levels of waste. Once again Schedule 1 shows a number of quantitative measures of these factors:

- The average total cycle time from customer enquiry to delivery should fall from 6 weeks in 2007 to 5 weeks in 2009. This indicates both internal efficiency and external effectiveness.

- Waste in the form of idle capacity of service personnel is expected to fall from 10% to 2% between 2007 and 2009. Also, service enquiries not taken up by customers, is expected to fall from 7.5% of enquiries in 2007 to 2.5% of enquiries in 2009. These are both examples of ways in which improved productivity may be measured. Both will be linked to the prevention and appraisal costs, which are intended to reduce the level of internal and external failure costs.

(b) The analysis of the 'gold standard' proposal shows a hierarchy of performance measures. The performance pyramid shown below indicates how strategies to assist in the achievement of corporate vision may be cascaded down through a number of levels. The analysis discussed and evaluated in section (a) consists of a number of interrelated areas of focus.

The marketing and financial success of the proposal is the initial focus for the achievement of corporate vision. Marketing and financial strategies must be formulated and inter-related. They must be linked to the achievement of customer satisfaction and high productivity at the next level in the hierarchy. Increased flexibility of methods should also be aimed for. This should help (internally) in achieving improved productivity and also (externally) in an improved level of customer satisfaction. High quality standards will improve customer satisfaction and in turn will assist in market retention and growth.

As discussed in part (a), customer satisfaction may be achieved through a more detailed focus on improved quality and delivery. Productivity may be improved through reductions in service cycle times and waste elements.

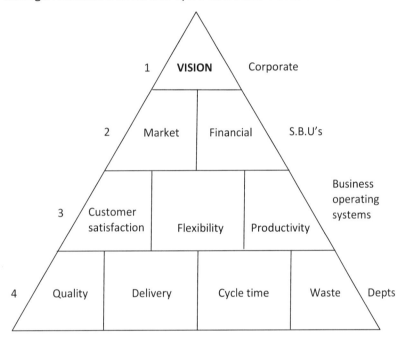